ENGLISH LANGUAGE AND LITERARY CRITICISM

ENGLISH LANGUAGE
AND
LITERARY CRITICISM

By

Dr. Ambreen Kharbe

Department of English

Samadiya College of Arts and Commerce

Bhiwandi

DISCOVERY PUBLISHING HOUSE PVT. LTD.

NEW DELHI-110 002

Published by:
Tilak Wasan

DISCOVERY PUBLISHING HOUSE PVT. LTD.
4383/4B, Ansari Road, Darya Ganj
New Delhi-110 002 (India)
Phone : +91-11-23279245, 23253475, 43596065
E-mail : discoverypublishinghouse@gmail.com
sales@discoverypublishinggroup.com
web : www.discoverypublishinggroup.com

***First Edition:* 2009**

***Reprinted:* 2020**

ISBN: 978-81-8356-483-0

English Language and Literary Criticism

Printed at:
Infinity Imaging Systems
Delhi

PREFACE

English Language and Literary Criticism has become a part of students studying English Literature. The book *English Language and Literary Criticism* has been written according to the syllabus prescribed by different Indian Universities for graduate and post-graduate students. However, the book is also useful for the students appearing for NET/SET and other competitive exams.

Being a student of English Literature it is very necessary to know the origin of English Language and its structure. Attempt has been made in short to trace the origin and history of English language beside focusing on its structure, its varieties and its importance in society.

Further the functions of literature and literary criticism along with contemporary literary theories and its approach to literature has been focused with due care with the discussion of the major critics.

The main aim of writing this book is to help the students studying English Language, English Literature and Literary Criticism making them understand the concepts and the subject more comprehensive and enjoyable for their studies.

Sincere thank are due to authors and publishers whose books have been consulted and freely drawn upon. I take this opportunities to express my indebtedness and gratitude to my husband.

Suggestions and comments for making the book more useful will be greatly appreciated.

Last but not least, I am grateful to Discovery Publishing House Pvt. Ltd. for undertaking the publication of this book.

Dr. Ambreen Safder Kharbe
M.A., EMBA, Ph.D

CONTENTS

ENGLISH LANGUAGE

LITERATURE AND LITERARY CRITICISM

CRITICAL THEORIES AND APPROACHES TO LITERATURE

ENGLISH LANGUAGE

1

History of English Language : Influence and Development from Anglo-Saxon to Modern Times

Introduction

Language is the expression of human personality in words, whether written or spoken. It is the universal medium alike for conveying the common facts and feelings of everyday life. The introduction of a system of recording thought and speech by writing (and later by printing) was a very important step forward and without it we would be very largely ignorant of the ways of life and the modes of thought of our ancestors. Language is evolutionary, not static. There is continuous change in the language. If we look at a passage from Chaucer (a fourteenth century writer) and compare it with the English that is spoken and written today, we find a great difference in this five hundred years or more; and if we go even further back to the Anglo-Saxon period, we find an even greater difference. In fact, Anglo-Saxon is much more unlike Chaucer's English than Chaucer's English is unlike ours. It should be realised that speech or language is the distinguishing characteristics of man as such and is one of the chief attributes which differentiate him from the other animal species.

The study of language cannot be isolated from other branches of study. The study of language can throw light on social history, and it has something to contribute to psychology, anthropology and sociology, just as in its turn it has much to gain from these studies. But, quite apart from the help that it can give to other studies, the study of language is a branch of knowledge of interest for its own sake, since it is the study of an important aspect of human behaviour. No two speakers of a language speak in exactly the same way, and a language does not exactly correspond with the speech of any one speaker of the language. It may therefore seem that a language is a rather unreal abstraction, like the 'average-man'. In fact, however, the lack of exact identity of speech-sounds is unimportant, since no ear is able to distinguish them with perfect accuracy. All that is necessary is that the speech-sounds used by different speakers of a language in pronouncing a particular word shall resemble each other so closely that most hearers think that the sounds are identical. A similar test may be used to define that much discussed abstraction standard English. Standard English is that form of English speech which so closely resembles the average pronunciation of most educated speakers as to seem identical with is to a hearer with a reasonably good ear.

The symbols which constitute a language may be spoken or written or they may consist of gestures. Gestures do not as a rule play a very important part in the language of civilized peoples, and from the point of view of the development of a language the spoken language is much more important than the written. One advantage which speech enjoys as compared with writing or gesture is that while we are speaking or listening the hands and eyes are left free. It is sometimes said that a further advantage of speech is that it is capable of a much wider range of expressiveness than either writing or gesture. It is true that a speaker can express subtle shades of meaning which cannot easily be expressed by means of writing or gesture, but it is doubtful whether speech can do this by reason of any inherent advantage which it possesses other forms of expression. It is more likely that the subtle meaningful variations of which speech is capable are the result of the use of speed as a medium of expression by countless generations of speakers. Writing and gesture are, like speech, capable of infinite variation, but these variations have not come to be associated with particular meanings.

Writing has some advantages which are not shared by speech. The chief of these is the ease with which it can be preserved and reproduced. It may be noticed that comparatively recent scientific inventions, the gramophone, the wireless and the tape recording machine, have done something to give to speech to advantages which writing has enjoyed for several centuries, but so far no invention has provided compensation for the fact that, whereas the ear can detect sounds only in succession, the eye can see a number of different objects at a single glance. As everyone who has listened to a lecture or a news bulletin knows to his cost, the listener has to accept the speed chosen by the speaker whereas the reader can go at his own speed, lingering over difficult passages and skipping very quickly over the passages of less interest or importance.

Nothing is known for certain, though very much has been speculated, of the origin of language. This is partly because thought and language cannot clearly be separated, since the one can scarcely seem to exist without the other. Therefore, the origin of language seems to be bound up with that of human thought. We must decide when and how man began to think, to know of the beginnings of language; and we must know when and how he began to speak, to decide on the origins of his existence as a thinking being.

History of English

Five events has shaped the history of English :

(1) The Anglo-Saxon Settlement : It's never easy to pinpoint exactly when a specific language began, but in the case of English we can at least say that there is little sense in speaking of the English language as a separate entity before the Anglo-Saxons came to Britain. Little is known of this period with any certainty, but we do know that Germanic invaders came and settled in Britain from the north-western coastline of continental Europe in the fifth and sixth centuries. The invaders all spoke a language that was Germanic (related to what emerged as Dutch, Frisian, German and the Scandinavian languages, and to Gothic), but we'll probably never know how different their speech was from that of their continental neighbours. However, it is fairly certain that many of the settlers would have spoken in exactly the same way as some of their north European neighbours, and that not all of the settlers would have spoken in the same way.

The reason that we know so little about the linguistic situation in this period is because we do not have much in the way of written records from any of the Germanic languages of north-western Europe until several centuries later. When Old English writings begin to appear in the seventh, eighth and ninth centuries there is a good deal of regional variation, but not substantially more than that found in later periods. This was the language that Alfred the Great referred to as 'English' in the ninth century.

The Celts were already resident in Britain when the Anglo-Saxons arrived, but there are few obvious traces of their language in English today. Some scholars have suggested that the Celtic tongue might have had an underlying influence on the grammatical development of English, particularly in some parts of the country, but this is highly speculative. The number of loanwords known for certain to have entered Old English from this source is very small. Those that survive in modern English include *brock* (badger), and *coomb* a type of valley, alongside many place names.

(2) The Scandinavian Settlements : The next invaders were the Norsemen. From the middle of the ninth century large numbers of Norse invaders settled in Britain, particularly in northern and eastern areas, and in the eleventh century the whole of England has a Danish king, Canute. The distinct North Germanic speech of the Norsemen had great influence on English, most obviously seen in the words that English has borrowed from this source. These include some very basic words such as *take* and even grammatical words such as *they*. The common Germanic base of the two languages meant that there were still many similarities between Old English and the language of the invaders. Some words, for example *give* perhaps show a kind of hybridization with some spellings going back to Old English and others being Norse in Origin. However, the resemblances between the two languages are so great that in many cases it is impossible to be sure of the exact ancestry of a particular word or spelling. However, much of the influence of Norse, including the vast majority of the loan-words, does not appear in written English until after the next great historical and cultural upheaval, the Norman conquest.

(3) 1066 and after 1066 : The centuries after the Norman conquest witnessed enormous changes in the English language.

In the course of what is called the Middle English period, the fairly rich inflectional system of Old English broke down. It was replaced by what is broadly speaking, the same system English has today, which unlike Old English makes very little use of distinctive word endings in the grammar of the language. The vocabulary of English also changed enormously, with tremendous numbers of borrowings from French and Latin, in addition to the Scandinavian loanwords already mentioned, which were slowly starting to appear in the written language. Old English, like German today, showed a tendency to find native equivalents for foreign words and phrases (although both Old English and modern German show plenty of loanwords), whereas Middle English acquired the habit that Modern English retains today of readily accommodating foreign words. Trilingualism in English, French and Latin was common in the words of business and the professions, with words crossing over from one language to another with ease. One only has to flick through the etymologies of any English dictionary to get an impression of the huge number of words entering English from French and Latin during the later medieval period. This trend was set to continue into the early modern period with the explosion of interest in the writings of the ancient world.

(4) Standardization : The late medieval and early modern periods saw a fairly steady process of standardization in English south of the Scottish border. The written and spoken language of London continued to evolve and gradually began to have a greater influence in the country at large. For most of the Middle English period a dialect was simply what was spoken in a particular area, which would normally be more or less represented in writing—although where and from whom the writer had learnt how to write were also important. It was only when the broadly London standard began to dominate, especially through the new technology of printing, that the other regional varieties of the language began to be seen as different in kind. As the London standard became used more widely, especially in more formal contents and particularly amongst the more elevated members of society, the other regional varieties came to be stigmatized, as lacking social prestige and indicating a lack of education.

In the same period a series of changes also occurred in English pronunciation (though not uniformly in all dialects), which go under the collective name of the great vowel shift. These were purely linguistic 'sound changes' which occur in every language in every period of history. The changes in pronunciation weren't the result of specific social or historical factors, but social and historical factors would have helped to spread the results of the changes. As a result the so-called 'pure' vowel sounds which still characterise many continental languages were lost to English. The phonetic pairings of most long and short vowel sounds were also lost, which gave rise to many of the oddities of English pronunciation, and which now obscure the relationships between many English words and their foreign counterparts.

(5) Colonization and Globalization : During the medieval and early modern periods the influence of English spread throughout the British Isles, and from the early seventeenth century onwards its influence began to be felt throughout the world. The complex processes of exploration, colonization and overseas trade that characterized Britain's external relations for several centuries became agents for change in the English language. This wasn't simply through the acquisition of loanwords deriving from languages from every corner of the world, which in many cases only entered English via the languages of other trading and imperial nations such as Spain, Portugal and the Netherlands, but through the gradual development of new varieties of English, each with their own nuances of vocabulary and grammar and their own distinct pronunciations. More recently still, English has became a *lingua franca,* a global language, regularly used and understood by many nations for whom English is not their first language. The eventual effects on the English language of both of these developments can only be guessed at today, but there can be little doubt that they will be as important as anything that has happened to English in the past sixteen hundred years.

English Language

In its historical sense, the name *English* is now conveniently used to comprehend the language of the English people from their settlement in Britain to the present day, the various stages through which it has passed being distinguished as Old, Middle, and New or Modern English. English is a West Germanic language originating mainly in England, and the first language for most people in Australia, Canada, the Commonwealth Caribbean, Ireland, New Zealand, the United Kingdom and the United States. It is used extensively as a second language and as an official language throughout the world, especially in commonwealth countries and in many international organisations.

Modern English is sometimes described as the first global lingua franca. English is a dominant international language in communications, science, business, aviation, entertainment, radio and diplomacy. The influence of the British Empire is the primary reason for the initial spread of the language for beyond the British Isles. Since World War II, the growing economic and cultural influence of the United States has significantly accelerated the adoption of English. A working knowledge of English is required in certain fields, professions, and occupations. As a result, over a billion people speak English at least at a basic level. English is one of six official languages of the United Nations.

The English language belongs to the Western sub-branch of the Germanic branch of the Indo-European family languages. The question as to which is the nearest living relative of English is a matter of discussion. Apart from such English-lexified cereole languages such as Tok Pisin, Scots (spoken primarily in Scotland and parts of Northern Ireland) is not a Gaelic language, but is part of the Anglic family of languages, having developed from early Northern Middle English. It is Scot's indefinite status as a language or a group of dialects of English which complicates definitely calling it the closest language to English. The closest relatives to English after Scots are the Frisian languages, which are spoken in the Northern Netherlands and Northwest Germany. Other less closely related living West Germanic languages include German, Low Saxon, Dutch, and Afrikaans. The North Germanic languages of Scandinavian are less closely related to English than the West Germanic languages.

Many French words are also intelligible to an English speaker (though pronunciations are often quite different) because English absorbed a large vocabulary from Norman and French, via Anglo-Norman after the Norman conquest and directly from French in subsequent centuries. As a result, a large portion of English vocabulary is derived from French, with some minor spelling differences (word endings, use of old French spellings, etc.), as well as occasional divergences in meaning, in so-called "faux amis", or false friends.

Old English or Anglo-Saxon and Modern English are, for all practical ends, distinct languages, as much so, for example, as Latin and Spanish. No amount of familiarity with Modern English, including its local dialects, would enable the student to read Anglo-Saxon, three-fourths of the vocabulary of which have perished and been reconstructed within 900 years, nor would a knowledge even of these lost words give him the power, since the grammatical system, alike in accidence and syntax, would be entirely strange to him. Indeed, it is probable that a modern Englishman would acquire the power of reading and writing French in less time than it would cost him to attain to the same proficiency in Old English; so that if the test of distinct languages be their degree of practical difference from each other, it cannot be denied that "Anglo-Saxon" is a distinct language from Modern English. But when we view the subject historically, recognizing the fact that living speech is subject to continuous change in certain definite directions, determined by the constitution and circumstances of mankind, as an evolution or development of which we can trace the steps, and that, owing to the abundance of written materials, this evolution appears so gradual in English that we can nowhere draw distinct lines separating its successive stages, we recognize these stages as merely temporary phases of an individual whole, and speak of the English language as used alike by Cynewulf, by Chaucer, by Shakespeare and by Tennyson. It must not be forgotten, however, that in this wide sense the English language includes, not only the literary or courtly forms of speech used at successive periods, but also the popular and, it may be, altogether unwritten dialects that exists by their side. Only on this basis, indeed, can we speak of Old, Middle and Modern English as the same *language,* since in actual fact the precise *dialect* which is now the cultivated language, or "standard English", is not the descendant of that dialect which was the cultivated language or 'English" of Alfred, but of a sister dialect then sunk in comparative obscurity,—even as the direct descendant of Alfred's English is now to be found in the non-literary rustic speech of Wiltshire and Somersetshire.

Some of the important characteristics of language are stated below—Language is a conventional, arbitrary system of sounds used for communication in a human linguistic community.

Language is a system at many levels. All languages have two levels, called *duality of patterning*. This consists of meaningful and meaningless components.

(a) Meaningless Components, the Phonemic System : Phonemes are the smallest meaningless components that constitute the sound system of a language.

(b) Meaningful Components, or Morphosyntax : Morphemes are the smallest meaningful components of a language. For example, the words *cats* consists of two morphemes [cat] and [–s]. Morphemes can be grammatical or lexical (affixes and function words). They can be free (able to stand alone) or bound (complete only when combined with morphemes. Bound lexical morphemes (or affixes) can be either derivational (used to create new words) or inflectional (used to signal grammatical relationships). *Syntax*—governs the way words come together to create sentences. The syntax of English has become less *synthetic* (grammatical structures are signals primarily by inflectional endings) and more *analytic* (grammatical structures are signaled primarily by word order and function words).

Language is a human activity. Though animals can communicate in a primal way, they do not have innate language abilities that allow for an unlimited number of novel utterances. Though some apes have been taught to use sign language (a paralanguage, or parallel system of communication), the breadth of idea that they express are limited.

Language is *arbitrary.* Aside from echoic words, there is no intrinsic relationship between words and the objects or concepts that they represent.

Language is *conventional*. Language is passed down from one generation to the next. It is the nature of language to change. Notions of absolute correctness are imposed by writers, linguists, scholars etc. and may slow down but do not prevent the natural process of language evolution.

Language is *sound.* Linguists are primarily concerned with speech. Writing is a secondary activity.

Let us now have a brief survey of English Language, its influence and development from Anglo-Saxon to Modern Times. Before going to the Anglo-Saxon Period or Old English it is necessary to have a glance on the Indo-European Language tree.

The Indo-European Language Tree

Linguists have traced most western and some non-western languages back to a common source, called the Indo-European language. Nothing remains of this language, but with the similarities that exist among the surviving branches of it, scholars are able to draw conclusions about it. For instance, look at the word for *father* in the following languages: Duth "vader"; Gothic "fadar"; Greek "pater"; Sanskrit "pitar"; English "father". In addition, look at the similarities in the following languages for the word *brother* : Sanskrit "bhratar"; German "Bruder"; Dutch "broeder"; Irish "brathair"; Old Slavic "bratu"; Greek "phrater"; English "brother". Clearly there is a connection among these words—and probably a common language from which all of them developed. These similar words—linguistic cousins that have a common source—are called cognates, and they go back to the mother tongue that we call Indo-European. From such a study of cognates, linguists conclude that many of the languages still in existence were at one time connected to a language that no longer exists.

There are two theories about the origins of the Indo-European people. One is called the *Kurgan* theory, and it states that the Indo-Europeans lived some 6000 years ago, in and around the Russian steppess. The theory is that they were a warlike people and spread their language through a series of military conquests. The people the Indo-Europeans subjugated were forced to speak the language of their conquerors in order to carry on trade and to survive in an environment controlled by invaders. This is sometimes called the sword theory because it is based on the use of the sword as a weapon for its spread.

The second theory is called the *Anatolian* theory, and it states that the Indo-Europeans lived approximately 10,000 years ago in Anatolia, the present-day Turkey. This is also referred to as the plough theory because it is based on the idea that the Anatolians were agricultural people, and they spread their influence not though war but through their advancements in farming, by the use of the plough.

Wherever and whenever they lived, Indo-Europeans migrated in different directions throughout Europe and Asia. When they moved, they obviously found differences in weather, vegetation, wildlife, and food in the regions in which they settled. Each group, then, created its own words for these discoveries, and the longer these groups lived in the separate regions, the more their languages differed from one another in vocabulary, stress and structure. As a result, people who migrated to the northern regions—for instance, the Norwegians (members of the North Germanic branch of the Indo-European tree) developed many words for snow and ice, as well as words for trees, shrubs, and animals found in cold climates. On the other hand, people who settled in southern areas, like Italy (members of the Italic branch of the Indo-European tree) encountered warmer weather, different trees, shrubs, and animals. Over centuries, the vocabulary, stress, and even structure of their language grew distinct from their northern counterparts. And this would have been true for the early speakers of Russian, Polish, Spanish, French, German, and so on, accounting for the profound differences among many of these languages.

Indo-European refers also to those languages which once were dialects of the language which cover a larger part of Europe and part of Asia. They are—

(a) Indian : In this language, we find the *Veda* (1500 B.C.), the oldest literature in any Indo-European (I.E.) language. The *Veda* consists of four groups of texts, the *Rig-Veda* oldest. Vedic Sanskrit is fully declined and thus is important in reconstruction the original I.E. language *Panini,* a fourth century grammarian, gave Sanskrit a fixed literary form.

(b) Iranian : Because speakers of this group probably traveled with speakers of Indian, the two language bear strong similarities and are sometimes grouped as one. Iranian is not as pure on example of I-E because it contains elements from other, non I.E. languages. This language has two main branches : *Avestan,* the language of the *Avesta,* the sacred text of the Zorastrians (1000 B.C. for the oldest of two parts, the *Gathas*), and *Old Persian,* which has a large Arabic mixture today. (Note that Indian and Iranian are often grouped together.)

(c) ***Armenian :*** Not closely linked to any other I-E language, Armenian is important to us because it shows a certain shifting of consonants analogous to *Grimm's Law* and lack grammatical gender. The earliest example of this language is a 5th century translation of the Bible.

(d) ***Albanian :*** Formerly grouped with Hellenic, this language was recognized as an independent I-E language only in the 20th century. Out knowledge of this language, which dates back only to 1500 A.D., is hampered by the fact that it contains a mixture of many other languages.

(e) ***Hellinic :*** The earliest Greek literary works are the heroic *Odyssey* and *Illiad* (8th century A.D.). Though there are five principal dialect group *Ionic* became the most important. *Attic,* a subdialect of Ionic and the dialect of Athens, became dominant by the 5th century B.C. It became the basis of a *koine,* or common Greek dialect. The language of the New Testament, it is the basis of Byzantine literature. Today, two varieties of Greek are in existence, the *Pure,* which attempts to restore the ancient vocabulary and inflections, are *demotic,* the popular, natural language.

(f) ***Italic :*** *Latin* became the dominant language of this branch. The languages that derive from Latin are known as *Romanic* or *Romance* languages. *Vulgar Latin* is the variety spoken in the streets of Rome, which is represented today by *Italian. Classical Latin* is a literary language with an elaborate and artificial vocabulary. The Romance languages as we know them descend not from classical, but from Vulgar Latin. In addition to Italian, four other Romanic languages are dominant : *French,* which originally consisted of a number of dialects. The Parisian, or *Ile-de-France* dialect, became the official and litera language and, since the 13th century, has been standard French. Two main dialects named for the pronunciation of the word *yes* divide North and South France : langue d'oc (the language of the Troubadours, today known as Provincial and *langue d'oil.* The other three are Spanish, Portuguese, and Romanian. Spanish and Portugue are quite similar, while Romanian is the Eastern most of the Romance languages.

(g) Balto-Salvic : These two language groups have enough similarities to merit their consideration as one classification and were probably nearly identical until the 7th or 8th century. The *Baltic* branch includes *Prussian* (now extinct), *Lettish* (the language of about a million in Latvia), and *Lithunian*. Of these, Lithunian is most important of a study of I-E languages because it preserves very old features. Three main divisions are *West* (Slovak, Czeck, and Polish, which is the largest), *South* Serbo, Croation, Slovenian, and Bulgarian), and *East* (Great Russian is the largest, the official and literary language of Russia).

(h) Tocharian : A wrinkle in the Statem-Centum split theory, Tocharian is a Ceytum (West) language which is located in Asia. This language exists only in a few fragmentary texts and is a twentieth century addition to the I-E family.

(i) Annatolian (Hittite) : The discovery of this language in the early twentieth century proved Saussure's theory that proto-Indo-European must have certain phonological units called *laryngeals.*

(j) Celtic : Various social forces have greatly diminished this once extensive language so that today it is spoken only by a small minority in France and the British Isles. This language consists of three main groups : *Gallic,* which is the language of the Celts in Gaul who were conquered by Caesar; *Gaelic,* spoken by the earliest Celtic settlers in England and represented by Irish, Scottish-Gaelic and Mann (extinct since WWII); and *Britannic,* represented by modern Cornish (extinct in the 18th century), Welsh, and Breton.

(k) Germanic : No documents record the earliest form of this language. It has been reconstructed by philologists and is thus termed *proto-Germanic Grimm's Law,* though it has been refined by Karl Verner and others and though it is still debated accounts for certain differences and connects Germanic to the other I-E languages. Three languages descend from proto-Germanic : The *East* branch includes Danish and Swedish. The earliest remnants of the Germanic branch are in this language, a translation of the Gospels and parts of the New Testament by *Ulfilas* (311-383). The *North* branch is subdivided into a *North West* (Icelandic and Norwegian) and *North East* (Danish and Swedish) branch due to dialectical changes apparent by the 11th century. Old Icelandic is the most literary offshoot of this branch, as a body of heroic poetry

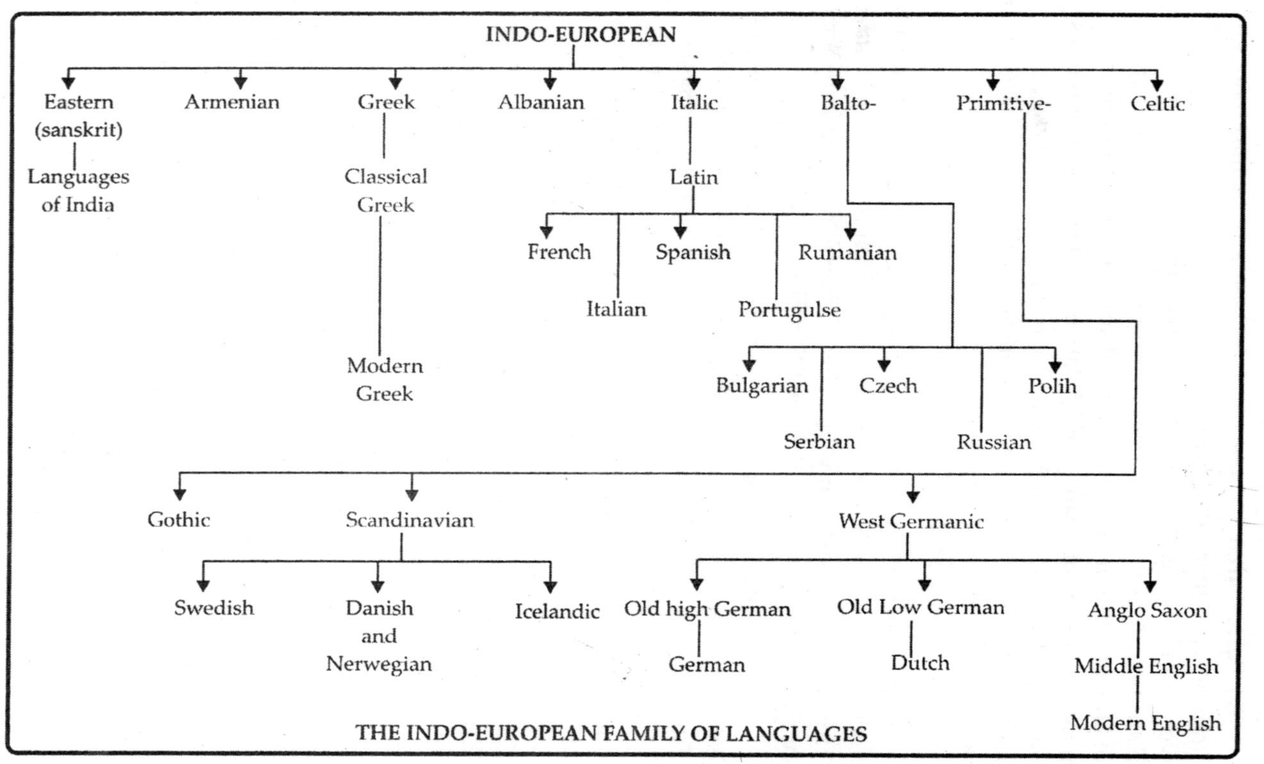

THE INDO-EUROPEAN FAMILY OF LANGUAGES

is preserved by settlers from Norway around 874. Prominent are the *Prose Edda* and *Poetic Edda* compiled in the 12th century by Snorri Sturluson.

The *West* branch is of most significance to us, for it is from this branch that English descends. The West branch is subdivided into two branches due to a *second* (or *High German*) *sound shift*. Analogous to Grimm's Law, this sound change entailed [p, t, k, d], which were changed to other sounds in the mountainous southern regions, but now in the lowlands. *High German*, popularized by Luther's translation of the Bible, became the literary language of Germany. *Low German* includes *Old English*, *Old Frisian* (closely related to Old English), *Old Franconian* (the basis of modern Dutch, Flemish, and Afrikaans), and *Old Saxon* (modern Low German).

Old English or Anglo-Saxon (450-1150)

Perhaps England has been inhabited for 50,000 years, yet English has been spoken for only 1,500.

Time Line

Upto 5000 B.C.	—	Paleolithic Man
2000 B.C. – 1500 B.C.	—	Neolithic Man (may have been the Basques)
1500 B.C. – 500 B.C.	—	Bronze Age (Celts are the first Indo-European speakers in England that we know of)
55 B.C.	—	Julius Caesar attacks England after conquering the Celts in Gaul. He doesn't succeed in conquering the Celts in England.
43 A.D.	—	Emperor Claudius gradually conquers the Celts in England.
61 A.D.	—	Celtic uprising led by Bodicae, widow of a Celtic chief.
75 – 85 A.D.	—	Conquest was said to have been completed under the Roman governor Agricola.

410 A.D.	–	Approximate date of Roman withdrawal.
499 A.D.	–	Approximate date of the Germanic invasions coming from continental Denmark and the low countries. The tribes included the Angles, Jutes, Saxons and Frisians. We have this date and know a little about their culture through Bede's *Ecclesiastical History of the English People,* completed in 731. The entries in the Chronicle indicate only in a general way the succession of settlements which extended over a century. We know that the nature of the Germanic invasion was different from the Roman one, as the former displaced the Celts, while the later ruled them.
789 A.D.	–	Invasion of Norwegians, Danes and Swedes in England. Their language was probably not all that different from the Angles, Saxons, Jutes and Frisians, and this Old English period lasted until approximately 1150 A.D.

Anglo-Saxon Civilization

This civilization was founded on comitatus relationship between lord and theign, and it was organized according to *earls* and *ceorls*. In times, various tribes combined and allied in small kingdoms, seven of which were eventually recognized as the *Anglo-Saxon Heptarchy*. The Heptarchy included Mercia, East Anglia, Northumbria, Kent, Essex, Sussex and Wessex. Of these, Wessex became the dominant, first under the Egbert (800-839) and more prominently under king Alfred (871-889).

Language

The various dialects spoken by the Germanic tribes are known as Pre-Old English. The term *England* developed later from the tribal name *Angles,* possibly because this kingdom was dominant. The term *Anglo-Saxon* referred to the West Germanic tribes generally. Old English was not entirely uniform and four main dialects were predominant : Northumbrian, Mercain, West Saxon and Kentish. Nearly all of Old English literature is preserved in the West Saxon dialect. The most significant work from the period is the epic poem *Beowulf.* During these early years, English was a heavily inflected language; that is nouns, verbs, adjectives, and adverbs took different forms, dependent on if they were singular or plural, past or present tense, in the nominative genititive, dative, or accusative cases. A modern remnant of inflection can be found in our pronouns. For example, as a subject, the masculine singular third-person pronoun is *he.* In its possessive form, *he* becomes his; in its objective form, *he* becomes *him.* When a word changes to reveal different forms like this, we call this inflection. Old English also had hundreds of irregular verbs.

A modern example of an irregular verb is "swim" because it changes its form : present tense *swim,* past tense *swam,* and past participle have, has, or had *swum.* This is also a type of inflection, called conjugation. Although our modern English grew out of Old English, for us today, Old English is a foreign language. We would need a dictionary for us to understand virtually every word of it. An example appears below :

Nu sculon herigean
heofonrices weard
Meotodes meahte and his
modge-panc
(Now we must praise
heaven's kingdom's
Guardian
The Measurer's might and
his mind plans)

A Few Primary Characteristics of Old English

Spelling and Pronunciation :

(1) the long vowels have undergone extensive change due to the great Vowel Shift.

(2) different letters.

(3) there were no unstressed syllables; primary stress usually occurred on the first syllable.

Wordstock

Nearly 85% of Old English words are no longer in use. Those that remain are basic elements of our vocabulary. Also absent are many borrowings from Latin and French. However, language was still poetic mainly through the use of compounds called *kennings.*

Development and Foreign Influences on Old English

Old English was not static, and its usage covered a period of approximately 700 years – from the Anglo-Saxon migrations that created England in the fifth century to some time after the Norman invasion of 1066, when the language underwent a dramatic transition. During this early period it assimilated some aspects of the languages with which it came in contact, such as the Celtic languages and the two dialects of Old Norse from the invading Vikings, who were occupying and controlling large tracts of land in northern and eastern England, which came to be known as the Danelaw.

(i) Germanic Origins : The most important force in shaping Old English was its Germanic heritage in its vocabulary, sentence structure and grammar which it shared with its sister languages in continental Europe. Some of these features were specific to the West Germanic language family to which Old English belongs, while some other features were inherited from the Proto-Germanic language from which all Germanic languages are believed to have been derived.

Like other West Germanic languages of the period, Old English was fully inflected with five grammatical cases (nominative, accusative, genitive, dative, and instrumental, though the instrumental was very rare), which had dual plural forms for referring to groups of two objects (but only in the personal pronouns) in addition to the usual singular and plural forms. It also assigned gender to all nouns, including those that describe inanimate objects ; for example *sēo sunne* (the Sun) was feminine, while *se mōna* (the Moon) was masculine (cf. modern German *die Sonne* vs. *der Mond).*

(ii) Celtic Influence : Traditionally, many maintain that the influence of Celtic on English has been small, citing the small number of Celtic loanwards taken into the language. The number of Celtic loanwards is of a lower order than either Latin or Scandinavian; distinctive Celtic traits have been argued to be clearly discerible from the post-Old English period in the area of syntax. Very msager, Celtic words are preserved primarily in place names. There are two main groups of words :

1. Popular words that the Anglo-Saxons learned through everyday contact with Celtic natives, and
2. Those that were introduced through Irish missionaries in the North.

(iii) Latin Influence : A large percentage of the educated and literate population (monks, clerics, etc.) were competent in Latin, which was the scholarly and diplomatic *lingua franca* of Europe at the time. It is sometimes possible to give approximate dates for the entry of individual Latin words into Old English based on which patterns of linguistic change they have undergone. There were at least three notable periods of Latin influence. The first occurred before the ancestral Saxons left continental Europe for Britain. The second began when the Anglo-Saxons were converted to Christianity and Latin-speaking priests became widespread. The third and largest single transfer of Latin-based words happened after the Norman invasion of 1066, after which an enormous number of Norman words entered the language. Most of these Oil language words were themselves derived from Old French and ultimately from classical Latin, although a notable stock of Norse words were introduced, or re-introduced in Norman form. The Norman conquest approximately marks the end of Old English and the advent of Middle English.

One of the ways the influence of Latin can be seen is that many Latin words for activities came to also be used to refer to the people engaged in those activities, an idom carried over from Anglo-Saxon but using Latin words. This can be seen in words like *militia, assembly, movement* and *service.*

The language was further altered by the transition away from the runic alphabet (also known as *futhorc* or *fuporc*) to the Latin Latin alphabet, which was also a significant factor in the developmental pressures brought to bear on the language Old English words were spelt as they were pronounced; the "silent" letters in many Modern English words, such as the *k* in *knight,* were in fact pronounced in old English. For example, the *c* in *cniht,* the old English equivalent of *knight,* was pronounced. Another side effect of spelling words phonetically was that spelling was extremely variable—the spelling of a word would reflect differences in the phonetics of the writer's regional dialect, and also idiosyncratic spelling choices which varied from author to author, and even from work to work by the same author. Thus, for example, the word *and* could be spelt either *and* or *ond.*

Old English spelling can therefore be regarded as even more jumbled than modern English spelling, although it can at least claim to reflect *some* existing pronunciation, while modern English in many cases cannot. Most present day students of Old English learn the language using normalised versions and are only introduced to variant spellings after they have mastered the basics of the language.

(iv) Viking Influence/Scandinavian Influence: It was the three main attack periods :

1. The period of the early raids. Recorded by the Anglo-Saxon chronicle in 787 and continuing intermittently until 850.
2. The work of large armies; widespread plundering. In 850, a Danish fleet arrives, captures Canterbury and London, and ravages the countryside. A West Saxon army defeats them, but soon they resume attacks. Short after Alfrel's accession to throne, Wessex is attacked. At one point, Alfred has to hide on the marshes. He regathers troops and later attacks and defeats Guthrum and the Danish army. After this defeat, the Danes agree to sign the treaty of Wedmore (878), which defined the line to the east of which the foreigners were to remain. Their designated land was known as the Danelaw.
3. The period of political adjustment and assimilation from 878-1042. Guthrum frequently broke faith, but situations improved under the reign of Alfred's son, Edgar (900-25) and grands on Athselstan (925-39).

Towards the end of the century, new invasions begin. A Viking fleet arrives in 1991 and is recorded in the Battle of Maldon. In 994, Olaf became king of Norway and was joined by the Danish King Svein in a new attack on London. Svein succeeds in conquering England, as they can no longer buy him off. In 1014, he seizes the English throne and became king, driving off Aethelred the unready. The Old English period ends with Svein's son, Cnut, as king of England.

The second major source of loanwords to Old English were the Scandinavian words introduced during the Viking invasions of the 9th and 10th centuries. In addition to a great many place names, these consist mainly of items of basic vocabulary, and words concerned with particular administrative aspects of the Danelaw (that is, the area of land under Viking control, which included extensive holdings all along the eastern coast of England and Scotland). The Vikings spoke Old Norse, a language related to Old English in that both derived from the same ancestral Proto-Germanic language. It is very common for the inter-mixing of speakers of different dialects, such as those that occur during times of political unrest, to result in a mixed language, and one theory holds that exactly such a mixture of Old Norse and Old English helped accelerate the decline of case endings in Old English. Apparent confirmation of this is the fact that simplification of the case endings occurred earliest in the North and latest in the southwest, the area farthest away from Viking influence. Regardless of the truth of this theory, the influence of Old Norse on the English language has been profound : responsible for such basic vocabulary items as *sky, leg,* the pronoun *they,* the verb form *are,* and hundreds of other words.

Grammar

Anglo-Saxon had a very complicated grammar. There were two declensions of the adjective—strong and weak—and for its nouns, like modern German, it had three-gender system, but fixed very arbitrarily, so that the word for *girl,* in the face of all logic and commonsense, was neuter, while of the two words for woman one was neuter and the other masculine. It was, too, a highly inflected language, though throughout the period of process of leveling-out took place, so that by A.D. 1000 some of the inflexions were tending to disappear and the was was being haved for considerable simplification in the Middle English period that was to follow. To take an example : there were originally a number of different declensions of the noun, but the most common was that in which the nominative and accusative plural ended in *–as* and the genitive singular in *–es*. As time went on many more nouns were made to conform to this type, and therein is to be found the reason why the last majority of words in modern English form their plural by the addition of *s*, and why we make our genitive with an apostrophe *s*. The plural and genitive endings, in fact, are all that remain in modern English nouns of the elaborate. Anglo-Saxon system of inflexions, though in the case of the pronouns they have been more fully preserved.

Spelling and Pronunciation of Old English

There are certain genuine differences of pronunciation between Old English and Modern English. Some of them call for comment. The symbol *f* represents in Old English both sounds *f* and *v* and therefore *v* symbol was not in use. When *f* occurs in the middle of a word before a voiced sound, and is not doubled, it is generally pronounced *v*. Examples are *giefan* (give), *seafan* (seven), *lifde* (live). In all other positions *f* symbol is pronounced *f* as in fxder (father), *hæft* (heft, hand).

The symbol *i* is difficult to interpret. Sometimes it is a semi-vowel as in the words *gear* (year), *geong* (young). Sometimes it is a stop as in *god* (good), *ges* (geese) and yet sometimes it is a fricative sound produced by narrowing the air-stream, as in words like *fugol* (word) *lagu* (law). The letter *h* represents a stronger and mofle articulate sound than what it is today. When we read Old English we must remember that every symbol is pronounced. In this sense, Old English is phonetic in character.

Phonology

The inventory of classical Old English (*i.e.* the West Saxon) surface phones, as usually reconstructed, is as follows.

	Bilabial	Labiodental	Dental	Alveolar	Postalvolar	Palatal	Velar	Glottal
Stop	pb			td			kg	
Affricate					tʃ (dʒ)			
Nasal	m			n			(*n*)	
Fricative		f (v)	θ (σð)	s (z)	ʃ	(Ç)	(×) (r)	h
Approximant				r		j	w	
Lateral Approximant				l				

The sounds marked in parentheses in the chart above are allophones:

- [dƷ] is an allopone of /j/ occurring after /n/ and when geminated.
- [ŋ] is an allophone of /n/ occurring before /k/ and /g/
- [v, ð, z] are allophones of /f, θ, s/ respectively, occurring between vowels or voiced consonants.
- [ç , x] are allophones of /h/ occurring in coda position after front and back vowels respectively.
- [r] is an allophone of /g/ occurring after a vowel, and, at an earlier stage of the language, in the syllable onset.

Monophthongs	Short		Long	
	Front	Back	Front	Back
Close	i. y	u	i: y:	u:
Mid	e (ϕ)	o:	e: (ϕ):	o:
Open	æ	a	æ:	a:

The front mid rounded vowels /q (:)/ occur in some dialects of old English, but not in the best attested Late West Saxon dialect.

Diphthongs	Short (monomoraic)	Long (bimoraic)
First element is close	i y	i: y
Both elements are mid	e o	e:o
Both elements are open	æ a	æ:a

Morphology

Unlike modern English, Old English is a language rich with morphological diversity and is spelled essentially as it is pronounced. It maintains several distinct cases: The nominative, accusative, genitive, dative and (vestigially) instrumental, remnant of which survive only in as few pronouns in modern English.

Syntax:

Word Order:

The word order of Old English is widely believed to be subject-verb-object (SVO) as in modern English and most

Germanic language is (not including German and Dutch). The word order of old English however, was not very important due to the aforementioned morphology of the language, so long as declension was correct it did not matter whether you said "My name is .... " as " Mīn nama is ...." or "Nama mīn is ...."

Questions

Due to its similarity with old Norse, it is believed that the word order of Old English changed when asking a question, from SVO to VSO, *i.e.* swapping the verb and the subject.

"You are ...." becomes "Are you .... ?"

" *Pū bist* ...." becomes "*Bist pū* .... ?"

Literature

Old English Literature, though more abundant than literature of the continent before AD 1000, is nonetheless scanty. In his supplementary article in the 1935 bosthumous edition of Brights' *Anglo-Saxon Reader*, Dr. James Hulbert Writes:

> In such historical conditions, an incalculable amount of the writings of the Anglo-Saxon period perished. What they contained, how important they were for an understanding of literature before the Conquest, we have no means of knowing: the scant catalogs of monastic librarier do not help us, and there are no references in extant works to other compositions.............. How incomplete our materials are can be illustrated by the well-known fact that, with few and relatively unimportant exceptions, all extant Anglo-Saxon poetry is preserved in four manuscripts.

Old English was one of the first vernacular languages to be written down some of the most important surviving works of Old English literature are *Beowulf*, an epic poem; the Anglo-Saxon Chronicle, a record of early English History; and Caedmon's Hymn, a Christian religious poem. There are also a number of extant prose works, such as sermons and saints' lives, Biblical translations, and translated Latin works of the early Church Fathers, legal documents, such as laws and wills, and practical works on grammar, medicine, and geography. Still, poetry is considered to be the heart of Old English literature. Nearly all Anglo-Saxon authors are anonymous, with a new exceptions, such as Bede and Caednon.

Some lines from Beowulf are translated which have slightly different meanings in a modern context:

	Original	*Translation*
(1)	Hwaet! wē Gār -Dena in geār -dagum,	What ! We [of] Gar-Danes (lit, spear-danes) in yore-days,
(2)	peod-cyninga, prym gefrunon	[of] people—kings, trim (glory) apried (have learned of by asking or "prying").
(3)	hu ja alpelingas ellen fremedon	how those athelings (princes) arm-strong feats framed (made).

Translation of *The Lord's Prayer*—presented in the standardised West Saxon literary dialect.

	Original	*Translation*
(1)	Fæder ure pu pe eart on heofonum	Father ours, thou that art in heaven,
(2)	Si pin nama gehalgod	Be thy name hallowed
(3)	To beume pin rice,	Come thy rich (Kingdom)
(4)	gewurpe din willa, on eardan swa swa on heofonum	Worth (manifest) thy will, on earth also as in heaven
(5)	Urne gedaeghwamlican hlaf syle us todaeg,	Our daily loaf sell (give) us today,

Middle English (1150-1500)

The last successful invasion of England occurred in 1066 A.D., when William the Conqueror, a Norman Frenchman, won the battle near Hastings. It's interesting to note that although the Normans came from northwestern France—and brought the French language into England with them—they had many years earlier originated from Scandinavia, from which former invaders of England had come. Therefore, their French was not the Midland

French but more of a guttural French. For approximately two hundred fifty years, this form of French had an influence on the English language, as any language of a conqueror affects the subjugated people. French particularly had its influence in government, among the upper classes, and among merchants who wanted to trade and sell goods to the wealthy leaders of England who spoke French. Linguists estimate that between 1250 and 1400, approximately 10,000 French words entered the English language. Here is a sample of that influence, the first group dealing with military matters: *peace, enemy, arms, battle, combat, skirmish, siege, defense, ambush, retreat, soldier, guard, spy, captain, lieutenant, defend.* The following word that refer to cuisine have entered the English language : *dinner, supper, appetite, taste, beef, mutton, biscuit, almonds, orange, lemon, cherry, peach, jelly, mustard, vinegar.* These originally French words refer to fashion: *fashion, dress, habit, gown, robe, garment, cape, cloak, coat, collar, veil, train, petticoat, lace, buckle, blue, brown, vermilion, scarlet.* And these French words refer to government—*crown, state, majesty, realm, royal, sovereign, tyrant, court, council, parliament, assembly, statute,* and *treaty.*

This second significant period in the English language is known as Middle English, and it ranges from 1150 A.D. to 1500 A.D. The most significant poet of this period is Geoffrey Chaucer, the author of the *Canterbury Tales.*

During this period, the English language lost much of the complexity that it had possessed in the Old English period. For instance, the use of inflection waned, and many of the irregular verbs used during Old English became regular. These changes were probably due less to the direct influence of French and more to the changes that had already begun by the late Old English Period into early Middle English. By the middle of the fourteenth century, English—not French—was once again the major language in England. This was due to political changes in England, as well as the hundred-year war between England and France. Later in the century, when Geoffrey Chaucer wrote the *Canterbury Tales,* he satirized the pretentiousness of characters in the tales who speak French. Although most of us would initially have trouble reading Middle English, with a bit of guidance, we can understand many of the words—and the general meaning of the text. This is illustrated in the example below :

Whan that April with his
showres soote
The droughte of March hath
perced to the roote,
And bathed every veine in
surch licour.
Of which vertu engendred is
the flowr:

Grammar

One change that brought about important differences between Old and Middle English was in part due to foreign influence. This was the decay of the Old English inflexional system. The weakening of the vowels of lightly stressed syllables had begun in the Old English period, and it is probable that the confusion of inflexional endings was increased by the presence in England of large numbers of Scandinavians and, to a lesser extent, by the presence of speakers of French. Many words had identical stem-syllables in English and Scandinavian, differing only in the inflexional endings. It is natural that, when the speakers of the two languages intermingled, inflexional endings should suffer.

The decay of inflexional endings had an influence on syntax. So long as inflexions served to indicate the cases of nouns, word-order was comparatively unimportant, but when nominative and accusative came to be identical in form, a fixed word-order was necessary in order to make clear the important distinction between 'The man killed the lion' and 'The lion killed the man'. One of the devices used to replace inflexional endings was the greater use of prepositions, and this development became even more marked in the Modern English period.

Another important change which took place in early Middle English was the loss of grammatical gender. In Old English, as in Modern French and German, the gender of nouns had no connexion with their meaning and was sometimes in direct contradiction to it. Thus, *wifmann*, 'woman' was masculine, white *wif* 'woman' and *cild* 'child' were neuter. Already in Old English we find the beginnings of natural gender, as in King Alfred's preface to the translation of Gregory's *Pastoral*, where the neuter pronoun *hit* is used to refer to the masculine noun *wīsdōm*. The gender of an Old English noun was often indicated by the form of an adjective or pronoun agreeing with it. When the decay of inflexions made it impossible to distinguish the gender of a noun in this way, the tendency of replace grammatical gender by natural gender was accelerated. The introduction of the personal pronoun *she*, first appeared in the middle of the twelfth century in the East-Midland dialect and subsequently spread to others.

Phonology

Dialectical differences play a more important part in Middle English than in either Old English or Modern English. They are less important in Old English because of the scarcity of non-West-Saxon texts; they are less important in Modern English because of the rise of standard English, a single dialect which had acquired greater, importance than the other dialect. The important development that took place was that in the Midland and the southern dialects the long *ā* of Old English in such words as *hām*, *stān*, *hōf* (pronounced with the same vowel as the modern *pslam*) became long *ō*. It was often represented orthographically by a double *o* (*hoom*, etc.), but was pronounce roughly the same as it is today in the words *home, stone,* and *loaf*, which of course, are the direct descendants of these Middle English forms. This change, which had already started in late Old English itself, appears to have been perfected by about 1250.

An examination of Middle English metrical writings will show that in the case of the majority of words introduced from French, not only was the vowel sound retained but until fairly late in the period the foreign accentuation was also preserved. The following few lines, with the French loan-words italicised and the accentuation marked, will serve as examples:

And bathed every veyne in swich *licóur,*
So priketh hem *natúre* in hir *couráges,*
Thanne longen folk to gon on *pilgrimáges,*
Of adventúres than whilorn han bifalle.

Another phonetic development which had commenced in the late Old English period and was completed in the Middle English was the lengthening of short vowels when they stood in open syllables, and the shortening of long ones in closed syllables, so that we can say that by the end of the thirteenth century almost all vowels in open syllables were long, either because they had been so originally or because they had been lengthened, while almost all vowels in closed syllables were short, for the same two reasons. Hence the modern difference in pronunciation between *tilling* and *tiling, canning* and *caning, laddy* and *lady*, etc. In Middle English the final *e* had a phonetic value, as is obvious from the poetry of the time, and thus they were disyllabic words, with their first syllable an open one. And the same is true of verbs like *meet, greet, sleep,* etc., which at first sight would seem to be closed syllables. Today it is true, they are closed; but in the Middle English period they had the infinitive termination *–en,* which 'opened' them.

In a trisyllabic word the vowel of the first syllable was shortened even though that syllable was an open one. Hence we get *hōly day* (two words), but *hōliday* (one word). Vowels before the combination *st* were normally short in Middle English, in Conformity with the rule laid down above : cf. the modern *best, fist, lost, rust,* etc. Nevertheless in a large number of Modern English words the vowel is long before this combination : e.g., *fast, least, priest, ghost, host,* etc. The lengthening probably came from an inflected form, or from the plural, where the *st* combination was regarded as belonging to the second syllable, thus leaving the first syllable an open one; e.g. *hō -stes, gō -stes, prē -stes,* etc.

Glide consonants were developed in a number of words especially after nasal consonants. The glide consonant was usually *b* or *p* next to *m,* and *d* or *t* next to *n*. Examples are *thumb* (OE *pūma*) and the related word *thimble* (OE *pȳmel*), *empty* (OE *āmetig*), *thunder* (OE *punor*). In *listen* (OE *plysnan*) and *glisten* (OE *glisnian*) the *t* has since been lost again in pronunciation, although it is kept in spelling.

Modern English – 1500 Present

Beginning in 1500 A.D., English moved into its third stage, called Modern English. During this century, prominent writers created poetry and drama in England, among them were Edmund Spenser, Christopher Marlowe, and William Shakespeare. Born in 1564, Shakespeare had the most profound effect on English; he possessed on enormous vocabulary, experimented with language, and through his sonnets, poems, and plays had a profound effect on the development of English. Most modern readers have little trouble reading poetry or prose from this period, just as most modern readers and speakers are grateful that during this time, the language became simpler than its Old English and Middle English forms. Because of the influence of Shakespeare and the economic and military power that England achieved under Queen Elizabeth I, the English language increased in its international importance.

Writers and thinkers became concerned about the profound changes in the language that had taken place in just five hundred years. Literate people in Shakespeare's day would not have been able to read Old English and some would have been able to read Old English, and some would have had trouble reading Chaucer's Middle English. In addition, until about 1650, English spelling had not been standardize, and often prominent writers would spell the same words differently. To prevent such inconsistencies from continuing, writers began to call for the standardization of the language. As early as the sixteenth century, they began this movement by writing grammar texts and guides to spelling. However, the interest in standardization reached its peak in the eighteenth century.

One of the principal proponents of standardization was Jonathan Swift, the author of *Guilliver's Travels*. In 1712, he proposed that something like an English academy be created, similar to the one that had been established in France. The members of the academy would function as a kind of language police who would determine what words could enter the language, what practices should be discarded, and what rules should be applied to it. This kind of grammar is referred to as perspective grammar; that is, it is authoritative and governed by rules; it functions something like the prescription that a doctor writes out for you for the improvement of your language skills. Other influential authors agreed with swifts prescriptive grammar were John Dryden and Joseph Addison, for instance but despite the movement to establish a language academy, the academy was never approved. Many grammarians, however, wrote books that advocated prescriptive rules that speakers and writers were told to abide by. Some of these rules had little or no logical basis; others were dictated by the rules used for Latin, and by analogy they were applied to English.

When the academy idea failed, English writers like Nathaniel Bailey in 1721 and Samuel Johnson in 1755 created dictionaries to be used as guidelines for the standardization of spelling and definations. Noah Webster did the same thing for American English. In the 1780's, he wrote books to help Americans with their spelling, grammar, and reading. In 1828, he published his influential *An American Dictionary of the English Language,* in which he showed that American English was considerably different from British English. For some modern examples of how words differ between American and British English, consider the following : What Americans call the *trunk* of a car, the English call the *boot,* what Americans call the *hood* of a car, the English call the *bonnet,* what Americans call a *truck,* the English call a *lorry,* what American call an *elevator,* the English call a *lift*. Many other modern examples exist.

Just as in Swift's day, the argument continues today that the English language is losing its purity and that the media and younger generations have abused it. But these arguments have raged for hundreds of years and, no doubt, will continue to rage. The counter argument to "the loss of purity" or "the decline of standards" faction is that for a language to remain alive and vibrant, it must change to fit new ideas, technologies, and generations. This latter approach to language is often referred to as descriptive grammar. That is, that while they maintain an historical standard, grammar texts should also faithfully record how language is used by various speakers of it, regardless of whether the usage is "good grammar" or "bad grammar". For instance, conservative speakers of the language use the word like only as a preposition : "People like her become upset by the use of poor grammar." In this sentence, *her* is the object of the preposition *like*. However, many modern speakers use *like* as a subordinating conjunction, with a subordinate clause following it : "He treated me like I wasn't even there. Conservative speakers and writers maintain the use of the subjunctive mood in the following use of the verb "to be" : "If I were you, I would not do that." Many other speakers and writers disregard the subjunctive mood : If I *was* you, I wouldn't do that, "Hundreds of other examples of these differences appear in the language, particularly when we think of new technologies. For instance, our language has words like *windows, mouse, cursor, download, upload,* and many others that have taken on a different meaning when they are applied to computers. Recently a new dictionary included the word *McJob* to indicate a job that pays poorly and offers little future for its holder; the word stems from the jobs offered by the fast-food franchise McDonald's.

Grimm's Law–1822

In 1822, the German folktale collector and philologist (an old word for linguist) Jakob Grimm clarified what an earlier Danish linguist Rasmus Rask had discovered about the similarities within certain languages. Jacob, along with his brother, is the author of *Kinder und Hausmarchen* (we know it as Grimm's Fairy Tales), and he drew attention to a similarity between consonants in Sanskrit, Greek and Latin—and those in certain Germanic languages, including English. Grimm said that the "p" in some Indo-European languages over time became an "f" in Germanic languages. This is how he showed the relationship between the Latin *piscis* (meaning fish) and the German *Fisch* and English *fish.* He also showed the "t" in the Latin *tres* (three) became the "th" in the English *three.* Similarly, the Latin *centrum* (hundred) became the English *hundred.* In further mutations of these changes, the German *offen* became the English *open,* the German *essen* becomes the English *eat.*

Jakob Grimm's observations about the connections among these languages have become known as Grimm's Law; It's an important development in the explanation of how these languages have evolved.

In 1453 Constantinople, hitherto the seat of European learning, fell to the Turk, and the scholars who were assembled there fled to western Europe, bringing with them as much of their libraries as they could manage to rescue and transport. They settled at first mainly in Germany and Italy and so started that intellectual awakening of Europe which has come to be known as the Renaissance. It was a classical Renaissance, and mainly a Latin one; hence the chief effect of it upon the vocabulary was from Latin origin or from Latin roots.

In the wake of the Renaissance followed the Reformation, and this again, though its importance was primarily religious and political, had its effect upon the language. The bitter religious controversies to which it gave rise during the next two centuries were productive of numerous words—most of them expressing odium or disapproval—which became current through contemporary polemics and so gained a permanent niche in the vocabulary, though no doubt there must have been many more which failed to survive their day and generation. Since England had, officially at least, became a Protestant country, most of these terms naturally applied to Catholics. The Catholic mind was just as fertile, but the soil in England, from the time of Elizabeth, being a Protestant soil, these never had a chance to take root—save possibly the word *heretic,* which actually existed earlier but came into more general use after the middle of the sixteenth century. *Papist* and *papistical* both belong to the earlier part of the same century; so does *Romish*. *Puritan* first made its appearance in 1567 and was usually employed with a suggestion of disapproval, as when Shakespeare uses it of Malvolio in *Twelfth Night.* A very important outcome of the Reformation was the various English translations of the Bible, the chief being Tyndale's in 1526, and, more important, the Authorised Version in 1611. Perhaps the latter was more influential and helped in creating some kind of standardization of the English language. Bible contributed to lot of metaphor and a stock of household phrases.

The contribution of Shakespeare and his contemporaries reflect not only the Renaissance culture and the Protestant Reformation, but also a growing national consciousness. On the other hand voyages and discoveries of new land brought different parts of world and men in contact. The invention of printing had a far-reaching effect upon the development of the language. Three aspects of it may be noticed here, viz.,

1. It tended to establish a 'standard' language and to discredit dialect.
2. It served to popularise and give currency to new coinages and newly introduced words.
3. It tended to fix spelling, about which there had been a great deal of uncertainty before.

The Elizabethan love-poetry was largely Petrarchan. There were also the medieval and Platonic strains in Elizabethan love-poetry. Love-poetry started characterising by increasing realism. Thus woman which was treated as a goddess, began to be treated mere as a creature of flesh and blood. The language of poetry had grown too poetic, and a conventional and stereotyped pharseology was used by poet after poet. Classical mythology was freely exploited for decoration and imagery. Marlowe introduced blank verse in his poetic drama. Many of the Renaissance poets tried to exploit ancient Greece and Rome and tried their hand in writing epic. But it was left only for Milton to complete this great task is it is rightly said "the English epic begins and ends with Milton."

Ben Jonson was a classicist by temperament as well as by his erudition. He is the real founder of Comedy of Manners.

The year 1890 is regarded as a landmark in the literary and social history of England. It ushered in an era of rapid social change which was observed in every sphere of life. Industrialisation and urbanisation brought in their wake their own problems. There have risen problems like the problem of over-crowding, housing shortage, a significant increase in vice and crime, fall in the standards of sexual morality, and a rapidly increasing ugliness. Early 20th century poetry vividly reflects all these effects of industrialisation. Boredom of city life, degradation of human life, loneliness are all brought together and can be seen in poem like *The Waste Land.* Nationalism was no longer regarded as enough, and imperialism came in for great deal of criticism. E.M. Forster in his *Passage to India* advocates relationships between nations, as well as between individuals, based on equality and the felling heart. The disintegration of faith and traditional beliefs led writers like D.H. Lawrence. The modern age has witnessed a phenomenal rise in literacy. Cheap books, magazines, papers increased the spread of education at a universal level. There has been an increase in vulgarity, brutality and coarseness. The modern poetry is constantly experimenting with new verse forms and poetic techniques. The use of slang and colloquialism has become common, the language and rhythm of poetry approximate more and more to those of common speech, the bonds of metre have been loosened, and the use of *verse libre* has become increasingly common. No rules of rhyme or metre are followed, stresses vary according to emotion, and verse rhythm is replaced by sense rhythm. Symbols, often purely personal, are used in abundance to express pure sensations, and visions, and the result is increased vagueness and obscurity of such poets as Yeats and T.S. Eliot. Modern English novel introuduced new technique, style, themes in the novel. Henry James, Joseph Conard, James Joyce, and Virginia Woolf, revolutionised the technique of the novel with their probings into the sub-conscious giving rise to stream-of-consciousness technique. The modern novel is realistic. The choice between capitalism and communism, science and religion, God and the Atom Bomb, is a confused one, and the result is the baffled and confused man giving out the theory of 'Absurdity'. The realism of the modern novel also gave rise to the treatment of sex.

Vocabulary

Of all word-languages English probably has the vocabulary which is the most copious, heterogeneous and varied. The Renaissance brought the turning of the best minds directly to the ancient civilization of Greece and Rome, and hence a direct influence from Classical Latin as distinct from the Latin of the Middle Ages. In Queen Elizabeth's time it was quite natural for educated men to use Latin terms or affixes unconsciously in their ordinary English speech. Shakespeare has been regarded as the inventor of the terms *castigate, auspicious* and *critic* because they appear to have been first recorded in his plays. The common misuse of *whom* for *who* by journalists and others is largely due to this Latinate tradition still influencing people who no longer have any real contact with Latin grammar. Again in metre we see the influence of an artificial Latin tradition. For English metre is based on stress or emphasis, not on quantity or length of syllable, yet teachers and text-books of metre still speak of *jambs* and *trochees* and *dactyls*; terms based on quantitative notions of syllables taken from Latin prosody and not at any time appropriate to English tradition or usage. Milton, in the Preface to his *Paradise Lost,* speaks of his own blank verse as observing 'fit quantity of syllable, though his real intention should have been on the appropriate arrangement of stress. Among the common Latin words which came into the language in the modern period since 1500, are as follows :

Sixteenth Century : *exist, genius, area, fungus, miser, circus, vacuum, medium, species, ignoramus, vagary.*

Seventeenth Century : *torpor, specimen, arena, apparatus, focus, album, complex, minimum, status, lens, pendulum.*

Eighteenth Century : *nucleus, inertia, alibi, ultimatum extra, insomnia, bonus* (noun), *via* (preposition), *deficit.*

Nineteenth Century : *opus, ego, moratorium, referendum, bacillus.*

Greek having been the European language which most fully and effectively developed the expression of philosophical ideas, it is natural that philosophical and related terms should, even though coming to English in Latin dress, have been founded upon Classical Greek originals. Before the close of the Middle Ages, English had acquired from Greek, *academy, atom, Bible* (Greek *biblos* 'book'), *diphthong, harmony, tragedy, tyrant* and *theatre.* The sixteenth century provided *irony, alphabet, drama, elegy, dilemma, chorus, pathos, laryax, epic* and *theory*. The next century gave *orchestra, pandemonium, museum, hyphen, dogma* and *clinic;* while the eighteenth produced *bathos* and *philander.* The last century saw the coining or adaptation of *phase, pylon, acrobat, therm* and *agnostic.* Many of the foregoing came through Latin or French, and most are now part of what may be termed the *Common European* vocabulary. Like Latin words in English, those from Greek are sometimes so far absorbed into the native complex as to be capable of new formations in English with English prefixes and suffixes that may be attached to English words. Thus, just as we have *un*propitious (Latin *propitus*), humane*ness* (Latin *humanus*) and concurrently (Latin *concurrentem*) where the Italicized elements are English, or *post*-war, and *infra*-red—in which the words are English with Latin prefixes, so too we have the Greek prefixes *anti* (against) and *hyper* (beyond) joined to English words in *anti*-British and *hyper*-sensitive; the Greek negative prefix *a* – is in *amoral*, and the Greek element–*ology* can be added to words of Latin English origin, as in *sociology* (Latin *socius*).

With Latin, French is one of the great fundamental formative influences on the English vocabulary. The development of French in modern English shows well how vocabulary may indicate the history, especially the social history, of a nation; and in the following illustrations of French borrowings since 1500, this should be particularly borne in mind. Besides the military and naval terms which the history of the period might lead one to expect, we find trading and social words. The following are some sixteenth-century French words which have remained in common use, but it must be remembered that this period was not outstanding for French influence : *pilot, sally, partisan, cache, volley, indigo, moustache, piquant, machine.* The seventeenth century was of mere significance. Dryden, the most widely representative author and critic of the later seventeenth century, was an enthusiastic follower in his earlier life of French dramatic models; it was he who first used the French word *correct* (as an adjective) : and he devoted a whole play, his *Mariage a la Mode,* to making fun of the Frenchified English women of the age. At the same time the borrowings of military technical terms and others of commerce, continued. Here are some words—*dragoon, stockade, parole, ballet, burlesque, liaison, par excellence, muslin, soup, group.* The eighteenth century continued its influence whereas the nineteenth century was the richest of all periods in French loans since Middle English times, especially in terms of art and letters, of textiles and furniture, with the usual borrowing of military terms. A few examples are—*barrage, parquet, cheval glass, motif, profile, restaurant, menu, chef, elite, faire.*

Phonology

As a rule Modern English sound-changes are not reflected in spelling, and it is therefore often difficult to date them. The most important of the independent sound-changes that have taken place since the Middle English period are those affecting the long vowels. All the long vowels have changed very considerably, but the distinction between one vowel and another has been preserved, except that Modern English open and close $\bar{e}$ have fallen together. It is possible to detect two general tendencies in the development of the Middle English long vowels in Modern English : they have become more close and they have tended to become diphthongs. In the following account of the changes in detail, the Middle English (ME) long vowels have been arranged in an order to bring out the symmetry between front and back vowels.

Modern English (ME) $\bar{a}$ was fronted to [æ:] in the fifteenth century, and this was raised to [ɛ:] in the sixteenth century and to [e:] in the seventeenth century. At the beginning of the eighteenth century this [e:] was diphthongized to [ei] and this diphthong has remained to the present day. Since Old English (OE) $\bar{a}$ has become [⊃:] in Middle English, the $\bar{a}$ which underwent the series of changes here outlined was not developed from OE $\bar{a}$, but occurred in the main in French loan-words, such as *cage* and *fame*, or in words, such as *name* and *acre*, in which early Modern English Short *a* had been lengthened in an open syllable.

Modern English [⊃:] was raised to [o:] in the early sixteenth century, and this was diphthongized to [ou] at the beginning of the eighteenth century, as in *home, stone* and *oath*. Modern English [o:] was raised to [u:] in the fifteenth century. This has remained to the present day in the pronunciation of some speakers, but many speakers in the south diphthongize the vowel to a sound approximating to [uw], especially when it occurs in final positions. Examples are *goose, cool* and *do.*

The development of Modern English (ME) [i:] was parallel to that of ME [u:]. It was diphthongizer to [ij] in the first half of the fifteenth century, and since that time the two elements of the diphthong have gradually become wider apart. Probably the stages were : [ij] became [ei] in the sixteenth century, and this became [i] at the beginning of the seventeenth century and [ai] in the eighteenth century. Examples are *life, shine* and *child.*

The independent changes affecting short vowels are—The Middle English back open vowerl [a], spelt *a,* was fronted to [æ] about the end of the sixteenth century, but a back vowel has generally remained in the North until the present day, as in *glad* and *apple.*

ME *o* has changed little since the Middle English period, though it has probably become somewhat more open. From the fifteenth to the eighteenth century there are spellings which suggest that *o* had been unrounded, and this unrounding is common in American speech and in some English dialects, but in standard English [æ], resulting from the unround of ME *o,* is found in only a few words, such as *Egad, strap, sprat, nap* (of cloth).

The Middle English diphthongs *eu* and *iu* and Anglo-Norman [y:] spelt *u,* all fell together as [iu] in late Middle English. During the sixteenth century this [iu] became [ju:], and in most positions this is the usual pronunciation at the present day, although [iu] has remained in some dialects. Examples are *few, neuter, due* and *steward.*

ME *ai* has fallen in with ME *ā* although there is some difference of opinion about the date when the two sounds fell together. Some grammarians think that ME *ai* and *ā* fell together *as* [æ:] in the fifteenth century, but others think that ME *ai* never became a monophthong and that ME *ai* and *ā* remained distinct until they fell together as [ei] in the seventeenth century.

ME *au* became [ɔ:] through the intermediate stage [ɔu] by about the end of the sixteenth century. The first element of the diphthong was rounded by the influence of the second element, and the second element, being lightly stressed, then disappeared. Examples are *awe, hawk* and *autumn.*

Beside these independent changes, many dependent changes have affected Modern English vowels. The most important of these changes are those caused by a following *l* or *r*.

ME *o* and [ɔ:] have become [ou] before *l*, as in *bolt, toll, bowl, cold,* old.

The development of *u* before *l* is less clear. Before *ld* or *lt, u* has become [ou], as in *shoulder, boulder, poultry.* Before other *l*-groups, *u* seems not to have been affected, as in *dull, wool, wolf.*

The influence of *r* on preceding vowels was even more marked than that of *l*. Short vowels have been lengthened and have generally also undergone a change in quality when followed by *r* belonging to the same syllable, but they have generally not been affected when the *r* (often spelt *rr*) was intervocalic. Hence we have *car* beside *carry* and *her* beside *herring*. The changes in detail are :

ME *a* become (ae) by an independent change, and in the seventeenth century this [ae], when followed by *r,* was lengthened to [ae:], which became [a:] in the eighteenth century, as an *arm, sharp, garden.*

ME *o* became [ɔ:] before *r* in the seventeenth century, as in *for, horse.*

Labial consonants tend to cause rounding of following vowels, and the influence of preceding labials often prevented the sixteenth-century change of [u] to [^] or led to the restoration of the rounded vowel, especially when the vowel was followed by [ʃ], [tʃ], or *l*, as in *full, pull, bull, pulpit, bushel* and *butcher*. Occasionally, as in *cushion*, the rounded vowel is found before [ʃ], even when there is no preceding labial consonant. The unrounded vowel is often found in later loan-words such as *bulb, pulse, fulminate.*

Many consonants have disappeared in Modern English. Perhaps the most important change of this kind is the loss of *r* medially before consonants and finally unless the next word begins with a vowel and belongs to the same breath-group. This change took place in the eighteenth century, but the *r* is always kept in spelling as in *arm, heard, order.* The *r* is usually silent before consonants, as in *I fear them*, but is pronounced before vowels, as in *I fear it*. This pronunciation of final *r* when the next word begins with a vowel is known as 'linking *r*'. Some speakers have extended the use of *r* by analogy to words where there is no historical justification for it, and where there is no *r* in spelling, with the result that *r* may be heard after *India* in a phrase like *India* and *China*. This misuse *r* is known as 'intrusive *r*'.

Initial *h* is generally pronounced as an aspirate in present day English. The two groups of words where it is regularly omitted are French loan-words like *hour* and *honour*, and lightly stressed words. In both these groups the initial *h* is sometimes restored in pronunciation by the influence of the spelling, as in *hotel, he, him*. In the pronoun *it* (OE *hit*) initial *h* has disappeared in both spelling and pronunciation because of the lack of stress.

Initial *k* and *g* disappeared in pronunciation in the late seventeenth century when immediately followed by *n*, as in *knave, knight, gnaw, gnash, gnat.* Initial *w* disappeared in pronunciation before *r* in the eighteenth century, as in *write, wrestle, wreath*. The consonant *w* often disappeared between *s* and a back rounded vowel and at the beginning of a lightly stressed syllable from the beginning of the Modern English period and occasionally even earlier, but in most words *w* has been restored either by the influence of the spelling or on the analogy of related words. The loss of *w* in pronunciation has proved lasting in *sword* and in place-names like *Norwich* and *Southwark.* Early spellings like *solen* and *sowlen* for *swollen*. Show loss of *w* which has later been restored, possibly on the analogy of *swell*.

Syntax

One of the most important changes in English syntax since Old English times has been the growing importance of word-order. English syntax has been influenced a good deal by that of foreign languages, chiefly Latin and French. Until recent years the grammarians who formulated the rules of 'good' English had been trained in the study of Latin syntax and, consciously or unconsciously, they sought to make English sentences conform to the pattern of Latin sentences. Similar influences were at work on many English authors who, until about the end of the seventeenth century, generally held the view that Latin was a more respectable language than English. Thus we find that Dryden in the first edition of his *Essay of Dramatic Poesy* had many sentences ending with prepositions, but in later editions he revised these sentences, altering, for example, *the age I live in to the age in which I live.* The first version represents natural English syntax and is an idiom of long standing in the language; the revised form is the result of applying the rules of Latin syntax to English, and, perhaps, of remembering the etymological meaning of the word 'preposition'. It may be noted that many people are indirectly influenced by the rules of Latin syntax without realizing the ultimate source of that influence.

In Old English there were several different genitive endings, varying according to the declension. The ending *–es* or *–'s* is the only one that has survived into Modern English, and this has been supplemented by a new construction consisting of the preposition *of* followed by the uninflected form of the noun. The original meaning of *of* was 'from', but when the *of*-phrase is used today, the original meaning of the preposition is not as a rule remembered. Since the Old English period the *of*-phrase has been constantly encroaching on the genitive in *–s*, and in present day use the latter is almost confined to persons and personified object and to a few set phrases, such as *at my wits end.* There is a difference in word-order between the two constructions : the genitive is *–s* usually precedes the noun which governs it, whereas the *of*-phrase follows the governing noun. Sometimes we find the *of*-phrase used together with the genitive in *–s*, as in *This is a book of my brother's.* There is a similar construction with possessive pronouns, as *He is a friend of mine, It is no business of theirs.*

One special form of the genitive which has grown up during the Modern English period is known as the group genitive. This consists of the addition of the genitive inflexion to the last word of a group of words that can be regarded as expressing a single idea even though it belongs logically to an earlier noun in the group. Thus, we say *somebody else's book, the King of England's son* and *the Wife of Bath's Tale,* but in the early manuscripts of the *Canterbury Tales* we find either *the Tale of the Wyf of Bathe* or *the Wyves Tale of Bath.* The group genitive has come into existence because in Modern English the inflected genitive is generally placed immediately before the governing noun, whereas in Old English the position of the genitive was more variable.

During the Modern English period the auxiliary *do* has come to be used in number of specialized functions. One of these is to add emphasis to a statement, as in *I do like mangoes.* A similar use of *do* is to strengthen an imperative, and in this construction *do* can be used with the verb *to be,* as in *Do be quiet*! Another use of *do* is in negative statements. The construction with *do* is normal with all full verbs, but not with auxiliaries. Thus we say *I do not know* but *I will not agree to it.*

Thus many developments and different influences of foreign languages on the growth of English language right from Anglo-Saxon Old English to Modern English has been noted. Still the researches are going on and the grammarians, linguists play their own role in the development of English Language.

2

Technological and Non-European Influence on English Language

> English must be practiced as an open field rather than a linguistic prisonhouse where involuntary anglo-phones do hard time behind the steel bars of alien grammar.
>
> —Joe Lockard

The English language has been the linear tongue of colonial discoveries, racial cruelties, invented names, simulated tribal cultures, and the unheard literature of dominance in tribal cultures; at the same time, this mother tongue of paracolonialism has been a language of liberation for many tribal people.

Anthropologists and linguists believe that language is the key to a culture. Used in the anthropological sense, the word 'culture' means "the characteristic features of a particular stage of advancement in civilization." The dividing line between culture and civilization is rather thin and it is not possible to define one of these without reference to the other. Civilization, for instance, is defined as "the culture characteristic of a particular time or place." All the resources of a—language sounds, vocabulary, grammar, syntax and other—reveal the culture of the people who speak that language as their mother tongue. This concept of the inter-relationship of language and culture was brilliantly summed up by the Sapir-Whorf hypothesis: "language structures reality." If Eskimo has three different words for *snow*, if some African languages have only two words for the seven colours of the rainbow, if Hopi has no past tense, if English has a large number of transitive verbs, if Indian languages have more kinship terms than English, these features reflect reality as apprehend by the speakers of those languages. The language Americans speak is by the same token, the key to American culture, American civilization, American experience or American way of life. In the similar way different culture have different words which has a great influence in making up of English language.

American Contribution

The use of English in the United States was inherited from British colonization. The first wave of English-speaking settlers arrived in North America in the 17th century. During that time, there were also speakers in North America of Dutch, French, German, Norwegian, Spanish, Swedish, Scots, Welsh, Irish, Scottish, Gaelic, Finnish, as well as numerous Native American Languages.

In many ways, compared to English English, North American English is conservative in its phonology. Some distinctive accents can be found on the East Coast, partly because these areas were in contact with England, and imitated prestigious varieties of English English at a time when those varieties were undergoing changes. Most North American speech is rhotic, as English was in most places in the 17th century.

North America has given the English lexicon many thousands of words, meanings, and phrases. Several thousand are now used in English as spoken internationally; others, however, died within a few years of their creation. The process of coining new lexical items started as soon as the colonists began borrowing names for unfamiliar flora, fauna, and topography from the Native American languages. Examples of such names are *opossum, raccoon, squash* and *moose* (from Algonquian). Other Native American loanwords, such as *wigwam* or *moccasin,* describe artificial objects in common use among Native Americans. The languages of the other colonizing nations also added to the American vocabulary; for instance, *cookie, cruller, stoop,* and *pit* (of a fruit) from Dutch; *levee, portage* ("carrying of boats or goods") and (probably) *gopher* from French; *barbecue, stevedore,* and *radeo* from Spanish.

Among the earliest and most notable regular "English" additions to the American vocabulary, dating from the early days of colonization through the early 19th century, are terms describing the features of the North American landscape; for instance, *run, branch, fork, snag, bluff, gulch reck* (of the woods), *barrens, bottomland, notch, knob, riffle, rapids, watergap, cutoff, trail, timberline* and *divide.* Already existing words such as *creek, slough, sleet* and (in later use) *watershed* received new meanings that were unknown in England.

The word *corn,* used in England to refer to wheat (or any cereal), came to denote the plant *Lea mays,* the most important crop in the U.S., originally named *Indian corn* by the earliest settlers; wheat, rye, barley, oats, etc. came to be collectively referred to as *grain* (or *bread-stuffs*). Other notable farm related vocabulary additions were the new meanings assumed by *barn* (not only a building for hay and grain storage, but also for housing livestock) and *team* (not just the horses, but also the vehicle along with them), as well as, in various periods, the terms *range,* (*corn*) *crib, truck, elevator, sharecropping* and *feedlot.*

With the new continent developed new forms of dwelling, and hence a large inventory of words designated real estate concepts (*land office, lot, outlands, waterfront,* the verbs *locate* and *relocate, betterment, addition, subdivision),* types of property (*log cabin, aclobe* in the 18th century; *frame house, apartment, tenement house, shack, shanty* in the 19th century; *project, condominium, town house, split-level, mobile home, multi-family* in the 19th century), and parts thereof (*driveway, breezeway, backyard, dooryard; clapboard, siding, trim, baseboard; stoop* (from Dutch), *family room, den;* and in recent years, *HVAC, central air, walkout basement).*

Ever since the American Revolution, a great number of terms connected with the U.S. political institutions have entered the language; examples are *run, gubernatorial, primary election, carpetbagger* (after the Civil War), *repeater, lame duck* and *fork barrel.* Some of these are internationally used (*e.g. caucus, gerrymander, filibuster, exist poll*).

The rise of capitalism, the development of industry and material innovations throughout the 19th and 20th centuries were the source of a massive stock of distinctive new words, phrases and idioms. Typical examples are the vocabulary of *railroading* and *transportation* terminology, ranging from names of roads (from *dirt roads* and *back roads* to *freeways* and *parkways*) to road infrastructure (parking lot, overpass, rest area), and from automotive terminology to *public transit* (*e.g.* in the sentence "riding *the subway downtown"*); such American introductions as *commuter* (from *communication ticket*), *concourse, to board* (a vehicle), *to park, double-park* and *parallel park* (a car), *double decker* or the noun *terminal* have long been used in all dialects of English.

Finally, a large number of English colloquialism from various periods are American in origin; some have lost their American flavour (from *OK* and *cool* to *nerd* and *24/7*); while others have not (*have a nice day, sure*); many are now distinctly old-fashioned (*swell, groovy*). Some English words now in general use, such as *hijacking, disc jockey, boost, bulldoze* and *jazz*, originated as American slang. Among the many English idioms of U.S. origin are *get the hang of, take for a ride, keep tabs, take a shine to, inside track, stiff upper lip,* etc.

American English has always shown a marked tendency to use substantive as verbs. Examples of verbed nouns are *interview, advocate, vacuum, lobby, expense, room, pressure, profile, buffalo, express* (mail), *factor* (in mathematics), *author* (which disappeared in English around 1630 and was revived in the U.S. three centuries later) and, out of American material, *proposition, graft* (bribery), *bad-mouth*, vacation, *major, backpack, intern, ticket, dope* and *OD*. Beside it number of slang words used by African-American too has a great influence on English Language.

Indian Contribution

Indian English is product of cultural, linguistic and other factors exerting pressure on the English language in India. In recent years the mass media such as the radio, film, television and VCRs have brought the native variety of English nearer home and provided more exposure to this language to thousands of Indians.

Indian English abounds in many Indianisms to express the cultural milieu—*e.g. cousin-brother, cooling glasses, delink*, use of jwellery for married woman—*mangalsutra, veni* (a string of flower put on the hair of woman). Indian English is replete with a whole lot of loanwords from Indian languages which the media make popular. Under this category we have *bandh, gherao, goonda, lathi, naxallite,* words which we notice in the newspapers almost everyday. The compounds made with Indian words are more amusing: *lathi* charge, *double* roti, *tiffin* carrier etc. The use of eatables such as vada pav, mango chusnis, etc. are included in English words.

The Indian myth and mythological names is the other contribution to English language, *e.g.*, Nag Puja, Lord Rama, Krishna, Vishnu, Sita, Ravan, etc. Different festivals and its related myth—Holi, Daserra, Buddha Purnima, etc. As India is a multi-religious, multi-cultural, multi-lingual country there is a lot of variety in the words of Indian English. Religious terms such as Hinduism, Sikhism, Buddhism etc. are the examples.

Russian Contribution

Prominent personalities of the Russian Revolution and political life have left their mark on English. Lenin, the leader of the Russian Revolution and founder of the communist state, gave *Leninism* and *Leninist.* His disciple, Leon Trotsky, preached immediate words-wide revolution by the proletariat. This type of revolution came to be known as *Trotskyis* and its advocates, *Trotskyites.* The Czar and his rule contributed a few words. The word, Czar (Tsar) derived from Latin Caesar, was used in English as early as the 16th Century, but *Czarina* (Czaritza), *Czarevitch* (son of a Czar). *Czarist* and *Czardom* came later. Czar became synonymous with a despot. *Ukase* is an imperial order or official decree having the force of law in Czarist Russia. It belongs in the category of words like 'fiat', 'diktat', 'firman', the 'Pope's bull' or the Ayotollah's 'fatwa'. *Boyar* is a member of the aristocratic class.

The Russian Revolution of 1917-20 made a number of words well known all over the world. *Bolshevik, Commissar, duma, kulak, pogrom, presidium* and Soviet belong to this group. Certain words of Russian origin gained wide currency after World War II. The Communist Information Bureau which was established during 1947-56 by the Communist Parties of nine European countries for "mutual advice and coordinated activity" appears as a portmanteau word, *cominform*. Similarly, *Comintern* is a blend of Communist International. *Politburo* is a shortened form of two Russian words; it stands for the "executive committee and chief policy-making body of the Communist party in the Soviet Union." *Comecon* is the Russian counterpart of EEC.

There are a few words of descriptive of the unique geographical features of the Soviet Union. *Steppe* is an arid, level land without forests; *taiga* is used for Siberian pine-forest; *Zastruga* is a furrow made by wind in loose snow. The fauna of Russia have given a few words : *borzoi* is a wolfhound; *Caracul* is a sheep of central Asia; *Astrakhan* caps are made from the fur of the young of this animal.

Other aspects of Russian life are revealed in a number of words which are used occasionally in English : *balalaika* (a sort of guitar), *borsch* (beat soup), *dache* (a country house or villa). A dacha is a symbol of bureaucratic status and it has a political connotation. *Izba* means a loghouse, *kibitza* (covered cart/sledge), *mir* (village), *shashlik* (a kabab), *Kvas* (rye beer) and *vodka* ('a colourless, unaged liquor of neutral spirits distilled from rye or wheat'). It is interesting to note that vodka is cognate with the Sanskrit *udaka; voda* in Russian means water.

Other Borrowings

From Arabic : alcohol, alchemy, alembic, algebra, alkali, cipher, elixir, sugar and syrup (all related to chemistry, mathematics and medicine), emir, fakir, gazelle, giraffe, harem, hashish, lute, mosque, sultan etc.

From Hebrew : camel, cinnamon, sapphire and words biblical in nature like amen, cherub, Jehorah, rabbi, pharisee, sabbath and seraph.

From Persian : magic, paradise, tulip, lilac, jasmin, orange, azure, scarlet, baksheesh, satrap, etc.

From Indian : Indian contribution to English vocabulary is no less important than the other major foreign influences. From its many languages English has very often taken over such terms like brahmin, bandahna, bungalow, calico, chutney, curry, indigo, juggernaut, jungle, loot, pyjama, kurta, rajah, sandal, coolie, polo, verandah and many others.

From Peru : jerky, pampas, puma, quinine.

From Brazil : boorish, chimpanzee, voodoo, zebra.

From Africa : banana, dengue, trek.

From Native American : alpaca, canoe, chocolate, cocaine, coyote, Eskimo, Igloo, racoon, tomato, potato, wigwam etc.

From Gaelic : bard, bog, glen, keen, pet, slew, slob, slogan etc.

From Japanese : judo, kamikaze, karaoke, karate, origami, sake, sushi, tsunami, tycoon.

Impact of Science on English

The Renaissance in English marked the widening of the mental horizon, for it was an age of humanism and also adventure. The emotional element in speech and writing which characterized the Elizabethan English style was undergoing change during the 17th century owing to scientific thinking. English prose which was conditioned by Latin was slowly becoming referential. The change was from rhetorical to the plain style during the 17th century. Though scientific thinking was responsible for plain style, other areas of knowledge namely philosophy, history and criticism were benefited by it.

The need for words in the field of science resulted in scientists seeking recourse to Latin and Greek vocabulary. Sometimes both Greek and Latin elements were joined and new words were created. Various branches of science, organisms, substances, plants, animals, instruments, measurements, medical states needed terms to signify what they signified and hence scientists went into shape new words.

The growth of science had been steady in the English speaking country that words started streaming in. Though scientific words account for the jargon in the respective field, the frequent use of certain terms have penetrated even into the rural areas of countries where English is spoken and the commoners of villages have access to usage of certain words; cholestrol, acidity, cardiology, chloroform, coma, anemia, diphtheria, pathology, laboratory are some of the words even a villager in any English speaking country is comfortable with. Given below are words related to different disciplines.

Medical Terms : Immunology, microbiology, oncology, neurology, vaccination, syndrome, asthma, bronchitis, cataracts, flu, constipation, diabetes, diarrhoea, hepatitis, migraine, shingles, tinnitus, ulcer, warts etc.

Electrical, Automobile Terms : Amplifier, switch, plug, wire, current, dynamo, spark, tension, gear, clutch, bonnet, bumper, suspension, garage etc.

Psychological Terms : Nihilism, Electra complex, Oedipus complex, neurosis, psychosis, schizophrenia, lunacy, introvert, extravert, catharsis, ego, id, libido, superego, trauma, personology, etc.

General Words Related to Science : Agriculture, horticulture, survey, trigonometry, anatomy, physiology, epidemic, antiseptic, cocaine, antidote, calorie, alkali, radium, antenna, frequency, broadcast, microphone, telephone, telegraph etc.

Computer Words : Hardware, software, programme, database, file, disk, chip, windows, desktop, internet, browsing, e-mail, password, pad, menu, modem, etc.

Influence of Printing on English Language

Linguists have always acknowledged that the invention of printing had exerted a great influence on languages. Among other things, printing helped to develop a 'standard' language and a more codified form of spelling.

Printing which was introduced into England by Caxton in 1476, helped to increase the spread of knowledge and literary level among the British public as more and more people had better access to reading materials. Over the centuries, as more English texts were printed, such as novels, dictionaries, the Bible and other documents, the English language gradually gained popularity and established itself as the national language of England. Apart from the advent of printing, political, social and economic factors also contributed to the development of English as a national language. The speakers attitude towards the language, the status of the language itself as well as colonialism later enhanced English position as an international language today.

Linguists Harry and Taylor have pointed out that through printing Caxton played a very significant and instrumental role in establishing English as the national language of England. They suggest that by adopting the dialect of London and the South-East as the English for his books, Caxton took a decisive step forward in establishing that particular variety as 'the English language.' We get the idea that Caxton as the first printer in England was highly responsible for imposing some form of uniformity to the English language simply by default. His choice of the dialect of the Southeast Midlands has given us the present form of standard English.

Before doing any printing, Caxton had to choose a variety of language, which should be understood by a lot of people, and not an exclusive language like Latin, which was the language of the elite. In Caxton's time, Latin, the *lingua franca* of Europe, was already a dying language. Independent states throughout Europe no longer gave much importance to Latin and Greek as in the past. The French, Italian, Spanish, German, Portuguese and Dutch had established their national identities and their own languages. Naturally, the British needed a language to call their own too.

According to Harris and Taylor, when Laxton started printing he realized that variations in English dialects posed some difficulties for users of the language. But he also knew that a single dialect had to be chosen to 'unite' the people of England. Despite the difficulties he faced in terms of orthography and the lack of authoritative guidance on the English grammars, Laxton managed to produce many English translations of French works.

Paradoxically Caxton's works would help to instill a consciousness of national identity among the English people, as they would come across and question some alien values in the translated works printing thus opened up the minds of the people to foreign ideas and knowledge.

Harris and Taylor point out that 'printing was the technological foundation of the European Renaissance.' In other words, printing revived the tradition of learning. Consequently, it let to unprecedented mass communications and the dissemination of information on a very wide scale. As printing became widespread, the standard variety of English also spread to all corners of England. As the masses became familiar with the spelling system and grammar introduced by Caxton, the language became more nationalised.

In the 15th century many people had an inferiority complex with regard to the English language. Greek and Latin were still regarded as superior to English. But by the 16th century, through the activities of Renaissance scholars who produced many grammar books on English, gained a higher status. The British had changed their attitude towards the language. It was now pursued and studied with fervour. During this period, English writers developed a greater loyalty and pride in the English language. This sense of pride was a direct result of the Reformation period.

A later version of the English Bible and the Book of Common Prayer in 1549 became the focus of service in the New Church of England. The English Bible itself became a main agent in standardizing the language. The Authorized (King James) version in 1611 was acclaimed by some as representative of the golden height achieved by early modern English. Printing made the spread of a thick book like the Bible possible to a wide audience within a short time. This helped to keep the language in constant usage. In retrospect, the Reformation contributed to the development of the English language as a national language by focusing on the use of English rather than Latin or other European languages.

Today English has reached a status which not many, languages have achieved. Starting from its humble origin as a language spoken by the Anglo Saxons who were not highly 'civilized' compared with the Romans, the language has developed into what it is now, an important language of science and the Internet. Caxton's introduction of printing into England remains a crucial turning point in the development of the English langauge. Besides setting a standard, it eventually turned English into an international language.

Internet and English/Cyber-English

The Internet is perhaps the most revolutionary invention since the printing press more than 500 years ago. It is for more powerful than the latter technologically, socially and linguistically. Its impact on the contemporary world is difficult to assess now. It is changing the modes of communication, methods of work, forms of entertainment, patterns of trade, and way of learning. The internet is a world-wide, publicly owned network of interconnected computer networks that transmit information. It is the largest computer network with more than a hundred million hosts throughout the world.

This electronic, global and interactive medium is fundamentally different from both speech and writing as we have known these two human activities. Modern technology has spread and preserved the written word across space and time. Telegraphy and teleprinting carried the written messages over long distances. The Internet came 10,000 years after writing was invented. The web is an encyclopedia of human knowledge; it is designed for multi-media interaction among computer users anywhere in the world. The Internet has various functions such as encyclopedia reference, archiving, advertising, self-publishing, news, games, reporting, creative writing, commercial transactions, films and entertainment.

The global sweep of English on the Internet has introduced many new words into English. A few examples *surfers, digiterati, netizens, weboids, spam, to geek out.* New coinages are made by joining two words: *double-click, cyberspace, hypertext.* New blends are obtained by combining *net* and *etiquette,* into *netiquette, information* and *entertainment into infotainment.* Spelling is simplified on the American pattern. The plural suffix *–s* is spelt as –z in words like *serialz.* The latter *f* is replaced by *ph* in *freak* which is spelt as *phreak.* The hyphen is eliminated in compound words like *flowerpot.* The period which is rarely used in the text has new uses in the Internet. It is a vital part of the e-mail addresses. The use of acronyms like FAQ and ISP is increasing. Certain letters or symbols have become popular and these are used to make up a whole range of new-looking or new-sounding words. On the analogy of *e-mail* a number of new words have become fashionable : *e-cash, e-text, e-merge, e-lapse, e-quip.* The symbol @ comes in handy to replace at in many words : *@ tract, @ Home.*

Cyber-English, the language of the nets, demands a common comprehension where no similar communicative need existed before. Born in the primitive command-and-control Arpanet and its Pentagopese argot, cyber-english emerged from the nuke-hardened, military cellars and now projects American world power overtly. Other world englishes, the more modest englishes of orality and textuality, function as subsumed and minor epistemologies, as necessary preparation for cyber-english. English is local; cyber-english is global.

A superdominant English specifically intrinsic to a computer-mediated technology base, cyber-english has rapidly come to serve as a transmission belt for 'free market' ideologies. Free expression and free exchange, in one view, inevitably will be furthered by common linguistic understanding. In *The Search for the Perfect Language,* Umberto Eco points out that this consociation of commercial advantage and free expression with the English language has been current since at least the seventeenth century, arguably the most profoundly imperial century in European history.

The colonial pursuit of geopolitical rationalization has historically relied on over-languages to endorse a politics of subordination. Cyber english, the first world English without a territorial base, has reformulated classic notions of universal imperial benefit. Viewed as a stage in this historiographic continuum, cyber-english is the latest extension of a centuries-long drive towards extinction of small tribal languages and consolidated expansion for a few languages of power.

English commodification on the nets involves not only such stratified language production regimes, but relies equally upon dialogic capacity. That is, a learned cyber-english semiotic ability denominates surplus value. An Indian woman who keyboards English texts has a severely limited role in cyber-english commodification because she cannot participate further in its production or interrogate its social purposes. The value of her Indian English lies in monologism, which surplus value attaches to an unavailable dialogism.

The dialogic freeze-out upon which cyber-english has been constructed differentiates cybercity from previous global forms of English production and mass consumption. Talkie-era Hollywood films, even as they were screened for colonial eyes in outdoor Phillipine theatres where the audience sat on logs, promised an opportunity to participate in American materialism *if* those

English lessons were learned. Computer technology, whose economies rely on expensive capitalizations rather than inexpensive film tickets, has expanded the space of anglophone monologism by presuming a fascination with English online textuality instead of English-language entertainment. Cybercity and cyber-english limit dialogism to those high end westernized consumers who can speak from within a technological paradigm that demands lexical participation. From this perspective, then, surplus dialogism in cyber-english can be described more succinctly as the domain of command and control.

3

Structure of English Language

Every human knows at least one language, spoken or signed. Linguistics is the science of language including the sounds, words, and grammar rules. Words in languages are finite, but sentences are not. It is this creative aspect of human language that sets it apart from animal languages, which are essentially responses to stimuli.

The rules of a language, also called grammar are learned as one acquires a language. These rules include *phonology,* the sound system, *morphology,* the structure of words, *syntax,* the combination of words into sentences, *semantics,* the ways in which sounds and meanings are related, and the *lexicon,* or mental dictionary of words. When you know a language, you know words in that language, *i.e.* sound units that are related to specific meanings. However, the sound and meanings of words are arbitrary. For the most part, there is no relationship between the way a word is pronounced (or signed) and its meaning.

Knowing a language encompasses this entire system, but this knowledge (called *competence*) is different from behaviour (called *performance*). You may know a language, but you may also choose to not speak it. Although you are not speaking the language, you still have the knowledge of it. However, if you don't know a language, you cannot speak it at all.

There are two types of grammars : descriptive and prescriptive. Descriptive grammars represent the unconscious knowledge of a language. English speakers, for example, know that "me likes apples" is incorrect and "I like apples" is correct, although the speakers may not be able to explain why. Descriptive grammars do not teach the rules of a language, but rather describes rules that are already known. In contrast, prescriptive grammars dictate what a speaker's grammar should be and they include teaching grammars, which are written to help teach a foreign language.

There are about 5,000 languages in the world right now, and linguistics have discovered that these languages are more alike than different from each other. There are universal concepts and properties that are shared by all languages, and these principles are contained in the *Universal Grammar,* which forms the basis of all possible human languages.

The structure of language is very complex. Language has an internal structure consisting of two sub-structures—sound and meaning, also known as expression and content. It is the network of association between expression and content that structures language. Neither sound nor ideas alone are language. Expression is the system of sounds, words, phrases, sentences as spoken, heard, felt or imagined independently of their particular meanings. The expression system is most completely observable in spoken language. Content is the system of classified units of cultural meaning and their combination and relations in a language or ideas, social situations, meanings, the fact or fantasies about man's existence, the things man reacts to and tries to convey to his follows.

We speak English but do we know where it comes from? Studying on this subject I leared where it comes from and how it has developed. The history of English begins a little after A.D. 600. The ancestors of the language were wandering in the forests of northern Europe. Their language was a part of Germanic brancih of Indo-European Family.

The people talking this language spread the northern coast of Europe in the time of Roman Empire. Among this people the tribes called Angels, Saxons, Jutes which is called Anglo-Saxons come to England. The first Latin effect was in that period. Latin effected the language with the merchants traveling the tribes. Some of the words taken from Latin are; kettle, wine, cheese, butter, cheap.

Also in the 14th century Rome Empire weakened because Goths attacked to Mediterranean countries of Roman Empire and Anglo-Saxons attacked to empire. On the other hand the Celtic tribes in Scotland and Wales developed. At the end in 410 the last Roman emperor left the island to Celtic and Anglo-Saxon. Celtic and Anglo-Saxons fought for 100 years and Anglo-Saxons killed all the Celtics. In 550 Anglo-Saxons established England. During Roman Empire Latin wasn't the native language of the kingdom because people in the country were talkling Celtic.

When Anglo-Saxons became Christian in 597 they learned Latin. According to the effects to English, the history of the language is divided into three; Old English (7th century–1100), Middle English (1100–1450/1500), Modern English (1500–now). In some books Modern English is divided into two-Early Modern (1500-1700), Late Modern (1700-now).

Old English

When England was established there were several kingdoms and the most advanced one was Nurthumbria. It was this period that the best of the Old English literature was written, including the epic poem Beowulf.

In the 8th century Nurthumbrian power declined, West Saxons became the leading power. The most famous king of the West Saxons was Alfred the Great. He founded and established schools, translated or caused to be translated many books from Latin into English.

After many years of hit-and-run raids between the European kingdoms, the Norseman landed in the year of 866 and later the east coast the island was Norseman's. Norse language effected the English considerably. Norse wasn't so different from English and English people could understand Norseman. There were considerable inter-changes and word borrowings (sky, give, law, egg, outlaw, leg, ugly, talk). Also borrowed pronouns like they, their, them. It is supposed also that the Norseman influenced the sound structure and the grammar of English.

Old English has some sound which we don't know have now. In grammar, Old English was much more highly inflected than Middle English because there were case endings for nouns, more person and number endings for nouns, more person and number endings of words and a more complicated pronoun systems, various endings for adjectives. In vocabulary Old English is quiet different from Middle English. Most of the Old English words are native English which weren't borrowed from other languages. On the other hand Old English contains borrowed words coming from Norse and Latin.

Middle English

Between 1100-1200 many important changes took place in the structure of English and Old English became Middle English. The political event which effected the administration system and language was the Norman conquest. In 1066 they crossed the channel and they became the master of England. For the next several years, England was ruled by the kings whose native, language was French. On the other hand French couldn't become the national language because it became the language of the court, nobility, polite society, literature. But it didn't replace as the language of the people. English continued to be the national language but it changed too much after the conquest.

The sound system and grammar wasn't so effected but vocabulary was effected much. There were word related with government : parliament, tax, government, majesty; church word: religion, parson sermon; words for food : veal, beef, mutton, peach, lemon, cream, biscuit; colors : blue, scarlet, vermilion; household words : curtain, chair, lamp, towel, blanket; play words : dance, chess, music, leisure, conversation; literary words : story, romance, poet, literary; learned words : study, logic, grammar, noun, surgeon, anatomy, stomach; ordinary word for all sorts : nice, second, very, age, bucket, final, gentel, fault, flower, court, sure, move, surprise, plain.

Middle English was still a Germanic language but it is different from Old English in many ways. Grammar and the sound system changed a good deal. People started to rely more on word order and structure words to express their meaning rather than the use of case ystem. "This can be called as a simplification but it is not exactly. Languages don't become simples, they merely exchange one kind of complexity for another". For us Middle English is simpler than Old English because it is closer to Modern English.

Early Modern English

Between 1400-1600 English underwent a couple of sound changes. One change was the elimination of a vowel sound in certain unstressed positions at the end of the words. The change was important because it effected thousands of words and gave a different aspect to the whole language.

The other change is what is called the great vowel shift. This was a systematic shifting of half a dozen vowels and diphthongs in stressed syllables. For example, the word *name* had in Middle English a vowel something like that in the modern word *father;* ... etc. The shift effected all the words in which these vowels sound occured. These two changes produced the basic differences between Middle English and Modern English. But there are several other developments that effected the language. One was the invention of printing. It was introduced to England by William Caxton in 1475. After this books became cheaper and cheaper, more people learned to read and write and advanced in communication.

The period of Early Modern English was also a period of English Renaissance, which means the development of the people. New ideas increased. English language had grown as a result of borrowing words from Frénch, Latin, Greek.

The greatest writer of the Early Modern English period is Shakespeare and the best known book is the King Jones version of the *BIBLE.*

Recent Developments

In order to establish the language they develop a dictionary. The first English Dictionary was published in 1603. Another product of the 18th century was the invention of English Grammar. As English is replaced with Latin as the language of scholarship, it was felt to control the language.

The period were English develodped most is the Modern English. In that period the people speaking that language increased too much. Now, English is the greatest language of the world spoken natively and as a second language. What will happen in the future? It'll continue to grow, may be it will be the universal language.

(i) Morphology : Etymologically speaking, 'morphology' means 'to science or study of shapes'. Geomorphology is concerned with the study of the physical features of the earth surface. In linguistics, the shapes concerned are the shapes of words. Words could be considered to have a shape in a number of different ways. They have shape in terms of their sounds, or a phonological shape; they have a shape in terms of their letters, or an orthographic shape; and they have shape in terms of the meaningful units from which they are constructed. Morphology is concerned with the relationship between the last kind of shape and the first two. It is primarily concerned with recurrent shapes (either phonological or orthographic) which are associated with constant meaning. Thus in the words 'walk, walks, walked, walking,' the shape 'walk' recurs with the same meaning; in the set 'pole, polar, polarize, polarization,' the shape (polic)' recurs with a constant meaning, and in, the set 'chewing, coughing, jumping, mailing, the shape '-ing' recurs with a constant meaning (even though it may be difficult to specifiy what that meaning is). Since morphology is concerned with linking phonological shape to meaning, it is clearly closely connected with the study of phonology. It is also closely connected with the study of syntax, since many of the meaningful elements that are found in words have syntactic functions, for example, the '-ed' in 'walked'. Morphology is thus Janus-like.

Although it is frequently difficult to draw a firm line between the two, morphology is often discussed in two categories inflection and derivation. Inflection is concerned with those constituents of words most closely related to syntax, while derivation is concerned with the structure of lexical words. Derivational morphology is thus sometimes termed 'lexical' morphology.' Traditionally derivational morphology and compounding are classified together as 'word-formation'; in recent work, however, word formation (usually without the hypen) has come to be a label for all morphology, inflectional as well as derivational.

In drawing parallels between the sets or 'paradigms' shown below, morphologists also study a lack of change of shape when a change would be expected, and changes of phonological shape which have the same effect as the addition of elements, or which accompany such addition.

bright	clean	long
brighten	clean	lengthen
brightness	clearness	length

One of the fascinations of morphology as an area of study is the way in which it overlaps with many other areas of linguistic study. It overlaps with phonology in the whole area of morphophonemics, where the question is raised to whether 'gene' and 'generate' have any more in common than 'mean' and 'menstruate'. It overlaps with syntax in a number of ways, but especially in the study of clitics where the '-'ll' in 'she'll' acts phonologically as part of a single word, but syntactically as a separate word, and compounding where what are otherwise two words function together as one, and it may not be clear whether 'girl-friend' (sometimes written 'girlfriend' or 'girl friend') is one word or two. It has implications in lexicology, stylistics, and pragmatics and is much studied by psycholinguists for the light it can throw on language acquisition and processing.

The grammatical description of many, if not all, languages is conveniently divided into two complementary sections; morphology and syntax. The relationship between them, as generally stated, is as follows : morphology accounts for the internal structure of words, and syntax describes how words are combined to form phrases, clauses and sentences.

There are many words in English that are fairly obviously analyzable into smaller grammatical units. For example, the word "unacceptability" can be divided into un-, accept, abil- and -ity (abil being a variant of -able). Of these, at least three are minimal grammatical units, in the sense that they cannot be analyzed into yet smaller grammatical units un-, abil-, and ity. The status of accept, from this point of view, is somewhat uncertain. Given the existence of such forms as accede and accuse, on the one hand, and of except, exceed, and excuse, on the other, one might be inclined to analyze accept into ac- (which might subsequently be recognized as a variant of ad-) and -cept. The question is left open. Minimal grammatical units the un-, abil-, and -ity are what

Bloomfield called morphemes; he defined them in terms of the "partial phonetic-semantic resemblance" holding within sets of words. For example, "unacceptable," "untrue", and "ungracious" are phonetically (or, phonologically) similar as far as the first syllable is concerned and are similar in meaning in that each of them is negatively by contrast with a corresponding positive adjective ("acceptable", "true", "gracious"). This "partial phonetic-semantic resemblance" is accounted for by noting that the word in question contain the same morpheme (namely, un-) and that this morpheme has a certain phonological form and a certain meaning.

Bloomfield's definition of the morpheme in terms of "partial phonetic-semantic resemblance" was considerably modified and, eventually, abandoned entirely by some of his followers. Whereas Bloomfield took the morpheme to be an actual segment of a word, others defined it as being a purely abstract unit, and the term morph was introduced to refer to the actual word segments. The distinction between morpheme and morph (which is, in certain respects, parallel to the distinction between phoreme and phone) may be explained by means of an example. If a morpheme in English is posited with the function of accounting for the grammatical difference between singular and plural nouns, it may be symbolized by enclosing the term plural within brace brackets. Now the morpheme [plural] is represented in a number of different ways. Most plural nouns in English differ from the corresponding singular forms in that they have an additional final segment. In the written form of these words, it is either –s or –es (*e.g.*, "cat"; "cats"; "dog"; "dogs", "fish"; "fishes"). The word segments written s or –es are morphs. So also is the word segment written in "oxen". All these morphs represent the same morpheme. But there are other plural nouns in English that differ from the corresponding singular forms in other ways (*e.g.*, "mouse"; "mice"; "criterion"; "criteria"; and so on) or not at all (*e.g.*, "this sheep "these sheep"). Within the post-Bloomfieldian frame work no very satisfactory account of the formation of these nouns could be given. But it was clear that they contained (in some sense) the same morphemes as the more regular plurals. Morphs that are in complementary distribution and represent to same morpheme are said to be allomorphs of that morpheme. For example, the regular plurals of English nouns are formed by adding one of three morphs on to the form of the singular: /s/, /z/ or /iz/ (in the corresponding written forms both /s/ and /z/ are written –s and /iz/ is written –es). Their distribution is determined by the following principle : if the morph to which they are to be added ends in a 'sibilant" sound (*e.g.*, s, z, sh, ch), then the syllabic allomorph. |iz| is selected (*e.g.*, fish-es | fiš -iz|, match-es [mač - iz]; otherwise the nonysyllabic allomorphs are selected the voiceles allomorph |s| with morphs ending in a voiceless consonant (e.g., cat-s/kat-s) and the voiced allomorph |z| with morphs ending in a vowel as voiced consonant (*e.g.*, flea-s/fli-z/, dog-s/dog z/). These three allomorphs, it will be evident, are in complementary distribution, and the alteration between them is determined by the phonological structure of the preceeding morph. Thus the choice is phonologically conditioned.

Very similar is the alteration between the three principal allomorphs of the past participle ending, /id/, /t/, and /d/, all of which correspond to the -ed of the written forms. If the preceding morph ends with /t/ or /d/, then the synllabic allomorph /id/ is selected (*e.g.*, wait-ed/ weit-id/). Otherwise, if the preceding morph ends with a voiceless consonant, one of the nonsyllabic allomorphs is selected—the voiceless allomorph /t/ when the preceding morph ends with a vowel or voiced consonant (*e.g.*, row-ed/rou-d/; tame/ teim-d/). This is another instant of phonological conditioning. Phonological conditioning may be contrasted with the principle that determines the selection of yet another allomorph of the past participle morpheme. The fina/n/ of show-n or see-n (which marks them as past participles) is not determined by the phonological structure of the morphs show and see. For each English word that is similar to "show" and "see" in this respect, it must be stated as a synchronically inexplicable fact that it selects the /n/ allomorph. This is called grammatical conditioning. There are various kinds of grammatical conditioning.

Alteration of the kind illustrated above for the allomorphs of the plural morpheme and the /id/, /d/, and /t/ allomorphs of the past participle is frequently referred to as morphophonemic. Some linguistics have suggested that it should be accounted for not by setting up three allomorphs each with a distinct phonemic form but by setting up a single morph in an intermediate morphophonemic representation. Thus, the regular plural morph might be said to be composed of the morphophoneme /Z/ and the common past-participle morphs of the morphophoneme /D/. General rules of morphophonemic interpretation would then convert /Z/ and /D/ to their appropriate phonetic form according to context. This treatment of the question foreshadows, on the one hand, the stratificational treatment and, on the other, the generative approach, though they differ considerably in other respects. An important concept in grammar and, more particularly, in morphology is that of free and bound forms. A bound form is one that cannot occur alone as a complete utterance (in some normal context of use). For example, -ing is found in this sense, whereas wait is not nor is waiting. Any form that is not bound is free. Bloomfield based his definition of the word on this distinction between bound and free forms. Any free form consisting entirely of two or more smaller free forms was said to be a phrase. (*e.g.*, 'poor John" or "ran away"), and phrases were to be handled within syntax. Any free form that was not a phrase was defined to be a word and to fall within the scope of morphology. One of the consequences of Bloomfield's definition of the word was that morphology became the study of constructions involving bound forms. The so-called isolating languages, which make no use of bound forms (*e.g.*, Vietnamese), would have no morphology.

A free morpheme has to pass two tests:

- it has to be a content word
- it cannot contain any other morphemes

The word "language" is an example of a free morpheme. It is defined in the dictionary as having lexical meaning, and it cannot be divided into any other morphemes.

A bound morpheme is defined by two qualities :

- it is not a content word
- it is always bound to another morpheme, either a face morpheme, or sometimes another bound morpheme.

The word "languages" is an example of combination of [free morpheme] + [bound morpheme] = [language + s]. "Language" is a free morpheme, and "s" is a bound morpheme. 'Context' plays an important part in defining morphemes. The suffix "s" on the word "language-s" is a morpheme because it has meaning in the context of the words itself-plurality, more than one. As a contrast, the [s] on "sheep" is NOT a morpheme, because it has no independent meaning other than defining a speech sound, /s/.

Within the category of bound morphemes are two sub-categories, derivational morphemes and inflectional morphemes. Derivational morphemes create a new word when added to another morpheme. For example, "read" is a free morpheme. Add the derivational suffix-er to the end of it, and you get "reader", which is a [free morpheme] + [derivational morpheme] = [a newly derived word]. Looking at the word "reader", you can see that it is indeed a different and unique dictionary entry compared to "read", so it meets the text to be a derivational morpheme.

Inflectional morphemes do not derive a new word when added to another morpheme—they only change the word's grammatic properties such as tense, gender, and case. For example, "read" is a free morpheme. Add the inflectional suffix -s to the end of it, and you get "reads", which is a [free morpheme] + [inflectional morpheme] = [the past tense of a word].

Roughly speaking, inflectional constructions can be defined as yielding sets of forms that are all grammatically distinct forms of single vocabulary items, whereas derivational constructions yield distinct vocabulary items. For example, "sings", "singing", "sang", and "sung" are all inflectional forms of the vocabulary item traditionally referred to as "the verb to sing"; but "singer", which is formed from "sing" by the addition of the morph -er (just as "singing" is formed by the addition of -ing), is one of the forms of a different vocabulary item. When this roughly distinction between derivation and inflection is made more precise, problems occur. The principal consideration, undoubtedly, is that inflection is more closely integrated with and determined by syntax. But the various formal criteria that have been proposed to give effect to this general principle are not uncommonly in conflict in particular instances, and it probably must be admitted that the distinction between derivation and inflection, though clear enough in most cases, is in the last resort somewhat arbitrary.

Bloomfield and most linguists have discussed morphological constructions in terms of processes. Of these, the most widespread throughout the languages of the world is affixation; *i.e.* the attachment of an affix to a base. For example, the word "singing" can be described as resulting from the affixation of -ing to the base sing. (If the affix is put in front of the base, it is a prefix; if it is put after the base, it is a suffix; and if it is inserted within the base, splitting in into two discontinuous parts, it is an infix.) Other morphological processes recognized by linguists need not be mentioned here, but reference may be made to the fact that many of Bloomfield's followers from the mid-1940s were dissatisfied with the whole notion of morphological processes. Instead of saying that -ing was affixed to sing they preferred to say that sing and -ing co-occured in a particular pattern or arrangement, thereby avoiding the implication that sing is in some sense prior to or more basic than –ing. The distinction of morpheme and morph (and the notion of allomorphs) was developed in order to make possible the description of morphology and syntax of a language in terms of "arrangements" of items rather than in terms of "processes" operating upon more basic items. Nowadays, the opposition of "processes" is, except among the stratificationalists, almost extinct. It has proved to be cumbersome, if not impossible, to describe the relationship between certain linguistic forms without deriving one from the other or both from some common underlying form, and most linguists no longer feel that this is in any way reprehensible.

Important Characteristics of Morphology

1. The minial meaningful sound unit of combination is called morph and the study of morph is called morphology.
2. Commonly the word is identified as the smallest meaningful unit of language, but linguists believe that the word can be divided into smaller meaningful parts called morphemes. Some of these smaller units can also occur by themselves as words, others can't. The former type are called free and the latter bound morphology.
3. Some morphemes signal a grammatical function rather than meaning. Such grammatical morphemes can also be free or bound.

4. Morphemes are often, but not always, represented by clearly identifiable phonological or orthographic material. Hence they are best treated as abstract rather than concrete entities.

5. The relationship between morphemes and words is seen as one of realization and not composition. Combinations of two or more morphemes may be realized as a single word. (*e.g.* killed, taken, horses).

6. Grammatical morphemes perform grammatical functions, *i.e.* they play a role in the rules which set out how words are to combine to form structure.

7. Grammatical morphemes also contribute to meaning but in a different : they modify the meanings a lexical morphemes in certain standard ways, *e.g.*, changing reference to plural, making it definite, changing time reference to past, etc.

8. Bound lexical morphemes contribute to meaning by modifying the meanings of the lexical morphemes to which they are attached, but these modifications are neither fixed nor regular (as in the case with the modifications made by bound grammatical morphemes).

9. Morphemes and combination of morphemes are realized as word. This process is called word-formation. All languages reveal certain pattern of word-formation, new words are being regularly created on these patterns.

10. Words are called simple, complex, compound or compound complex depending on whether they realize a single free morpheme, a free morpheme plus one or more than one bound morpheme, two or more free morphemes or two or more free morphemes plus one or more bound morphemes respectively. In some cases, two bound morphemes, of which one is a bound base, may also be realized as a complex word.

    e.g. Simple : boy, sing, kind, write

    Complex : boys, singing, kindness, writers

    Compound : playboy, birdsong

    Compound-Complex: hot-bloodedness, writer-producer.

11. Affixes are morphs which represent bound morphemes. They can be subdivided into prefixes and suffixes.
12. Prefixes and affixes attached to the beginning of the stem; suffixes are affixes attached to the end of the stem.
13. A stem can consist of free morpheme base, a bound morpheme base, a base consisting of one free plus one or more bound morphemes, or of two or more free morphemes.
14. The inflectional morphology of English describes the bound grammatical morphemes of English, the grammatical rules in which they figure, the paradigms they form, and the various phonological and orthographic forms into which they are realized.
15. The derivational morphology of English describes the bound lexical morphomes of English, the categories of the stems with which they can be combined, the categories of the resulting forms, the meaning changes brought about in this process, and the phonological/orthographic shapes these morphemes acquire.
16. Derivational prefixes are classified on the basis of the meaning criterion into Negative, Reversative, Privative, Pejorative and a few other types.
17. Morphemes may or may not have meaning, may or may not have a phonological representation (un-) has a negative meaning in unfriendly, unhealthy, unable, unemployed and many other words but is meaningless in under. (-e) has a constant meaning in teacher, heater, reader, writer, speaker, leader etc. But it would be difficult to pin down any constant meaning for (spect) in respect, inspect, circumspect and spectacle or for (pro) in protest, professor, prospective, progress, process etc. In plural words like sheep, fish, we have two morphemes in each words; the first Morpheme in each case has a phonological representation but the second one has no phonological representation and is called zero morphome.
18. Morpheme may be Monosyllabic as (man) and (a/an/the) or Polysyllabic as (happy) and (nature).

19. When words belonging to one grammatical category are used as words of another category we have 'conversion'. A word cannot undergo conversion if it has already undergone inflection but it can still undergo conversions if it has undergone derivation.

20. The syntactic approach describes the formation of compounds in terms of the grammatical categories of the words that are combined into compounds. However, not all words belonging to those grammatical categories can be combined with each other. Moreover, some kinds of combinations are more productive than others.

21. The semantic approach describes the compounds in terms of the relationships between the meaning of the words combined. The meaning of a compound is always more than the sum of the meaning of its constituent words. However, usually the meanings of the constituent words provide some lead into the meaning of the compound.

22. The syntatic-semantic (generative) approach believes that compounds are generated freely from sentential structures and therefore do not need to be listed in the dictionary. The same rules that restrict the combination of words in sentential structures also restrict it in compounds. No separate rules are needed.

23. Coining and meaning-change are two other ways in which new words have been added to the English language.

24. There are five coining processes which have been particularly fruitful: back-formation, reduplication, blending, clipping and acronym formation. Back-formation refers to the process by which a word is derived from another word by dropping an affix, sometimes a supposed affix. Reduplication involves repetition of the whole or part of the root. Blends are words coined by combining elements from two other words. Clipping means shortening of a word by dropping some part of it. Acronyons are words formed from the first letters of a series of words usually constituting a name, provided these letters form a pronunceable 'word'.

25. Meaning change is a non-morphological process of word-formation.

II. PHONOLOGY

Phonology (Greek- phōnē), voice, sound + (logos, words, speech, subject of discussion), is a subfield of linguistics which studies the sound system of a specific language (or languages), whereas phonetics is about the physical production and perception of the sounds of speech, phonology describes the way sounds function within a given language or across languages.

An important part of phonology is studying which sounds are distinctive units within a language. In English, for example /p/ and /b/ are distinctive units of sound, (*i.e.*, they are *phonemes* the difference is *phonemic*, or *phonematic*). This can be seen from minimal pairs such as "pin" and "bin", which mean different things, but differ only in one sound. On the other hand, /p/ is often pronounced differently depending on its position relative to other sounds, yet these different pronunciations are still considered by native speakers to be the same "sound". For example, the /p/ in "pin" is aspirated while the same phoneme is "spin" is not. In some other languages, for example Thai and Quechua, this same difference of aspiration or non-aspiration does differentiate phonemes.

In addition to the minimal meaningful sounds (the phonemes), phonology, studies how sounds alternate, such as the /p/ in English described above, and topics such as syllable structure, stress, accent and intonation.

The principles of phonological theory have also been applied to the analysis of sign languages, even though the phonological units are not acoustic. The principles of phonology, and for that matter, language, are independent of modality because they stem from an abstract and innate grammar.

The most obvious aspect of language is speech. Speech is not essential to the defination of an infinitely productive communication system, such as is constituted by a language. But, infact, speech is the universal material of human language, and the conditions of speaking and hearing have, throughout human history, shaped and determined its development. The study of speech sounds and of the physiology of speaking is called phonetics: Articulatory phonetics relates to the physiology of speech and acoustic phonetics to the physics of sound waves, their transmission and reception.

Phonetics covers much of the ground loosely referred to in language study as pronunciation. But, from a rather different point of view, speech sounds are also studied in phonology. Every language make use of a very wide range of the articulation and resultant sounds that are available within the human vocal and auditory resources. Each language uses a somewhat different range, and this is partly responsible for the difficulty of learning to speak a foreign language and for speaking it "with an accent." But mere repertoires of sounds are not all that is involved. Far fewer general classes of sounds are distinctive (carry meaning differences) in any language than the number of sounds that are actually phonetically different. The English sounds at the beginning and end of "tot" and in the two places in "stouter" are all different, though these differences are not readily noticed by English speakers; and, rightly, the same letter is used for them all-similar statements could be made about most or all of the other consonant and vowel sounds in English.

What is distinctive in one language may not be distinctive in another or may be used in a different way; this is an additional difficulty to be overcome in learning to speak and undersand a foreign language. In Chinese and in several other languages loosely called tone languages, the pitch, or tone, on which a syllable is said helps to distinguish one word from another: ma in northern Chinese on a level tone means "mother", or on a rising tone means "hemp" and or a falling tone means "to curse". In English and in most of the languages of Europe (though not all-Swedish and Norwegian are exceptions) pitch differences do not distinguish one word from another, but form part of the intonation tunes that contribute to the structure and structural meaning of spoken sentences.

Language differ in the ways in which consonant and vowel sounds can be grouped into syllables in words. English and German tolerate several consonant (before and after a single vowel: "strengths" has three consonants sound before and three after a single vowel sound (ng and th for one sound each). Italian does not have such complex syllables, and in Japanese and Swahili, for example, the ratio of consonant and vowel sounds in syllables and in words is much more even. Speakers of such languages find English words of the sort just mentioned very hard to pronounce, though to an Englishman they are perfectly "natural", "natural" in his context meaning "within the sounds and sound sequences whose mastery is acquired in early childhood as part of one's mother tongue." All these considerations relating to the use of speech sounds in particular languages fall under the general heading of phonology; phonology is often regarded as one component of language structure.

With the great progress made in phonetics in the late 19th century, it had become clear that the question whether two speech sounds were the same or not was more complex that might appear at first sight. Two utterances of what was taken to be the same word night differ quite perceptibly from the occasion of the utterance to the next. Some of this variation could be attributed to a difference of dialect or accent and is of no concern here. But even two utterances of the same word by the same speakers might vary from one occasion to the next. Variation of this kind, though it is generally less obvious and would normally pass unnoticed, is often clear enough to the trained phonetician and is measurable instrumentally. It is known that the "same" word is being uttered, even if the physical signal produced is variable, in part, because the different pronunciations of the same word will cluster around some acoustically identifiable form. But this is not the whole answer, because it is actually impossible to determine norms of pronunciation is purely acoustic terms. Once it has been decided what counts as "sameness' of sound from the linguistic point of view, the permissible range of variation for particular sounds in particular contexts can be measured, and within certain limits, the acoustic cues for the identification of utterances as "the same" can be determined.

What is at issue is the difference between phonetic and phonological (or phonemic) identity, and for these purposes it will be sufficient to define phonetic identity in terms solely of acoustic "sameness." Absolute phonetic identity is a theoretical ideal never fully realized. From a purely phonetic point of view, sounds are more or less similar, rather than absolutely the same or absolutely different. Speech sounds considered as units of phonetic analysis in this article are called phones, and, following the normal convention are represented by enclosing the appropriate alphabetic symbol in square brackets. Thus [p] will refer to a 'p' sound (*i.e.,* what is described more technically as a voiceless, bilabial stop); and [pit] will refer to a complex of three phone – a 'p' sound, followed by an 'i' sound, followed by a 't' sound. A phonetic transcription may be relatively broad (omitting much of the acoustic detail) or relatively narrow (putting in rather more of the detail), according to the purpose for which it is intended.

Phonological, or phonemic, identity was referred to above as "sameness of sound from the linguistic point of view." Considered as phonological units—*i.e.,* from the point of view of their function in the language – sounds are described as phonemes and are distinguished from phones by enclosing their appropriate symbol (normally, but not necessarily, an alphabetic one) between two slash marks. Thus /p/ refers to a phoneme that may be realized on different occasions of utterance or in different contexts by a variety of more or less different phones. Phonological identity, unlike phonetic similarity, is absolute : two phonemes are either the same or different, they cannot be more or less similar. For example, the English words "bit" and "pit" differ phonemically in that the first has the phoneme /b/ and the second has the phoneme /p/ in initial position. As the words are normally pronounced, the phonetic realization of /b/ will differ from the phonetic realization of /p/ in a number of different ways : it will be at least partially voiced (*i.e.,* there will be some vibration of the vocal cords), it will be without aspiration (*i.e.,* there will be no accompanying slight puff of air, as there will be in the case of the phone realizing /p/), and it will be pronounced with less muscular tension. It is possible to vary any one or all of these contributory differences, making the phones in question more or less similar, and it is possible to reduce the phonetic differences to the point that the hearer cannot be certain which word, "bit" or "pit", has been uttered. But it must be either one or the other; there is no word with an initial sound formed in the same manner as /p/ or

/b/ that is halfway between the two. This is what is meant by saying that phonemes are absolutely distinct from one another—they are discrete rather than continuously variable.

How it is known whether two phones realize the same phoneme or not is dealt with differently by different schools of linguists. The "orthodox" post-Bloomfieldian school regards the first criterion to be phonetic similarity. Two phones are not said to realize the same phoneme unless they are sufficiently similar. What is meant by "sufficiently similar" is rather vague, but it must be granted that for every phoneme there is a permissible range of variation in the phones that realize it. As far as occurrence in the same context goes, there are no serious problems. More critical is the question of whether two phones occuring in different contexts can be said to realize the same phoneme or not. To take a standard example from English : the phone that occurs at the beginning of the word "pit" differs from the phone that occurs after the initial /s/ of "spit". The "p sound" occuring after the /s/ is unaspirated (*i.e.*, it is pronounced without any accompanying slight puff of air). The aspirated and unaspirated "p sounds" may be symbolized rather more narrowly as [ph] and [p] respectively. The question then is whether [ph] and [p] realize the same phoneme /p/ or whether each realize a different phoneme. They satisfy the criterion of phonetic similarity, but this, though a necessary condition of phonemic identity, is not a sufficient one.

The next question is whether there is any pair of words in which the two phones are in minimum contrast (or opposition); that is, whether there is any context in English in which the occurence of the one rather than the other has the effect of distinguishing two or more words (in the way that [ph] versus [b] distinguishes the so-called minimal pairs "pit" and "bit", "pan" and "ban" and so on). If there is, it can be said that, despite their phonetic similarity the two phones realize (or "belong to") different phonemes—that the difference between them is phonemic. If there is no context in which the two phones are in contrast (or opposition) in this sense, it can be said that they are variants of the same phoneme—that the difference between them is nonphonemic. Thus, the difference between [ph] and [p] in English is nonphonemic; the two sounds realize, or belong to, the same phoneme, namely /p/. In several other language—*e.g.*, Hindi—the contrast between such sounds as [ph] and [p] is phonemic however. The question is rather more complicated that it has been represented here. In particular, it should be noted that [p] is phonetically similar to [b] as well as to [ph] and that, although [ph] and [b] are in contrast, [p] and [b] are not. It would thus be possible to regard [p] and [b] as variants of the same phoneme. Most linguists, however, have taken the alternative view, assigning [p] to the same phoneme as [ph]. Here it will suffice to note that the criteria of phonetic similarity and lack of contrast do not always uniquely determine the assignment of phones to phonemes. Various supplementary criteria may then be invoked.

Phones that can occur and do not contrast in the same context are said to be in free variation in that context, and, as has been shown, there is permissible range of variation for the phonetic realization of all phonemes. More important than free variation in the same context, however, is systematically determined variation according to the context in which a given phoneme occurs. To return to the example used above : [p] and [ph], though they do not contrast, are not in free variation either. Each of them has its own characteristic positions of occurence, and neither occurs, in normal English pronunciation, in any context characteristic for the other (*e.g.*, only [ph] occurs at the beginning of a word, and only [p] occurs after s). This is expressed by saying that they are in complementary distribution. (The distribution of an element is the whole range of contexts in which it can occur.) Granted that [p] and [ph] are variants of the same phoneme /p/, it can be said that they are contextually, or positionally, determined variants of it. To use the technical term, they are allophones of /p/. The allophones of a phoneme, then, are its contextually determined variants and they are in complementary distribution.

The post-Bloomfieldians made the assignment of phones to phonemes subject to what is now generally referred to as the principle of bi-uniqueness was also held to imply that, if a given phone was assigned to a particular phoneme in one position of occurence, then it must be assigned to the same phoneme in all its other positions of occurence; it could not be the allophone of one phoneme in one context and of another phoneme in other contexts.

A second important principle of the post-Bloomfieldian approach was its insistence that phonemic analysis should be carried out prior to and independently of grammatical analysis. Neither this principle nor that of bi-uniqueness was at all widely accepted outside the post-Bloomfieldian school, and they have been abandoned by the generative phonologists.

Phonemes of the kind referred to so far are segmental; they are realized by consonantal or vocalic (vowel) segments of words, and they can be said to occur in a certain order relative to one another. For example, in the phonemic representation of the word "bit", the phoneme /b/ precedes /i/, which precedes /t/. But nonsegmental of words and utterances may also be functional in a language. In English, for example, the noun "import" differs from the verb "import" in that the former is accented on the first and the latter on the second syllable. This is called a stress accent : the accented syllable is pronounced with greater force or intensity. Many other languages distinguish words suprasegmentally by tone. For example, in Mandarin Chinese the words hào "day" and haŏ "good" are distinguished from one another in that the first has a falling tone and the second a falling-rising tone; these are realized, respectively as (1) a fall in the pitch of the syllable from high to low and (2) a change in the pitch of the syllable from medium to low and back to medium. Stress and tone are suprasegmental in the sense that they are "superimposed" upon the sequence of segmental phonemes. The term tone is conventially restricted by linguists to phonologically relevant variations of pitch at the level of words. Intonation, which is found in all languages, is the variation in the pitch contour or pitch pattern of whole utterances, of the kind that distinguishes (either of itself or in combination with some other difference) statements from questions or indicates the mood or attitude of the speaker (as hesitant, surprised, angry, and so forth). Stress, tone and intonation do not exhaust the phonologically relevant suprasegmental features found in various languages, but they are among the most important.

A complete phonological description of a language includes all the segmental phonemes and specific which allophones occur in which contexts. It also indicates which sequences of phonemes are possible in the language and which are not : it will indicate, for example, that the sequences /bl/ and /br/ are possible at the beginning of English words but not /bn/ or /bm/. A phonological description also identifies and states the distribution of the suprasegmental features. Just how this is to be done, however, has been rather more controversial in the post-Bloomfieldian tradition.

Description and Classification of English Sounds

Speech sounds, that is the sounds which occur in various words we use in our English speech are broadly divided into two categories, namely, *vowels* and *consonants.* In the production of the vowels the air comes out freely through the mouth. There is no closure of the air-passage and no narrowing of a degree that would cause audible friction. All other sounds are called consonants.

There are 24 consonants in the variety of British English known as R.P. or Receivied Pronunciation. Of the native accents we have chosen R.P. as a model because—

(*i*) it is a native accent of English which is very widely understood and accepted.

(*ii*) it is used by most dictionaries to indicate the pronunciation of words.

(*iii*) there is no pan-Indian accent which can serve as a model or which is being used by lexicographers at present.

(*iv*) it is an accent that most recognised 'good' speakers in India, (for examples, AIR and Doordarshan news readers) tend to approximate to for national and international intelligibility.

(*v*) owing to historical reasons, we have not been exposed to other native accents as much as we have been to the educated southern-eastern British accent. In other words, other native accents such as Educated Scottish, General American, Educated Canadian and Australian have not been easily accessible.

For the description of *consonants* we have to indicate :

1. The air-stream mechanism;

2. The state of the glottis, *i.e.*, whether the sound is *voiceless* or *voiced;*
3. The position of the soft-palate, *i.e.* whether the sounds are *oral, nasal* or *nasalized;*
4. The place of articulation, that is where the closure or narrowing takes place; (the lower lip and the tongue are called active articulators because they are moving during the production of speech sounds. The upper lip and the entire roof of the mouth are the passive articulators because the active articulators move in their direction).
5. The manner of articulation, that is the kind of closure or narrowing (also called stricture).

As far as (1) is concerned, all English sounds are produced with agressive lung air.

As far as (2) is concerned the following consonants are *voiceless* :

/p, t, k, tʃ, f, θ, s, ʃ, h/

The others are *voiced,* namely :

/b, d, g, dz, v, ð, z, 3, m, n, η, l, r, j, w/

All the vowerls and diphthongs are voiced.

As far as (3) is concerned all the English consonants and vowels except /m, n, η/ are oral. /m, n, η/ are nasal consonants.

According to (4) place of articulation the consonants can be classified as follows :

Bilabial : Articulated by the two lips, *e.g.*, English /p, b, m, w/

Labio-dental : Articulated by the lower lip against the upper teeth; *e.g.*, English /f, v/

Dental : articulated by the tip of the tongue against the upper teeth *e.g.* English /θ, ð/

Alveolar : articulated by the blade of the tongue against the teeth-ridge; *e.g.* English /t, d, s, z, n, l/

Post-alveolar : articulated by the tip of the tongue against the back of the teeth ridge; *e.g.* English /r/

Palato-alveolar : articulated by the blade of the tongue against the teeth-ridge with the front of the tongue raised towards the hard palate; *e.g.* English /tʃ, dʒ, ʃ, z/

Palatal : articulated by the front of the tongue against the hard palate; *e.g.* English /j/

Velar : articulated by the back of the tongue against the soft palate; *e.g.* English /k, g, η/

Glottal : produced by an obstruction or narrowing between the vocal cords; *e.g.* English /h/

In (5) Manner of articulation refers to the way in which the passage of the air is closed at the place of articulation or there may be only a narrowing that causes friction. According to the manner of articulation, consonants can be classified as follows :

Plosive : There is a complete closure of the air passage, pressure is built up and then the air is released suddenly with explosion *e.g.* English /p, b, t, d, k, g/

Affricates : There is a complete closure of the air passage in the mouth, then the organs are separated slowly so that friction is heard; *e.g.* English /tʃ, dʒ/

Nasals : There is a complete closure in the mouth; the soft palate is lowered and the air escape through the nose; *e.g.* English /m, n, η/

Roll : The active articulator makes a number of rapid taps against the passive articulator. Some people pronounce English /r/ by making the tip of the tongue strike against the teeth-ridge a number of times.

Flap : There is only one tap made of the tip of the tongue against the teeth ridge. English /r/ in *very* is pronounced in this manner.

Lateral : There is complete closure in the middle of the mouth but the air escapes along the sides of the tongue without any friction, *e.g.* English /l/

Fricatives : The active articulator is brought so close to the passive articulator that there is a very narrow gap between them. When the air passes through this narrow passage audible friction is produced *e.g.* English /f, v, θ, ð, s, ʒ, f, z, h/ and English /r/ in words like *train* and *draw.*

Frictionless Continuants : There is no closure or friction but the sound has a consonantal function *e.g.* English /r/ in words like *rain, red,* etc.

Semivowels : A vowel glide with a consonantal function *e.g.* English /j, w/ (In the present day terminology frictionless continuants and semi vowels are referred to as *Approximants* after Peter Ladefoged (1975).

In R.P. the 24 consonants when classified according to manner of articulation, fall into the following groups :

Plosives (6)	/p, b, t, d, k, g/
Affricates (2)	/tʃ, dʒ/
Nasals (3)	/m, n, η/
Lateral (1)	/l/
Fricatives (9)	/f, v, θ, ð, s, z, ʃ, ʒ, h/
Frictionless continuent (1)	/r/
Semi vowels (2)	/j, w/

When classified according to the place of articulation, they fall into the following groups :

Bilabial (4)	/p, b, m, w/
Labio-dental (2)	/f, v/
Dental (2)	/θ, ð/
Alveolar (6)	/t, d, n, l, s, z/
Post-alveolar (1)	/r/
Palato-alveolar (4)	/tʃ, dʒ, ʃ, z/
Palatal (1)	/j/
Velar (3)	/k, g, η/
Glottal (1)	/h/

Nine consonants are voiceless :

/p, t, k, tʃ, f, θ, s, ʃ, h/

the remaining 15 are voiced :

/b, d, g, dʒ, m, n, η, l, v, ð, z, ʒ, r, w, j/

Classification of English Consonants

Place/ Manner	*Bilabial*		*Labiodental*		*Dental*		*Alveolar*		*Post-alveolar*		*Palato-alveolar*		*Palatal*		*Velar*		*Glottal*	
	vl	*vd*	*vl*	*vd*	*vl*	*vd*	*vl*	*vd*	*vl*	*vd*	*vl*	*vd*	*vl*	*vd*	*vl*	*vd*	*vl*	*vd*
Plosive	p	b					t	d							k	g		
Affricate											tʃ	dʒ						
Nasal		m						n								η		
Lateral								l										
Fricative			f	v	θ	ð	s	z			ʃ	ʒ						h
Frictionless Continuant										r								
Semivowel		w												j				

vl = Voiceless
vd = Voiced

I.P.A. symbols have been used in the above table. Consonants are listed below with common key words showing their sounds and their occurence in the initial, medial and final positions. A blank space in the table indicated the non-occurence of a consonant in that position. The three-term description is given in the right hand column.

Consonant	*Initial*	*Medial*	*Final*	*Vl/Vd*	*Place*	*Manner*
p	pin	spin	ship	voiceless	bilabial	plosive
b	bit	clubs	hub	voiced	bilabial	plosive
t	take	stone	lit	voiceless	alveolar	plosive
d	day	heads	lid	voiced	alveolar	plosive
k	key	sky	talk	voiceless	velar	plosive
g	go	eggs	bag	voiced	velar	plosive
tʃ	chain	fetched	teach	voiceless	palato-alveolar	affricate
dʒ	jail	barged	barge	voiced	palato-alveolar	affricate
m	main	small	sum	voiced	bilabial	nasal
n	nail	snake	shine	voiced	alveolar	nasal
ŋ	things	sing	voiced	voiced	velar	nasal
l	late	slate	tell	voiced	alveolar	lateral
f	fan	sphere	half	voiceless	labio-dental	fricative
v	view	thieves	live	voiced	labio-dental	fricative
θ	thin	months	bath	voiceless	dental	fricative
ð	then	bathes	clothe	voiced	dental	fricative
s	sit	taste	loss	voiceless	alveolar	fricative
z	zoo	buzzed	lose	voiced	alveolar	fricative
∂	ship	wished	fresh	voiceless	palato-alveotar	fricative
ʒ	–	division	rouge	voiced	palato-alveolar	fricative
h	hat	behave	–	voiceless	glottal	fricative
r	run	shrewd	–	voiced	post-alveolar	frictionless constinuant
w	win	swin	–	voiced	bilabial	semi-vowel
j	yes	tune	–	voiced	palatal	semi-vowel

Vowels

During the articulation of vowel sounds, the lung-air escapes through the mouth without any friction because there is neither any obstruction or narrowing in the mouth. The vocal cords are normally vibrating, so vowels are *voiced.* They are articulated with a structure of open approximation. The active articulator that is the tongue is raised in the direction of the passive articulator that is the palate. For this purpose the tongue is divided into three parts: front, centre and back and the palate into : hard palate, centre palate (*i.e.* the part of the roof of the mouth between the hard palate and the soft palate) and soft palate. Remember, in the formation of the vowels there is no contact of the tongue with the roof of the mouth and the soft palate is in the raised position so that the nasal cavity is shut off and therefore the vowels are oral, not nasalized.

To describe a vowel following criteria has to be taken into account—

(*a*) The part of the tongue raised during its articulation (front, central, back);

(*b*) The height to which it is raised (close, half-close, half-open and open);

(*c*) The position of the lips (unrounded and rounded).

We can describe a vowel using a three term descriptive label, the three terms indicating the three criteria mentioned above. Thus a *back half-open rounded vowel* would mean that

(*i*) the back of the tongue is raised in the direction of the soft palate;

(*ii*) it is raised to a point between the close and open positions but closer to open;

(*iii*) the lips are rounded.

Diphthongs

The description of vowels given above shows that the tongue remains unchanged during the process of their production, and therefore their quality remains unchanged. A diphthong is called a vowel glide because during the course of its production the tongue first takes the position required for the articulation of a certain vowel and then moves or glides quickly towards the position required for the articulation of another vowel. The vowels in English words *buy, boy, cow* and *poor* are some examples of diphthongs.

Since vowels that change their quality are called diphthongs, vowels that do not change their quality are called *monophthongs* or *pure vowels.*

Remember, a diphthong is not a sequence of two monophthongs because it occupies only one syllable we can conclude that—

(*i*) Vowels are voiced sounds;

(*ii*) They are oral sounds, *i.e.* the soft palate is raised and the nasal cavity is closed;

(*iii*) The quality of vowels depends on the part of the tongue raised, which gives us front vowels, central vowels and back vowels and on its height which gives us close, half-close, half-open and open vowels;

(*iv*) According to the position of the lips, vowels are either unrounded or rounded.

(*v*) The tongue changes its position through a smooth glide during the articulation of diphthongs. They occupy one syllable.

In R.P. there are twenty vowels made up of twelve pure vowels or monophthongs and eight vowel-glides or diphthongs. These are listed below (in I.P.A. symbols) with key words illustrating their occurence in the initial, medial and final positions. A blank space in the table indicates the non-occurence of a vowel in that position. The three-term description of pure vowels is given in the right hand column.

Vowels	*Initial*	*Medial*	*Final*	*Part of the tongue raised*	*Height of the tongue*	*Rounded/ unrounded*
Pure Vowels						
i:	east	seen	key	front	close	unrounded
I	it	hit	duty	centralized front	half-close	unrounded
e	end	lend	—	front	between half-close and half-open	unrounded
æ	and	land	—	front	just below the half-open	unrounded
a:	arm	harm	car	back	open	unrounded
⊂	on	cot	—	back	just above open	rounded
⊃:	all	caught	saw	back centralized	between half-open and half-close	rounded
u	—	put	—	back	just above half-close	rounded
u:	ooze	choose	shoe	back	close	rounded
^	up	cup	—	central	between open and half-open	unrounded
3:	earn	turn	sir	central	between half-close and half-open	unrounded
∂	ago	police	tailor	central	short	unrounded

Diphthongs

Diphthongs	*Initial*	*Medial*	*Final*
eI	eight	straight	stray
∂u	oak	joke	slow
ai	ice	mice	my
au	out	shout	how
⊃i	oil	boil	boy
i∂	ear	beard	clear
e∂	air	shared	care
u∂	—	cured	poor

Of the 12 monophthongs, 7 are short /*i.e.*, æ, ⊃, u, ʌ, ∂ / and 5 long, /i:, a:, ⊃:, u:, 3:/. Diphthongs are all long vowels.

III. SOUNDS OF ENGLISH—INTONATION, ACCENT

Linguistics attempt to make accurate statement about the system of language currently in use in any speech community. All languages change in the course of time. Written records make it clear that 15th century English is quite noticeably different from 20th century English as in 15th century French or German from modern French or German. It was the principal achievement of the 19th century linguists not only to realize more clearly than their predecessors the unbiquity of linguistics change but also put its scientific investigation on a sound footing by means of the comparative method.

Since the beginning of the 19th century, when scholars observed that there were a number of systematic correspondences in related words between the sounds of the Germanic languages and the sounds of what were later recognized as other Indo-European languages, particular attention has been paid in diachronic linguistics to changes in the sound systems of languages. Certain common types of sound change, most notably assimilation and dissimilation, can be explained, at least partially, in terms of syntagmatic, or contextual, conditioning. By assimilation is meant the process by which one sound is made similar in its place or manner of articulation to a neighbouring sound. For example, the word "cupboard" was presumably once pronounced, as the spelling indicates, with the consonant cluster pb in the middle. The p was assimilated to b in manner of articulation (*i.e.,* voicing was maintained throughout the cluster) and subsequently the resultant double consonant bb was simplified. With a single b in the middle and in unstressed second syllable, the word "cupboard", as it is pronounced nowadays, is no longer so evidently a compound of "cup" and "board" as its spelling still shows it to have been. The Italian words notte "night" and otto "eight" manifest assimilation of the first consonant to the second consonant of the cluster in place of articulation (cf. Latin nocte (m), octo). Assimilation is also responsible for the phenomenon referred to as umlaut in the Germanic languages. The high front vowel i of suffixes had the effect of fronting and raising preceding back vowels and, in particular, of converting an a sound an e i of suffixes had the effect of fronting and raising preceding back vowels and, in particular, of converting an a sound into an e sound. In Modern German this is still a morphologically productive process (cf. Mann "man" : Männer "men"). In English it has left its mark in such irregular forms as "men" (from* manniz), "feet" (from *fotiz) and "length" (from *langa). Dissimilation refers to the process by which one sound becomes different from a neighbouring sound. For example, the word "pilgrim" (French pelerin) derives ultimately from Latin peregrinus; the I sound results from dissimilation of the first r under the influence of the second r. A special case of dissimilation is haplology, in which the second of the two identical or similar syllables is dropped. Examples include the standard modern British pronunciations of "Worcester" and "Gloucester" with two syllables rather than three and the common pronunciation of "library" as if it were written "libry". Both assimilation and dissimilation are commonly subsumed under the principle of "ease of articulation." This is clearly applicable in typical instances of assimilation. It is less obvious how or why a succession of unlike sounds in contiguous syllables should be easier to pronounce than a succession of identical or similar sounds. But a better understanding of this phenomenon, as of other "slips of the tongue", may result from current work in the physiological and neurological aspects of speech production.

Not all sound change is to be accounted for in terms of syntagmatic conditioning. The change of p, t and k to f, θ (the th sound in "thin"), and h or of b, d, g, to p, t and k in early Germanic cannot be explained in these terms. Nor can the so-called Great Vowel Shift in English, which, in the 15th century, modified the quality of all the long vowels (cf. "profane" : "profanity"; "divine" : "divinity"; and others). Attempts have been made to develop a general theory of sound change, notably by the French linguist Andre Martinet. But no such theory has yet won universal acceptance, and it is likely that the causes of sound change are multiple. Sound change is not necessarily phonological; it may be merely phonetic. The pronunciation of one or more of the phones realizing a particular phoneme may change slightly without affecting any of the previously existing phonological distinctions; this no doubt happens quite frequently as a language is transmitted from one generation to the next. Two diachronically distinct states of the language would differ in this respect in the same way as two coexistent but geographically or socially distinct accents of the same language might differ. It is only when two previously distinct phonemes are merged or a unitary phoneme splits into two (typically when allophonic variation becomes phonemic) that sound change must definitely be considered as phonological. For example, the sound change of p, to f, t to θ (th), and k to h, on the one hand, and of b to p, d to t, and g to k, on the other, in early Germanic had the effect of changing the phonological system. The voiceless stops did not become fricatives in all positions; they remained as voiceless stops after s. Consequently, the p sound that was preserved after s merged with the p that derived by sound from b. (It is here assumed that the aspirated p sound and the unaspirated p sound are to be regarded as allophones of the same phoneme). Prior to the Germanic sound shift the phoneme to be found at the beginning of the words for "five" or "father", also occured after s in words for "spit" or "spew"; after the change this was no longer the case.

Word-stress/accent

Word stress in English is by and large unpredictable, it is possible to frame rules for primary stress on words with some derivational suffixes. Not all the derivational suffixes affect stress. We need to know the suffixes that affect stress and those that do not affect stress. When words are fitted into utterances they contribute to the rhythm of English. Utterances have strings of words, some of which are stressed and some are not. While the stressed syllables in words tend to occur at roughly regular intervals of time, the unstressed syllables between them are weakened. Indeed some words that are predisposed to being unstressed even have weak forms.

In English words can have one or more than one syllable. In English for example, there are words with two, three, four, five, six or even seven syllables. The words, *point, lost, threat, salt, grade* all have one syllable. In an English word of more than one syllable, one of the syllables is pronounced with *greater prominence* than the other (s). The syllables that is pronounced more prominently than the other(s) in the same word is said to be *accented* or to *receive the accent.*

The factors responsible for prominence are:

(1) Loudness : The breath force used by a speaker are the greater muscular energy involved is heard as greater loudness or stress. In a word of more than 3 syllables several degrees of articulatory energy is used. For example, in 'calculation' one of the syllables is heard as the loudest of all and that is *la*. The syllable *cal* is heard as the second loudest. Listeners can perceive two degrees of loudness clearly and therefore the majority of listeners are in agreement regarding two degree of stress. Listeners seldom agrees as to which syllables have the third, fourth or fifth degree of loudness because these degrees of loudness are not clearly perceptible to the naked ear.

(2) Pitch Change : In English stress alone is not an efficient marker of prominence. If we change only the loudness, the perceptual effect of stress is not very strong. The pattern of accent in a word becomes clearer when the syllable that is prominent is associated with pitch change. For example, the word 'insult' as a noun is recognised not only because the speaker uses extra breath force and thus stresses the first syllable, but also because there is a pitch change on the first syllable. In other words when the word 'insult' is said, the first syllable, in addition to being heard as louder than the second syllable, carries pitch change, that is, a movement of pitch from high to low or low to high. The pitch change is generally indicated by a slanting line above and before the stressed syllable if the word is said with a falling pitch as shown on the word 'insult'. It is generally marked with a slanting line below and before the stressed syllable if it is said with a rising pitch, like this—insult. However, when a word is said in isolation we generally use a falling pitch.

(3) A third factor that plays an important part in prominence is the quality of a vowel. A syllable will tend to be prominent if it contains a vowel that is different from the vowels in the neighbouring syllables. If we take a nonsense word like /ta : ta : ta : ta:/ and change one of the vowels, we get /ta : ti : ta : ta :/. The odd syllable /ti : /will be heard as more prominent. Indeed, in words of more than one syllable, the syllable that has a vowel that is different from the weak vowels, particularly /ə / and also /I/ and /u/ in weak syllables, stands out against a background of these weak syllables, and is often a stressed syllable.

(4) Another factor that is responsible for prominence is the quantity or length of syllables. If one of the syllables in a word of more than one syllable is made longer than the others, there is quite strong tendency for that syllable to be heard as prominent.

Prominence, than is produced by 4 main factors (1) loudness, (2) pitch, (3) quality and (4) quantity. Generally, these factors work in combination, though syllables may sometimes be made prominent by means of only one or two of them. Experiments have shown that these factors do not have equal importance; the strongest effect is produced by pitch, and length is also a powerful factor. Loudness and quality have much less effect.

In a polysyllabic English word more than one syllable is accented. The syllable on which the pitch change takes place is said to receive *primary accent* or *tonic accent*. The other prominent syllable in the same word is said to receive *secondary* accent. For example, in the word examination /Ig-zæmi-nei-ʃn/, the fourth syllable /nei/ has the maximum prominence and is said to carry the primary accent. The second syllable /zæ/ has the next degree of prominence and is said to receive secondary accent.

Primary accent is marked with a vertical bar *above* and *in front* of the syllable to which it refers. Secondary accent is marked with a vertical far *below* and *in front* of the syllable to which it refers. Here are some words with both primary and secondary accents marked :

Examination	/Ig, zæmi' neiʃn/
International	/,Intə' næʃ ənl /
Organization	/, ɔ: gənai 'Zeiʃn/
Admiration	/, ædmI' rei'ʃən/
Determination	/dI, t3: mI' neiʃ ən /
Combination	/,ɔmbI' neiʃ ən /
Psychologically	/,saikə'Iɔdʒ Ikəll
Confidential	/,kɔfI'denʃ əl /

Rules of Accent Placement

1. If a word has two syllables, the primary stress falls on the first-syllable.

   'able, 'package, 'private, 'happy,, 'doctor some exceptions :

   a'bout, de'light, ca'nal, sham'poo, su'preme

2. 3-syllable words may be accented on the first, second or third syllable :

   (*a*) Accent on the first syllable
   'accident, 'bicycle, 'calculate

   (*b*) Accent on the second syllable
   ex'ception, con'trastive, de'liver, ho'rizon

   (*c*) Accent on the third syllable
   disap'point, enter'tain, under'stand

If a two syllable word functions as a noun/adjective, it is accented on the first syllalde, and if it functions as a verb, it is accented on the second syllable :

3. *Word*	*Noun/Adjective*	*Verb*
absent	/'æbsənt/	/əb/sent/
compound	/'kɔmpaund/	/kəm'pound/
Conflict	/'kɔnflIkt/	/kəm'flikt/
desert	/'dezət/	/dI'z3:t/
increase	/'Inkri:s/	/In'kri:s/

4. Words with weak prefixes are always accented on the root :

abroad	/ə'b⊃ :d/
alone	/ə'lə un/
below	/bI'lə u/

5. The inflectional suffixes *–ed, –es* and *–ing* do not affect the accent :

–ed	re'late	re'lated
–es	suc'cess	suc'cesses
–ing	'happen	'happening

6. The derivational suffixes *–age, –ance, –en, –er, –ess, –ful, –hood, –ice, –ish, –ive, –less, –ly, –ment, –ness, –or, –ship, –ter, –ure,* and *–zen* do not normally affect the accent :

–age	'carry	'carriage
–ance	ap'pear	ap'pearance
–en	'light	'lighten
–er	per'form	per'former
–ess	'actor	'actress
–ful	'beauty	'beautiful
–hood	'brother	'brotherhood
–ice	'coward	'cowardice
–ish	'yellow	'yellowish
–ive	a'buse	a'busive
–less	'colour	'colourless
–ly	'certain	'certainly
–ment	a'chieve	a'chievement
–ness	'bitter	'bitterness
–or	col'lect	col'lector
–ship	'author	'authorship
–ter	'laugh	'laughter
–zen	'city	'citizen

7. Words ending in *–ion* take the primary accent on the last syllable but one :

   ,admi'ration, ,appl'cation, ,deco'ration

8. Words ending in *–ic, –ical, –ically, –ious, –ias* and *–ially* take the primary accent on the syllable preceding the suffix :

-ic	ter'rific
-ical	'optical
-ically	'chemically
-ious	,cere'monious
-ial	me'morial
-ially	dra'matically

9. Words ending in -ity take the accent on the third syllable from the end :

a'bility	ratio'nality	gene'rosity
ac'tivity	mo'rality	,possi'bility

10. A compound is accented on the first syllable of the first word, but a noun phrase is accented on the first syllables of both the words :

Compound	*Noun Phrase*
'blackbird	'black 'bird
'copperplate	'copper' plate
'grandmother	'grand' mother
'goldfish	'gold'fish

The above description of the rules of accentual patterns shows that accent in English is both *fixed* and *free*. It is fixed in the sense that every word has its own fixed accentual pattern. It is free in the sense that some words are accented on the first syllable, some on the second syllable, others on the third syllable, and so on. Accent generally falls on the root syllable and not on a prefix or suffix. Accented syllables are also called stressed.

Intonation

In linguistics, 'intonation' is the variation of pitch when speaking. Intonation and stress are two main elements of linguistic prosody.

Many languages use pitch semantically, for instance to convey surprise and irony or to change a statement to a question. Such languages are called *intonation languages.* English and French are well-known examples. Some languages use pitch to distinguish words; these are known as tonal languages. Chinese, Thai, and Hausa are examples. An intermediate position is occupied by languages with tonal word accent, for instance Norwegian or Japanese.

Rising intonation means the pitch of voice increases over time; *falling intonation* means that the pitch decreases with time. A *dipping intonation* falls and then rises, whereas a *peaking intonation* rises and then falls.

Stress and intonation are linked phenomena; they work together to give the effect of 'prominence' or accent. Accented syllables can be said with level pitch or with a change in pitch. An accented syllable said on level pitch is described as having a *static tone,* whilst an accented syllable on which a pitch change takes place has a *kinetic tone.* The syllable which initiates a kinetic tone is called the *nucleus* and is said to have *nuclear* or *tonic* accent. Thus the sentence.

They 'came at/ 'night.

Would be said with a high level tone on *came* and a falling nucleus or falling kinetic tone, on *night.* In a tone group the last prominent syllable will be the nucleus and the changing tone may be *falling, rising, falling-rising* and *rising-falling.* These tones are marked in the text and their graphic representations are given below :

(1) Level (static) Tone

Marked with a symbol 'above and in front of the syllable to which it refers :

'Those

'Have

(2) Moving (Kinetic) Tones

(*a*) *Falling tone* is marked with a symbol \ in front of the syllable to which it refers :

'Then

'Do

(*b*) *Rising tone* is marked with a symbol / in front of the syllable to which it refers :

,These

,Car

(*c*) *Falling-rising Tone* is marked with a symbol V above and in front of the syllable to which it refers :

v Try v Soft

(*d*) *Rising-falling Tone* is marked with a symbol ^ above and in front of the syllable to which it refers :

^ Yes of ^ course

Uses of Tones

Every utterance has one or more than one tone group and every tone group has its own pattern of pitch variation. This pattern depends on the number of accented syllables in a particular tone group, the location of the tonic syllable in it, and the nature of the change of pitch direction on the tonic syllable.

Intonation performs a linguistic function in very much the same way as grammar does. In the organization and communication of meaning, it is complementary to grammar. It performs the following three functions :

(a) Grammatical Function : With the help of intonation, the hearer can make out whether a particular utterance is a statement or a question, a command or a request. It also tells the hearer whether a tone-group is a complete or incomplete utterance. Look at the following sentences :

He is ar'riving 'late. (Falling tone-statement)

He is ar'riving, late (Rising tone-question)

'Shut the 'door. (Falling tone-command)

'Shut the , door. (Rising tone-request)

'When you , come here /I'll' get you what you want.

(The first tone group-rising tone-incomplete utterance. The second tone group falling tone-complete utterance).

(b) Attitudinal Function : With the help of intonation, we can find out the mood or attitude of the speaker-whether he is bored, annoyed, interested in the subject of conversation or sarcastic, polite, assertive, incredulous or querulous etc.

'When can you, come? (a plain neutral, normal question)

'When can you, ,come? (expresses politeness and even deference)

(c) Accentual Function : Intonation enables the speaker to make any part of his utterance prominent in accordance with the meaning he wants to convey. This he can do by choosing the appropriate nucleus.

I 'hate 'woman (However, I like men or children)

I 'hate 'women. (Insists on the statement)

'I hate 'women. (Although my brother is very fond of them).

1. Falling Tone : A falling tone is used :

(*a*) In ordinary statements:

He's 'just been pro'moted.

It's 'seven o' 'clock.

(*b*) In wh-questions said in a natural way :

'Where are you 'going?

'What can I 'do for you?

(*c*) In commands :

'shut the 'window.

'come 'here.

(*d*) In exclamation :

'Good 'heavens!

'What a fine 'weather!

2. Rising Tone : The rising tone is used

(*a*) In yes/no type questions :

Are you 'leaving for 'Delhi to, day ?

Is 'father 'at, home?

(*b*) In requests :

'Pass me the 'salt 'please.

'shut the ,door.

(*c*) Wh-questions showing politeness, friendliness and personal interest :

'How is you ,son?

'Why didn't you' 'come and ,see me?

(*d*) In incomplete, utterances :

It's 'seven O' , clock..... (but she hasn't got up yet)

If you 'don't come in , time .... (I'll leave)

(*e*) In tag-questions asking for information :

'These are 'nice/,aren't they?

(3) Falling-rising Tone : This tone indicates that something is implied - something is not expressed in the utterance and the listener should understand more than a literal interpretation of the words. It may imply an insult, an apology, an unpleasant news, or doubt on the part of the speaker. The fall and the rise may occur within the same syllable or on different syllables.

If you 'don't be ˇhave / (I'll punish you) (Incomplete statement)

(He has three daughters). He has ˇfour.

(Correction of information)

You 'musn't 'go like ˇthis. (warning)

He's ˇgood. (but I can't trust him)

(4) Rising—falling Tone : The rise reinforces the meaning conveyed by the following fall. The initial rise may indicate warmth, anger or sarcasm.

It was ^horrid. (enthusiastic agreement)

'What has he been ^doing? (suspicion)

'Go and 'break you ^head. (haughtiness)

'How ^good for you! (sarcasm)

The uses of tones are summarised in the following diagram

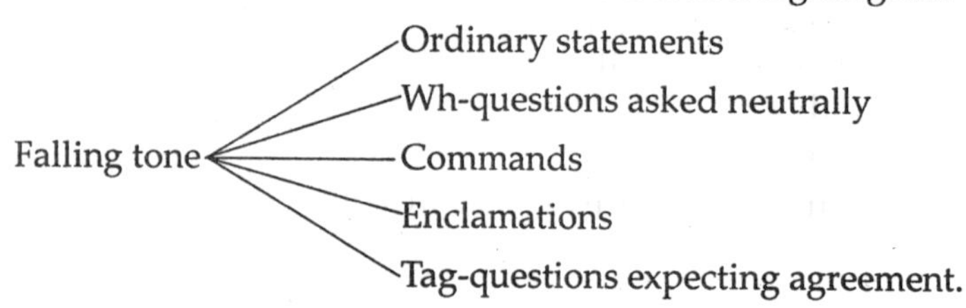

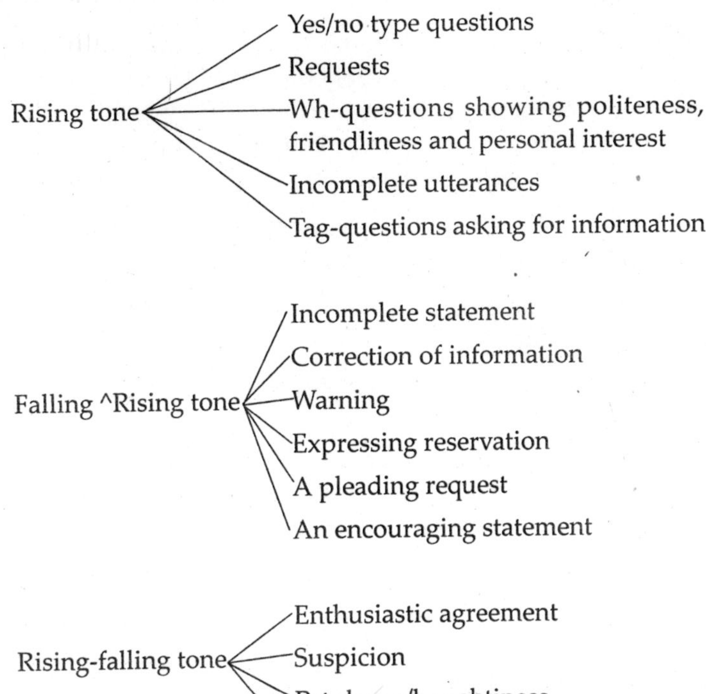

SOCIOLINGUISTICS

We all use language everyday. We all are creative in the use of language. We use a variety of ways for a variety of purpose. Language is actually a great mystery. The mysterious nature of language begins to unfold itself when you realize that it cannot be studied in isolation. It is used in society and therefore, we need to study language in relation to society. Language is what members of a society speak. But what is a society? A society comprises of a group of individuals who are normally drawn together for a certain purpose or purposes. Whatever may be the purpose, the use of language is undoubtedly an integral part of being human. Infact, an inability to use language appropriately or adequately can effect ones status in society, and may even alter one's personality.

Language cannot exist and develop outside society. What lyrics are to music, language is to society. The relationship between the two is that of interdependence. To ignore the influence of language on society or of society on language would give only an incomplete picture of the relationship that language and society share. The main concern of sociolinguistics is to examine this complex relationship between language and society.

Some of the questions that sociolinguists investigate are :

1. Is language static or variable ?
2. To what extend are social factors responsible for language variation?
3. How is it that people are able to communicate despite variation?
4. Are standard languages different from dialects.
5. Why should each social context be examined in its own right ?
6. Are there any homogenous societies in reality ?
7. Can language be used as a tool for power in all spheres of social life, like education, religion, and administration, etc. and lead to social exploitation ?
8. Can language initiate a social change ?
9. Why do languages change ?
10. Is language planning essential ?

Language is probably the most important instrument of socialization that exists in all human societies and cultures. It is largely by means of language that one generation passes on to the next its myths, laws, customs and beliefs, and it is largely by means of language that the child comes to appreciate the structure of the society into which he is born and his own place in that society. As a social force, language serves both to strengthen the links that bind the members of the same group and to differentiate the members of one group from those of another. In many countries there are social dialects as well as regional dialects, so that it is possible to tell from a person's speed not only where he comes from but what class he belongs to. In some instances social dialects can transcend regional dialects. This is notable in England, where standard English in the so-called Received Pronunciation (RP) can be heard from members of the upper class and upper middle class in all parts of the country. The example of England is but an extreme manifestation of a tendency that is found in all countries : there is less regional variation in the speech of the higher than in that of the lower socioeconomic classes. In Britain and the United States and in most of the other English-speaking countries, people will almost use the same dialect or not. (Relatively minor adjustments of vocabulary may, however, be made : an Englishman speaking to an American may employ the word "elevator" rather than "lift" and so on. In many communities throughout the word, it is common for members to speak two or more different dialects and to use one dialect rather than another in particular social situations. This is commonly referred to as code-switching. Code-switching may operate between two distinct languages (*e.g.*, Spanish and English among Puerto Ricans in New York) as well as between two dialects of the same language. The term diglossia (rather than Bilingualism) is frequently used by sociolinguists to refer to this by no means uncommon phenomenon.

In every situation, what one says and how one says it depends upon the nature of that situation, the social role being played at the time, one's status vis-a-vis that of the person addressed, one's attitude towards him, and so on. Language interacts with nonverbal behavior in social situations and serves to clarify and reinforce the various roles and relationships important in a particular culture. Socio-linguistics is far from having satisfactorily analyzed or even identified all the factors involved in the selection of one language feature rather than another in particular situations. Among those that have been discussed in relation to various languages are : the formality or informality of the situation; power and solidarity relationships between the participants; differences of sex, age, occupation, socioeconomic—class, and educational background; and personal or transactional situations. Terms such as style and register (as well as a variety of others) are employed by many linguists to refer to the socially relevant dimensions of phonological, grammatical, and lexical variation without one language. So far there is very little agreement as to the precise application of such terms.

Just as it is difficult to draw the boundary between linguistics and psycholinguistics and between psychology and psycholinguistics, so it is difficult to distinguish sharply between linguistics and sociolinguistics and between sociolinguistics and sociology. There is the further difficulty that, because the boundary between sociology and anthropology is also unclear, sociolinguistics merges with anthropological linguistics.

It is frequently suggested that there is a conflict between the sociolinguistics and psycholinguistic approach to the study of language, and it is certainly the case that two distinct points of view are discernible in the literature at the present time. Chomsky has described linguistics as a brand of cognitive psychology, and neither he nor most of his followers have yet shown much interest in the relationship between language and its social and cultural matrix. On the other hand, many modern schools of linguistics that have been very much concerned with the role of language in society would tend to relate linguistics more closely to sociology and anthropology than to any other discipline. It would seem that the opposition between the psycholinguistic and the sociolinguistic viewpoint must ultimately be transcended. The acquisition of language, a topic of central concern to psycholinguists, is in part dependent upon and in part itself determines the process of socialization; and the ability to use one's native language correctly in the numerious socially prescribed situations of daily life is as characteristics a feature of linguistic competence, in the broad sense of this term, as is the ability to produce grammatical utterances. Some of the most recent work in sociolinguistics and psycholinguistics has sought to widen the notion of linguistic competence in this way. So far, however, sociolinguistics and psycholinguistics tend to be regarded as relatively independent areas of research.

Sociolinguistics is thus the subdiscipline of linguistics which deals with the relationships between language and society. It has close connections with the social sciences, in particular, sociology, anthropology, social psychology, and education and encompasses the study of multilingualism, social dialects, conversational interaction, attitudes to language, language change, and much more. Sometimes the field is subdivided into macro and microsociolinguistics, with the macro-domain sometimes also referred to as the sociology of language. Macrosociolinguistics takes society as its starting point and deals with language as a pivotal factor in the organization of communities. Microsociolinguistics begins with language and treats social forces as essential factors influencing the structure of languages. Some also distinguish between theoretical and applied sociolinguistics. The former is concerned with formal models and methods for analyzing the structure of speech communities and speech varieties, and providing a general account of communicative competence. Applied sociolinguistics deals with the social and political implications of fundamental inequalities in language use in various areas of public life, for example, school, courts, etc.

It may be surprising to lay person that orthodox historical linguistics has not taken very much account of social factors in attempting to explain linguistic change. Some experts insist that social factors are of little relevance, and that the causes of change are to be found in phenomena that are more central to language structure, for example, 'natural' phonetic processes. However, there is one important difficulty, which applies especially to the explanation of sound change. This is that if one does not take social factors into account, there appears to be little reason why sound change (and some other kinds of change) should take place at all. If, at some time, the sound [a] should change to [o] in all relevant words, the language has not gained anything by the change, as one tiny segment of sound cannot be 'better' or more efficient than another. Indeed, it can be argued that change is dysfunctional, since, when a change is introduced by some section of speech community, it is in principle possible that the new form will not be immediately understood. However, change is continuously in progress, and its operation has greatly altered the sound systems and structural characteristics of languages in the course of history : Old and Middle English, for example, were clearly very different in pronunciation and grammar from twentieth-century English, and language change can be very rapid.

It seems that the causes of change are not to be found in the structure of languages as such, but in the behavior of speakers. As speakers in social groups manifestly attach great social importance to quite small differences in pronunciation, which are arbitrary in linguistic terms (*i.e.,* one sound is just as good as another), sociolinguists argue that collecting and analyzing the language of live speakers in social groupings can be used to advance the understanding of the causes of linguistic change. The basic problem to be solved is known as the 'actuation problem', and it can be stated thus :

> Why do changes in a structural feature take place in a particular language at a given time, but not in other languages with the same feature, or in the same language at other times?

Thus, one might ask why the French language has lost many final consonants in the course of history, while Spanish and Italian have preserved them, and (at the dialectical level) why some dialects of English have lost final and pre-consonant [r] in words such as *car, card,* while others (for example, Scottish and North American English) have retained it. Although the actuation problem cannot be completely solved, sociolinguists attempt to come closer to understanding it.

Most changes in language, as far as is known, take place without self-conscious attempts being made by speakers to implement them; yet, paradoxically, they must in some way be implemented through speaker activity, as the new forms are accepted and used by new generations of speakers. Self-conscious institutional intervention in language is generally known as 'language planning.' Another phenomenon that may be brought about by institutional intervention is language standardization; from a socialinguistic point of view, standardization can be seen as an attempt to impose uniformity on a phenomenon which is by nature variable (language), and part of its purpose is to prevent linguistic change. Sociolinguistics have up until the time of writting been mainly interested in change that comes about 'naturally', without conscious intervention.

Three main approaches can be distinguished. The first is associated with the work of anthropological linguists, and focuses on 'language shift'—the replacement of one language by another, perhaps with discernible effects on one or both languages. Work in this tradition traces the replacement patterns as they progress through bilingual populations. It is typically found that some social groups (*e.g.,* females as against males, or a particular social class) lead in the shift, and that the recessive language is replaced by the incoming language in different social situations at different rates : for example, the recessive language normally persists in domestic environments after it has been replaced in most other functions. The study of recessive languages in these situations is referred to as the study of 'language death'. Typically, these languages undergo a great deal of internal change during the process.

The second approach to language change focuses on monolingual situations in much greater linguistic detail, and is associated with the name of William Labov. It can be called quantitative social dialectology, as it makes use of quantification to reveal patterns of variation in terms of the social characteristics of the speakers studied—age, sex, and social class, for example. By this means, linguistic changes in progress can be detected and traced in fine detail as they diffuse in an orderly way through populations of speakers. These studies usually focus on quite small communities of speakers, and they have shown that, in order to understand linguistic changes, one must first think of changes as coming about in the speech community rather than in the national language as a whole. That is, changes originate not in 'English', but in some localized variety of English. From localized situations, they may diffuse much more widely, and these wider patterns of diffusion are also studied.

The third relevant approach concerns Pidgin and Creole languages. Like the first approach, this involves contact between languages, except that the replacement of one language (an established native language) is abrupt—it is brought about by upheaval of populations who are then thrown together with strangers in situations where there is no common language. Creoles are normally based on colonial languages such as English or Portuguese, with much reduced syntax. Pidgin and Creole studies have greatly advanced the understanding of universals of language change, particularly syntactic universals.

So far, theoretical advances in traditional historical linguistic concerns have come mainly from work in the second approach above. They have been chiefly concerned with sound change and have borne in mind the traditional neo-grammarian axioms, which propose that sound change is phonetically gradual and lexically abrupt. In this view, change is believed to proceed by imperceptible degrees affecting all members of a word-class at the same time (*e.g.*, all words with the vowel [a], as in *bat, band, hand* etc.). Many sociolinguistics patterns however, have proved to be different from this : they are lexically gradual and phonetically abrupt, and sound change is often observed to spread gradually through the relevant lexicon, affecting some words before others. Similarly, phonetic differences are not necessarily imperceptible, but may be quite marked. The relevance of these traditional concerns is a matter of debate; what is certainly clear is that sound change is *socially* gradual. It spreads gradually through populations of speakers.

Influenced by Labov, many attempted accounts of language change have used social class as a background to their arguments. Change has been seen as spreading upward and downward from some central point in the social-class hierarchy, and social-class differentiation seems to have been thought of as a cause of change. Sex differentiation in language has also been cited as an equally important variable in linguistic change, as males and females are always found to differ in speech, usually with females using more 'careful' or less 'vernacular' speech than males.

Argumentation based on the idea of varying solidarity within and between communities and operationalized in terms of social network has been used to propose a theory that can account for different language situations—encompassing those studied by the three approaches enumerated above. This suggests that, as close and solidary personalities in communities result in dialect maintenance and resistance to change, linguistic change is facilitated by the development of large numbers of weak ties. If this model is used in interpretation, it appears to account in a coherent way for situations of different orders of magnitude. It is proposed that :

> Linguistic change is slow to the extent that the relevant populations are well established and bound by strong ties, whereas it is rapid to the extent that weak ties exist in populations.

Although traditional historical linguistics neglected speakers (partly because it did not have access to tape recorders), languages that have no speakers do not change. A theory of change must therefore have a place of speakers, and it has been proposed that a distinction should be drawn between innovations and changes in language. An innovation is an act of the speaker, which may or may not lead to a *change,* which is something that is embedded in the language system. In order to make progress here, one must attempt to understand the way in which some innovations in some circumstances can become changes, whereas others fall away without trace. Although the actuation problem is still a very long way from being solved, it is to be hoped that the typical sociolinguistic focus on speaker behaviour will make further contributions to linguists' understanding of the nature of linguistic change.

Sociolinguists examine the variable nature of language. They believe that language is not a static entity but is dynamic. Language variation can be investigated at any of the levels: phonological, morphological, syntactic, semantic or disourse. Variation may be due to a number of factors like geographical separation, sex, age, education, social class, caste etc. or because of style and register differences. Languages can also vary according to the situation or the social context which is considered to be of utmost importance in sociolinguistics.

Another concern of sociolinguists has been to regard language as a marker of group solidarity and group identity. An individual creates his/her identity in terms of the social group or groups he/she belongs to. He/she shares certain social and linguistic norms with the other members of the social group. There is, therefore, a sort of conformity to a social group. Yet, the uniqueness of each individual's experience of language and the society he/she belongs to enables him/her to filter his/her experience of new situations in his/her own way. This obviously means that since no two individuals are alike or have the same experience, they interpret situations in different ways and construct mental maps according to their own interpretation. Hence, there are as it were, two forces operating, one leading to similarities between individuals by conforming to a social group or groups and their norms and the other leading to individual differences. These forces are often referred to as conformity and individualism. The amount of variation between speakers within a social group depends on the relative strengths of these two forces.

Language is also often used as a tool of power in all spheres of social life, be it education, religion, media, administration and so on. Language of the rich and the powerful is often made a 'standard' variety at the cost of all other varieties, which are in no way linguistically inferior. Sociolinguists in India are increasingly getting concerned with the standardization of language in the social content and keen to bring about a social change in keeping with our sociolinguistic reality.

The study of sociolinguistics is partly empirical and partly theoretical. It must be founded on an adequate data base like censuses, documents, surveys, and interviews. To conclude, Fishman's description of sociolinguistics appears to be quite apt and interesting. He considers sociolinguistics to encompass everything from 'who speaks (or writes) what language (or what language variety) to whom and when and to what end.'

VARIATION AND VARIETIES OF ENGLISH

The word language contains a multiplicity of different designations. Two senses can be distinguished : language as a universal species-specific capability of mankind, and languages as the various manifestations of that capability, as with English, French, Latin, Swahili, Malay and so on. There is, of course, no observable universal language over and above the various languages that have been or are spoken or written: but one may choose to concentrate on the general and even the universal features, characteristics, and components of different languages and on the ways in which the same sets of descriptive procedure and explanatory theories may be applied to different languages. In so doing one may refer to language (in general) as one's object of study. This is what is done by linguists, or linguistic scientists, persons devoting themselves to the scientific study of languages (as opposed to the popular sense of polyglots, persons having a command of several different languages).

Language by its nature is dynamic and variable. There is no such thing as uniformity in language. Not only does the speech of one community differ from that of another, but the speech of different individuals of a single community, even members of the same family, is marked by individual pecularities. These individual pecularities are known as the 'dialect'. Where constant communication takes place among the people speaking a language, individual differences become merged in the general speech of the community, and a certain conformity prevails. The differences may be slight of the separation is slight and we may have merely local *dialects* on the other hand, they may become so considerable as to render the language of one district unintelligible to the speakers of another. In this case we may have the development of separate languages. Even where the differentiation as gone this far, it is usually possible to recognise a sufficient numbers of common features which the resulting languages still retain in common to indicate that at one time they were one.

Dialects

No two person speak exactly alike, and within the area of all but the smallest speech communities (groups of people speaking the same language, there are subdivisions of recognizably different types of language) called dialects, that do not, however render inter-communication impossible nor markedly difficult. Because inter comprehensibility lies along a scale, the degree required for two or more forms of speech to quality is dialects of a single language, instead of being regarded as separate language is not easy to quantify or to lay down in advance, and the actual cut of point must in the last resort be arbitrary. In practice, however, the terms dialect and language can be used with reasonable agreement. One speaks of different dialects of English Southern, British, English, Northern British English, Scottish English, Midwest American English, new England American English, Australian English, and so on, with, of course, many more delicately distinguished subdialects within these very general categories but no one would speak of Welsh and English or Irish and English as dialects of a single language, although they are spoken within the same area and often by people living in the same villages as each other.

The expansion of the British Empire and—since World War II—the primary of the United States have spread English throughout the globe. Because of that global spread, English has developed a lost of English dialects and English-based creole language and pidgins.

The major varieties of English include, in most cases, several subvarieties, such as Lockney slang within British English; Newfoundland English within Canadian English, and African American Vernacular English ("Ebonics") and Southern American English within American English. English is a pluricentric language, without a central language authority like France's Academie Francaise and although no variety is clearly considered the only standard, there are a number of accents considered to be more prestigious, such as Received Pronunciation in Britain.

Scots developed—largely independently—from the same origins, but following the Acts of Union 1707 a process of language attrition began, whereby successive generations adopted more and more features from English causing dialectalisation. Whether it is now a separate language or a dialect of English better described as Scottish English is in dispute. The pronunciation, grammar and lexis of the traditional forms differ, sometimes substantially, from other varieties of English.

Because of the wide use of English as a second language, English speakers have many different accents, which often signal the speaker's native dialect or language. Just as English itself has borrowed words from many different languages over its history, English loanwords now appear in a great many languages around the world, indicative of the technological and cultural influence of its speakers. Several pidgins and create languages have formed.

Using an English base, such as Jamaican Creole, Nigerian Pidgin, and Tok Pisin there are many words in English coined to describe forms of particular non-English languages that contain a very high proportion of English words. Franglais, for example, is used to describe French with a very high English word content; it is found on the Channel Islands. Another variant, spoken in the border bilingual regions of Quebec in Canada, is called Fr English.

Southern Hemisphere native varieties of English began to develop during the 19th century, with the colonization of Australian and South Africa. Australian English, New Zealand

English and South African English are non-rhotic dialects closely related to one another and to the English spoken in Southeastern England. The vocabularies of these dialects are also similar to that of English, with some differences and several terms that are peculiar to each country; Australian English features also a number of North American words. Differences in grammar and usage are mostly limited to colloquial speech.

Canadian English is regarded as one of two sub-varieties of North American English (the other being U.S. English) ; however, it also features many elements of British English that are not founcl in the United States.

The Carribean : Carribean English is influenced by the English-based Creole verieties spoken, but they are not one and the same. There is a great deal of variation in the way English is spoken with a "Standard English" at the top of the social scale and creoles at the bottom. These dialects have roots in 17th century English and African languages: unlike most native varieties of English, West Indian dialects often tend to be syllable-timed rather than stress-timed.

Africa : Several dialects of West African English exist, with a lot of regional variation and some influence from indigenous language. West African English lends to be syllable-time, and its phoneme inventory is much simpler than that of Received Pronunciation: this sometimes affects mutual intelligibility with native varieties of English. A distinct East African English is spoken in countries such as Kenya or Tanzania.

Small communities of native English speakers can be found in Kenya, Zimbabwe, Botswana and Namibia, the dialects spoken are similar to South African English. The present Republic of South African has been occupied successively by Bushmen, Hottentots, Bantus Portuguese, the Dutch and the English. From these sources and especially from Dutch and its South African development, Africaan the English language has acquired several features while *apartheid* and *veldt* have become a part of the English vocabulary, bittong (meat), *lekk* (nice), *gogga* (insect), *donga* (ravine), *kopje* (Chill) remain uniquely South African with little international appeal. In pronunciation, South African English has been influenced by Afrikaans and to a lesser extent by numerous Scottish school masters.

West African English is remarkable for its variety. With as yet no identifiable standard, it is difficult to draw the line between an incorrect usage and a local variant. In Nigeria, English exists alongside Hausa, Igbo, Yoruba and scores of smaller languages. The distinctive accent of Nigerian English has been influenced by the first language of the people—Yoruba and Igbo in the South and Hausa in the North. *Follow* is pronounced as (fə/ə) due to vowel harmony in Igbo, while Hausa speakers tend to break up clusters by inserting vowels so that 'screw' becomes (sukuru), *beat* and *bit* have the same tense vowel. This produce a large number of homophones in Nigerian and other African varieties-*leave-live, seen-sin, Don't sleep on the floor—Don't slip on the floor.*

In East Africa the most important African language is the Bantu Kiswahili due to which the East African variety has acquired some of its characteristic phonological patterns—for example the lack of [ð] and [θ] as in *this/thing* which pronounced as *zis sig*.

America : The Northern and Southern dialects of American English emerged from primary settlements in the eastern United States, and the Midland and western from secondary settlements to the south and west. The Northern dialects had their source in Massachusetts; the southern dialects, in Virginia and the Carolinas. Originating in Pennsylvania, the Midland dialects are an extension from the northern area. Today, these three are the strongest regional divisions in American speech, although now Midland seems everywhere to be a blend of Northern and southern features, having lost most of its distinctiveness. In the same, way north and west of Texas, Oklahoma and Arkanas, the western dialect area combine features from the other three areas. The northern and southern dialects obtained in the seventeenth century, with the Massachusetts, Carolina and Virginia colonies reflecting the Puritan/Royalist division in England. The Midland dialect area grew with the development of the Old Frontier in the eighteenth century. The western dialect area is a social product of the nineteenth century, following the Louisiana Purchase.

Asia : India has the world's largest English speaking population, although most speakers of Indian English are not native speakers. Indian English phonology is highly variable; stress, rhythm and intonation are generally different from those of native varieties. There are also several pecularities at the levels of morphology, syntax and usage, some of which can also be founded among educated speaker. Certain pronunciation result from the influence of Indian languages. Speakers of Hindi habitually pronounce words like *station* with an initial vowel (iste: en) Words and phrases that strike British and American speakers as strange are natural expressions of cultural context absent in the west-expression such as these *bow my forehead, fall at your feet, policewala, mother of my daughter.* It follows logically that the varieties of English spoken in Nepal, Bangladesh, Pakistan and Sri Lanka, etc. will be conditioned by the culture and native languages of their own countries.

The development of English in Singapore, Malaysia, Hong Kong is interesting because of the influence of Chinese, Malay, Tamil and the language policies of the various Governments. In Hong Kong English is much less used for oral communication than in Singapore. English in Singapore and Malaysia is marked by the omission of *be* both as a copula (*This coffee house-very cheap*) and auxiliary (*my brother-working*), differences of syntax in the word order of questions (*May I ask where is the counter*?) and difference of stress.

Thus dialects are varieties of English co-related to particular spatial points. If the geographical barriers between regions are slight, then dialectical variations between regions are also negligible and the speech of one region is largely comprehensible to the inhabitants of the neighbouring regions. But if the geographical barriers are significantly large, then with time dialects develop into separate independent languages and a great deal of comprehensibility between varieties as lost.

Pidgin and Creole

Pidgin and Creole are new languages varieties, which developed out of contacts between colonial non-standard varieties of a European language and several non-European languages around the Atlantic and in the Indian and Pacific Oceans during the seventeenth to nineteenth centuries. Pidgins typically emerged in trade colonies which developed around trade forts or along trade routes, such as on the coast of West Africa. They are reduced in structures and specialized in functions (typically trade), and initially they served as non-native *lingua francas* to users who preserved their native vernaculars for their day-to-day interactions. Some pidgins have expanded into regular vernaculars, especially in Urban settings, and are called 'expanded pidgins' example include *Bislama* and *Tok Pisin* (Melanesia) and Nigerian and Cameroon Pidgin English. Structurally, they are as complex as Creoles. The latter vernaculars developed in settlement colonies whose primary industry consisted of sugar cane plantations or rice fields, which employed massive non-European slave labor. Examples include *Cape Verdian Criolou* (lexified by Portuguese) and Papiamentu in Netherlands Antilles (apparently Portuguese-based but influenced by Spanish): Haitian, Mauritian, and Seychellois (lexified by French) Jamaican, Guyanese, and Hawaiian Creole, as well as Gullah in the USA (all lexified by English); and *Saramaccan* and *sranan* in Surinam (lexified by English, with the former heavily influenced by Portuguese and the latter by Dutch). Through Melanesian pidgins are associated with sugar cane plantations, they apparently originated in trade settings and were adopted on the plantations.

The term *Creole* and *pidgin* have also been extended to some other varieties that developed during the same period out of contacts among primarily non-European languages. Examples include Delaware pidgin Chinook Jargon, and Mobilian in North American Sango, (Kikongo-) Kituba, and Lingala in Central Africa, Kinubi in Southern Sudan and in Uganda and Hiri Motu in Papua New Guinea. In the original, lay peoples naming practice, the term *jagron* was an alterate to pidgin. However, some creolists claim that pidgins are more stable and jargons are an earlier stage in the 'life-cycle, that putatively progresses from Jargon, to Pidgin, to Creole, to Post-Creole by progressive structural expansion, stabilization, and closer approximations of the *lexifier* - the language, which contributed the largest part of a Creoles lexicon.

The term *'Creole'* was originally coined in Iberian colonies, apparently in the sixteenth century in reference to nonindigenous people born in American colonies. It was adopted in metropolitan Spanish, then in French and later in English by the early seventeenth century. By the second half of the same century, it was generalized to descendants of Africans or Europeans born in Romance colonies. Usage varied from one colony to another. The term was also used as an adjective to characterize plants, animals and customs typical of the same colonies.

Among the earliest claims that Creoles developed from Pidgins is the following statement in Bloomfield: 'When the Jargon (*i.e.,* Pidgin) has become the only language of the subject group, it is a creolized language'. Hall reinterpreted this, associating the vernacular function of Creoles with nativization. Thus, Creoles have been defined inaccurately as 'nativized Pidgins' *i.e.,* Pidgins that have acquired native speakers and have therefore expanded both their structures and functions and have stabilized. Hall then also introduced the pidgin-crocle 'life-cycle' to which De Camp added a 'post-Creole' stage.

The languages from which the Pidgin is derived are simplified, and vocabulary and grammatical complexities have been reduced. A Pidgin is characterized by a small vocabulary of between a few hundred and a thousand or so words drawn largely from the superstrate language (the language of the socially dominant group), and a reduction of many grammatical features such as inflectional morphology. The grammar typically comes largely from the substratum language (s) of the socially subordinate group. In addition to retaining some features found in the input varieties speakers must bring some general and possibly innate principles to bear on the task of learning to communicate under such circumstances. Often vocabulary and pronunciation conventions from other languages (other than the one on which the pidgin is based) are introduced into the Pidgin by those who use it.

Initially a Pidgin is nobody's mother tongue. But since this is the only language of communication and interaction among a diverse group of people, the frequency of its use slowly increases as does the number of its speakers. The Pidgin no longer remain only the language of the work place but also becomes the language of the home. It is then passed on to the Newer generations who learn the Pidgin as their mother-tongue. A functional switch of languages takes place, and when this happens, a Pidgin become a *Creole.*

The process of *Creolisation* is the reverse of the process of Pidginisation. A Pidgin is a highly reduced language, strictly confined to the work place. But when it develops into a Creole, a functional expansion of the language takes place and it becomes the language of the home, of the market, of personal and informal interaction. Because of increased demands on the language, its vocabulary expands, grammatical structures become more elaborate and *elaboration* and *expansion* take place – possessive markers, markers of intensity, tense markers, pronominal forms all comes in but in an altered form from that of the parent pidgin.

Register

Language varies as its function varies, it differs in different situations. The name given to a variety of language distinguished according to use is *register*. Registers are sets of vocabulary items associated with discrete occupational or social groups. Doctors, airline, pilots, bank managers, sales clerks and grocers use different vocabularies. Of course one person may control a variety of registers; he can be a stockbroker and archaeologist, or a mountain climber and an economist. A register shows what you are doing. Register studies language variation according to use in specific situations.

J. C. Catford says, "By register we mean a variety correlated with a performer's role on a given occasion." A person plays a series of different social roles and uses varieties of language which correspond to different situations, different speakers and listeners or readers and writers and so on. Thus register are stylistic functional varieties of a dialect or language. They account for what people do with their language.

Besides, the event or state of affairs, it is the convention that determines that a certain kind of language is appropriate to a certain use. Dialects differ in substance, but register differ in form. The crucial criteria of any given register are to be found in its grammar and it lexis. For example, 'cleanse' puts us in the language of advertising, 'probe' of newspapers, 'tablespoonful' of recipes or prescriptions, 'neckline' of fashion reporting or dress making instructions. Newspaper headlines, church services, sport commentaries and popular songs exhibit specific grammatical characteristics.

Linguistic events are manifested in a particular dialect and register and the registers between them cover the total range of our language activity. Registers are defined by their formal properties. It is, therefore, useful to introduce a classification along three dimensions, each representing on aspect of the situations in which language operates and the part played by language in them. Registers may be distinguished according to field of discourse mode of discourse and style of discourse.

Field of Discourse refers to the area of operation of the language activity, that is the subject matter. According, we can recognize register such as politics and personal relations and technical registers like biology and mathematics. When the language plays a minor part, the field of discourse refers to the whole event. In this sense there is a register of domestic chores. Register classified according to field of discourse include both the technical and the non-technical: shopping and games-playing as well as medicine and linguistics. Technical registers are used in discussion and non-technical as a means of achievement.

Mode of discourse refers to the medium or mode of the language activity and this determines the role played by the language activity in the situation. The primacy distinction on this dimension is that into spoken and written language. In medieval times the difference between the written and spoken varieties was very wide, but in modern languages the two modes are extremely close. The written and spoken modes are by no means formally identical. They differ both in grammar and lexis. We can recognize further registers such as the language of newspapers, of advertising, of conversation and of sports commentary. The classification of modes of discourse is variable in delicacy. We may first identify 'the language of literature' as a single register, but at the next step we can separate the various genres, such as prose fiction and light verse as distinct registers within it. The register of journalism may be subclassified into reportage, editorial comment, feature writing and so on. The third dimension of register classification is *style of discourse,* which refers to the relations among the participants. They suggest a primary distinction into colloquial and polite, but this dimension being a sort of a continuum more delicate cuts with categories such as 'casual', 'intimate' and 'deferential' have been suggested.

The participant relations that determine the style of discourse may be temporary or permanent. The most temporary relationship holds between participants at a party or in a train and the most permanent between parents and children. Relations between teacher and than pupil or labour and management lie intermediately. Some such registers may show more specific formal properties others. For example, in most languages some lexical items tend to be used more by one sex than the other but in Japanese there are grammatical features which are restricted to the speech of one sex only.

The study of registers is crucial both to our understanding of how language works and in application to literary analysis, machine translation and language teaching.

Jargon

Sometimes, as in the case of criminal argots, part of the function of special language is deliberately to mislead and obstruct the rest of society and the authorities in particular: they may even become wholly impenetrable to outsiders. But this is not the role or main purpose of most specialized varieties of language. Professions whose members value their standing in society and eager to render their services to the public foster their own vocabulary and usage, partly to exchange the dignity of their profession and the skills they represent but partly also to increase their efficiency. An example of this is the language of the law and of lawyers. The cultivation and maintenance of specialized types of language by certain professions should not be regarded as trivially or superficially motivated In general usage, languages are necessarily imprecise, or they would lack the flexibility and infinite extensibility demanded of them. But for certain purposes in restricted situations much greater precision is required, a part of the function of the particular style and vocabulary of legal language is the avoidance, so far as may be possible, of all ambiguity and the explicit statement of all necessary distinctions. This is why legal texts, when read out of their context, seem so absurdly pedantic and are an easy target for ridicule. Similar provision for detail and clarity characterizes the specialist jargons of medicine and of the sciences in general and also of philosophy. Indeed, one might regard the formulas of modern, symbolic logic as the result of a consciously developed and specialized written language for making precise the relations of implication and inference between statements that, when couched in everyday language, are inexact and open to misinterpretation. Some would go as far as to say that traditional metaphysics is no more than the result of misunderstanding everyday discourse and that the main purpose of philosophy is to resolve the puzzles that arise from such misunderstandings.

The use of specialized types of language in fostering unity is also evidenced in the stereotyped forms of vocabulary employed in the playing of certain games. Tennis scores use the sequence "love, 15, 30, 40, and game", cricketers verbally appeal to the umpire when a batsman may be out by calling "How's that"? and the ways of being out are designated by stereotypes, "run out", "leg before wicket," "stumped", and so forth. The esoteric language of horse racing and its associated wagering of money is well known, though not readily understood by outsiders.

The ancient but persistent recognition of the power of language is apparent in the respect for correctness in the use of language in any sphere of life having supernatural connections. Those credited with such connections employ special formulas and rigidly prescribed modes of diction: examples of the language of magic and of magicians are widespread, ranging from the usages of shamans and witch doctors to the ritual "abracadabra" of the mock magic displayed by conjurors at children's parties. The efficacy of religious worship and of prayers is frequently associated with the strict maintenance of correct forms of language, taught by priests to their successors, lest the ritual become invalid. In ancient India the preservation in all its supposed purity of the language used in the performance of certain religious rituals (Sanskrit) gave rise to one of the world's most important schools of linguistics and phonetics. In the Christian churches one can observe the value placed by Church of England and Episcopalian churchmen on the formal English on the Authorized version of the Bible and of the Book of Common Payer, despite recent attempts at replacing these rituals forms of language by forms taken from modern spoken vernaculars

Slang

Slang first emerged in abundance where diverse peoples met at the cultural crossroads of the ancient market city, it flourished in the more diverse and occupationally interdependent medieval city. For the same but more complex reasons in the nineteenth century, slang become part of the life of modern cities, or more validly today, of modern society in general. By its very nature slang emerges from the organization of diverse society and in small ways serves both to maintain and to change social structures, or the power relationships among social groups. Slang is a necessary and inevitable cultural product of a plural, complex, dynamic, and highly interdependent modern society.

The word 'slang', of uncertain origin, has been dated to about 1750 and was soon thereafter defined at least once as 'street language'. Slang originally denoted cant, or the restricted speech of the low, often criminal classes of society. However, the idea of slang gradually evolved to denote other subcultural speech, both high and low, as well as more general but conventional vocabulary. By 1890 slang had taken on its present sense of a level of language below standard and of a body of lexemes derived from yet lower and more restricted levels of speech. The more general idea of popular speech, which includes slang, is today coming into a newer and wider use by language scholars. Popular speech encompasses older forms of folk speech, which are associated with rural society and with the oral tradition, and newer forms of folk speech, often slang, which are associated with cities and modern society and with the mass media. Sociologically speak, slang is the urban part of popular speech and has historically found many of its incentives and referents in the socially diverse urban setting.

Dictionaries usually characterize slang by describing its informality, unconventionality, emphemerality, ellipsis, bizarre metaphors, playfulness and the like. People of a Whitmanesque bent have said that slang is the poetry of everyday life and the free and natural speech of the common people. While slang expression is acute, the metaphors occasionally brilliant, and it sometimes alliterates and rhymes, slang is more a level or register of speech than a poetic form of the folk. For practical lexicographers, slang is a 'place', a way station and a proving ground for cheeky new words and phrases. Slang is 'below' standard and 'correct' informal usages and socially is less acceptable in formal discourse. On the other hand, slang is more widely used or at least more widely understood than restricted subgroup speech, such as regional and social dialects argot, cant, or jargon. In this sense, slang is 'above' subcultural speech, where so much slang began its upward and outward-bound career into general usage.

The role of slang in subcultural confrontation has long been known but perhaps not generally appreciated. Slang is a class of language used, among other social and psychological uses, to deny allegiance to genteel, elite, and proper society and to its standard linguistic forms. Slang is thus used to assert social opposition, ranging from the most vicious and hostile verbal aggression to the gentlest, teasing contrariness and playful disruptiveness. The utterance of subcultural words and phrases is also a way to seek bonds with sympathetic orders and, as a new group, to oppose or just to break with the dominant tone of discourse. Slang in any case is used earnestly of playfully in order to lower, or to shift laterally, the register of discourse slang also facilitates a variety of distinctive interactions in modern society, insofar as it retains widely recognizable subgroup origins and meanings. Slang is used to manage the multiple, overlapping, and shifting identifies of modern life—a world of 'masks and mirrors'.

Modern slang is a distinct level or register of language that arose during the Great Transformation from homogeneous rural to heterogeneous urban society. While in principle, general slang can arise in any situation of social difference, the modern industrial city in the nineteenth century intensified every material condition that creates slang: the aggregation of large and variegated social groupings, their proximity and high visibility to one another, the complexity of their economic interdependencies and the necessity and desirability of contact and exchanges of every sort. Heavy migration and settlement in ethnic enclaves of the great cities influenced slang throughout the nineteenth century and are influencing it again in the 1990s. To this potent mix was added the intensifying ingredient of common knowledge of the city through the mass media, especially the newspapers and the comics and, in another medium, the popular cultures of minstrelsy and vaudeville.

More than half of historical American slang, it has been estimated, cane from the chiefly male sub-cultural speech of lumberjacks, railroaders, musicians, hoboes, sportsmen, show business, teenagers, college students, ethnic minorities, the military, and various deviant subcultures, such as criminals and drug users.

In the past slang has been used more by men than by women and more by younger than by older people. In this sense, general slang itself was a semirestricted vocabulary of youthful male subculture and reflected its distinctive social construction subcultures merge a little in their social experiences. Much historical slang came from stressful male social worlds of the barroom and brothel, the life of tramps and hoboes, rough occupations, the military, sports, and deviant subcultures. Sociolinguists report that, until the 1970s at least, women used less slang than men and, even if they knew its meaning, used it in fewer social situations. Proper English signaled proper behavior and the avoidance of slang reflected the greater pressures on women toward conventional behavior, at least in mixed company.

These subcultural walls are breaking down as women move into male preserves and so into situations of greater cultural variety and clash, which prompted male slang in the first place. Even low-register sexual and scatalogical expressions used as slang hardly raise an eyebrow in gatherings of sophisticated young men and women. Such vulgar and taboo expressions were formerly the restricted speech of male subculture, which is today losing its exclusiveness and isolation. Yet slang remains to some extent the province of the young—of socially engaged young men and women. The cultural boundaries of yet other social categories—ethnic, class, style of life—are weakening as well slang will certainly retain a role in the inevitable cultural conflict among them.

English as Lingua-Franca (Bilingualism and Multilingualism)

The learning of a second and of any subsequently acquired language is quite a different matter. Except for one form of bilingualism, it is deliberate activity undertaken when one has already nearly or fully acquired the basic structure and vocabulary of one's first language. Of course, many people never do master significantly more than their own first language. It is only in encountering a second language that one realizes how complex language is and how much effort must be devoted to subsequent acquisition. It has been said that the principal obstacle to learning a language is knowing one already, and it may also be that the faculty of grammar construction exhibited in childhood is one that is gradually lost as childhood recedes.

Whereas every normal person masters his mother tongue with unconscious ease, people vary in their ability to learn additional languages, just as they vary in other intellectuals activities. Situational motivation, however, appears to be by far the strongest influence on the speed and apparent ease of this learning. The greatest difficulty is experienced by those who learn because they are told to or are expected to, without supporting reasons that they can justify. Given a motive other than external compulsion or expectation, the task is achieved much more easily. In Welsh schools it is found that English children make slower progress in Welsh when their only apparent reason for learning Welsh is that there are Welsh classes. Welsh children on the other hand, make rapid progress in English, the language of most further education, the newspapers, most television and radio, most of the better paid jobs, and of any job outside Welsh-speaking areas. Similar differences in motivation have accounted for the excellent standard of English, French, and German acquired by educated persons in the Scandinavian countries and in Holland, some countries whose languages, being by relatively few foreigners, are of little use in international communication. This attainment may be compared with the much poorer showing in second-language acquisition among comparably educated persons in England and America, who have for long been able to rely on foreigners accommodating to their ignorance by speaking and understanding English.

It is often held that children brought up bilingually in places in which two languages are regularly in use are slower in schoolwork than comparable monolingual children, as a greater amount of mental effort has to be expended in the mastery of two languages. This is by no means provide, and because much of a child's language acquisition taken place in infancy and in the preschool years, it does not represent an effort in the way that consciously learning a language in school does, and indeed it probably occupies a separate part of the child's mental equipment. The question of speed of general learning by bilinguals and monolinguals must be left open. It is quite a separate matter from the job of learning, by teaching at home or in school, to read and write in two languages, this undoubtedly is more of a labour than the acquisition of monolingual literacy.

Two types of bilingualism have been distinguished, according to whether the two languages were acquired from the simultaneous experience of the use of both in the same circumstances and settings or from exposure to each language used in different settings (an example of the latter is the experience of English children living in India during the period of British ascendancy there, learning English from their parents and an Indian Language from their nurses and family servants). However acquired, bilingualism leads to mutual interference between the two languages; extensive bilingualism within a community is sometimes held partly in grammar in the meanings of words. Bilinguals often speak their own languages each with "an accent" *i.e.* they carry into each certain pronunciation features from the other. The German word in "He comes tomorrow home" has been reported as an example of grammatical interference; and in Candian French the verb introduce has acquired from English the additional meaning "introduce, make acquainted" (which in metropolitan French is presenter).

Bilingualism refers to the proficiency in the use of more than one language. Till some time back it was believed that monolingualism, or the use of one language, was the norm in most parts (especially developed countries) of the world and that bilingualism was some kind of aberrant or unusual phenomenon. In recent times however, it has been gradually realized that all of us (including the so-called monolinguals) are essentially bilinguals, because even where one is supposedly using only one language (say English) one does control and employ several styles, registers and dialects of the same language. Strictly speaking, however, the term bilingualism is used to refer to situations where two or more distinct languages are involved. As a matter of fact, some people prefer to use the term bilingualism to refer to a two language situation, and use the term multilingualism for situations where two or more distinct languages are involved. The term 'bilingualism, has now, however, come to be accepted as the standard cover term for referring to all situations involving two or more languages. Another thing that one must remember is that the term bilingualism is used to refer to the learning or proficiency in and use of two or more languages. It is an individual accomplishment, and many characterize whole groups or communities or societies. Thus one can talk of bilingual individuals or communities that are characterized by wide-spread bilingualism. On the other hand, one uses the term multilingualism to refer to the presence of several languages in a country. For instance, when we say that India is a multilingual country, what we imply is that there are several languages spoken and used in India.

No one learns a language without a purpose. White the L1 (Mother tongue, it may be said) is acquired without any apparent purpose in mind, a second language is learnt for specific purposes. These purposes may range from restricted, rather limited use like interacting with neighbours, shopkeepers and like, or for seeking limited, though necessary information for getting about in a new place, or acquiring knowledge about other times, other people and other cultures, to a more extensive habitual use, along with ones L1, for almost all spheres and activities of life. It is useful to think of purposes for learning L2 in terms of the following:

(*a*) for interacting informally and casually with speakers of L2;

(*b*) for interacting with speakers of L2 in more formal settings;

(*c*) for purposes of academic advancement—reading books, consulting journals, listening to lectures, talks, etc;

(*d*) for getting access to both print and electronic media;

(*e*) for professionals/administrative purposes—for instance, for successfully functioning as a lawyer, a doctor, an engineer, a salesman, a government officer, an ambassador, etc.

(*f*) for interacting with peer group in casual, informal or intimate encounters, as well as, in more formal contexts;

It will be obvious from the foregoing that the L2 may serve either restricted or extended proposes relating to social, academic, professional and general purposes. In the context of becoming a bilingual in English (*i.e.* in addition to having one of the Indian languages as one's L1) all or some of the above purposes may motivate a person to learn it.

The term multilingualism can refer to an occurrence regarding an individual speaker who uses two or more languages, a community of speakers where two or more languages are used, or between speakers of different languages.

Multilingual speakers outnumber monolingual speakers in the world's population. A multilingual person, in the broadest defination, is anyone who can communicate in more than one language, be it active (through speaking and writing) or passive (through listening and reading). More specifically, the terms bilingual and trilingual are used to describe comparable situation in which two or three languages are involved. A generic term for multilingual persons is polyglot.

Multilingualism could be rigidly defined as being *native-like* in two or more languages. It could also be loosely defined as being *less than native-like* but still able to communicate in two or more languages.

Multilingual speakers have acquired and maintained at least one language during childhood, the so-called first language (L1). First languages (sometimes also referred to as mother tongue) are acquired without formal education, by mechanisms heavily disputed. Children acquiring two first languages since birth are called simultaneous bilinguals. Even in the case of simultaneous bilinguals one language usually dominates over the other. This kind of bilingualism is most likely to occur when a child is raised by bilingual parents in a predominantly monolingual environment. It can also occur when the parents are monolingual but have raised their child or children in two different countries.

Even if someone is highly proficient in two or more languages his so-called *communicative competence* or ability may not be as balanced. Linguists have distinguished various types of multilingual competence, which can roughly be put into two categories:

(*a*) For *compound* bilinguals, words and phrases in different languages are the same concepts. That means, a 'chien' and 'dog' are two words for the same concept for a French English speaker of this type. These speakers are usually fluent in both languages.

(*b*) For *coordinate* bilinguals, words and phrases in the speaker's mind are all related to their own unique concepts. That means, a bilingual speaker of this type has different associations for *chein* and for 'dog'. In these individuals, one language, usually the first language, is more dominant than the other, and the first language may be used to *think through* the second language. These speakers are known to use very different intonation and pronunciation features, and sometimes assert the feeling of having different personalities attached to each of their languages.

A sub-group of the latter is *subordinate* bilingual which is typical of beginning second language learners.

The distinction between compound and coordinate bilingualism has come under scrutiny. When studies are done of multilinguals most are found to show behavior intermediate between compound and coordinate bilingualism. Some authors have suggested that the distinctions should only be made at the level of grammar rather than vocabulary. Other use "coordinate bilingual" as a synonym for one who has learned two languages from birth and others have proposed dropping the distinction altogether.

Many theorists are now beginning to view bilingualism as a "spectrum or continuum of bilingualism " that runs from relative monolingual language learner to highly proficient bilingual speakers that function at high levels in both languages.

The potential multilingual speakers are:

(*a*) People with a strong interest in a foreign language

(*b*) People who find it necessary to acquire a second language for practical purposes such as business, information gathering (internet, mainly English), or entertainment (foreign language films, books or computer games).

(*c*) Language immersion children.

(*b*) Immigrants and their descendants. Although the heritage language may be lost after one or two generations particularly if the replacing language has greater prestige.

(*e*) Children of expatriates. However, language loss of the L1 and L2 in younger children may be rapid when removed from a language community.

(*f*) Residents in border areas between two countries of mixed languages where each language is seen of equal prestige, efforts may be made by both language communities to acquire an L2. Yet, in areas where one language is more prestigious than the other, speakers of the less prestigious language may acquire the dominant language as an L2. In time, however, the different language communities may likely become one, as one language becomes extinct in that area.

(*g*) Children whose parents each speak a different language, in multilingual communities. In unilingual communities, when parents maintain a different-parent/different-language household, younger children may appear to be multilingual, however, entering school will overwhelm the child with pressure to conform to the dominant community language. Younger siblings in these households will almost always be unilingual. On the other hand, in unilingual communities, where parents have different L1s, multilingualism in the child may be achieved when both parents maintain a one-language (not the community language) household.

(*h*) Children in language-rich communities where neither language is seen as more prestigious than the other and where interaction between people occurs in different languages on a frequent basis.

(*i*) Children who have one or more parents who have learned a second language, either formally (in classes) or by living in the country. The parent choses to speak only this second language to the child. One study suggests that during the teaching process, the parent also boosts his or her own language skills, learning to use the second language in new contexts as the child grows and develop linguistically.

Widespread multilingualism is one form of language contact. Multilingualism was more common in the past than is usually supposed, in early times, when most people were members of small language communities, it was necessary to know two or more languages for trade or any other dealings outside one's own town or village, and this holds true today in places of high linguistic diversity such as sub-Sharan Africa and India. Linguist Ekkehard Wolff estimates that 50% of the population of Africa is multilingual.

In multilingual societies, not all speakers need to be multilingual. When all speakers are multilingual, linguists classify the community according to the functional distribution of the languages involved-diglossia, ambilingualism, and bipart-lingualism.

Various, but not nearly all, Multilanguals tend to use code-switching, a term that describes the process of 'swapping' between languages. In many cases, code-switching is motivated by the wish to express loyalty to more than one cultural group, as holds for many immigrant communities in the New world. Code-switching may also function as a strategy where proficiency is lacking. Such strategies are common if the vocabulary of one of the languages is not very elaborated for certain fields, or if the speakers have not developed proficiency in certain lexical. Domains, as in the case of immigrant languages. Code-mixing presupposes competence in two languages not lack of it. It is not chaotic, but follows grammatical rules not of one language but two languages. There are restrictions on what can be mixed. Code-mixing is not arbitrary, but functional. It conveys the social meanings of identity and distancing with regard to speech participants and speech content.

In computing, software are said to be multilingual when the user interface language can be switched. Translating user interface is usually part of the software localisation process which also include other adaptations such as units and date conversion. Many software applications are available in several languages, with a total number of languages usually ranging from a handful (the most spoken languages) to dozens of languages, for the most popular applications (like office suite, web browser, etc). Due to the status of English in computing, software development nearly always requires using it, and so, almost all commercial software version is available in it.

Thus languages are a resource to enrich one's functionality. The communicative and social functions of the language are distributed over many languages in the multilingual arrangement of a country. Such an arrangement is true of a community and of individual also.

LITERATURE AND LITEARY CRITICISM

4

Nature, Functions and Scope of Literature

Literature is a body of written works. The name is often applied to those imaginative works of poetry and prose distinguished by the intentions of their authors and the excellence of their execution. Literature may be classified according to a variety of systems, including language, national origin, historical period, genre, and subject matter. Literature is the artistic expression of thought, which is replete with feelings and imagination. It is expressed in such an *untechnical* form as to make it intelligible and give aesthetic pleasure and relief to the mind of the common man. According to Lord Morley : "Literature consists of all the books where moral truth and human passion are touched with a certain largeness, sanity and attraction of form." In other words, literature heightens our awareness of human life. It enables us to look at nature with new eyes. It interprets with charm of language, the experiences and spiritual intutions of man.

Definations of the word *literature* tend to be circular. *The Concise Oxford Dictionary* says it is "writing whose value lies in the beauty of form or emotional effect." The 19th century critic Watter Pater referred to "the matter of imaginative or artistic literature" as a 'transcript, not of mere fact, but of fact in its infinitely varied forms." But such definations really assume that the reader already knows what literature is. And indeed its central meaning, at least, is clear enough. Deriving from the Latin *littera,* "a letter of the alphabet", literature is first and foremost mankinds entire body of writing; after that it is the body of writing belonging to a given language or people; then it is individual pieces of writing.

But already it is necessary to qualify these statements. To use the word *writing* when describing literature is itself misleading, for one may rightly speak of "oral literature" or "the literature of preliterate peoples." The art of literature is not reducible to the words on the page; they are there because of the craft of writing. As an art, literature is the organization of words to give pleasure; through them it elevates and transforms experience; through them it functions in society as a continuing symbolic criticism of values.

Literature is a form of human expression. But not everything expressed in words—even when organized and written down—is counted as literature. Those writings that are primarily informative—technical, scholarly, journalistic—would be excluded from the rank of literature by most, though not all, critics. Certain forms of writing, however, are universally regarded as belonging to literature as an art. Individual attempts within these forms are said to succeed if they possess something called artistic merit and to fail if they do not. The nature of artistic merit is less easy to define than to recognize. The writer need not even pursue it to attain it. On the contrary, a scientific exposition might be of great literary value and a pedestrian poem of none at all.

The purest (or, at least, the most intense) literary form is the lyric poem, and after it comes elegaic, epic, dramatic, narrative, and expository verse. Most theories of literary criticism base themselves on an analysis of *poetry*, because the aesthetic problems of literature are there presented in their simplest and purest form. Poetry that fails as literature is not called poetry at all but verse. Many novels—certainly all the world's great novels—are literature, but there are thousands that are not so considered. Most great dramas are considered literature (although the Chinese, possessors of one of the world's greatest dramatic traditions, consider their plays with few exceptions, to possess no literary merit whatsoever).

The Greeks thought of history as one of the seven arts, inspired by a goddess, the Muse Clio. All of the world's classic surveys of history can stand as noble examples of the art of literature, but most historical works and studies today are not written primarily with literary excellence in mind, though they may possess it, as it were, by accident.

The essay was once written deliberately as a piece of literature: its subject matter was of comparatively minor importance. Today most essays are written as expository, informative journalism, although there are still essays in the great tradition who think of themselves as artists. Now, as in the past, some of the greatest essayists are critics of literature, drama, and the arts.

Some personal documents (autobiographies, diaries, memoires, and letters) rank among the world greatest literature. Some examples of this biographical literature were written with posterity in mind, others with no thought of their being read by anyone but the writer. Some are in a highly polished literary style; others, concluded in a privately evolved language, win their standing as literature because of their cogency, insight, depth, and scope.

Many works of philosophy are classed as literature. The *Dialogues* of Plato (4th century B.C.) are written with great narrative skill and in the finest prose; the *Meditations* of the 2nd century Roman emperor Marcus Aurelius are a collection of apparently random thoughts, and the Greek in which they are written is eccentric. Yet both are classed as literature, while the speculations of other philosophers, ancient and modern, are not. Certain scientific works endure as literature long after their scientific content has become outdated. This is particularly true of books of natural history, where the element of personal observation is of special importance. An excellent example is Gilbert White's *Natural History and Antiquities of Selbourne* (1789).

Oratory, the art of persuasion, was long considered a great literary art. The oratory of the American Indian, for instance, is famous, while in Classical Greece, Polymnia was the muse sacred to poetry and oratory. Rome's great orator *Cicero* was to have a decisive influence on the development of English prose style. Abraham Lincoln's *Gettysbury Address* is known to every American schoolchild. Today, however, oratory is more usually thought of as a craft than as an art. Most critics would not admit advertising copywriting, purely commerical fiction, or cinema and television scripts as accepted forms of literary expression, although others would hotly dispute their exclusion. The test in individual cases would seem to be one of enduring satisfaction and, of course, truth. Indeed, it becomes more and more difficult to categorize literature, for in modern civilization words are everywhere. Man is subject to a continuous flood of communication. Most of it is fugitive, but here and there in high-level journalism, in television, in the cinema, in commerical fiction, in westerns and detective stories and in plain, expository prose-some writing, almost by accident, achieves an aesthetic satisfaction, a depth and relevance that entitle it to stand with other examples of the art of literature.

Literature is one of the instruments, and one of the most powerful instruments, for forming character, for giving us, characters armed with reason, braced by knowledge, clothed with steadfastness and courage, and inspired by that public spirit and public virtue of which it has been well said that they are the brightest ornaments of the mind of man. Bacon is right, when he bides us read not to contradict and refute, nor to believe and take for granted nor to find talk and discourse, but to weight and to consider. Thus, literature enables us to weigh and to consider.

Literature is classified, into two broad field—'Literature of Knowledge' and 'Literature of Power'. Literature of knowledge includes books dealing with history, travel, biography, philosophy and so on. Whereas, Literture of Power is the 'pure' literature and deals with all creative literature—the epics of Homer, Virgil, Milton, the plays of Greek dramatists—Sophocles, Euripedes; Shakespeare and other modern dramatist; the poems of Shelly, Keats and novels, and all imaginative literature. The characteristic, which distinguishes the creative literature with the literature of knowledge is that it contains the 'vision' of the art.

As regard to the function of literature, according to Pater, it is, "not to teach lessons, or enforce rules, or even to stimulate us to noble ends, but to, withdraw the thoughts for a little while from the machinery of life, to fix them, with appropriate emotions, on the spectacle of those great facts in man's existence which no machinery effects." Says, R.A. Scott-James, Pater in contrast with Arnold and Ruskin, almost reverses the order of values. "Art is no longer the servant, but is to be the master, the highest morality will be to enable as much as possible of life to be lived in the spirit of the artist." For Pater the problem of literature is the manner in which it represents an approach to life; and the whole task of criticism is to approach literature in the same way. "Literature and the arts for him are not merely a part of life; they seem to become the whole of life in so far as it is lives in the finer way of the spirit, and in so far as it is objectively expressed."

In some literatures (notably classical Chinese, Old Norse, Old Irish), the language employed is quite different from that spoken or used in ordinary writing. This marks off the reading of literature as a special experience. In the Western tradition, it is only in comparatively modern times that literature has been written in the common speech of cultivated men. The Elizabethans did not talk like Shakespeare nor 18th century people in the stately prose of Samuel Johnson or Edward Gibbon. The first person to write major works of literature in the ordinary English language of the educated man was Daniel Defoe. Thus literature help us to be a cultivated person.

Literature, like music, is an art of time, or "tempo" : it takes time to read or listen to, and it usually presents events or the development of ideas or the succession of images or all these together in time. The craft of literature, indeed, can be said to be in part the manipulation of a structure in time, and so the simplest element of marking time, rhythm, is therefore of basic importance in both poetry and prose.

The content of literature is as limitless as the desire of human beings to communicate with one another. The thousands of years, perhaps hundreds of thousands, since the human species first developed speech have seen built up the almost infinite systems of relationships called *languages*. A language is not just a collection of words in an unabridged dictionary but the individual and social possession of living human beings, an inexhaustible system of equivalents, of sounds to objects and to one another. Its most primitive elements are those words that express direct experiences of objective reality, and its most sophisticated are concepts on a high level of abstraction. Words are not only equivalent to things, they have varying degrees of equivalence to one another. Symbols are used to convey the meaning for example 'lion' is the symbol of 'courage', 'cross' the symbol of 'Christianity'. Thus literature help us to widen our horizon of thought.

As time goes on, literature tends to concern itself more and more with the interior meanings of its narrative, with problems of human personality and human relationships. Many novels are fictional, psychological biographies which tell of the slowly achieved integration of the hero's personality and of his disintegration, of the conflict between self-realization and the flow of events and the demands of other people. This can be presented explicity, where the characters talk about what is going on in their heads, either ambiguously and with reserve, as in the novels of Henry James, or overtly, as in those of Dostoyevsky. Alternatively, it can be presented by a careful arrangement of objective facts, where psychological development is described purely in terms of behaviour and where the reader's subjective response is elicited by the minute descriptions of physical reality, as in the novels of Stendhal and the greatest Chinese novels like the *Dream of the Red Chamber,* which convince the reader that through the novel he is seeing reality itself, rather than an artfully contrived semblance of reality.

Literature, however, is not solely concerned with the concrete, with objective reality, with individual psychology, or with subjective emotion. Some deal with abstract ideas or philosophical conceptions. Much purely abstract writing is considered literature only in the widest sense of the term, and the Philosophical works that are ranked as great literature are usually presented with more or less of a sensuous garment. Thus, Plato's *Dialogues* rank as great literature because the philosophical material is presented in dramatic form, as the dialectical outcome of the interchange of ideas between clearly dawn, vital personalities, and because the descriptive passages are of great lyric beauty. Karl Mark's *Das Kapital* approaches great literature in certain passages in which he expresses the social passion he shares with the Hebrew prophets of the Old Testament. Euclid's *Elements* and St. Thomas Aquina's *Summa theologica* give literary, aesthetic satisfaction to some people because of their purity of style and beauty of architectonic construction. In short, most philosophical works that rank as great literature do so because they are intensely human. The reader responds to Blaise. Pascal's *Pensees,* to Michel de Montaigne's *Essays,* and to Marcus Aurelius *Meditations* as he would to living men. Sometimes the pretense of purely abstract intellectual rigour is in fact a literary device. The writings of the 20th century philosopher Ludwig Wittgenstein, for example, own much of their impact to this appraoch, while the poetry of Paul Valery borrows the language of philosophy and science for its rhetorical and evocative power.

In preliterate societies oral literature was widely shared; it saturated the society and was as much a part of living as food, clothing, shelter, or religion. In barbaric societies, the ministrel might be a courtier of the king or chieftain, and the poet who composed liturgies might be a priest. But the oral performance itself was accessible to the whole community. As society evolved its various social layers, or classes, an "elite" literature began to be distinguishable from the "folk" literature of the people. With the invention of writing this separation was accelerated until finally literature was being experienced individually by the elite (reading a book), while folklore and folk songs were experienced orally and more or less collectively by the illiterate common people.

Elite literature continuously refreshes itself with materials drawn from the popular. Almost all poetic revivals, for instance, include in their programs a new appreciation of folk song, together with a demand for greater objectivity. On the other hand folk literature borrows themes and, very rarely; patterns from elite literature. Many of the English and Scottish ballads that date from the end of the Middle Ages and have been preserved by oral tradition share plots and even turns of phrase with written literature. A very large percentage of these ballads contain elements that are common to folk ballads from all over Western Europe; central themes of folklore, indeed, are found all over the world. Whether these common elements are the result of diffusion is a matter for dispute. They do, however, represent great psychological constants, archetypes of experience common to the human species, and so these constants are used again and again by elite literature as it discovers them in folklore.

Literature, like all other human activities, necessarily reflects current social and economic conditions. Class stratification was reflected in literature as soon as it had appeared in life. Among the American Indians, for instance, the chants of the Shaman, or medicine man, differ from the secret, personal songs of the individual, and these likewise differ from the group songs of ritual or entertainment sung in community. In the Heroic Age, the epic tales of kings and chiefs that were sung or told in their barbaric courts differed from the folktales that were told in peasant cottages.

The more cohesive a society, the more the elements—and even attitudes—evolved in the different class strata are interchangeable at all levels. In the tight clan organization that existed in late medieval times at the Scottish border, for example, heroic ballads telling of the deeds of lords and ladies were preserved in the songs of the common people. But where class divisions are unbridgeable, elite literature is liable to be totally separated from popular culture. An extreme example is the classical literature of the Roman Empire. Its forms and its sources were largely Greek—it even adopted its laws of verse patterning from Greek models, even though these were antagonistic to the natural patterns of the Latin language—and most of the sophisticated works of the major Latin authors were completely closed to the overwhelming majority of people of the Roman Empire.

Printing has made all the difference in the negotiability of ideas. The writings of the 18th century French writers Voltaire, Rousseau, and Diderot were produced from and for almost as narrow a caste as the Roman elite, but they were printed. Within a generation they had penetrated the entire society and were of vital importance in revolutionzing it.

Class distinctions in the literature of modern times exist more in the works themselves than in their audience. Although Henry James wrote about the upper classes and Emile Zola about workingmen, both were, in fact, members of an elite and were read by members of elite—moreover, in their day, those who read Zola certainly considered themselves more of an elite than did the readers of Henry James. The ordinary people, if they read at all, preferred sentimental romances and "penny dreadfuls". Popular literature had already become commercially produced entertainment literature, a type which today is also provided by television scripts.

Literature has an obvious kinship with the other arts. Presented, a play is drama; read, a play is literature. Most important have been based upon written literature, usually novels, although all the great epics and most of the great plays have been filmed at some time and thus have stimulated the younger medium's growth. Conversely, the techniques required in writing for film have influenced many writers in structuring their novels and have affected their style. Most popular fiction is written with "movie rights" in mind, and these are certainly a consideration with most modern publishers. Literature provides the libretto for operas, the theme for tone poems—even so anomalous a form as Friedrich Nietsche's *Thus Snake Zarathustra* was interpreted in music by Richard Strauss—and of course it provides the lyrics of songs. Many ballets and modern dances are based on stories or poems. Sometimes, music and dance are accompanied by a text read by a speaker or chanted by a chorus. The mid-19th century was the heydey of literary, historical, and enecdotal painting, though, a side from the surrealists, this sort of thing died out in the 20th century. Cross-fertilization of literature and the arts now takes place more subtly, mostly in the use of parallel techniques—the rational dissociation of the cubists or the spontaneous action painting of the Abstract Expressionists, for example, which flourished at the same time as the free-flowing uncorrected narratives of some novelists in the 1950s and '60s.

Literature studied as a reflection of the spirit of the age creates a new spirit for us. With its help, we travel into the minds of the other races and the minds of the other epochs. Thus it becomes a sort of sociological approach, a supplementary and commentary on history. Once we are steepped in the spirit of a by-gone age, we are able to enjoy even archaic books which otherwise would not appeal to us.

Literature has a national as well as a personal character and interest. Literature can be observed from age to age and its various transformations. It is not only an account of work done by a number of separate writers, but it is also an account of a great body of literature which in its totality, is to be regarded as the production of the genius of the people. Everything that for good or evil entered into the making of our nations life has also entered into the texture of its literature. Ordinary English history in English nation's biography and its literature is its autobiography. In the one we read the history of its actions and practical achievements : in the other the story of its intellectual and moral developments. As we survey the history of English literature through all its transformations, we are brought into direct and living contact with the motive forces of the inner life of each successive generation and learn at the first hand how it looks at life and what it thought about it, what were the things in which it was most interested and by which it was most willing to be amused, by what passions it was most deeply stirred, by what standards of conduct and of taste it was governed, and what types of character it deemed most worthy of its admiration." Thus literature is the revelation of the progressive mind as well as the spirit of the people.

Literature is simply a mirror of life, a reproduction and thus a social document. Chaucer is the representative poet of the 14th century. His masterpiece the *Canterbury Tales* reveals the political, economic and social conditions of the time. This poem has the true colour and aroma of the fourteenth-century England. Spenser's *The Faerie Queene* is a very useful document which conveys realistically Christian dogmas in the Elizabethan Age. Pope's *The Rape of the Lock* satirises the frivolities of his Age. T.S. Eliot's *The Wasteland* is an extremely moving but extremely depressing poem. It reveals the barrenness of England as it appears today. A historical knowledge of literature is almost indispensable for a complete appreciation of the poem. It is considered as the most important document of his age.

Literature acts as a great instructor and gives us moral education, *e.g.*, we learn certain behavioural norm from, characters and plays like 'Othello', 'King Lear', 'Dr. Faustus'. In our lifetime the total knowledge that we get is very little but we can enrich our experience by reading works of art and thereby becoming tolerant understanding and wise. It also helps us building our personality. Literature leads to catharsis (feeling of pity and fear)—purging emotions. Literature is a best teacher of morality because morals and philosophy teaches virtue by abstract ideas. Further the ideal world is so presented that it delights the reader and thus the moral value is driven.

Literature and Imagination

We read imaginative literature—novels, plays, poetry etc. because it is a work of art. And, as a work of art, it gives us aesthetic pleasure. But the question is whether it gives us aesthetic pleasure. But the question is whether it gives us a wider and deeper understanding of the world of reality, or whether it is a mere escape into a brilliant dream-world—an opium vision. As imaginative literature is an art, the answer is clear. For, art embodies the vision of the artist; and the value of a work of art lies in the vision of the artist. The vision is unique. It may be personal, and may not be objective, or give objective truth. Yet, it is a wider and deeper understanding of reality. The artist has imagination—a finer and keener imagination. And imagination is not a faculty of lying, but it is the instrument of the artist to penetrate to reality. It may be embodied in realistic art, or it may be romantic, and shed the light and glory of romance and beauty on Nature and everyday life. But realistic or romantic, it penetrates to reality.

Both wordsworth and Coleridge had imagination, in the supreme degree. Wordsworth had a realistic imagination, while Coleridge had a romantic imagination. The two friends divided the poetic realm between them. One would treat the natural as supernatural, while the other would treat the supernatural as natural—treat it in such a way that it could be believed as natural. So, we read 'The Ancient Mariner' of Coleridge, and Wordsworth's 'We are Seven', 'Ode on the Intimations of Immortality' and 'Tintern Abbey', and get from them a wider and deeper understanding of the world of Reality.

The literary artist is not confined to the lyric. He can be a novelist, or a dramatist. His experience and his vision can be conveyed adequately only in the extended medium. Of course, every novelist or dramatist is not a genius, or a great artist. But when we read a great novel like Hardy's "Tess", or Tolstoy's "War and Peace", or Shaws 'Man and Superman', or 'Back to Methuselan', we become conscious that we understand life—that we get a deeper, wider and truer vision of Reality. An artist creates his own world, and we enter it. Outwardly, it may be a realistic world, or it may be a romantic world. But essentially, it gives us a unique and truer vision of reality. It interprets it with genuine insight.

The romantic period emphasised the self, creativity, imagination and the value of art. This is in contrast to the Enlightenment emphasis on Rationalism and Empiricism. Its roots can be found in the work of Jean-Jacques Rousseau and Immanuel

Kant. Philosophers and writers associated with the Romantic movement include Johann Wolfgan von Goethe (1749-1832), Friedrich Wilhelm Joseph von Schelling (1775-1854), and George Wilhelm Friedrich Hegel (1770-1831) in Germany; Samuel Taylor Coleridge (1772-1834) and William Wordsworth (1770-1850) in Britain.

Philosophically romanticism represents a shift from the objective to the subjective : science claims to describe the objective world, the world understood from no particular viewpoint. Imagine three people looking at a landscape, one is a farmer, another a property developer and the third an artist. The farmer would see the potential for raising crops and livestock, the property developer the chance to build houses and the artist at the shades are subtleties of colour and form. None of these individuals is seeing the landscape objectively; they are seeing it from a particular or subjective viewpoint.

The move from the objective to the subjective is a result of Kant's idea that human beings do not see the world directly, but through a number of categories. We do not directly see "things-in-themselves". We only understand the world through our human point of view. If we agree with Kant we can never know things-in-themselves, we may as well discard them. This leads to Idealism; the belief that what we call the "external world" is somehow created by our minds.

The Englightenment's emphasis on the empirical deterministic universe left little room for the freedom and creativity of the human spirit. The romantic emphasis on art and imagination is a direct critical reaction to the mechanical view of some Enlightenment figures.

The romantic emphasis on the individual was reflected in ideas of self-realisation and nature. Wordsworth thought that the individual could directly understand nature without the need for society and social artifice, salvation is achieved by the solitary individual rather than through political movements. The preface to the second edition of *Lyrical Ballads* (1800), by Wordsworth and Coleridge was of prime importance as a manifesto of literary romanticism. Here the two poets affirmed the importance of feeling and imagination to poetic creation and disclaimed conventional literary forms and subjects. Thus, as romantic literature everywhere developed, imagination was praised over reason, emotions over logic, and intution over science-making way for a vast body of literature of great sensibility and passion. This literature emphasized a new flexibility of form adapted to varying context, encouraged the development of complex and fast-moving plots, and allowed mixed genres (tragicomedy and the mingling of the grotesque and the sublime) and freer style.

No longer tolerated, for example, were the fixed classical conventions, such as the famous three unities (time, place and action) of tragedy. An increasing demand for spontaneity and lyricism-qualities that the adherents of romanticism found in folk poetry and in medieval romance-led to a rejection of regular meters, strict forms, and other conventions of the classical tradition. In English poetry, for example, blank verse largely superseded the rhymed couplet that dominated 18th century poetry. The opening lines of the swash-buckling melodrama *Hernani* (1830; translated 1830), by the great French romantic writer Victor Hugo, are a departure from the conventional 18th century rules of French versification; and in the preface to his drama *Cromwell* (1827; translated 1896), a famous critical document in its own right, Hugo not only defended his break from traditional dramatic structure but also justified the introduction of the grotesque into art. In their choice of heroes, also, the romantic writers replaced the static universal types of classical 18th century literature with more complex, idiosyncratic characters; and a great deal of drama, fiction and poetry was devoted to a celebration of Rousseau's "common man."

The central interest of the romantic movement was the concern of nature and natural surroundings. Delight in unspoiled scenery and in the (presumably) innocent life of rural dwellers is perhaps first recognigable as a literary theme in such a work as "The Seasons" (1726-1730), by Scottish poet James Thomson. The work is commonly cited as a formative influence on later English romantic poetry and on the nature tradition represented in English literature, most notably by Wordsworth. Often combined with this feeling for rural life is a generalized romantic melancholy, a sense that change is imminent and that a way of life is being threatened. Such intimations were early envined in "Ode to Evening" (1747) by William collins, 'Elegy Written in a Country Churchyard "(1751) by Thomas Gray, and *The Borough* (1810) by George Grabbe. The melancholic strain later developed as a separate theme as in "Ode on Melancholy" (1820) by John Keats, or—in a different time and place—in the works of American writers, the novels and tales of Nathaniel Hawthorne, which probe the depths of human nature in puritanical New England, or the Macabre tales and melancholy poetry of Edgar Allan Poe.

In another vein in American literature, the romantic interest in untrammeled nature is found in such writers as Washington Irving, whose *Sketch Book of Geoffery* Cragon Gent (1819-1820), a collection of descriptive stories about the Hudson River valley, reflects the author's knowledge of European folktales as well as contemporary romantic poetry and the Gothic novel. The *Leather-Stockin Tales* by James Fenimare Cooper celebrate the beauty of the American Wilderness and the simple frontier life, in romantic fashion they also idealize the Native American as (in Rousseau's phrase) the "noble savage." By the middle of the 19th century the Nature tradition was absorbed by American literary transcendentalism, chiefly expressed in the essays of Ralph Waldo Emerson and Henry David Thoreau.

The trend toward the irrational and the supernatural was an important component of English and German romantic literature. It was reinforced on the one hand by disillusion with 18th-century rationalism and on the other by the rediscovery of a body of older literature—folktales and ballads—collected by Percy and by German scholars Jacob and Wilhelm Karl Grimm and Danish writer Hans Christian Andersen. From such material comes, for example, the motif of the doppelganger (German for double). Many romantic writers, especially in Germany, were fascinated with this concept, perhaps because of the general romantic concern with self-identity. Poet Heinrich Heine wrote, a lyric apocryphally titled " Der Doppelganger" *The Devil's Elixir*, a short novel by E.T.A. Hoffman, is about a double, and *Peter Schlemihl's* Remarkable story, by Adelbert von Chamisso, the tale of a man who sells his shadow to the devil, can be considered a variation on the theme. Later, Russian master Fyodor Mikhaylovich Dostoyevsky wrote his famous novel *The Double* (1846), an analysis of paranoia in a humble clerk.

By about the middle of the 19th century, romanticism began to give way to new literary movements: the Parnassians and the symbolist movement in poetry, and realism and naturalism in prose.

5

Critical Terminology and Ways to Analyze Literature

A. No critical approach is true or Inherently superior to any or all other critical approaches. The value of a particular approach depends upon its usefulness clarifying or enlarging experience at the moment to the person who is employing it.

B. Moyer Abram's list of critical approach to literature and the other arts:

1. Expressive (author's relation to his work):
   (*a*) to what extent is the work a product of the author's life (a correlation of the author's biography with the literary work).
   (*b*) what were the author's intentions, and were they fulfilled? (That the author's intentions are important is called the intentional fallacy.)
   (*c*) how did the author construct the work? (a study of the various sources for and versions of the literary work)
2. Pragmatic (the reader s relation to the work):
   (*a*) what value does the work have for the individual reader? (This may or may not be in accordance with the author's Intention.)
   (*b*) what specific knowledge and experience of the reader enable her/him to interpret the work and to share her/ his criticism with others?
3. Mimetic (the relation of the work to the universe or reality):
   (*a*) is the work true to life or reality (as conceived by the reader. and/or most people)?

(*b*) is the work a faithful representation or product of the period. in which it was written?

4. Obliciive (the relation of the parts of the work to each other and to the whole of the work):

(*a*) what is the relation of each part (word, line, stanza, section, mark of punctuation, sound, etc.) to every other part and to the whole work?

(*b*) treating the whole work and a part of English or of World literature, what is its relation to the whole how is it either a repetition, elaboration, or continuation of a literary tradition?

C. Analysis of style (ultimately all literary matters are reduceable to diction, syntax, and the variable of the Individual's experiences up to the moment she/he reads the work):

1. Diction (choice of words):

(*a*) elevated or low (in term of what the occasion demands)

(*b*) formal or colloquial (written or informally spoken)

(*c*) concrete or abstract (does the word represent something directly perceivable through one or more of the five sense or does it represent a conglomerate of sense experiences or a concept?)

(*d*) learned or simple (depends on number of syllables or frequency of use in everyday communication)

(*e*) repetition (can result in either emphasis or do-ouphasts)

2. Syntax (word order)

(*a*) regular (subject, verb, object) or irregular (for what purpose? emphasis, metrical or rime patterns?) Traditionally irregular syntax is justifiable for influencing meaning, but not justifiable for sound effects.

(*b*) simple or complex.

(*c*) dramatic : periodic (thought completed at end of sentence) or loose (thoughs completed early in sentence.

(*d*) balance (parallelism and antithesis)

(*e*) repetition

D. Analysis of Poetry:

1. Poetry is not to be equated with verse; opposing poetry is non-poetry; opposing verse is prose; there is poetic prose.
2. All art is selective, not a mere recording of experience, and as such may be considered the conscious work of the artist. Therefore, the critic of literature can and should assume that every work and mark in the work has a purpose. Any statement about the content or style of a work should be followed by at least one of two questions: Why? or How? The attention of the critic should center on how the literature is constructed, nor what it says. One might also paraphrase the work being studied and discuss the differences in diction and syntax that exist between the paraphrase and the original work.
3. Judge poetic excellence by:

   (*a*) the principle of decorum (the interdependence of matter and form, content and style, sense and sound- - making the rhythm, rime, diction, syntax, etc., parallel the meaning).

   (*b*) seeing whether the substitution, deletion, or addition of any word or the re-ordering of any words would improve the poem in anyway, especially its unity.
4. Methods of Analyzing Poetry:

   (*a*) Content : conceptual (ideas) or physical (things)

   (*b*) style

   (*c*) form (the informal, external, often traditional pattern or shape of the poem and structure (the internal organization of the content)

   (*d*) sound devices (repetition or interruption of sound patterns):-

I. end rime:

(*a*) the sonnet:

(i) Italilian or Petrarchan: abbaabba, cdecde (sestet has variations) (the emphasis is on its two part construction

(ii) English or Shakespearean: abab, cdcd, efef, gg; spenserian: abab, bcbc, cdcd, ee (emphasis on the four part construction: three quatrains as examples of a principle which is stated abstractly or concretely in the concluding couplet)

(*b*) the couplet: every two lines rime

(*c*) stanziac patterns:

1. rime royal: ababbcc
2. ottava rima : abababcc (an echoing rime with a stinger in its tail)
3. Spenserian stanza: ababbcbcc (last line in hexameter and usually has caesura which might have the same organization that the two quatrains in the previous part of the stanga have in relation to each other)
4. terza rima: 1 aba, bcb, cdc, ded, etc. 2) internal rime;

(*a*) alliteration (initial sounds of words)

(*b*) assonance (vowel sounds)

(*c*) consonance (consonantal sounds)

(*d*) end rimes within lines (ends-of words-riming words need not always occur at the ends of lines).

3. rhythm:

(*a*) phrasal and clausal

(*b*) syllabic: iambic (x/), trochaic (/x) anapestic (xx/), dactylic (/xx), spondaic (//)

(*c*) line lengths: monomenter (one foot), diameter (two feet), trimeter (three feet), tetrameter (four feet) pentamenter (five feet), hexameter (six feet)

(*d*) Special forms:

1. heroic couplet: rimed iamic pentameter
2. blank verse: unrimed iambic pentameter
3. free verse: unrimed and no regular line length

or metrical scheme (the problem : how to justify the length of each line)

4. Other concerns in sound

   (*a*) the quality (harshness or smoothness) of vowel and consonantal sounds

   (*b*) the peculiarity of their succession

   (*c*) the case or difficulty or transition between words

   (*d*) the silence between the sounds (a variable determined in large part by the reader, but also by the author's positioning of letters, words, and lines on the printed page)

   (*e*) figures of speech (comparison and associations) :

1. What is the subject matter of the imagery (does the author draw his images from the earth, sky, country, city etc.)?
2. What senses (sight, hearing, touch, smell, taste) are emphasized?
3. Classification :

   (*a*) When both parts of the comparison are present (sometimes referred to as horizontal predication or addition) :

   1. simile : direct comparison of two objects, using 'like' or 'as'
   2. metaphor : indirect comparison of two objects, using the verb "to be"

   (*b*) When only one part is present and the other or others are supplied by the reader (sometimes referred to as vertical substitution)

   1. Symbol : using a perceivable object—not human—to represent one or more unmentioned concepts or objects; the reader can be set off on a train of associations which may fluctuate between levels of non-perceivable subjects and concepts and perceivable objects and situations (such as tower..... isolation....island.....desert)

(*a*) check its consistency in the work (whether the symbol always represents the same thing and concepts throughout the work)

(*b*) if there is more than one symbol in the work-what are their relationships, which is most important?

2. connotations : meanings, qualities, and feelings suggested to the reader by a word of phrase
3. synecdoche : use of a part for the whole....."hand" for 11 man (now usually included under the term "metonymy").
4. metonymy : substitution of the name of one object for a closely associated second object..... "crown" for "king"
5. personification : attribution of human qualities to inanimate objects or abstract concepts.

(*f*) tone : the author's attitude toward (1) his subject matter (2) his audience, and occasionally, (3) himself the surest, quickest way to determine such attitudes is through a study of diction.

(*g*) satire : a negatively critical treatment of a subject, usually employing devices of humor, with a variety of tones possible on the spectrum from deeply serious to the light-hearted, from sharp condemnation to detached amusement. It usually urges reform and implies a set of values contrary to those being embodied and satarized. Pay attention to : the degree to which the writer implies that reform is possible or impossible, the inclusion or exclusion of the writer himself within the material being satirized; and the specific (John Smith) or general (mankind) nature of the object of the satire.

(*h*) devices of indirection and of multiplication :

1. ambiguity : two or more possible meanings from the same word or set of words.
2. irony :

(*a*) dramatic : the author implies different meaning from that of the speaker in the literary work.

(*b*) verbal :

1. a character's not realizing the significance of what he says.
2. a character's saying one thing and meaning the opposite.

(*c*) situational : incongruity between circumstances (what they are and what they should be or what they were expected to be)

(*d*) romantic : an author who is enthusiastic, inspired, and imaginative but also reflective, conscious, and critical of his/her ideas and self.

3. Paradox : contradictions
4. symbolism

E. Analysis of Narratives :

1. Character :

(*a*) the function of the character within the work (what would be missing if the character were removed from the work?), only for minor characters.

(*b*) balancing of characters (parallels and contrasts in personalities and beliefs between characters or in relation to a major character).

(*c*) consistency of character (does the character change in any way during the course of the narrative?)

(*d*) ways of creating character : the character's thoughts, words, actions, and opinions expressed by other characters about the character.

2. Plot : the following parts of a plot (1) are not all essential or necessarily present (2) may occur in different ordering, and (3) may involve conflict between ideas or concepts within characters rather than just between the characters themselves.

(*a*) situation (time and place)

(*b*) generating circumstances (what first interests the reader in the narrative)

(*c*) rising action (development of conflict between protagonist and antagonist) (*d*) climax (the triumph of the protagonist or antagonist)

(*e*) falling action (explanation and completion of the previous action)

3. Setting :

(*a*) function : (1) the influence of the setting on the characters (environmental influence or parallels between settings and characters such as a Man's room reflecting his character (2) the symbolic significance of the setting.

(*b*) substance : physical or mental

4. Point of view : the way the author tells his story : person and tense

(*a*) omniscient (author knows everything everywhere and usually uses the third person, past tense).

(*b*) personal narrative : major or minor character in the first person.

(*c*) dramatic (absence of author and omniscience....in its purest form : dialogue).

(*d*) stream of consciousness (a series of associations often omitting links between the associations, which are to be supplied by the reader; the greater the gap between associations, the more "difficult" the work).

5. Symbols.
6. Theme : the one major concept embodied in the narrative, a declarative statement.
7. Motifs : minor concepts woven throughout the narrative in repeated phrases, images, scenes, or situations.
8. Tone.
9. Satire.
10. Devices of Indirection and Multiplication.

F. Some Random subjects and Criteria for the Evaluating of Literature :

1. Balance : a psychological function of art is to produce a sense of balance for or in a reader, such a balance may

result either from the reader's perception of a balance within the work of art or from the reader's experiencing a sense of balance between himself and the work of art.

2. Open and closed-endedness : a narratives action may or may not be resolved or completed. Thematically any work of art may be unresolved or incomplete when it depends upon devices of indirection and multiplication. In a more general sense, every work of art is incomplete until the reader adds himself to it (which may or may not result is some kind of closed interpretation or perpetuation of open-endedness).
3. Complexity and simplicity : the values of having complexity in thoughts and structure in a work of art is to include as much and as diverse material as possible within the smallest given space thereby bringing all of the faculties of the reader into activity. When one calls a work simple or complex, he is usually commenting on whether or not a single, clear meaning is obvious upon a first reading. Actually whether a work is simple or complex depends upon the wishes of the reader : the "simple" can be made "complex" by the reader's bringing materials to the work, and the "complex" can be made "simple" by the reader's ignoring elements within the work and his own experiences. In like manner the concrete can be made abstract or the abstract made concrete by the activities of the reader and what he brings to bear upon the work.
4. Humor : the basis of all humor is incongruity. Incongruity can occur not only between elements within a work (character and setting, style and content) but also within a single element (high and low diction) or through such specific literary devices as irony and ambiguity or between the work and a special context the reader chooses to put the work into.
5. Mythmaking : a myth is any series of events....which of necessity must include characters and symbols—

which enables man to evaluate his experiences (form a set of values). Meaning, not historical authenticity, is of primary significance.

6. Novelty : experimentation in diction, sound devices, rhetoric, subject matter, or any combination thereof.
7. Unity and Disunity : the value of a unified, closely knit structure, every word and mark must be functional; hence brief works are most popular for such interpretations. And, in contrast, disunity or the lack of unity (through diversity of style and content, digressions, or stream of consciousness) often to promote freeplay and creativity by the reader.
8. Variety : the value of a variety in subject matter and forms of expression within the works of a single author, a quantitative as well as qualitative criterion.

6

Functions of Literary Criticism

The word 'criticism' is derived from the Greek word meaning. 'Judgement'; and hence criticism is the exercise of judgement, and literary criticism is the exercise of judgement on works of literature. Literary criticism is the study, analysis, and evaluation of imaginative literature. Everyone who expresses an opinion about a book, a song, a play, or a movie is a critic, but not everyone opinion is based upon thought, reflection, analysis, or consistently articulated principles. As people mature and acquire an education, their ability to analyze, their understanding of human beings, and their appreciation of artistic craftsmanship should increase. The study of literature is as essential component of this growth of reflection.

Sometimes students object to analysis and ask, "Why do we have to analyze everything? Why can't we just enjoy the books we read in English?" These are good questions, and there are some good answers for them. First, talking about an experience, actual or vicarious, is one way of increasing enjoyment. Second, sometimes talking about an experience involve recreating in words, but it can also involve the search for meaning, in short, analysis. Finally, as Socrates said, "The life which is unexamined is not worth living." Analysis, or examination, increases awareness and understanding; it is part of the maturation process. The analysis of literature has always been part of a liberal education. When a work of literature is studied without reference to history or to the life of author, the approach is intrinsic, or formalistic. However, literature is related to two other humanistic disciplines : philosophy and history. Philosophy explores basic, general ideas, such as truth, beauty, and goodness. History attempts to ascertain, what happened in the past and why it happened. Philosophy may help readers to understanding general ideas, or themes, of a literary work. History helps to elucidate the life and times of the author.

Traditionally, literary studies were conducted within the three humanistic disciplines of literature, history, and philosophy. In the twentieth century, the social sciences have been used to develop new approaches to criticism. Psychology has helped to illuminate the motivations of characters and the writers who create them. Sociology has revealed the relationships between the works the author produces and the society that consumes them. Anthropology has shown how ancient myths and rituals are alive and well in the plays, poems, and novels that are popular today. Literary criticism has been a social institution for many centuries. Different ages take different approaches, but the activity is constant. Authors are aware of criticism so that it is probably not entirely fair to say that the literary critic reads meanings into the texts that were never intended by the author. Literary criticism is not "reading between the lines"—it is reading the lines very carefully, in a disciplined and informed manner.

Criticism is a science and an art which has undergone changes and it had different objectives at different times. Literary criticism is the reasoned consideration of literary works and issues. It applies as a term, to any argumentation about literature, whether or not specific works are analyzed. Plato's cautions against the risky consequences of poetic inspiration in general in his Republic are thus often taken as the earliest important example of literary criticism. More strictly construed, the term covers only what has been called "practical criticism", the interpretation of meaning and the judgement of quality. Criticism in this narrow sense can be distinguished not only from aesthetics (the philosophy of artistic value) but also from other matters that may concern the student of literature : biographical questions, bibliography, historical knowledge, sources and influences, and problems of method. Thus, especially in academic studies, "criticism" is often considered to be separate from "scholarship." In practice, however, this distinction often proves artificial, and even the most single-minded concentration on a text may be informed by outside knowledge, while many notable works of criticism combine discussion of texts with broad arguments about the nature of literature and the principles of assessing it.

Shipley in his Dictionary of World Literature points out that the word criticism has been in use only since the seventeenth century, although the judgement it represents is recorded among the Athenians in the 5th century B.C. The defination being—"The conscious evaluation or appreciation of a work of art, either according to the critic's personal taste or according to some accepted aesthetic ideas......Increasingly it is stated as it was almost always (save among the Romantics) implied, that to set up as a critic is to set up as a judge of values." Edmund Goose on 'Criticism' states—"The term has come to posses a secondary and specialized meaning as a published analysis of the qualities and characteristics of a work in literature or fine art. A. Richardson asserts—"Literary criticism, consists in analysing writer's work explaining it by its causes, judging its aesthetic value. T.S. Eliot has said—"I assume that criticism is that department of thought which either seeks to find out what poetry is, what its use is, what desires it satisfies, why it is written and why read or recited : or which assesses actual poetry......[There are these two theoretical limits of criticism; at one of which we attempt to answer the question 'what is poetry?' and at the other 'is this a good poem'." 'Criticism' in the words of Walter Pater "is the art of interpreting art. It serves, as an intermediary between the author and the reader by explaining the one to the other. By his special aptitude and training, the critic feels the virtue of a masterpiece, disengages it, and sets it forth." Caryle said, "Criticism stands like an interpreter between the inspired and the uninspired; between the prophet and those who hear the melody of his words, and catch some glimpse of their material meaning, but understand not their deeper import."

The functions of literary criticism vary widely, ranging from the reviewing of books as they are published to systematic theoretical discussion. Though reviews may sometimes determine whether a given book will be widely sold, many works succeed commercially despite negative reviews, and many classic works, including Herman Melville's *Moby Dick* (1851), have acquired appreciative publics long after being unfavourably reviewed and at first neglected. One of criticism's principal functions is to express the shifts in sensibility that makes such revaluations possible. The minimal condition for such a new appraisal is, of course, that the original text survive. The literary critic is sometimes cast in the role of scholarly detective, unearthing, authenticating, and editing unknown manuscripts. Thus, even rarefied scholarly skills may be put to criticism's most elementary use, the bringing of literary works to a public's attention.

The variety of criticism's functions is reflected in the range of publications in which it appears. Criticism in the daily press rarely displays sustained acts of analysis and may sometimes do little more than summarize a publisher's claims for a book's interest. Weekly and biweekly magazines serve to introduce new books but are often more discriminating in their judgements, and some of these magazines, such as The (London) Times Literary Supplement andThe New York Review of Books, are far from indulgent toward popular works. Sustained criticism can also be found in monthlies and quaterlies with a broad circulation in "little magazines" for specialized audiences, and in scholarly journals and books.

Because critics often try to be lawgivers, declaring which works deserve respect and presuming to say what they are "really" about, criticism is a perennial target of resentment. Misguided or malicious critics can discourage an author who has been feeling his way toward a new mode that offends received taste. Pedantic critics can obstruct a serious engagement with literature by deflecting attention toward inessential matters. As the French philosopher-critic Jean-Paul Sarte observes the critic may announce that French thought is a perpetual colloquy between Pascal and Montaigne not in order to make those thinkers more alive but to make thinkers of his own time more dead. Criticism can antagonize authors even when it performs its function well. Authors who regard literature as needing no advocates or investigators are less than grateful when told that their works possess unintended meaning or are imitative or incomplete.

What such authors may tend to forget is that their works, once published, belong to them only in a legal sense. The true owner of their works is the public, which will appropriate them for its own concerns regardless of the critic. The critic's responsibility is not to the author's self-esteem but to the public and to his own standards of judgement, which are usually more exacting than the publics'. Justification for his role rests on the premise that literary works are not in fact self-explanatory. A critic is socially useful to the extent that society wants, and receives, a fuller understanding of literature that it could have achieved without him. In filling this appetite, the critic whets it further, helping to create a public that cares about artistic quality. Without sensing the presence of such a public, an author may either prostitute his talent or squander it in sterile acts of defiance. In this sense, the critic is not a parasite but, potentially, someone who is responsible in part for the existence of good writing in his own time and afterward.

Although some critics believe that literature should be discussed in isolation from other matters, criticism usually seems to be openly or covertly involved with social and political debate. Since literature itself is often partisan, is always rooted to some degree in local circumstances, and has a way of calling forth affirmations of ultimate values, it is not surprising that the finest critics have never paid much attention to the alleged boundaries between criticism and other types of discourse. Especially in modern Europe, literary criticism has occupied a central place in debate about cultural and political issues. Sartre's own what is literature? (1947) is typical in its wide-ranging attempt to prescribe the literary intellectual's ideal relation to the development of his society and to literature as a manifestation of human freedom. Similarly, some prominent American critics, including Alfred Kazin, Lionel Trilling, Kenneth Burke, Philip Rahv, and Irving Howe, began as political radicals in the 1930s and sharpened their concern for literature on the dilemmas and disillusionments of that era. Trilling's influential *The Liberal Imagination* (1950) is simultaneously a collection of literary essays and an attempt to reconcile the claims of politics and art.

Such a reconciliation is bound to be tentative and problematic if the critic believes, as Trilling does, that literature possesses an independent value and a deeper faithfulness to reality than is contained in any political formula. In Marxist states, however, literature has usually been considered a means to social ends and, therefore, criticism has been cast in forthrightly partisan terms. Dialectical materialism does not necessarily turn the critic into a mere guardian of party doctrine, but it does forbid him to treat literature as a cause in itself, apart from the working class's needs as interpreted by the party. Where this utilitarian view prevails, the function of criticism is taken to be continuous with that of the state itself, namely, furtherance of the social revolution. The critic's main obligation is not to his texts but rather to the masses of people whose consciousness must be advanced in the designated direction. In periods of severe orthodoxy, the practice of literary criticism has not always been distinguishable from that of censorship.

Although almost all the criticism ever written dates from the 20th century, questions first posed by Plato and Aristotle are still of prime concern, and every critic who has attempted to justify the social value of literature has had to come to terms with the opposing argument made by Plato in *The Republic.* The poet as a man and poetry as a form of statement both seemed untrustworthy to Plato, who depicted the physical world as a mere copy of the copy. Thus, literature could only mislead the seeker of truth. Plato credited the poet with divine inspiration, but this, too, was cause for worry; a man possessed by such madness would subvert the interests of a rational polity. Poets were therefore to be banished from the hypothetical republic.

In his Poetics—still the most respected of all discussions of literature—Aristotle countered Plato's indictment by stressing what is normal and useful about literary art. The tragic poet is not so much divinely inspired as he is motivated by a universal human need to imitate, and what he imitates is not something like a bed (Plato's example) but a noble action. Such imitation presumably has a civilizing value for those who emphasize with it. Tragedy does arouse emotions of pity and terror in its audience, but these emotions are purged in the process (Katharsis). In this fashion Aristotle succeeded in portraying literature as satisfying and regulating human passions instead of inflaming them.

Although Plato and Aristotle are regarded as antagonists, the narrowness of their disagreement is noteworthy. Both maintain that poetry is mimetic, both treat the arousing of emotion in the perceiver, and both feel that poetry takes its justification, of any, from its service to the state. It was obvious to both men that poets wielded great power over others. Unlike many modern critics who have tried to show that poetry is more than a pastime, Aristotle had to offer reassurance that it was not socially explosive. Aristotle's practical contribution to criticism, as opposed to his ethical defense of literature, lies in his inductive treatment of the elements and kinds of poetry. Poetic modes are identified according to their means of imitation, the actions they imitate, the manner of imitation, and its effects. These distinctions assist the critic in judging each mode according to its proper ends instead of regarding beauty as a fixed entity. The ends of tragedy, as Aristotle conceived them, are best served by the barmonious disposition of six elements : plot, character, diction, thought, spectacle, and song. Thanks to Aristotles' insight into universal aspects of audience psychology. Many of his dicta have proved to be adoptable to genres developed long after this time. Later Greek and Roman criticism offers no parallel to Aristotle's originality. Much ancient criticism, such as that of Ciero, Horace, and Quintilian in Rome, was absorbed in technical rules of exegesis and advice to aspiring rhetoricians. Horaces' verse epistle the Art of Poetry is an urbane amplification of Aristotles' emphasis on the decorum or internal propriety of each genere, now including lyric, pastoral, satire, elegy, and epigram as well as Aristote's epic, tragedy, and comedy. This work was later to be prized by Neoclassicists of the 17th century not only for its rules but also for its humour, common sense, and appeal to educated taste. On the sublime, by the Roman-Greek known as "Longinus", was to become influential in the 18th century but for a contrary reason : when decorum began to lose its sway encouragement could be found in Longinus for arousing elevated and ecstatic feeling in the reader. Horace and Longinus developed, respectively, the rhetorical and the affective sides of Aristotle's thought, but Longinus effectively reversed the Aristotelian concern with regulation of the passions.

In the Christian Middle Ages criticism suffered from the loss of nearly all the ancient critical texts and from an antipagan distrust of the literary imagination. Although there was no lack of rhetoricians to dictate the correct use of literary figures, no attempt was made to derive critical principles from emergent genres such as the fabliau and the chivalric romance. Criticism was in fact inhibited by the very coherence of the theologically explained universe. When nature is conceived as endlessly and purposefully symbolic of revealed truth, specifically literary problems of form and meaning are bound to be neglected. Even such an original vernacular poet of the 14th century as Dante appears to have expected his Divine comedy to be interpreted according to the rules of scriptural exegesis.

Renaissance criticism grew directly from the recovery of classic texts and notably from Giorgio Valla's translation of Aristotles' *Poetics* into Latin in 1498. Critics looked to ancient poems and plays for insight into the permanent laws of art. Sidneys *Defence of Poesie* (1595) vigorously argued the poet's superiority to the philosopher and the historian on the grounds that his imagination is chained neither to lifeless abstractions nor to dull actualities. Neoclassicism, however, connotes narrower attitudes that are at once literary and social : a wordlywise tempering of enthusiasm, a fondness for proved ways, a gentlemanly sense of propriety and balance. During 18th century the spirit of nationalism entered criticism as a concern for the origins and growth of one's own native literature and as an esteem for such non-Aristotelian factors as 'the spirit of the age." Romanticism tended to regard the writing of poetry as a transcendentally important activity, closely related to the creative perception of meaning in the world. The poet was credited with the godlike power that Plato had feared in him; Transcendental Philosophy was, indeed, a derivate of Plato's metaphysical Idealism. In the typical view of Percy Bysshe Shelley poetry "strips the veil of familarity from the world, and lays bare naked and sleeping beauty, which is the spirit of its forms." Wordsworth's preface to Lyrical Ballads (1800), with its definition of poetry as the spontaneous overflow of powerful feelings and its attack on Neoclassical diction, is regarded as the opening statement of English Romanticism. In England, however, only Cloridge in his Biographia Literaria (1817) embraced the whole complex of Romantic doctrines emanating from Germany; the British empiricist tradition was too firmly rooted to be totally washed aside by the new metaphysics. Most of those who were later called Romantics did share an emphasis on individual passion and inspiration, a taste for symbolism and historical awareness, and a conception of art works as internally whole structures in which feelings are dialectically merged with their contraries. Romantic criticism coincided with the emergence of aesthetics as a separate branch of philosophy, and both signalled a weakening in ethical demands upon literature. The lasting achievement of Romantic theory is its recognition that artistic creations are justified, not by their promotion of virtue, but by their own coherence and intensity. 20th century criticism made a shift from impressionism to formalism. New criticism has been the methodological counterpart to the strain of modernist literature characterized by allusive difficulty, paradox, and indifference or outright hostility to the democratic ethos. In certain respect the negemony of New Criticism has been political as well as literary; and anti-Romantic insistence on irony, convention, and aesthetic distance has been accompanied by scorn for all revolutionary hopes. In Hulme conservatism and classicism were explicitly linked. Romanticism struck him as "split religion", a dangerous exageration of human freedom. In reality, however, New Criticism owed much to Romantic theory, especially to Coleridge's idea of organic form, and some of its notable practitioners have been left of centre in their social thought.

Criticism deals with poetry, drama, novel and other literary forms, which deal with life directly. If creative literature is an interpretation of life through various forms of literary expression, criticism is an interpretation of that interpretation as well as of the forms of literature. This does not mean that criticism has nothing to do with life directly. Literature is interested in life and personality is one of the chief facts of life. Criticism, which tries to interpret the personality of a great writer as it is revealed in a literary work of art, truly deals with life as literature does.

Literary criticism has two major functions to perform, one of interpretation and the other of judgement. The history of criticism shows that these two functions were combined till recent times. A majority of critics have used interpretation as a means to reach judgement which they have thought to be the real and of criticism. The real aim of a critic is to penetrate the heart of a work, analyse it, evaluate it, separate the essential beauties, examine the artistic and moral principles that have guided the writer and expose all the cultural, historical, psychological, philosophical scenario of the author as well as his work. In a true sense it is a journey of exploration through self experience and the nature of literature.

According to Longinus—it is the creative imagination which modifies and transforms, and produces works of beauty. Longinus is the first of the critics to emphasise this aspect of great literature, such as the works of antiquity. In his practical criticism, Longinus makes use of both the historical and comparative methods. Criticism helps the reader to have better understanding of the text. It focusses on the laws and merits of the practice of the artists. It helps us in the task of easing or widening and deepening our response to what is best in literature. Another important function of criticism is that it builts a communication between an author and a reader. The communication of feelings, reasoning, understanding even though the writer may be obscure, recondite and difficult. The best example is T.S. Eliot's poem 'The Waste Land'. It was obscure and beyond the reach of ordinary reader to understand. But reviews literary criticism, has helped the readers to understand the poem though it is still controversial.

The function of criticism is not fault finding as it is supposed to be the layman. Its function is not to pick holes or favour appreciate favourite author but rather to interpret the personality of a writer through his work. Indiscriminate praise is as bad as indiscriminate fault finding. Throughout 17th and 18th centuries the critic was looked upon as a judge with no other duty than to pronounce upon the faults or merits of a work, which still persists. Criticism helps us for the comparative study of literature. The history and principles of Literary criticism from Plato, Aristotle to Eliot and Richard help us to come close to literature, its classics, the change in thoughts, movements, trends and characteristics in literature. It makes us aware of the richness of the past literature as T.S. Eliot has emphasised in his famous essay "Tradition and Individual Talent" that those artists are considered to be best who is attached with the past. There is no present without past. It is just because of literary criticism we are aware of the merits of the classics of all the ages. Criticism has made Chaucer, Shakespeare, Milton, Wordsworth, Pope, and others favourite of the readers as it has helped them to understand and gain aesthetic pleasure.

Evaluation, interpretation and explanation or elucidation are now considered as the chief functions of literary criticism. Atkins, comments in this connections—"Thus there is a criticism that deals with literature in the mass, that seeks to explain not only its nature and functions, but also the secrets of the literary craft, the principles that underline its creative process. Then too, there is a criticism that deals not so much with abstract questions of literature in general as with literature in the concrete, with specific literary works; and then it aims at discussing particular qualities, or at estimating the value of a given artistic performance. And again, criticism may aim at a yet more subtle treatment when it seeks to realise the manifold appeal of a work of art and to interpret it imaginatively, so that all who read may read with understanding. Criticism is, therefore, an activity of a many-sided kind; it may consist of theorising or judging, legislating or appreciating."

7

The Role and Qualifications of a Critic

The task of criticism is a very difficult and exacting one, and a critic in order to perform his task well, must be an exceptionally gifted and qualified individual. A critic, in the first place, is an ideal reader. But, criticism, in its etymological sense, is judgement, or valuation. Hence, criticism does not end with appreciation. The critic must also pronounce judgement on the work of art-on its significance, and how it compares with similar works of art. The critic is "minimally required to be a connoisseur", which means he must have a "sound knowledge" of the history of art, as Philip Weissman wrote in his essay *The Psychology of the Critic and Psychological Criticism* (1962) but "the step from connoisseur to critic implies the progression from knowledge to judgement. "The critic must make judgements because the art dealt with is generally new and unfamiliar—unless the critic is trying to reevaluate an old art with a fresh understanding of it—and thus of uncertain aesthetic and cultural value. The critic is often faced with a choice : to defend old standards, values, and hierarchies against new ones or to defend the new against the old. There are thus avant-grade critics, who become advocates of art that departs from and even subverts or destabilizes prevailing norms and conventions and becomes socially disruptive, as well as reactionary critics, who defend the old order of thinking and values and the socially established familiar art that goes along with them. Extreme innovators-artists whose work is radically different, even revolutionary-pose the greatest challenge to the critic. Such artists push the limits of the critic's understanding and appreciation or else force the critic to fall back on established assumptions in intellectual self-defeat. The greatest threat to art criticism is the development of defensive cliches-settled expectations and unquestioned presuppositions-about art, while the adventure of art criticism lies in the exposure to new possibilities of art and the exploration of new approaches that seem demanded by it.

The critic thus has a certain power of determination over art history, or at least great influence in creating the canon of art, as is evident, for example, in the naming by critics of many modern movements and in the "basic understanding" of the ostensibly incomprehensible unconventional artists who initiated them. The British critic Roger Fry, who created the name "Post-Impressionism" and wrote brilliantly and convincingly about Paul Cezanne, is a classic example. Art criticism may also encompass historiography; while "art history" is often spoken of as an objective field, art historians' own preferences cannot always be separated from their judgements and choices of emphasis, and this makes many art-historical narratives a subtler form of art criticism.

The French poet and critic Charles Boudelaire famously said, in his review of the salon of 1846, that "to be just, that is to say, to justify its existence, criticism should be partisan, passionate, and political, that is to say, written from an exclusive point of view, but a point of view that opens up the widest horizons. "In thus way, criticism is subjective as well as objective. It should be a matter of considered choice rather than arbitrary in its decisions of significance, but an emotional factor necessarily enters, as Baudelaire readily admitted. This can make criticism impressionitic or poetic as well as descriptive, analytic, and scholarly. Even the most journalistic criticism—and modern criticism is often a species of journalism—is rarely neutral and detached. The subjective affinities and cognitive interests of the critic and, however, subliminally, a critics' perception of social needs inevitably affect the content of criticism. In the 20th and 21st centuries, theoretical bases such as Marxism and feminism have often entered art criticism more directly, making the critics' perceptions of social needs more directly applicable to evaluations of art. As the German theorist Hans Robert Jauss wrote, every work of art exists within a social and historical "horizon of expectation." The aesthetic response elicited by the work often defends upon how much it does or does not conform to historically conditioned social expectations. Critical recognition and advocacy, as Jauss says, is a complicated response to an often complicated art. The history of art criticism is a narrative of the responses that made an aesthetic as well as social difference in the general perception and conception of art, often legitimating its changes in direction.

Since antiquity, philosophers have been theorizing about art, as well as criticizing it. Plato, for example, regarded art as an inferior form of knowledge, indeed, no more than an illusion of knowledge. In the Republic he describes the painter as a "creator of appearances", stating that "What he creates is untrue", a "semblance of existence" rather than a "real existence." Plato further writes that works of art are "but imitations thrice removed from the truth, and could easily be made without any knowledge of the truth, because they are appearances, only and not realities." Imitation-image-making-should not be "the ruling principle of [anyone's] life, as if he had nothing higher in him." One might all this metaphysical criticism : art is at best a way of simplifying and communicating complex ideas-philosophical truths—to the ignorent, according to Plato, although from the point of view of absolute truth, the artist is also profoundly ignorant.

Aristotle took a somewhat different approach to his theory of art, although he also regarded art as a form of imitation. In his *Poetics,* perhaps the most influential work on art ever written, he makes it clear that art is a moral issue, since it deals with human character. "The objects of imitation..... represent men either as better than in real life, or as worse, or as they are." He argues that imitation is a human instinct, and as such, works of imitative art, in whatever medium, move human beings deeply. Such works of art are evocative and cathartic; the viewer identifies and impathizes with the human beings and human situations depicted, feeling what they left, and learning from their experience, which is an essentialized imitation of what all might experience. Thus, the viewer pities those who suffer in tragedy—the highest form of art, since the tragic hero is a higher type of human being—while being terrorized by their suffering and the situations which cause it, for they are potentially the viewer's own, in spirit if not in actuality. For Aristotle, art is a lesson in life and, is such, is of great social and broadly human value. He was the first psychologically minded critic, and his idea of the inseparability of art and morality of art in the service of moral teaching—remained influential into the modern period. Thus their theories has helped the coming generation to analyse the text or the work of art.

As the critic is to be an ideal reader, it is essential that he should get a correct idea a clear, and undistorted view of the book, or of the author he is judging. Hence, some of the mental faculties to be expected of him, are that he must be alert, flexible, and he should be free from all sorts of bias. Criticism is often spoiled because the critic is not free from bias. A critic like Arnold, for instance, has a classical bias, while Cloridge has a metaphysical bias whereas Dryden is bias to Chaucer. Further, there are party, political bias which disorts the criticism in Reviews.

As a critic has to deal with a variety of books, he must have mental flexibility to react properly to all sorts of books. Most of the critics can deal with one or two forms of literature. It is sometimes said that Lamb was a drama-blind critic. He could see only the poetry in the plays of Shakespeare, and the Elizabethans, but he had no idea of the dramatic values.

Wide and many-sided reading is basic to most of the intrinsic qualifications that a critic should possess. Just as experience helps a person become mature on the path of life, a wide ranging and indepth reading of literature makes a critic more sound and dependable in his literary responses. Such reading enables a critic to recognize the literary qualities of a genius who makes a departure from literary tradition and conventional writing. A critic has to recognize a genius or what Eliot calls an individual talent, on first meeting him in his works. He should be quick in responding to a fresh and virgin sensibility. A proper estimate of an author always takes time, but a good critic comes up with it when he comes across a literary genius for the first time. According to Eliot the foremost quality which an ideal critic must have is a highly developed sense of fact. The sense of fact is a rare gift. It is not frequently met with, and it is very slow to develop. The value of a practitioner's criticism—say, that of, poet on his own art, 'workshop criticism' as Eliot elsewhere calls it—lies in the fact that he is dealing with facts which he understands, and so can also help us to understand them. Eliot's own criticism is such 'workshop criticism', and Eliot is all praises for such critics and their criticism. There is a large part of criticism which seeks to 'interpret' an author and his work. But most of such interpretation is no interpretation at all. It is mere fiction; the critic gives his views, his impressions of the work, and so is false and misleading. Eliot has no use for such "impressionistic criticism; it gives us no insight into the work under study. Further, the critic should be guided by facts and facts alone. He should approach the work of art with a free mind, unprejudiced by any theories or pre-conceived notions. Only then can he be completely objective and impersonal. It is in this way that criticism approximates to the position of science. It is only in this way that criticism becomes a co-operative activity, the critic of one age co-operates with critics of the previous ages in the common pursuit of truth.

Comparison and analysis are the two chief tools of the critic. But the critic should be careful in handling them. The critic must know how to compare and what to analyse. Critical truths are not permanent and universal. The truths of one age may not be convincing or even profitable to people of another age. Even when the now invalidated truths of the previous age have a great value, the critic should try to discover some other and profitable truths. According to Arnold a critic must know the best that is known and thought in the world : 'in the world' and not merely in his own country or in one or two countries. He must know the best not in literature alone, but in other subjects as well.

The critic performs a very important function. He rouses men out of their self-satisfaction and complacency, for such complacency is vulgarising and retarding. By shaking the complacency of men, he makes their mind dwell upon what is excellent in itself, and the absolute beauty and fitness of things. He raises above practical consideration by making them contemplate the ideally perfect. Practical considerations are vulgarising, they make men incapable of perceiving fine distinctions. Arnold refers to such incapacity as Philistinism, and it is criticism, in the true sense of the word, that can save us from it. The critic must rise above practical considerations, for such considertions impoverise the soul; he must always have ideal perfection as his aim, for it is only then that he can make others rise to it.

In the view of Wordsworth an ideal critic of poetry should possess the following qualities—(*a*) he must be both poetic and philosophical, (*b*) his affections must be free and kindly, (*c*) his understanding must be clear, and his judgement dispassionate, (*d*) his vision must not be clouded by his prejudices, literary, personal, or religious, (*e*) his sensibility must have been trained by a continuous study of poetry, and (*f*) he must be of a mature age. Even when a critic has all the above qualities he may not, be always correct and just in his judgement. Indeed, even the class of such critics includes both the worst and the best.

A good critic must be entirely impersonal and objective. He must not be guided by the "inner voice", but by some authority outside himself. A good critic must not be emotional. He must be entirely objective. He must try to discipline his personal prejudices and whims. He must have a highly trained sensibility, and a sense of structural principle, and must not be satisfied with vague, emotional impressions. Critics who supply only vague, emotional impressions, "opinion or fancy", are great corruptors of taste. An ideal critic must have a thorough understanding of the language and structure of a poem. He must also have an idea of the music of poetry, for a poet communicates as much through the meaning of words as through their sound. A critic must promote the enjoyment and understanding of works of art. He must develop both the aesthetic and the intellectual sensibilities of his readers. Criticism is of great importance in the work of creation itself. The poet creates, but the critic in him shifts; combines, corrects and expunges, and thus imparts perfection and finish to what has been created. No great work of art is possible without critical labour. The critic must have imaginative sympathy. He must be able to put himself in the place of the writer, and thus see things from his point of view, and share his vision of life. It is only through such imaginative sympathy that the real meaning and purpose of an author are to be understood, and the real significance of his work is to be brought. Not only must the critic approach the book in the proper attitude—the sympathetic attitude—but he must also have gusto or enthusiasm to convey his own appreciation to the readers. And he must be able to give reasons for his views—for the faith that is in him.

The critic is a man whose genius is less, which his charity is more. "Clarity is one of the finest essentials of the true critic." The artist is often limited in his sympathies. He may be a man of obsessions. But the critic is one who is tolerant, a generous and sympathetic. He is impartial in his attitude, has the power to understand and interpret, the power to enter into the states of consciousness and moods which are so far beyond the range of any individual artist. He has often to take within his province the most diverse temperaments among the artists and this demands the greatest width of sympathy. As Hazzlitt says, "The critic is a man of disinterested tastes and of liberal feelings."

One should not underrate a critic's qualities on the basis of a few blind spots in his otherwise sensitive response. If Charles Lamb is a worthwhile critic only in connection with romantic literatue, we should appreciate this quality as his strength and therefore accept his limitation with regard to the rest of the literature. A good critic always has such limitations; we should expect him to be good within his own limited range. A good critic is he who narrates the adventures of his soul among masterpieces.

Although a critic is expected to be a judge, his basic function is to interpret a work of art. He is, first and foremost, an interpreter of literature. He opens the entire world of imaginative experience and desire aesthetics pleasure from it. G. Wilson Knights analysis of Shakespeare's language or Caroline Spurgeon's brilliant study of Shakespearean imagery takes us to the heart of this plays. Many scholars considered Shakespeare's last plays as less artistic and neglected them as romance, but it credit of Derek Traversi to prove the artistic merit of the last plays like *The Tempest.* Though their method of analysis are different, all these critics are good in their own way.

Oscar Wilde summarising the qualities of a critic writes, "Who is the true critic but he who bears within himself the dreams, and ideas, and feeling of myriads of generations and to whom no form of thought is alien, no emotional impulse obscure? And who the true man of culture, if not he who by fine-scholarship and fastidious rejection has made instinct self-conscious and intelligent, and can separate the work that has distinction from the work that has it not, and so by contact and comparison makes himself master of the secrets of style and school, and understands their meanings and listens to their voice, and develops that spirit of disinterested curiosity which is the real root, as it is the real flower, of the intellectual life, and thus attains to intellectual clarity, and, having learned, 'the best that is known and thought in the world', lives with those who are the Immortals."

These are very exacting demands, so much so that E.E. Kellet says, "The perfect critic, then, was never born, and never will be born." And yet he must have one more qualification. He must have the gift of communication, the power of communicating his own aesthetic pleasure to his readers.

8

Aristotle—Plato on the Art of Imitation (Mimesis)

The term mimesis is derived from the Greek *Mimesis,* meaning to imitate. The Old English Dictionary defines mimesis as "a figure of speech, whereby the words or actions of another are imitated" and "the deliberate imitation of the behavior of one group of people by another as a factor in social change". Mimicry is defined as "the action, practice, or art of mimicking or closely imitating.......the manner, gesture, speech, or mode of actions and persons, or the superficial characteristics of thing". Both terms are generally used to denote the imitation or representation of nature, especially in aesthetics (primarily literary and artistic media).

When Western traditions of aesthetic thought, the concepts of imitation and mimeses have been central to attempts to theorize the essence of artistic expression, the characteristics that distinguish works of art from other phenomena, and the myraid of ways in which we experience and respond to works of art. In most cases, mimesis is defined as having two primary meanings—that of imitation (more specifically, the imitation of nature as object, phenomena, or process) and that of artistic representation. Mimesis is an extremely broad and theoretically elusive term that encompasses a range of possibilities for how the self-sufficient and symbolically generated world created by people can relate to any given "real", fundamental, exemplary, or significant world. Mimesis is integral to the relationship between art and nature, and to the relation governing works of art themselves. Michael Taussig describes the mimetic faculty as "the nature that culture uses to create second nature, the faculty to copy, imitate, make models, explore difference, yield into and become Other. The wonder of mimesis lies in the copy drawing on the character and power of the original, to the point whereby the representation may even assume that character and that power."

The word "mimesis" is post-Homeric: it does not occur in either Homer or Hesiod. Its etymology, as linguists maintain, is obscure. Most probably it originated with the rituals and mysteries of the Dionysian cult; in its first (quite different from the present) meaning the mimesis-imitation stood for the acts of cult performed by the priest-dancing, music, and singing. This is confirmed by Plato as well as by Strabo. The word which later came to denote the reproducing of reality in sculpture and theatre art had been, at that time, applied to *dance, mimicry,* and *music* exclusively. In Delian hymns, as well as in Pindar, this term was applied to music. Imitation did not signify reproducing external reality but expressing the inner one. It had no application then in visual arts.

In the fifth century BC. the term "imitation" moved from the terminology of cult into philosophy and started to mean reproducing the *external* world. The meaning changed so much that Socrates had some qualms about calling the art of painting "mimesis" and used words close to it such as "ek-mimesis" and "apo-mimesis". But Democritus and Plato had no such scruples and used the word "mimesis" to denote imitation of nature. To each of them, however, it was a different kind of imitation.

For Democritus mimesis was an imitation *of the way nature functions.* He wrote that in art we imitate nature: in weaving we imitate the spider, in building the swallow, in singing the swan or nightingale. This concept was applicable chiefly to industrial arts.

Another concept of imitation, which acquired greater popularity, was also formed in the fifth century in Athens but by a different group of philosophers: It was first introduced by Socrates and further developed by Plato and Aristotle. To them "imitation" meant the copying of the *appearances of things.* This concept of imitation originated as a result of reflection upon *painting and sculpture.* For example, Socrates asked himself in what way do these arts differ form the others. His answer was: In this, that they repeat and imitate things which we see (Xenophon's Comm. III, 10,1). So he conceived a new concept of imitation; he also did something more: he formulated the theory of imitation, the contention that imitation is the basic function of the arts (such as painting and sculpture). It was an important event in the history of thinking on art. The fact that Plato and Aristotle accepted this theory was equally important: thanks to them it became for centuries to came the leading theory of arts. Each of them, however, assigned a different meaning to the theory and, consequently, two variants of the theory, or rather two theories originated under the same name.

Plato in his early writings was rather vague in his use of term "imitation" : he applied it to music and dance (Laws 798 D) or confined it to painting and sculpture (*Republic* 597 AD); at first he called "imitative" only poetry in which, as in tragedy, the heroes speak for themselves (epic poetry describes and does not imitate, he said). Finally, however, he accepted Socrate's broad concept which imbraced almost the entire art of painting, sculpture, and poetry. Later, beginning with Book X of the *Republic,* his conception of art as imitating reality grew very extreme: he saw it as a passive and faithful act of copying the outer world. This particular conception was induced primarily by the then contemporary illusionist art of painting. Plato's idea was similar to what was in the nineteenth century advanced under the name of "naturalism". His theory was descriptive and not normative; on the contrary, it disapproved of the imitation of reality by art on the basis that imitation is not the proper road to truth (*Republic* 603 A, 605A; Sophist 235-D-236C).

Aristotle, seemingly faithful to Plato, transformed his concept and theory of imitation; he maintained that artistic imitation may present things either more or less beautiful than they are; it also may present them such as they could or ought to be; it can and ought to limit itself to their characteristics which are general, typical, and essential. Aristotle preserved the thesis that art imitates reality but imitation meant to him not faithful copying but a free and easy approach to reality; the artist who imitates can present reality in his own way. Aristotelian "imitation" was, in fact, the result of a fusion of two conceptions: The ritualistic and the Socratic. The idea of imitation, therefore, was just as applicable to music as to sculpture and theatre. Later theoreticians of art referred more often to Aristotle, but tended to uphold the simpler and more attractive conception of Plato's. Due to Aristotle's personal interests the theory of imitation was for centuries more concerned with poetry than with visual arts. To Aristotle "imitation" was, in the first place, imitation of human actions; however, it gradually became the imitation of *nature* which was to be regarded as the source of its perfection.

The ancient theory of imitation was founded on typically Greek premises; that the human mind is passive and, therefore, able to perceive only what exists. Secondly, even if were able to invent something which does not exist, it would be ill advised to use this ability because the existing world is perfect and nothing more perfect can be conceived.

In the Middle Ages other premisses were advanced, formulated early by Dionysius the Areopagite and by Saint Augustine. If art is to imitate, let it concentrate on the *invisible* world which is more perfect. And if art is to limit itself to the visible world, let it reach in that world for *traces of eternal beauty.* This may be better achieved by means of symbols than by imitating reality.

With the Renaissance the theory of imitation became again the basic theory of art and poetry, and only then reached its apogee. Saved from oblivion, it appeared as a revelation and made the most of privileges enjoyed by new ideas. Modern theory took the term *imitation* from the Romans: *imatazione* in Italian, *imitation* in French and English. At the very beginning of the fifteenth century, the dectrine of imitation was accepted earliest of all in the plastic arts. It appeared in L. Ghiberti's *Commentaries* (1436), where he spoke of having tried to imitate nature (*imitare la nature*) "as well as it was possible for him" (*I com,* ed. Morisani, II, 22). Leonardo da Vinci had even more radical views. According to him the more faithfully the painting depicts its object—(*conformita co'la cosa imitata: Tratt.* frag-*411*)—the more praiseworthy it is. These were the poineers who were followed by other Renaissance writers. The concept and theory of imitation did not enter Renaissance poetics until the middle of the sixteenth century, that is, only after Aristototle's *Poetics* had been fully accepted; from that time on it became the most essential element of poetics.

In 17th and early 18th century conceptions of aesthetics, mimesis is bound to the imitation of (empirical and idealized) nature. Aesthetic theory emphasized the relationship of mimesis to artistic expression and began to embrace interior, emotive, and subjective images and representations. In the writings of Lessing and Rousseau, there is a turn away from the Aristotelian conception of mimesis as bound to the imitation of nature, and a move towards an assertion of individual creativity in which the productive relationship of one mimetic world to another is renounced.

The nineteenth century laid the greatest stress on being faithful to nature (not to antiquity). Nevertheless, the term "imitation" which for ages played the leading part in the theory of art, disappeared suddenly, it acquired a pejorative meaning and was used to denote something unauthentic, faked-imitations of diamonds, marble, furs, etc., and could no longer be applied to art. It appeared in the other form such as "realism" and "naturalism" in the hands of writers like G. Planche, J. H. Champfleury and E. Zola.

In 20th century approaches to mimesis, authors such as Walter Benjamin, Adorno, Girad, and Derrida have defined mimetic activity as it relates it social practice and interpersonal relations rather than as just a rational process of making and producing models that emphasize the body, emotions, the senses, and temporality. The return to a conception of mimesis as a fundamental human property is most evident in the writings of Walter Benjamin, who postulates that the mimetic faculty of humans is defined by representation and expression. The repression of the mimetic relation to the world, to the individual, and to others leads to a loss of "sensuous similarity". In this war language may be seen as the highest level of mimetic behavior and the most complete archive of non-sensuous similarity: a medium into which the earlier powers of mimetic production and comprehension have passed without residue, to the point where they have liquidated those of magic.

Derrida uses the concept of mimesis in relation to texts-which are non-disposable doubles that always stand in relation to what has preceded them. Tents are deemed "nondisposable" and "double" in that they always refer to something that has preceded them and are thus "never the origin, never inner, never outer, but always doubled." The mimetic text (which always begins as a double) backs as original model and its inherent intertexuality demands deconstruction. "*Difference* is the principle of mimesis, a productive freedom, not the elimination of ambiguity; mimesis contributes to the profusion of images, words, thoughts, theories, and action, without itself becoming tangible." Mimesis thus resists theory and constructs a word of illusion, appearances, aesthetics, and images in which existing worlds are appropriated, changed, and reinterpreted. Images are a part of our material existence, but also mimetically bind our experience of reality to subjectivity and connote a "sensor experience that is beyond reference to reality."

Plato

Plato was born in Athens around 428 BC to an aristocratic family with a long and esteemed history of leadership. Plato's father Ariston descended from the early kings of Athens. His mother Perictione came from a similarly distinguished line that included the sixth-century legislator Solon.

Plato's father appears to have died when Plato was still a young child. His mother remarried to Pyrilampes, an associate of the statesman Pericles, being otherwise unable to support Plato and his siblings. Plato has political ambitions as a young man and appeared destined to follow the family tradition. He became disillusioned with Athenian politics, however, because both the Empire and its politics had begun to decline since the onset of the Peloponnesian War (several years before Plato's birth). Outside the political sphere, Plato enjoyed success in athletics and engaged in both poetry and drama. According to Aristotle, Plato also became familiar with the teachings of cratylus—a student of Heroditus—as well as those of other pre-Socratic thinkers such as Pythagoras and Parmenides. These teachings provided the young philosopher with an introduction to the foundations of Greek metaphysics and epistemology.

Around 409 BC, Plato met Socrates and became his devoted follower. He was the founder of the Academy in Athens. He is the major figure in the history of western philosophy. He is the earliest of thinkers to discuss poetry at length. He writes dialogues in dramatic form. He bequeaths to literary criticism the theory of imitation or mimesis, dominant in literary criticism until well into the 18th century. Plato has Socrates locate reality in what he calls the ideas or forms rather than in the world of appearances or phenomena experienced. Plato is the founder of moralistic and didactic criticism. He separates content from form, privileging content. Aside from administering the Academy, Plato expounded his more mature philosophic speculations in his works such as the *Phaedrus, Symposium, Euthydemus, Cratylus, Phaedo,* and *The Republic*. Relatively little is known about the final years of Plato's life. It is certain that Plato continued to lecture at the Academy, where Aristotle studied until Plato's death. The late Platonic dialogues include the *Sophist, Statesman, Critias, Philebus, Laws, and Timaeus*. The year of Plato's death is believed to be around 348 or 347 B C.

Aristotle: (384 BC-322 BC)

Aristotle was a Greek philosopher, a student of Plato and teacher of Alexander the Great. He wrote on many different subjects, including physics, metaphysics, poetry, theatre, music, logic, rhetoric, politics, government, ethics, biology and zoology. Aristotle was born in Stageria, Chalcidice in 384 BC. His father was the personal physician to King Amyntas of Macedon. Aristotle was trained and educated as a member of the aristocracy. At about the age of eighteen, he went to Athens to continue his education at Plato's Academy. Aristotle remained at the academy for nearly twenty years, not leaving until after Plato's death. He then traveled with Xenocrates to the court of Hermias of Atarneus in Asia Minor. While in Asia, Aristotle traveled with The pophrastus to the is land of Lesbos, where together they researched the botany and zoology of the island. Aristotle married Hermia's daughter Corniece) Pythias. Soon after Hermia's death, Aristotle was invited by Philip of Macedon to become tutor to Alexander the Great.

After spending several years tutoring the young Alexander, Aristotle returned to Athens. By 335 BC, he established his own school there, known as Lyceum. Aristotle conducted courses at the school for the next twelve years. It is during this period in Athens when Aristotle is believed to have composed many of his works. Aristotle wrote many dialogues, only fragments of which survived the works that have survived are in treatise form and were not, for the most part, intended for widespread publication, as they are generally thought to be lecture aids for his students. His most important treatises include *Physics, Metaphysics, Nicomachean Ethics, Politics, De Anima (On the soul)* and *Poetics*. These works, although connected in many fundamental ways, vary significantly in both style and substance.

Aristotle not only studies almost every subject possible at that time, but made significant contribution to most of them. In physical science, Aristotle studied anatomy, astronomy, economics, embryology, geography, geology, meteorology, physics, and zoology. In philosophy, he wrote on aesthetics, ethics, government, metaphysics, politics, psychology, rhetoric and theology. He also studied education, foreign customs, literature and poetry. His combined works constitute a virtual encyclopedia of Greek knowledge. It has been suggested that Aristotle was probably the last person to know everything there was to be known in his own time.

Both Plato and Aristotle saw, in mimesis, the representation nature. Plato wrote about mimesis in both *Ion* and *The Republic* (Books II & III & Book X). In *Ion* he states that Poetry is the art of divine madness, or inspiration. Because of the poet being subject to this divine madness, it is not his function to convey the truth. As Plato has it, truth is the concern of the philosopher only. As culture in those days did not consist in the solitary reading of books, but in the listening to 'performances' the recitals of orators (and poets), or the acting out by classical actors of tragedy, Plato maintained in his critique that theatre was not sufficient in conveying the truth. His was concerned that actors orators were thus able to persuade an audience by rhetoric rather than by telling the truth.

In Book II of *The Republic,* Plato describes Socrate's dialogue with his pupils. Socrates warns we should not seriously regard poetry as being capable of attaining the truth and that we who listen to poetry should be on our guard against its seductions, in as much as that the poet has no place in our idea of God.

In developing this in Book X, Plato tells of Socrate's metaphor of the maker of beds, the carpenter who is compared with God, the maker of Earth and Heaven and everything on it : There are three beds : one existing in nature (the Platonic ideal, a bed made by God); one made by the artistic imitator of God's idea, the carpenter; and one made by the painter or poet, who when copying the carpenter's work in their work become imitators thrice removed from the truth. The copiers only touch on a small part of things as they really are, where a bed may appear differently from various points of view, looked at obliquely or directly, or differently again in a mirror. So pointers or poets, though they may point or describe a carpenter or any other maker of things, know nothing of the carpenter's (the craftsman's) art, and though the better painters or poets they are, the more faithfully their works of art will resemble the reality of the carpenter making a bed, nonetheless the imitators will still not attain the truth (of God's creation).

The poets, beginning with Homer, far from improving and educating humanity, do not possess the knowledge of craftsmen and are mere imitators who copy again and again images of virtue and rhapsodise about them, but never reach the truth in the way the superior philosophers do.

Similar to Plato's writings about mimesis, Aristotle also defined mimesis as the perfection and imitation of nature. Art was not only imitation but also the use of mathematical ideas and symmetry in the search for the perfect, the timeless, and contrasting Being with becoming. Nature is full of change, decay, and cycles, but art can also search for what is everlasting and the first causes of natural phenomena. Aristotle wrote about the idea of four causes in nature. The first formed cause being like a blueprint, or in immortal idea. The second cause is the material, or what a thing is made out of. The third cause is the process and the agent, in which the artist or creator makes the thing. The fourth cause is the good, or the purpose and end of a thing, known as telos.

Aristotle's *Poetics* is after referred to as the counterpart to this Platonic conception of poetry. Poetics in his treatise on the subject of mimesis. Aristotle was not against literature as such; he stated that human beings are mimetic beings, feeling an urge to create texts (art) that reflect and represent reality.

Aristotle considered it important that there be a certain distance between the work of art on the one hand and life on the other; we draw knowledge and consolation from tragedies only because they do not happen to us. Without this distance, tragedy could not give rise to catharsis. However, it is equally important that the text causes the audience to identify with the characters and the events in the text, and unless this identification occurs, it does not touch us, as an audience. Aristotle hold that it is through *simulated representation,* mimesis, that we respond to the acting on the stage which is conveying to us what the characters feel, so that we may empathize with them in this way through the mimetic form of dramatic role play. It is the task of the dramatist to produce the tragic enactment in order to accomplish this empathy by means of what is taking place on stage.

In short, catharsis can only be achieved if we see something that is both recognizable and distant. Aristotle argued that literature is more interesting as a means of learning than history, because history deals with specific facts that have happened, and which are constingent, whereas literature, although sometimes based on history, deals with events that could have taken place, or ought to have taken place.

Aristotle thought of drama as being "an imitation of an action", that of tragedy as of "falling from a higher to a lower estate", and so being removed to a less ideal situation in more *tragic* average human being, and those of comedy as being worse.

Plato in Republic X states that poet does not appeal to reason but to the senses and passions (what is easily imitated). His creations have an inferior degree of truth. He impairs reason. It stirs the emotions instead of controlling them. Poetry feeds and waters the passions instead of drying them up. Homer is great but we should only admit in the state hymns to the gods and praises of famous men. Law and reason must reign, not pleasure and pain. We are aware of poetry charms, but we should not betray truth. Poetry has no use, only delight. Justice and virtue might suffer on account of the delight of poetry.

The first scandal in the *Poetics* is the initial marking out of dramatic poetry as a form of imitation. We call the poet of creator, and are offended at the suggestion that he might be merely someone recording device. As the painter's eye teaches us how to book and shows us what we never saw dramatis present things that never existed until he imagined them, and makes us experience worlds we could never have found the way to on our own. But Aristotle has no intention to diminish the poet. By imitation, Aristotle does not mean the sort of mimicry by which Aristophanes, say, finds syllables that approximate the sound of frogs. He is speaking of that imitation of action, and by action he does not mean mere happenings. Aristotle speaks extensively of praxis in the *Nicomachean Ethics*. It is not a word he used loosely, and in fact his use of the defination of tragedy recalls the discussion in the *Ethics*.

Plato believed that art is essentially an imitation of nature, therefore, art is at best—(1) useless and (2) potentially dangerous.

1. Art was Useless : It serves no valuable purpose in society. As a "Imitation of Nature" it added nothing our knowledge of the world nor to society. The same value could be added by simply by holding up a mirror to the world. Note that simply holding up a mirror would be far less costly and demand fewer resources than the "production of art", but would have the same approximate value. According to this line of thought, if art was basically an imitation of nature and it was "costly" one at that, it should be worth the time and money we put into it. But it is not concluded Plato. It was useless. (Add to this his metaphysics and we see that with art, the resultant product is an imitation of an imitation, thus barely real at all.)

(2) *Art was Potentially Dangerous for Several Reasons :* (*a*) Art was essentially *deceptive*. The whole aim of art was to deceive. Success was achieved when the spectator mistook an imitation for reality. Furthermore, artists were unconcerned with truth. It made no difference to the artists whether the images or stories they depicted were real.

(*b*) Art was mainly concerned with sensual pleasure. Art seems directed entirely towards pleasing the senses and ignoring the mind, intellect, or concepts. According to *Platonic Mind/Body Dualism*, our senses/body are the least valuable, least permanent, least "real" aspects of our personalities. According to Plato, our senses are also incapable of providing us with genuine knowledge since they only gather information from an ever-changing physical world and not the immaterial forces which guide, direct and sustain it. As such our senses, and consequently art, are "metaphysically" misguided since they are directed towards illusion and not "reality". Art serves to perpetuate and sustain this misdirection, keeping us ignorant of truth, justice, goodness and "real" beauty.

(*c*) Further, Art was *psychologically de-stabilizing*. Human existence is, in great part, a struggle to master the emotions and sensual urges by using reason and intellect according to Plato. Therefore, art was dangerous and counterproductive to this end since it appeals not to reason and intellect, but to the psychological forces which constantly try to over-through reason, namely passion and emotion.

(*d*) Art leads to immortality—Art was unconcerned with mortality, sometimes even teaching immoral lessons. Plato could site *The Illiad* as an example in which Achilles refuses to fight for his country out of spite. This story is told even though the poem glorifies Achilles as a hero. Plato worries that such art would encourage immortality in the citizens of this state. People might uncritically accept and admire immoral, vicious traits when they are attractively packaged by skilled artists (distinction between truth and illusion/physicians and cooks/beauty and glamour). Like a skilled chef, artists are only interested in pleasing the palate, even if it poisons the diner. Since (mimetic) art is institutionally divorced from truth, goodness or any concern with 'real' beauty, it creates an environment of superficial "flavours" where all sorts of atrocities can be made to seem a tempting confection.

(*e*) Art was politically dangerous, a treat to the common good. Similar to the point made earlier (*c*), Plato worried that strong art which appeals to emotions stirs up negative emotions which we are trying to control. But this is more than just a problem for the individual. A people with a history of "mania" would certainly view strong, emotion-stirring art as a threat to the good of state/community. It was therefore, correctly the concern of government. Remember, Greece had suffered from waves of mania, episodes of mass, irrational, emotional, destructive behavior. With this as precedent, it is not surprising that Plato was deeply concerned about dramatic arts which intentionally caused people to cry and weep presumably without any real reason. This is similar to the criticism raised by some today of the violence and sex in media. Like Plato, they argue that violence and sex in the media cause us to be more violent, sexually obsessed culture. Therefore, it affects not just the people who consume the violent images, but the entire community of which they are a part.

Thus Plato thought art was essentially was mimetic, and being so, that it had no positive value, but was pernicious (had negative values, teaching dangerous things).

Aristotle was Plato's most famous student and greatest critic. While disagreeing with much else that Plato said, Aristotle agreed that art was essentially an imitation of nature. But, he maintained, art was not useless nor dangerous.

First, and crucial to Aristotle's defense of art is his rejection of Plato's dualism. Man is not an "embodied" intellect, longing for the spiritual release of death, but rather and animal with, among all the other faculties, the ability to use reason. We must study humans as we would study other animals to discover what their "nature" is. Among the species, who are the thriving and successful and what activities do they engage in ? This is how to determine what is and is not appropriate for a human and for human societies.

(1) Art is not Useless, it is Natural : Aristotle claims that it is natural for human beings to imitate. Any human society which is healthy will be a society where there is imitative art. Nothing is more natural than for children to pretend. (Note: the inability or lack of desire to engage in spontaneous games of pretend is a symptom of developmental disability—perhaps Autism). Nothing is more natural than for human beings to create using their imagination. We could never eliminate art from healthy human society. Furthermore, since art is imitation, it is an imagination use of concepts; at its heart, art is "conceptual", "intellectual".

Art production and training is a necessary part of any education since it uses and encourages the imaginative manipulation of ideas. Further it is not merely copying particulars in nature, but the representation of ideals. This too requires the intellectual act of abstracting the essential nature from a group of particulars.

(2) Good Art is Not Dangerous : (*a*) Art is not entirely deceptive according to Aristotle because artists must accurately portray reality to be successful. Drama must accurately portray *psychological reality* in order for characters to be believable and their actions understandable. Convincing and powerful drama is convincing and powerful because it reveals some truth of human nature. It teaches effectively and it teaches the truth.

Also, Aristotle introduces the concept of "Organic Unity" the idea that in any good work of art each of the parts must contribute to the overall success of the whole. As in nature, there is a "unity in difference." In order for a work of art to be successful each element in the work must contribute to the oveall success of the work; there must be a "unity among the parts." This is the first time in western aesthetics that a *formal characteristic* is offered as a *value principle.* Aristotle believe that it follows from a mimetic reading of nature; just as in biological organism each element must contribute to the thematic development. This is another way in which works of art reflects or imitates reality.

(*b*) For reason stated above, Aristotle did not believe that art was solely concerned with the sensual pleasures, but rather was/should be an intellectual, conceptual affair. Furthermore, Aristotle did not believe that the mind was one thing and the body was something else. Aristotle did not suffer from the sort of "Mind Body Dualism" that Plato did and therefore Aristotle did not have the bias against physical pleasures that Plato did. The only way of acquiring knowledge at all, according to Aristotle, was through the senses and so developing, exercising and sharpening those senses through art was a healthy thing to do.

(*c*) Art is defined by Aristotle as the realization in external form of a *true idea,* and is generated out of the natural pleasure humans take in their innate ability to imitate and imagine as well as the pleasure humans feel in recognizing likenesses. Contrary to Plato, Aristotle claims that art is not merely "copying." Rather, in art, the artist *idealizes* nature and compensates for its deficiencies. It is an intellectual (cognitive) process where the artist seeks to make manifest the universal type in the individual phenomenon.

(*d*) Aristotle believed that drama was an excellent way of teaching morality. In a Greek Tragedy the main character always comes to a bad end because of a *character flaw.* Thus, Greek Tragedies teach moral truths : When trying to understand how tragedies achieve their peculiar effect (fear and pathos), he notes the psychology and morality on which they must be based. The main character must not be totally evil (or else we would not identify with him) nor must he be totally good (or else we would find his misfortune repugnant). Instead the main character must be basically good, but flawed and it is this flaw that is his undoing. Pathos is achieved because while we commiseratve with the fallen hero, we nevertheless understand that the outcome was inevitable and proper. The "moral truth" that all tragedies teach is that immoral actions or character flaws lead one to a tragic ending. In doing so, drama reinforces morality and the ultimately rational structure of the universe rather than challenging it.

One should bear in mind that Aristotle believed that drama imitated not only "events", but actions. As such they imitated intentions, psychological forces and the unseen "inner life" of persons. The art of dramatic poetry, though it is an imitation of human actions, it is not a mere "Chronicle" of events (history). While (un-philosophical) history is limited to what has actually happened, poetry depicts things in their *universal character.* "Poetry is more philosophical and more elevated than history" says Aristotle because "While the latter records what did happen, the former reveals what should happen and what must happen" according to the laws of the universe and human psychology.

Art does not teach us history because it is imitation, but because art imitates human actions, good art has to depict *character,* character tracts and personality. These latter things are real so it teaches us moral, psychological lessons; what it is imitating is real and applicable to our lives. We can learn a lot from these false stories because though they are false, they are in another sense "true".

The Mimetic Theory of Art was accepted by for generations by artists, philosophers, aestheticians, and art critics; that to say they believed that art was the faithful imitation of natural ideas.

In mimetic theory, the main criterion for the evaluation of art was how closely the work imitated real life. The standard for excellence was art's relation to something external to art, the "real world" or at least, the "real world idealized." Now this criterion implies that there is/are objective standards of realistic representation.

Further the adherents of the view also presumed that art had to "sing for its super", that is, that art had to perform some productive work (moral, religious, educational, social) in order to justify the amount of time, money and other resources that we typically spend on it.

9

Aristotle's Doctrine of Catharsis

Aristotle was the first person ever to write a treatise devoted to literary theory. Before his time others had practiced literary criticism in various simple forms, mostly to do with the use (and abuse) of literature as a vehicle for social, moral, religious and political deals, and Plato, his teacher, was the first to raise many of the questions which he himself sought to answer. But to Aristotle belongs the credit for recognizing that literature has its own set of principles, which can be discovered by careful analysis from this recognition came the *Poetics*.

This brief treatise does not deserve attention only for its pioneering qualities or its incisive comment about ancient epic and drama, it has also had a profound effect on the way we read and analyse literature today. Once the *Poetics* was rediscovered and published in about A. D. 1500, its concepts, methods of analysis and conclusions acquired fundamental importance among Renaissance and seventeenth century dramatists and literary critics in Italy, France and England. Interest in *the Poetics* has redouble recently, because it has been acknowledged as a crucial text in the continuing and vigorous debates about the nature and purpose of literature, and about language itself. Nor is this interest likely to decline in the future. Some aspects of Aristotle's theory (notably catharsis) are only now becoming clear in the light of new evidence. Moreover, his analysis has already proved flexible enough to be his time, like the detective novel; it would still be relevant even to a culture based exclusively on media like cinema or television. There is nothing outdated in Aristotle's construction of a complex yet challenging theory, except perhaps for the breadth of its foundations. These include his own careful analysis of human action, speech and thought, and many aspects of his wider philosophy. Because of this exceptional breadth, as well as his remarkably acute reasoning, Aristotle has much to offer that is still timely about literature and its relation to life, topics which are no less vital now than they were twenty-three centuries ago when he wrote.

Aristotle theorized in his work *Poetics* that tragedy results in a catharsis (emotional cleansing) of healing for the audience through their experience of these emotions in response to the suffering of the characters in the drama. He considers it superior when a character passes from good fortune to bad rather than the reverse; at the time, the term "tragedy" was not yet fixed solely on stories with unhappy endings.

Catharsis is a Greek word meaning "purification" or "cleansing" derived from the ancient Greek gerund *kocooipeiv* transliterated as *Kathairein* to purify, purge, and "adjective *Katharos*" "pure or clean".

The term in drama refers to a sudden emotional breakdown or climax that constitutes overwhelming feelings of great sorrow, pity, laughter any extreme change in emotion that results in the restoration, renewal and revitalization for living.

The term 'catharsis' referred to a form of emotion cleansing was first used by Aristotle in his work *Poetics*. It refers to the sensation, or literary effect, that would ideally overcome an audience upon finishing watching a tragedy (a release of pent-up emotion or energy). In his previous works, he used the term in its medical sense (usually referring to the evacuation of the "Katamenia" the menstrual fluid or other reproductive material). Because of this, F.L. Lucas maintains that *catharsis* cannot be properly translated as *purification* or *cleansing*, but only as *purgation*. Since before poetics *cathoarsis* was purely a medical term, Aristotle is employing it as a medical metaphor. "It is the human soul that is purged of its excessive excessive passions" Lessing sidesteps the medical aspect of the issue and translates *catharsis* as a purification, an experience that brings pity and fear into their proper balance: "In real life he explained, men are sometimes too much addicted to pity or fear, sometimes too little; tragedy brings them back to a virtuous and happy mean." Tragedy is then a corrective; through watching tragedy the audience learns how to feel these emotions at the proper levels. Some modern interpreters of the work infer that catharsis is pleasurable because audience members felt *ekstasies* (literally; astonishment, meaning: *trance*) from the fact that there existed those who could suffer a worse fate than them was to them a relief. Any translator attempting to interpret Aristotle's meaning of the term should take into account that *Poetics* is largely a response to Plato's claim that poetry encourages men to be hysterical and uncontrolled. In response to Plato, Aristotle maintains that poetry makes them less, not more, emotional, by giving a periodic and healthy outlet to their feelings.

In literary aesthetics, catharsis is developed by the conjunction of stereotyped characters and unique or surprising actions. Throughout a play we do not expect the nature of a character to change significantly, rather pre-existing elements are revealed in a relatively straight forward way as the character is confronted with unique actions in time. This can be clearly seen in Oedipus Rex where King Oedipus is confronted with ever more outrageous actions until emptying generated by the death of his mother-wife and his act of self-blinding. As a literary effect, catharsis should be compared with the equivalent effects for epic and poetic forms of Kairosis and Kenosis.

In contemporary aesthetics catharsis may also refer to any emptying of emotion experienced by an audience in relation to drama. This exstasis can be perceived in comedy, melodrama and most other dramatic forms. Deliberate attempts, on political or aesthetic bases, to subvert the structure of catharsis in theatre have occurred. For example, Bertold Brecht viewed catharsis as a pap for the bourgeois theatre audience, and designed dramas which left significant emotions unresolved, as a way to force social action upon the audience. In Brecht's theory, the absence of a cathartic resolving action would require the audience to take political action in the real world in order to fill the emotional gap they experience. This technique can be seen as early as his agit-prop play *The Measure Taken*.

Poetics provides no explicit reply to Plato's argument that tragedy, comedy and epic stir up our emotions, which we should instead seek to control. Since this aspect of his attack on poetry is so important, scholars have rightly assumed that Aristotle tried to answer it.

Aristotle accepted that these kinds of poetry have powerful emotional effects on the audience, since he often says so in the *Poetics*. In fact he defines the function of tragedy as the "Catharsis" of emotions *i.e.* their "purgation" or "purification"; the presence of catharsis in his definition of tragedy proves its importance to his theory, but he gives no further explanation. In a passage on the use of music and poetry in education (*politics* VIII 7. 1341b37-40), he speaks briefly of catharsis and promises a bull account of it is the poetics; since no such account appears in that part of the text we still have, he is most probably referring to its second book (can comedy) now lost. The *On Poets* seems also to have discussed this question. If we are to understand his poetic theory completely, this gap needs to be filled.

Scholars have tried to reconstruct Aristotle's view of catharsis in two ways, either by comparing what he says in Politics VIII with his account of the emotional effects of tragedy in the *Poetics,* or by searching for later writers who knew his theory directly or indirectly; both approaches are valuable. The relevant passages from the *Politics* and from these later writers are newly collected, translated and equipped with notes in this volume; some of them have not appeared in English before. Since the later writers who talk about catharsis seem to have known the theory from the more widely read *On Poets* rather than from *Poetics II.*

The interpretation of catharsis which has prevailed until very recently is that advanced by Jacob Bernays, in a famous essay published in 1857. At *Politics* VIII. 1342 a 4-16 Aristotle explains tragic catharsis by comparing it with the healing of people suffering from hysterical outbreaks of emotion (*enthousasmos*); these people are cured by 'cathartic songs', which *arouse* their emotions and thereby relieve them. Bernays concluded that the catharsis we obtain from tragedy is a similar process of psychological healing; we all have build-ups of undesirable commotions of pity and terror which can be aroused and then released by watching tragedy.

Bernay's medical interpretation allows the theory of catharsis to answer Plato's point that poetry stimulates undesirable emotions, but it is otherwise unsatisfactory. His view makes catharsis an accidental by product of tragedy, rather than something essential to its nature, as Aristotle implies by including it in his definition of tragedy (*Poetics* L1 a b 27). According to Bernay's theory the best audience for a tragedy, in terms of its emotional effect, would surely be an audience of people who are emotionally disturbed and unbalanced. This seems peculiar; in the

Poetics Aristotle implies several times that ordinary audiences are inferior to the man of judgement, who is no doubt a philosopher, and therefore less subject to emotional disturbance. The Poetics assumes normal audiences in normal emotional states, and nowhere suggests that we go to the theatre for the same reason that we visit the doctor. Moreover, Bernays assumes that the emotions are inherently undesirable, just as Plato thought; but we see that Aristotle did not regard them as necessarily undesirable in themselves.

The term *catharsis* has also been adopted by modern psychotherapy, particularly Freudian psychoanalysis, to describe the act of expressing deep emotions often associated with events in the individual's past which have never before been adequately expressed. Catharsis is also an emotional release associated with talking about the underlying causes of problem (it was first mentioned by Aristotle: catharsis associated with audience watching tragic plays).

Another meaning under the heading of purging can concern body and soul—in it concerns efforts made to come to terms with guilt and sin, penance such as by chastisement (in modern use of that word, the meaning of punishment has taken over from the original sense of purification), such as practiced by flagellants; a testimony to the age of this use is the very name of the Cathars (a medical sect).

In Mysticism, the end of human life and of philosophy is to realize the mystical return of the soul to God. Freeing itself from the sensuous world by katharsis, the purified human soul ascends by successive steps through the various degrees of the metaphysical order, until it units itself in a clear and completely conscious contemplation to the One, and unifies into the state of ecstasies.

Thus in the neo-Platonism of Plotinus, the first step in the return of the soul to God is the act by which the soul, withdrawing from the world of sense by a process of purification (Katharsis) free itself from the trammels of matter. A point to note here is that psychology and philosophy were not separate in classical philosophy (Greek through Roman Period). Thus in classical mysticism, as well as current mystical traditions, Katharsis is a process leading to the transcending of psychological as well as spiritual, traumas and negativities.

As catharsis might be a purgation, fear can obviously be an insidious thing undermines life and poisons it with anxiety. It would be good to flush this feeling from our systems, bring it into the open, and clear the air. This may explain the appeal of horror move that they redirect our fears toward something external, grotesque, and finally ridiculous, in us puncture them. On the hand, fear might have a secret allure, so that what we need to do is the desire for the thrill that comes wit fear. The horror movie also provides a safe way to join and satisfy the longing to feel afraid, and go home afterward satisfied, the desire is purged, and temporarily by being bed. Our souls are so many-headed that opposite satisfactions may be at the same time, but I think these two really are opposite. In the first sense of purgation, the horror movie is a kind of medicine that does its work and leaves the soul healthier, while on the way its sense is a potentially addictive drug. Either explanation may account for the popularity of the movies among teenageres, since fear is so much a fact of that time of life. For those of us who are older, the tear-jerker may have more appeal, offering a way to purge the regrets of our lives with sentimental outpouring of pity. As with fear, this purgation too may be either medicinal or the like.

This idea of purgation, in its various forms, is what we usually mean when we call something cathartic. People speak of watching football, or boxing, as a catharsis of violent urges, or can shouting match with a friend a useful catharsis of buried resentment. This is a practical purgation that drama may also serve but it has no particular connection with beauty or truth, to be going this purgative way, a drama has no need to be good in any other way. No one would be tended to confuse the feeling at the end of a horror movie with what Aristotle calls "the tragic pleasure" to call such a movie a tragedy. But the English word catharsis does not contain everything as in the Greek word. Let us look at other things it might mean.

Catharsis in Greek can mean purification. While purging something getting rid of it, and purifying something means getting red with worse or baser parts of it. It is impossible that tragedy purifies the feelings themselves of fear and pity. These arise in us in crude ways, attached to sorts of objects. Perhaps the poet educates our sensibilities, our powers to fell and be moved refining them and attaching them to less easily discernible objects. There is a line in *the Wasteland*, "I will show you fear in a handful of dust." Alfred Hitchcood once made us all, in little shudder when we took showers. The poetic imagination is limited only by its skill, and turn any object into a focus for any feeling. Some people turn to poetry to find delicious and exquisite new ways to feel old feelings, and consider themselves to enter in that way into a purified state. It has been argued that this sort of thing is what tragedy, and the tragic pleasure all about, but it does not match up with my experiences. Sophocles does make us fear and pity human knowledge when we watch the *Oedipus Tyrannus*, but this is not a refinement of those feelings but a discovery that they belong to a surprise object. Sophocles is not training our feelings, but using them to show us something worthy of wonder. The tragic pleasure is a paradox. As Aristotle says, in a tragedy, a happy ending does not make happy at the end of the play the stage is often littered with bodies, and we feel cleansed by it.

The Poetics indicates that poetry's arousal of the emotions is connected with the core of Aristotle's poetic theory i.e. his concept of representation. This is especially evident when he says that the tragic poet must aim to bring about the pleasure that comes from pity and terror by means of representation (53b12). Pity and terror are painful emotions in themselves, but much depends on why we feel them. Aristotle is distinguishing between experiencing pity and terror in real life, which is not pleasant, and experiencing them because the tragic representation which leads to the pleasure proper to tragedy. Similarly at 48b10-12 he says that we derive pleasure from seeing representations even of things that are painful to look at in actuality. According to the argument of the *Poetics*, if the action represented (the plot) is correctly structured, it will arouse in the audience the correct emotional response; in the case of tragedy this is pity and terror. If the action is badly structured, it will arouse the wrong emotional response, which Aristotle calls "shock" or "revulsion" (52b36) literally "dirtiness"—the opposite, surely, of *catharsis*, which means "cleansing" or "purification". This show that the theory of catharsis is not an accidental appendage to the rest of Aristotle's literary theory, but an essential part of it.

To progress further, we need to consider Aristotle's general view of the emotions. Plato tended to regard them as merely irrational, but Aristotle considered them an important factor in taking correct decisions and forming good character. In his Ethics he argues that we should feel the correct emotion towards the right object, at the right time to the proper degree and so forth. There are things about which it is right to feel e.g. anger, pity or terror; such correct emotional reactions as proper compassion, justified anger and the right degree of courage can and should affect decision or moral choice. It is important to feel the emotions lightly. For example, if we feel too much fear, we are cowardly, but we feel too little we are foolhardy; only if we feel fear to the correct extent, no more no less, are we courageous. Such correct reactions, attain the means between the extremes; in Aristotle's view, this is where virtue lies, e.g. Courage is the virtue lying at the mid-point between the extremes, namely cowardice and foolhardiness, which are both errors relative to it.

For Aristotle, one of the main factors in the building of good character is to develop a settled disposition to feel emotion correctly, since this will lead to good decisions, Just as, in Aristotle's moral theory, we become good by habitually doing good, so too by feeling emotion appropriately (towards the right object, at the right time etc.) we become habituated to having the right emotional responses, those emotional responses which attain the mean between the extremes; these help us to take the correct decisions, so that we come nearer to the mean, where virtue lies, and become virtuous in character.

Now poetry offers an obvious way in which we can learn these responses without the hazardous process of undergoing in actuality the experiences represented in poetry. By responding emotionally to the representation, we can learn to develop the correct emotional responses. Aristotle says precisely this about music, *in which he includes poetry*, at *Politics* VIII 5. 134 Oa 14-25, translated in this volume as Testimonial A(i) on catharsis.

Thus poetry undoubtedly has an educative and moral function, that is, it helps to form character. This may seem to have little to do with catharsis, but the later writers indicate that it did. Thus Proclus, explicitly referring to Aristotle, says that tragedy and comedy make it possible to satisfy the emotions in due measure and by satisfying them, to keep them tractable for *education*. The remarkable new text about catharsis from Herculaneum states "poetry is useful with regard to virtue, *purifying*, as we said, the [related] part [of the soul]" [*on poets*]. This text even indicates that catharsis applies no less to errors in the intellectual virtue of practical intelligence, than to errors of character and emotion, like excessive fear: poetry contributes to virtue as a whole, which in Aristotle's moral theory depends on both intellect and character. Catharsis and the mean in terms of the emotions are also linked by Iambilihus and the *Tractatus Coislinianus*.

Unfortunately Aristotle himself never states this clearly in his surviving works; but it accords with his theories of character and education, and also with the general sense of his discussion of catharsis in the *Politics*. There he says that music (and poetry) confer three benefits, the education of children, catharsis and entertainment. Like the songs used for healing abnormal emotional states, which produce a catharsis in hysterical people, tragedy produces "a sort of catharsis of pity and terror, but this affects everybody, insofar as we are all prone to excess in the emotions to some degree. From this statement it surely follows that tragedy reduces these emotions so that they are no longer excessive and divergent from the mean, but in due proportion and in accord with it. Both kinds of catharsis are homeopathic; both work on the emotions by arousing the emotions, just as we treat a fever by piling on blankets.

If the interpretation advanced above is right, tragedy confers the other two benefits as well.

It is obviously a form of entertainment, a concept which Aristotle associates not merely with relaxation but also with acquiring intelligence. However, like the poetry used in education (which surely includes Homer), tragedy also habituates us to feel the correct emotional as well as intellectual responses to the people and actions it represents; this is important for the development of good character and virtue. Thus catharsis falls in between—and combine—education and entertainment.

If this ethical aspect of catharsis is accepted Aristotle's theory becomes a complete answer to Plato and a far more subtle and sophisticated one. The above interpretation seems superior to Bernays; because it accords better with Aristotle's view of the emotions and their relation to character, it shows how catharsis is an integral part of poetry, as a representation of actions which arouse the emotions, and it explains how catharsis can benefit everyone, not just people who are emotionally unstable.

Taking tragedy as an example, the cathartic process works as follows. By representing pitiable, terrifying and other painful events, tragedy arouses pity, terror and other painful emotions in the audience, for each according to his won emotional capacity, and so stimulates these emotions as to relieve them by giving them moderate and harmless exercise, thereby bringing the audience nearer to the mean in their emotional responses, and so nearer to virtue in their characters; and with this relief comes pleasure. Comedy works on the pleasant emotions in the same way.

CRITICAL THEORIES AND APPROACHES TO LITERATURE

10

Sociological Approach

Sociological approach to literature, takes into account, the author's social origin and the socio-cultural background in which he is born and brought up. It is an attempt to relate the author with the social surroundings, because the social surroundings affect the author's sensibility and goes on in the making of the literary creation by that author. The study of this background—of the social surrounding naturally, helps the reader to understand the literary creation a great deal, as it places the book/the creation in a proper perspective. This approach is the oldest approach as old as the Homeric epics for man and society is something which has even been present. But a systematic and deliberate efforts to relate the two has been rather late only after the development of Sociology as an independent social science. Because Sociology studies in detail and is a systematic way the relationship between the man and his social surrounding. Marx and Engels added a new dimension to sociological approach with their emphasis on means and methods of production and their impact on the society and ultimately on the individual sensibility. Marxist approach became an important aspect of sociological approach of literary criticism and it exercised considerable influence throughout the world quite for sometime and soon abated as most of the exponents of Marxist approach withdrew themselves from the movement.

Sociological criticism is a next step to historical criticism. It assumes a close relationship between society and literature. Sociological criticism considers the writers and their literature as direct products of the sociological forces in the. History of the period. Therefore, sociological critics believes that sociological conditions of Elizabethan England produced Shakespeare and

Shakespearean drama. According to sociological criticism the writer is not a free agent; inspiration is nothing but an illusion or it may be only a different name for sociological forces giving birth to an idea in the writer's mind. The writer naturally obeys the forces and drives of the time. His only source of inspiration is the sociological condition of particular time.

Sociological criticism has a two way influence.

1. Sociological forces give birth to a writer and produce literature.
2. Literature also shapes and mould society. This approach has got the following a deficiency—
   (*a*) Here literature simply becomes one of the factors in the Sociological forces.
   (*b*) As political and Economic forces mould the material outlook of man, similarly literature as a sociological factor moulds man's thinking.
   (*c*) Literature moulds social thinking; social thinking produces literature and thus the cycle of social change goes on.
   (*d*) In other words sociological criticism asserts that the writer is a product of sociological forces and is himself a sociological force.

The basic principle behind sociological criticism is as old as criticism itself e.g. Plato in his "Republic" recognizes the sociological aspect and function of literature. Similarly Aristotle also considers the Sociological aspect of literature in his "Poetics". However they consider it only with reference to the influence which the poet and his poetry can have on society and not vice-versa. Modern sociological criticism takes a different view of the matter. It says that the poet and writer simply give back to society what they have first received from it.

The father of modern sociological criticism John Baptista in his book "Principles of a New Criticism" develops this approach. He states that the sociological factors in the history of the times determine the tone and temper of the writer. Herder in Germany took literature as the product of national and temporal conditions.

In England, Pope and Johnson tried to explain Shakespeare in terms of the culture and sociology of his age. In France, Modern de Stael, Michelet and Renan gave socio-historical interpretation of literature. Thus sociological criticism has a long history, however the man who first gave theoretical basis for sociological criticism is H.A. Taine, the French critic and historian. According to him there are three controlling factors which determine the character of literature—

1. Race—which means the national and racial characteristics.
2. Milieu-which means the trend or the flow of social events.
3. Moment-which means the demands and compulsion of the moment.

Thus the sociological criticism tried to find correlation between the individual authors and the circumstances of the social and cultural era in which they live and write. They try to find, the relation of a literary whole to the segment of the society, to which the work is addressed. Literature represent life and life is in large measure, a social reality. The poet, too is a member of society, possessed of a specific social status. He receives some degree of recognition and reward, he addresses and audience with the help of literature which has a social function or use. Thus, a large majority of the question raised by literaty study are social questions, questioning tradition and conventions, norms and genre, symbols and myths. Questions are asked about the relations of literature to a given social situation in economic, social and political system. Attempts are made to describe and define the influence of society on literature and to prescribe and judge the position of literature in society.

Literature studied as a reflection of the spirit of the age creates a new spirit for us. With its help, we travel into the minds of the other races and ther minds of the other races and the minds of other epochs. Thus it becomes a sort of sociological approach, a supplementary and commentary on history. Once we are steeped in the spirit of a by-gone age, we are able to enjoy even archaic books which otherwise would not appeal to us.

We do not find any interest in the novels of Richardson or Fielding, if they are studied as the books of social facts. Even we do not find charm in the *Spectator, The Faerie Queene* and *Arcadia,* if they are studied for understanding the ages of their respective authors. Thus it is an admitted fact that if the work of a writer merely reflects the spirit of his times, it cannot be a great literature. It is a very useful piece of valuable material for the sociologist and the historian. It is entirely devoid of the virtue of permanence and universality. The literature of the Greeks should not appeal to an Indian or a German mind if its historical factor is taken into consideration. Similarly, Shakespeare should not be regarded a great dramatist, if he simply and purely reflects the Elizabethan period. The essence of literature lies in the individual approach of the author, his personality which will dominate over other influences. Undoubtedly, the author is shaped by the spirit of his age, but he has also got the capabilities to mould his period. A great man of letters is the creature as well as the creator of the age in which he exists. Thus we talk of the age of Shakespeare, the age of Dryden, the age of Pope, the age of Wordsworth, the age of Bernard Shaw, and so on. Milton's *Paradise Lost,* was a great challenge to the age of cynicism, low morals and satirical literature. This mighty book does not reveal the time-spirit of his age. Milton revolted rather than expressed the spirit of his times. Similarly, in spite of all the atmosphere of heroism, noble ideas, and love of song and drama, the Elizabethan age could not produce another Shakespeare. The original, mysterious and incommunicable element of personal genius of Shakespeare made him the dramatist for all ages and time. It is this factor which gives an abiding and universal appeal to the work of a great writer.

W.H. Hudson strongly supports the sociological approach. The very fact that the important writers of a common era share common features of their writing, however diverse their personality and show the heavy influence of their contemporary society on their creative faculty. Shakespeare in spite of his unique creative talents, had a lot in common with Marlowe, Jonson, Fletcher and Webster.

The dependence of the author on the audience/reader is even greater. One interesting and important case is that of theatre goers. The type of theatre-audience has always determined the type of drama in English literature. The comic episodes of Shakespeare's historicals and tragedies were written to satisfy the groundlings. The obscenity and profligacy of the 18th century Comedy of

Manners are traced to the taste of the audience of the period, decline in drama at the beginning of the 19th century is associated with the theatre goer's disgust with this type of drama. The role of such social institutions and associations as the salon, the café, the club, the academy and the university in creating an audience response is studied. It is said that in modern America, the women are the active determinants in deciding literary taste. The rise of the novel in 18th century in England is traced to the leisure enjoyed by women of the contemporary society.

Another important factor of sociological criticism is that—literature to a great extent reveals the type of contemporary society, gives interesting sociological data and documents. Chaucer is the representative poet of the 14th century. His masterpiece the *Canterbury Tales* reveals the political, economic and social conditions of the time. This poem has the true colour and aroma of the fourteenth century England. He holds the mirror upto the life of his time. The Prologue to this poem gives us the background of the action and movement of the pilgrims who make up the company. All these pilgrims represent the whole of English society of the fourteenth century.

Being the product of his age, Spenser was not lacking in the defects of the Renaissance. This age has certain drawbacks, such as exaggeration; diffuseness and prolixity which are the common literary Flaws. It was the fashion on this age to give an elaborate story with certain anecdotes in it. Spenser devised the story of *The Faerie Queen* in this manner. It is a story with so many anecdotes which make it diffusive and prolix. In a nutshell, he was deeply affected by the Renaissance. His works were the embodiment of the high ideals which were directly taken from the Italian poets and Greek philosophers. The influence of the Reformation could be also seen in this great epic *The Faerie Queen,* which is a very useful document which conveys realistically Christian dogmas. The book itself is the outline history of the Reformation in England. Marlowe's plays especially *Doctor Faustus* is a best example of Renaissance play. Milton was as much a child of the Renaissance as of the Reformation. Milton's *Lycidas* is directly associated with the Renaissance and its classicism.

Pope was for a whole generation 'the poet of a great nation.' He was a remarkably clear and adequate reflection of the spirit of the age in which he lived. There was hardly on ideal, a belief, a doubt, a fashion, a whim of Queen Anne's time that is not neatly expressed in his poetry. *The Rape of the Lock* is one of the greatest of mock-heroic poems. It pictures the frivolities of the time. In it all the pecularities of society are pictured in the minutest detail and satirized with the most delicate wit. It is perfect in its way as expressing the artificial life of the age—its cards, parties, toilettes, lap-dogs, tea-drinking, snuff-taking and ideal vanities.

The French Revolution brought to Europe the hope of political freedom and social reconstruction. Though the hope was dashed to the ground with the accession to power of Napoleon, its place was taken by the enthusiasm of the struggle of the nations against old regimes. Wordsworth was deeply saturated with the dogmas of the French Revolution. The Prelude analyses as well as communicates the progress of Wordsworth's political sympathies. The French Revolution stirred in him republican sympathies, which were strengthened by his visit to France. Shelley was also the most melodious singer of the Revolution and the poet of revolutionary idealism.

Tennyson was the representative poet of the Victorian Age. This works reflect the tendencies, the aspirations and the problems that agitated the minds of men of his age. *The Dickens World* by Humphery House is the most admirable work of sociological criticism. The author makes his points by aulternating between sections giving account of the changing historical scenes in Docken's days and illustration of the reflection of this changing scenes in Dickens novels. Dicken's *Oliver Twist* discusses the problem of child labour, warehouse, gangsters in the society, and other social evils of the day. Dicken's *A Tale of Two Cities* records the history of the period.

Sociological approach to a literary work is more helpful to fiction than to poetry, for the obvious reason that fiction, particularly novel deals largely with social issue while poetry tends to communicate a more private vision of reality. Robinson, Crusoe, on finding himself alone on an island, did not seek to exploit his loneliness by meditation on the relation between man and the universe. His task was to recreate in this distant isolation the skeleton at least of the civilization he had left behind him. The novelist, at least a majority of them, draw their material out of the social conventions. The eighteenth and nineteenth century novel, therefore, is particularly a happy hunting ground for the sociological critic.

On the other hand, a sociological approach has been bought to bear on poetry mostly by the Marxists. However, such critics like F.W. Bateson in his *English Poetry : A Critical Introduction* discusses Gray's *Elegy Written in a Country Churchyard* from sociological point of view which is in sharp contrast in method with Cleanth Brooks analysis of the poem in *The Well Wrought Urn*. T.S. Eliots poem *The Waste Land* poses a difficult problem while being looked at from sociological point of view. First, because it is 'modern' and Modernism does not really bother much about society, while it could be said that the Moderns turned inward as a result of what they described the disgusting social realities. From that point of view a novel like *Ulysses* or *Women in Love*, or Pound's *Mauberley Poems* could be looked at from sociological viewpoint and could be linked with society but generally Modern literature calls is another approach—*Forma Approach* as it is called, because it stresses too much form, style and technique. A poem like *The Waste Land* which is a landmark of modern poetry is famous for its technical complexity so much so that when the poem appeared for the first time in 1922. It annoyed many readers of poetry even the serious reader who asked the poet to add certain notes to the poem. Eliot did the likewise, but the notes themselves become a subject of study and research rather than the original poem. Apart from this technical aspect the poem is also famous for the poet's concern for the contemporary society. The poet really draws the sociology of his time throughout the poem. The early decades of this century had seen the decline of religious faith and moral decay. The early, warmth in human relation has disappeared, and money had come to play a prominent part in human transaction. The traditional concept of love change into a mere desire for sex. Even the sexual act—the relationship between man and woman had become purely mechanical. The institution of marriage came to be undervalued and the relationship between the spouses had become strained. This was the sociology of the time when Eliot wrote the poem and the sociology is very much present throughout the poem. The entire poem is about sociology of the time which Eliot looked upon as distorted and devoid of human/spiritual/moral values. The distorted state of affairs in society made him sad, gloomy. It was, however, an inevitable outcome of various fators which worked togethers to produce what Eliot calls *The Waste Land.*

Sociological Criticism and Marxism

Although the sociological approach to literature has been widely used by the critics in the earlier, it was with the spreading of the ideas of Karl Marx that this approach became a scientific method of literary interpretation. In the twentieth century Marxist critics emphasized the relationship between literature and society and the social change evidenced in literature. Literature, so far, was considered a reflection of society but society undergoes a continuous process of change which would inevitably be projected in literature. Marx and Engels thought that the essence, the nature and function of literature and art, could be understood only by relating it to the prevailing social conditions and by analyzing the social system as a whole. Literature and art, as considered by them, are forms of social consciousness and social change is bound to create changes in literature and art.

In the Marxist Approach, Marx never formulated a sociology of art but his incidental discussions of literature and art concern a wide range of aesthetic, political and economic issues. The Marxist critic is very clear about his stance from which he writes : the text has to be read in the light of an all informing philosophy. It has to be seen in relation to a Marxist view of history in which the idea of class struggle is central.

According to Marxist, the view that literature, particularly poetry, is an expression of divine inspiration or an inner subjective pressure of a mysterious nature is untrue and untenable. In fact the nature and mode of economic production create social relations in which men enter to form class relations and these class relations formed, legitimatized and fostered in a particular way, on the mental level, become the ideology of the society. In the Marxist view literature and art try to stabilize the ideology, which in its turn, mediates between the *praxis* (social practice) of the ruling class and its consciousness. When the productive relations enter into contradiction there would arise new forms of consciousness, new ideologies to be stabilized by new forms of art and literature.

Christopher Caudell and Raymond Williams have made valuable contribution to sociological criticism in general and

Marxist criticism in particular. Althusser's major contribution lies in his efforts at redefining the concept of ideology.

The demerits of Marxist criticism are—

1. This type of criticism makes the writer a tool of Marxist Philosophy.
2. This type of criticism is very likely to produce the propagandist literature.
3. It would make the writer a slave to the sociological force of his time.
4. Marxist criticism may give rise to capitalist-oriented criticism also.

Socialist Feminism

As a form of sociological criticism, feminist criticism shares some qualities with Marxist approaches. Both are critical of society, as it is presently constituted. Both are concerned with the lives of those oppressed or marginalized by the dominant culture. Both investigate literature as a means of bringing about changes in attitudes and ultimately in society. Socialist feminists set three main goals for themselves. They are—

1. To achieve a combination of breadth and precision, so that all forms of oppression are explored and that exploration is anchored in women's experiences. Here the stress is on finding out different forms of oppression of women; either within the family or outside. Then to develop a common agenda for women's movements.
2. To develop explicit and adequate methods for social analysis by standing in on expanded notion of historical materialism. All types of socialist feminisms rely on historical materialism. Throughout history material culture, system of production are owned by one class (capitalist) and used it as a weapon to exploit labour class. This labour also include labour class women. Hence, socialist feminists aim to find out different methods to gain information and to use it.
3. To treat ideas as equal to material production in determining human affairs. This is specially with reference to women.

An important idea of socialist feminism is that in a capitalist society marriage and patriarchal family acts like a capitalist unit. On a smaller scale it reproduces conflict and contradiction of wider society. Wives are like labour class and the patriarchal head of the family is like an exployer or owner of the unit. Yet socialist feminist do not look of men as their enemies. This is because they say like women are exploited in capitalist society and men act as the agents of the system. In the process, men are also oppressed. Hence, men and women should unite together to fight against the system.

This is general socialist movement. Within this separate feminist movement was felt necessary because in the existing movement men activist were not interested in women's problems or issues. To them class conflict and labour movement were important. They ignored the double oppression of women as workers and housewives. Perhaps some of these men activists are also the agent of the system and responsible for women's oppression in family. This is the most active group among feminist. Using Marx and Engel's frame-work they have observed and analyzed women's problems. Oppressed women's involvement in the struggle, is achieved by socialist feminist.

The sociological criticism thus lets us know the social factors which have influenced literary techniques and tastes. Literature is not only the effect of social causes but also the cause of social effects. But we must understand that literature does not confine itself to socials truth only. More important than the social realism is the artistic truth. Therefore when a critic says that a writer is a representative of his age he should underscore the fact that a writer reflects through his work not only the spirit of his age but also the quintessence of human nature and thus lays bare his individual talent. The writer as the representative of his age is to be appreciated for his artistic truth rather than for social realism.

The sociological approach thus helps the reader to see why certain poets and dramatists wrote as they did not what the moral pattern of their work really is. The sociological approach illuminates the reader about the differences between contemporary writers. The sociological criticism thus helps to increase the reader's literary perception and to explain the origins of the literary works.

11

Psychoanalytic Criticism

Critics, rhetoricians, and philosophers since Aristotle have examined the psychological dimensions of literature, ranging from an author's motivation and intentions to the effect of texts and performances on the audience. The application of psychoanalytic principles to the study of literature, however, is a relatively recent phenomenon, initiated primarily by Freud and, in other directions, by Alfred Adler and Carl Jung. The notion of the "unconscious" was not in itself new, and it can be found in many thinkers prior to Freud, notably in some of the Romantics such as Schlegel, in Schopenhauer and in Nietzsche. Freud's fundamental contribution was to open up the entire realm of the unconscious to systematic study, and to provide a language and terminology in which the operations of the unconscious could be expressed.

Most psychoanalytic methods produce texts, and most use texts such as dreams, narrative, slips of tongue, jokes, but also bodily symptoms for their investigations. Freud employ Greek myths (most prominently Oedipus and Narcissus) for his crucial concepts. Jung scrutiniscs fairy tales and folklore, eastern and western religion, even alchemy. Neither differentiates between stories by actual patients and those inherited by literature and culture. This trend continues into the late twentieth century, as is evident in Lacan's analyis of Eagar Allan Poe's story 'The Purloined Letter'. Eventually, psychoanalytic text themselves have become objects of analysis, as in the writings of Abraham and Torok, who, analyse Freud's analysis of the psychological case study the 'Wolf Man'.

Text-based in its methods, psychoanalysis shares with literature the poieses of images and expressions, the poetics of their arrangements, the grammar of narratives, but also theory of inter-pretation. The latter frequently abandons the idea of an origin of symptoms (in empirical fact or transcendent metaphysics and instead refers to other texts, previous traumas or archetypal images and stories that are closely related to myth. Modern literary theory calls this 'intertexuality'. Psychoanalytic theories also refer to their material in literary terms: the poetry of dreams, the drama of urscenes, and the narratives that emerge from them. Moreover they have inspired texts in all these genres: from the poetry of Sylvia Plath via Thitchcok's psycho-drama to fiction such as D.M. Thomas The White Hotel and the works of Angela Carter.

Psychoanalytic thought add a great deal to the study of literature. What Psychoanalysis can contribute to literature are as follows.

(1) Psychoanalysis is a "talking cure"; language and narrative are fundamental to it. In a sense psychoanalytic therapy is the re-narratization of a Person's life.

(2) As psychoanalysis deals with language and with interpretation, it introduces a significant approach to the hermeneutics of suspicion, the idea that there are motives and meanings which are disguised by and work through other meanings. The "permeneutics of suspicion" (Paul Ricoeur's term) is not limited to psychoanalytic thought but is found in structural thought generally ...... the idea that we look, to understand action, to sub-texts, not pre-texts.

(3) Psychoanalysis deals with motives, especially hidden or disguisted motives: as such it helps clarify literature on two levels, the level of the writing itself, and the level of character action within the text. A 'companion' level to the level of writing, is the level of reading; both reading and writing as they respond to motives not always available to rational thought, can be illumined by psychoanalytic thought.

(4) Psychoanalysis opens the nature of the subject : who it is who is experiencing, what our relationships of meaning and identity are to the psychic and cultural forces which ground so much of our being. This understanding, particularly in terms of Lacan's sense that the subject is ex-centric to itself, is very important in contemporary

understandings of reading, meaning, and the relation of literature to culture.

(5) Psychoanalysis examines the articulation of our most private anxieties and meanings to culture and gives us a perspective on them as cultural formations.

(6) Psychoanalysis looks to culture as informative of our deepest psychic levels.

(7) Psychoanalysis deals with the relations of 'body meanings (what Kristeva would call, in her formulation, the 'semiotic') and derives to symbol or cultural, meaning.

(8) Psychoanalytic thought is part of the project of much 20th Century thought to 'correct' the Cartesian mind/body split, to see humans as bodily, incarnate beings. Psychoanalysis tends to read this split as a de racination of the self from its vital and formative being.

(9) Psychoanalysis constitutes one approach to the questions of good and evil, and especially of suffering and error, which plague us as humans.

Psychoanalytic criticism adopts the method of "reading" employed by Freud and later theorists to interpret texts. It argues that literary texts, like dreams, express the secret unconscious desires and anxieties of the author, that a literary work is a manifestation of the authors own the within a literary work, but it is usually assumed that all such characters are projections of the author's psyche.

One interesting facet of this approach is that it validates the importance of literature, as it is built on a literary key for the decoding Freud himself wrote, "The dream-thoughts which we first come across as we proceed with our analysis often strike us by the unusual form in which they are expressed; they are not clothed in the prosaic language usually employed by our thoughts, but are on the contrary represented symbolically by means of similies and metaphors in images resembling those of poetic speech."

Like psychoanalysis itself, 'this critical endeavor seeks evidence of unresolved emotions, psychological conflicts, guilts, ambivalences, and so forth within what may, well be a disunified literary work. The author's own childhood traumas family' life, sexual conflicts, fixations. amd such will be traceable within the behavior of the characters in the literary work. But psychological material will be expressed indirectly, disguised, or encoded as in dreams through principles such as "symbolism" (the repressed object represented in disguise), "condensation" (several thoughts or persons represented in a single image' and "displacement" (anxiety located onto another image by means of association.

Psychological critics view works through the lens of psychology. They look either at the psychological motivations of the characters or of the authors themselves, although the former is generally considered a more respectable approach. Most frequently psychological critics apply Freudian psychology to works but other approaches (such as Jungian approach) also exist. A Freudian approach often includes pinpointing the influences of a characters (the instinctual, pleasure seeking part of the mind), (the part of the mind that represses the id's impulses), and the (the part of the mind that controls but does not repress the id's impulses releasing them in a healthy way). Freudian critics like to point out the sexual implications of symbols and imagery, since Freud's believed that all human behavior is motivated by sexuality. They tend to see images, such as ponds, flowers, cups, and caves as female symbols; whereas objects that are longer than they are wide are usually seen as male. Dancing, riding and flying are associated with sexual pleasure. Water is usually associated with birth, the female principle, the maternal, the womb, and the death wish.

Freud was aware of the problematic nature of language itself, its openness and materiality, its resistance to clarity and its refusal to be reduced to any one-dimensional "literal" meaning. His own writings contain many literary allusions and some of his major concepts, such as the Oedipus complex' were founded on literary models such as *Oedipus Rex* and *Hamlet*. Freud's own literary analyses tend to apply his models of dream interpretation to literary texts, viewing the latter as expressions of wish fulfillment and gratifying projections of the ego of an author. Subsequent psychologists and literary critics, developing the Freud's ideas have extended the field of psychoanalytic criticism to encompass: analysis of the notives of an author, of readers and fictional characters, relating a text to features of the author's biography such as childhood memories, relationship to parents; the nature, of the creative process; the psychology of reader's responses to literary texts; interpretation of symbols in a text, to unearth latent meanings; analysis of the connection between various authors in a literary tradition; examination of gender roles and stereotypes; and the functioning of language in the constitution of the conscious and unconscious. What underlies nearly all of these endeavors is the perception of a broad analogy, fostered by Freud himself between the psychoanalytic process and the production of a narrative. In a sense, the psychoanalyst himself creates a fiction: triggered by a patient's neurosis and recollection of traumatic events, the psychoanalyst creates a coherent narrative about the patient withen which the traumatic even can take its place and be understood.

After Freud, psychoanalytic criticism was continued by his biographer Ernest Jones, whose book *Hamlet* and *Oedipus* interpreted 'Hamlet's indecisive behavior in killing his uncle in terms of his ambivalent feelings toward his mother. In an extended defensive of Freud's initial interpretation, Jones sought to prove how the appeal of Shakespeare's play could be accounted for through Hamlet's Oedipal conflict, which he saw as a direct expression of Shakespeares own unresolved Oedipal complexs. These unconscious Oedipal desires then in turn resonate with the unconscious desires of the audience,'which he urges, accounts for the play's universal appeal and timelessness. Jone's interpretation was ingenious but it rested upon a number of fallacies and a large degree of speculation about Shakespeare's life. In order to assert that Hamlet has an unresolved Oedipal conflict we must first assume that he a "real" person rather than a character on the stage. Jones, therefore, must insist on the verisimilitude of Shakespeare's text and ignore its literary and dramatic quality. Second, the critic must accept that the text is merely a symptiom of the author's particular neurosis. Another of Freud's disciples, Otto Rank, produced *The Myth of the Birth of the Hero,* which reaffirmed Freud's notion of the artist producing fantasies of wish fulfillment, and which compiled numerous myths on subjects such as incest, and on the notion of the hero. Ella Freeman Sharpe treated language and metaphor from a psychoanalytic perspective. Melanie Klein modified Freudian theory of sexuality, rejecting the primacy of the Oedipus complex and elaborating a they of the drive.

Marie Bonaparte wrote a large study of Edgar Allon Poe, attributing much of his creative disposition to the loss of his mother when he was a child. In *The Life and Work of Edgar Allan Poe: A Psychoanalytic* Interpretation, Marie Bonaparte argued that the literary work is analogous to a dream or a symptom and thus can be seen to reveal the author's psychopathology. Bonaparte identifies two incidents that irrevocably marked Poe's life: first, the sight of his dead mother and his subsequent infatuation with her; second, a night he spent in the same room as a consumptive rice and the desire this aroused in him. These two instances can be seen to recur in Poe's fiction, albeit in disguised forms, thus his key to understanding Poe's work is deeply repressed sadonecrophilia. As with Jones, Bonaparte uncovers some interesting insights into Poe's life and work but she also shares the problem of directly equating the fictional text with the biography of the author. This problem is further compounded by the analogy between the literary text and the dream.

Another generation of literary critics—not necessarily Freudians-drew upon psychoanalysis in their interpretations of literary texts. These included I.A. Richards, William Empson, Lionel Trilling, Kenneth Burke, and Edmund Wilson, who in various ways searched texts for latent content. Harold Bloom's theory of literary influence as mediated through "anxiety" drew upon Freud's account of the Oedipus complex. Poets and critics such as Robert Graves and W.H. Auden (who wrote a poem in memory of Freud) also had recourse to Freudian concepts in their prose writings. Indeed, the Freud's ideas was so pervasive that it can be seen in the very conception of character in many modern novelists, such as William Faulkner and James Joyce. Interestingly, D.H. Lawrence appears to have arrived independently at idea very similar to Freud's, as for example in his novel *Songs and Lovers*, where Oedipal feelings figure powerfully.

Wilson's comments that the question of creativity can lead us to focus on the psychology of the author might suggest that a text helps to explain the life and concerns of an author and vice versa. For example, Edmund Wilson argues that Sophocles wrote the play *Philoctetes* because he identified with the character. Both Sophocles and Philoctetes experienced madness, Wilson explains, and both were "persons of mysterious virtue, whom their follows are forced to respect." Just as Philoctetes suffered nobly from his physical ailment and went on to win the campaign for the Greeks, Sophocles rose above accusations of incompetence and earned the applause of his fellow men.

Wilson Says that Sophocles used the character of Philoctetes to symbslize both madness and nobility. Thus, Wilson might claim that this character was "overdetermined" This term was used by Freud in his work on dream analysis and refers to the process by which one image takes on more than one meaning. A Freudian literary critic might say that this process was also involved when Joseph Conrad wrote *Heart of Darkness*. The critic Frederick Karl notes that Conrad utilizes the jungle as a symbol not only of what we fear, but also of what we destroy. Through this symbol, Conrad voices his concerns on both political policy and the irrationality of human behavior.

The influence of psychoanalysis has extended into nearly all dimensions of modern literary theory. Simon O Lesser furnished a psychoanalytic account of the reading process. Influenced by Lesser Norman Holland used ego psychology and the notion of the literary texts as fantasy to elaborate his version of reader-response criticism, studying the manner in which texts appeal to the repressed fantasies of readers. Where Freud located the meaning of literary texts in the unconscious fantasy of the author, the ego psychologists see meaning as deriving from what is publicly shareable and socially enclosed. In other words, meaning does not rest in the psyche of the author but in the conventions between reader and text, this kind of criticism is closely aligned with *reader-response theory*. In *The Dynamics of Literary Response* (1968) Norman N. Holland initially argued that the literary text was a kind of fundamental fantasy shared by both author and reader but in subsequent revisions of his work, *Poem in Person* and *Five Readers Reading*, he placed the emphasis for meaning firmaly on the side of the reader. In line with ego psychology, Holland has been concerned with the way in which readers adapt their identity in the process of interpretation and thereby confirm a sense of self and autonomy.

Feminist critics such as Juliet Mitchell have used Freud's ideas in their explanations of the operations of patriarchy; others, such as Kristeva, have modified his notions in undertaking their analyses of language and gender. Members of the Frankfurt School of Marxist thinkers, such as Herbert Marcuse, have enlisted Freudian concepts in their analyses of mass culture and ideology. Other significant theorists include Normean O. Brown, Winnicott, and Gilles Deleuze and Felix Guattare, who have explored the ideological bases of psychoanalysis.

Sigmund Feud

Sigmund Freud was born in 1856 to Jewish parents in Moravia, a small town in what is now the Czech Republic. His father was somewhat aloof and authoritarian while his mother was a warmer and more accessible figure. He took his medical degree in 1881, and was drawn to only one branch of medicine, psychiatry. His acquaintance with the physician Josef Breuer had an enormous impact on his thinking. Within a few years Freud had turned his attention to the study of nervous diseases. Initially influenced by Jean-Martin Charcot's investigations of hysteria, Freud developed the idea that neuroses might have a psychological rather than physiological origin. Freud setted in Venna in 1886 as a specialist in nervous diseases. In 1895 Freud and Breuer jointly published their findings as *Studies on Hysteria,* a texts which stressed the emotional life of the patient, distinguished conscious and unconscious mental acts, and introduced the idea of "conversions" whereby a symptom was viewed as arising from the damming up of an emotional affect or impulse. Freud eventually arrived at a number of conclusion. Firstly, in considering the actiology (the causes and origins) of neuroses, he reasoned that it was not just any kind of emotional excitement behind these but specifically excitement of a sexual nature. Thus, all neuroses, he claimed, derived from disturbances of the sexual function. Freud eventually abandoned hypnosis in favor of what he would call psychoanalysis though he retained his practice of asking the patient to lie upon a sofa with the analyst seated unseen behind him.

Early Psychoanalysis: Hysteria, Dreams and Case Studies

In 1885-86 Freud studied with the famous neurologist Jean-Martin Charcot at the Salpetriere (a mental asylum for hysterical women in Paris), a period in which his interests shifted from neurology to Pathology, and during which he observed the use of hypnotic suggestion in the treatment of hysteria. Current theory held that derived hysteria from interited mental degeneration, "bad blood", abuse of alcohol or syphilis but Charcot showed that hysterical symptoms would vanish when patients were hypnotised, proving that the cause was psychological rather than physiological. After observing the work of Liebault and Bernheim in Nancy in 1889, Freud concluded that hypnosis was of limited therapeutic value and his emphasis shifted to the use of free association as an analytic technique. In 1895, with his friend Josef Breurer, Freud published *studien uber Hysterie* (*studies on Hysteria,* 1936), a report of five case histories, with essays exploring the causation and psychotheraphy of hysteria, in which Freud and Breuer stressed the function of sexuality and repression, the effect of pre-pubertal sexual seduction in causing neurotic illness, and their ability to remove symptoms once the patient could be persuaded to remember and talk about the experience which was its original cause. Freud subsequently abandoned reduction theory in favours of a theory of fantasised in which Freud is accused of concealing actual child abuse).

Freud first deployed the term psychoanalysis in a paper written a French in 1896. The following year he began his self-analysis, after the death of his father at the age of 81. This process of self-analysis is intimately bound up with his landmark work, *Die Traumdeutung* (The Interpretation of Dreams) in which he declared that "the interpretation of dreams is the royal road to a knowledge of unconscious activities of the mind." According to Freud the motive force behind each dream is a repressed wish that seeks a fulfillment it cannot achieve in waking life. To find expression, the wish uses material from recent experiences, day, residues, somatic stimuli and early memories relating to infantile erotic desire. The dream wish also deploys symbols drawn from cultural sources and "typical" symbols that appear to feature in the dreams of many *patients*. Freud's discussion of these recurrent symbols in dreams for example, long objects (cigars, swords, pens) are taken to represent the penis, whilst enclosures or receptacles (caves, drawers, pockets) stand for the female genitals-gave rise to "vulgar Freudianism" according to which all dream-images can be interpreted through a reductive code. Freud however, stressed the need to contextualize image and symbols in the course of dream-interpretation. Freud's main focus is on the form of desire in dreams: the meaning of dreams lies not in their manifest content, but in the ways in which repressed wishes and latent dream-thoughts are disguised and distorted by what he terms the dream-work. The dream-work transforms or translates the latent content of the dream into a manifest form that the dreamer can remember (and relate in the analytic situation). The four central-features of the dream-work are condensation, displacement, considerations of respectability and secondary revision. Condensation involves the creation of composite structures and figures within the dream, through a process of connecting and synthesising disparate thoughts. It involves overdetermination, the combination of often widely divergent thoughts and wishes. In displacement, which Freud (borrowing from Nietzsche) describes as a "transvaluation of psychical values", elements of high intensity and value in the latent dream are replaced by ideas which are of lesser value in the manifest dream. Thus the manifest dream presents only a distorted form of latent dream-wish. Considerations of representability or the means by which dream-thoughts are represented in the dream, is the third component of the dream-work. The language of representation, the way in which images are formed, in the manifest dream resembles a rebuswilt-a chain of idegrams or pictographs that leaves the dreamer (and, in turn the dream-interpreters) to forge her/his own syntactical connections. The final aspect of dream-work is secondary revision, another distorting activity that acts as both editor and censor of the dream. In secondary revision, the dream loses some of its apparent absurdity and discon nectedness, and approximates "to the model of an intelligible experience". In order to understand the underlying dream-wish, the analyst must decipher the multiple disguises, digressions and distortions the wish undergoes in the dream-work. The dream, like the neurotic symptom, is a "compromise formation" in which the unconscious wish both resists and succumbs to censorship and prohibition. Since the dream-work is predominantly a matter of word and image, the technique of dream-interpretation is akin to literary analysis, but Freud strongly imphasises the reducible distance between conscious and unconscious thought: dreams do not want to be understood, and the full meaning of dream can never be deciphered.

The *Interpretations of Dreams* brought psychoanalysis to an international audience. In 1904, Freud published Zur

Psychpothologie des Alltagslepens (*The Psychopathology of Everyday Life*), in which he discusses the steps of the tongue (parapraxes), apparently chance actions and apparently innocent forgetting of words that reveal how the unconscious threads itself into the fabric conscious, working life. Two more major works followed in 1905: *Derwitz and Seine Beziehugh Zum Unbewussten* (trans A.A. Brill as Wit and its Relation to the Unconscious, 1916: now usually entitled *Jokes and Their Relation to the Unconscious*) and Drei *Abhandleungen zur sexualtheorie* (*Three Contributions to the Sexual Theory,* 1910), which includes the famous "Dora" case study. In addition to the "Dora" study, Freud published a number of other case histories: "Little Hans" and the "Rat Man" (both 1909), Schreber (1911), the " Wolf Man" (1918) and "A case of Homosexuality in a Woman" (1920). In the case of "Dora" the eighteen-year old Ida Bauer Dora appeared to exhibit the classic symptoms of hysteria, including fainting spells and the loss of her voice for periods of time. The analysis revealed that Dora was an unwilling participant in a complicated sexual and emotional tangle involving her father and family friends. Her father was having an affair with Frau K. with whom Dora was closely involved, and Herr K. had made several sexual advances to Dora by the time she was sixteen, occasionning bouts of hysterial behavior. While Dora told Freud that she felt manipulated by the adults around her and he accepted her versions of events-Freud repeated this manipulation by insisting that Dora actually loved Herr K. and her hysteria was generated by her repressed desires for him. Dora contested Freud's interpretation, and the analytic relationship proved highly combative, with Dora finally terminating the analysis. This case history reveals a number of central issues for the analytic situation: it involves (sometimes unequal) power relations, it can be subject to an exchange of desires between patient and analyst (termed transference by Freud) and it demonstrates that each analysis, as Freud admitted, constitutes a provisional interpretation rather than scientific orthodoxy.

Sexuality

As the case studies demonstrate, Freud regards neurotic and hysterical symptoms as deriving primarily, although not exclusively from sexual desires. He showed how the neurosis of adulthood were related to childhood desires, and their frustration or prohibition by parental and social forces. This focus on infantile sexuality, and children's fascination with bodily satisfaction, was the most contentious area of his theory. For Freud, the earliest stage of development is that of polymorphous perversity. The infant only slowly learns to distinguish between inner and outer worlds, and individuation is a process of learning that there is a boundary separating ones body from external reality. During this process the child also learns that her/his desires are not always satisfied, and that she/he needs to communicate this lack or insufficiency to others. For Freud, the primordial form of (sexual) satisfaction for the child is found in the mother's breast, which provides food and comfort, and places the child at the centre of parental attention. Freud terms this first phase of erotic gratification the oral stage. The child next discovers the satisfaction of defecation, in this and stage the child's growing self-awareness is tied to its control over excretory functions. The child's ability to evacuate bodily waste can be read as a form of gift to its parents. The third phase of erotic development that Freud identifies is the genital stage, when the infant becomes aware of the genitals as a source of stimulation.

The first objects of the child's desire are the parents, and this desire places the child in the Oedipal scenario that Freud shapes every family, and is the common determinant of subject-formation. He termed the recurrent pattern in which the child desires the parent of the opposite sex, and expresses jealousy or even murderous hatred towards the other parent, the Oedipus complex. The baby covets the mother's attention, and desires to have her love exclusively, but soon realises that the father is a love-rival, and this competition provokes a longing to kill or displace the father. This wish to have the mother and remove the father remains unfulfilled, however, the powerful father threatens to punish the child-symbolically castrate him—for his illicit desires, and to protect himself the child must accept the prohibition of his impulses. Freud calls this fear of the loss of the penis the castration complex and sees it as establishing a renunciation of the instincts which continues adulthood, where the subject recognises the restrictions placed by social codes and institutions on the satisfaction of his wishes. Problematically, this universal pattern of psycosexual development is based on the model of the male child, and presumes the normaloy of a heterosexual rather than homosexual orientation. The injunction against incestuous desire for the mother centres on the threat of castration, the removal of the organ of sexual satisfaction for the little boy. How, then, does the little girl negotiate the Oedipal stage? Even if the scenario is reversed for her—she desires the father and hates the mother—the nature of the threat of castration still causes conceptual difficulties for Freud. He argues that the little girl treats her lack of a penis as an indication that she has already been castrated and the cause of this lack appears to be her mother, who did not give one to the girl and similarly lacks a penis. In frustration the girl turns to her father who can at least provide a baby as a substitute for her missing penis. Thus, while boys develop a certain anxiety, girls develop penis envy. This hypothesis has proved highly controversial for many other psychoanalysts and later feminist critics.

Freud's Oedipal story may be open to strenuous critique, and this aspect of his sexual theory has predominated in accounts of his ideas. Yet, given that it draws on a literary source, and shows how early sexual fantasies can exhibit, mythic qualities, the Oedipal drama demonstrates that sexual development can be regarded as a matter of narrative and fantasy rather than biology, and in these stories the body is read by the subject both literally and metaphorically. Equally, in his early work on sexuality, Freud proposes no distinction between the development of boys and girls, and sees the achievement of "normal" sexuality as a reduction of the polymorphous desire characteristic of infancy. In *Three Essays on Sexuality* he argues that, in the process of subject-formation, masculinity and feminity are flexible positions rather than immutable essences, and heterosexuality is not a biological imperative. The channelling of desire form the libidinal maelstrom of infancy to normative adult behavior is a complex and conflictual process. Freud also points out that every form of sexual relation—even the innocent kiss (the mouth, after all, is the opening to the digestive tract)—bears a trace of perversion. Therefore, rather than representing polar opposites, normal and "aberrant"sexuality are closely related. So, in some respects, Freud's greatest scandal lay in questioning fixed definations of gender and sexuality, even if many of his assumptions are phallic and normative.

The Theory of the Instincts

Freud's continuing observations led him to believe that the Oedipus complex was the nucleus of the neuroses. It was both the climax of infantile sexual life and the foundation for all of the later developments of sexuality. This in turn brought Freud to believe that neurotics failed to overcome that were resolved by normal people. In other worlds psychoanalysis expressed the psychology of the normal human mind. Before the Oedipal phase in which the libido is attached to images of the parents, there is a period of *narcissism* or self-love in which the subject's libido has his own ego for an object. This state, Freud surmised, never completely ceases, and for all of his life his libido moves back and forth from the self to objects in the world. In other words, narcissistic libido is continually being transformed into object-libido and vice versa, as well exemplified in the state of being in love, where the subject can range between self-sacrifice and self-indulgence. These considerations led Freud to reformulate the mechanism of repression. The main agency of repression, urged Freud, was the instincts of self-preservation or the "ego-instincts." It is precisely these instincts which constitute the narcissistic libido. In the process of repression, narcissistic libido is opposed to the object-libido, the self-preservative instincts defend themselves against the demands of object love.

In some of his later works, such as *Beyond the Pleasure Principle* (1920), *Group Psychology and the Analysis of the Ego* (1921), and The *Ego and the Id* (1923), Freud considered a new account of the operation of the instincts. He used the word *eros* (Greek for "love") to designate the instincts of self-preservation as pertaining to both the individual and the species. He opposed this instinct to another instinct of death or destruction, which he called *thanatos* (Greek for "death"). He viewed these two forces as engaged in a constant struggle, which is the broader context of our mental experience.

Freud and Culture

Around 1907 Freud's interests in the implications of psychoanalysis began to extend over the entire domain of culture. He sought to apply psychoanalytic principles to the study of art, religion, and primitive cultures. In his studies of religion, Freud viewed obsessional neurosis as a distorted private religion and religion itself as a universal obsessional neurosis. In studies such as *Totem and Taboo* (1912-1913) Freud explored taboos or prohibitions in primitive cultures, and analogized the various postulates of primitive beliefs with neurosis. In works such as *Civilization and its Discontents* (1930) Freud suggested the extension of the analysis of neurosis in individuals to the examination of the imaginative and cultural creations of social groups and peoples. Some of Freud's disciples, such as Ernest Jones and Otto Rank, followed through the implications of psychoanalytic theory in the realms of literary analysis, mythology and symbolism. All in all, Freud hoped that psychoanalysis, while yet underdeveloped, might offer valuable contributions in the most varied regions of knowledge.

Freud's Literary Analysis

Even in his earlier work, Freud had appealed to literary texts—notably *Oedipus Rex* and *Hamlet*—not only to exemplify and illuminate, but even to ground some of his theoretical notions. He saw Sopocle's play *Oedipus Rex* as expressing a "universal law of mental life," and interpreted fate in that play as the materialization of an "internal necessity." He also saw the Oedipus complex as governing the tragedy of *Hamlet*, though he later altered his views on this play. As for poetic and artistic creation in general, Freud wrote a paper, "Creative Writers and Day-Dreaming" (1907), which viewed works on art as the imaginary satisfactions of unconscious wishes, just as dreams were. What the psychoanalyst can do is to piece together the various elements of an artist's life and his works, and to construct from these the artist's mental constitution and his instinctual impulses. Freud conducted such an analysis of Leonardo da Vinci's picture of *The Madonna and Child with St. Anne* (1910). His lengthy examination of Leonardo da Vinci's character generated a prototype for Psychoanalytic biography. He wrote a psychonalytic account of the novella *Gradiva* by the German author Willhelm Jensen, as well as psychological readings of other works. In 1914 he published (anonymously) an acute reading of the "meaning" of Michelangelo's statue of Moses in Rome. Notwithstanding his own readings of literary and artistic texts, Freud never claimed that psychoanalysis could adequately explain the process of artistic creation. In his paper "Dostoevsky and Parricide" (1928), he stated:

"Before the problem of the creative artist analysis must, alas, lay down its arms."

According to Freud the creative writer engages himself in a kind of play: "He creates a world of phantasy which he takes very seriously—that is, which he invents with large amounts of emotion-while separating it sharply from reality". Freud divides creative writers into two broad groups: Those who, "like the ancient authors of epics and tragedies, take over their material ready-made," and those who "seem to originate their own material." Oddly, Freud states that he will choose for analysis "not the writer a most highly esteemed by the critics, but the less pretentious authors of novels, romances and short stories," who have the "widest and most eager circle of readers of both sexes". Behind this preference may lie the fact Freud's immediate audience consists of laymen, and also a desire to examine creative writing as a phenomenon in popular culture rather than a professional or academic elite. It is clear, also, that Freud often offended the academic establishment; he sometimes observed that the popular reception of his works was more telling than its assessment by experts. Whatever the reason behind Freud's focus on popular fiction, it is surely questionable whether his claims can be unproblematically extended to higher forms of literature.

Freud acknowledges that certain kinds of novels, such as the naturalistic novels of Emile Zola, seem to "stand in quite special contrast to the type of the day-dream." Here, he concedes, the hero plays only a small active role and" sees the actions and sufferings of other people pass before him like a spectator". How can such novels accord with the model of the daydream? Freud's answer (again characteristics) is to say that *some* daydreams are precisely like naturalistic novels: in these dreams "the ago contents itself with the role of spectator." A cynical observer might remark that it would be, difficult for a novel not to conform with Freud's model, since that model itself can be modified to accord with the nature of the novel in question.

Of all Freud's essay on art and literature, "Das Unheimliche" (1919; 'The Uncanny", 1925) has enjoyed the greatest critical afterlife, partly because it eschews this emphasis on the psychoanalysis of the author. In this essay, Freud sets out to trace the nature of the uncanny, "that class of the frightening which leads back to what is known of olf and long sets out to trace the nature of the uncanny, " that class of frightening which leads back to what is known of old and long familiar. The initial part of the essay shows how definitions of the German word *"heimlich"* (homely, familiar, cherished) can coincide with its opposite *"unheimlich"* (unhomely, weird, concealed, secret). Freud traces the experience of the uncanny to the "primary narcissis", of early childhood and to an animistic, conception of the universe amongst 'primitive' and superstition cultures, a formative phase of human history that corresponds to the early stages of infantile development. He discusses many of the characteristics features and situations associated with the uncanny, such as the uncertain boundaries between living and inanimate bodies, the figure of the double, involuntary repetition, the occult and womb phantasies. Freud demonstrates the significance for psychoanalysis of many of these uncanny phenomenon through a discussion of E.T.A. Hoffman's short story, "The Sand Man" which revolves round Nathaniel, a student haunted by his memories of the Sand-Man, a figure of dread in nursery tales who is reputed to steal children's eyes when they refuse to go to bed. This imaginary figure finds its living embodiment in a "real" Sandman the sinister lawyer Coppelius, who visits Nathaniels home and is subsequent implicated in the death of his father. Later, while at university, Nathienal believes that he has recognised the Sand-Man in the guise of Coppola, an optician who sells him an eyeglass with which he spies a beautiful automaton, Olympia. Nathaniel's infatuation for Olympia becomes conflated with his obsession with Coppelius, and he is eventually driven to madness and suicide as a result of this skewed vision. Freud concludes that the uncanny effect of "The Sand-Man" derives from anxiety about losing one's eyes and its connection with the castration complex of childhood, a reading that has been disputed by a number of critics. Despite some of Freud's hesitancies in analysing the properties of the uncanny, the essay has become hugely influential for literary and cultural critics over the last thirty years. More generally, while the "classic" Freudian approach to aesthetics has come to be regarded as a reductive, many of Freud's essays have proved sources of rich fascination for literary critics and theories, and his case studies are now often read in terms of their literary qualities. Freud himself was awarded the Goethic prize for literature in 1930.

CARL GUSTAV JUNG

Archetypal Criticism

The controversy between Freud and Jung introduced the first major schism in the newly established discipline. While Freud assessed the evolution of the individual in a particular cultural setting, Jung extended his theories to the history of humanity. Both aspire towards universal validity. While Freud's scenarios are consequently based on the family (itself), in its nuclear variety, the product of the nineteenth century), Jung employs anthropological models that seemingly encompass all cultures. Ultimately, both remain troubled by the challenge of historicity. Freud requires a starting point for his libidinal impasses in the conflicts of an imaginary ur-tribe, a scenario that he outlines in *Totem and Taboo.* Jung posits an 'always already' in the shape of an inherited collective set of images, values and meanings that he calls *archetypes.* This pseudo-genetic model of a, collective unconscious is thus indebted to Darwin's theory of evolution. Neither Freud nor Jung can ultimately answer the question concerning the origin of ur-scenes and archetypes. Jung's most prominent archetypes are those of *anima* and *animus,* representing feminine and masculine qualities, respectively. Archetypes have fascinated many scholars, mainly because they exists in abundance in cultural and literary artefacts.

While Freud's model is ultimately based on conflict, Jung uphold's harmony as its starting point and ultimate goal. In order to posit an orginally harmonious self, Jung separates this self from culture and society. Like Freud, Jung refuses to define an essence of art, although he also regards artistic creativity as crucial for his ideas. Jangian concepts resemble the purification rituals of primitive cultures and many religions. They are clearly anti-rational, and indeed often vilify consciousness, contrary to at least early Freudian theories that see it as the safe haven into which libidinal chaos has to be translated. Like Freud, Jung splits human experience into planes, the rational one where archetypes must be recognised in their significance, and the underlying dream-like would in which archetypes are formed. He often describes the latter in terms of formlessness and water. In its 'back to nature' mysticism, Jangian theories have informed important cultural trends of twentieth century, such as Rudolph Steiner's Anthropomorphical movement. They also fascinated writers intent on using primitivism as a critique of modern civilisation, such as D. H. Lawrence. The seemingly higher spirituality that resulted from the disregard of society and the simultaneous chastising of the libidinous self also appealed to authors such as W. B. Yeats.

The essentialism of Jungian archetypes also resurfaces in some post structuralist feminist theories. While Camille Paglia rather unsubtly reasserts the anti-cultural force of sexuality (in terms that have long been employed by misogynist positions), even a more complex theorist such as Helene, Cixous with her concepts of writing in mother's milk and fluid feminity harks back to archetypal models.

Maud Bodkin offers an alternative, but equally problematic use of Jungian concepts in literary studies—Her *Archetypal Patterns in Poetry* (1934) returns Jungian models to the individual, in particular the artistic individual, who finds self-realisation in art with the helps of archetypal symbolism. Great art in turn enables its audience to achieve similar fulfillment through empathic interpretation. Apart from the obvious intentional fallacy of such a reading, the conceptual problem is again that recurring cultural images are taken to represent pre-cultural truths. Yet these 'truths' are only every realised inside culture and inform and often strengthen the idealogical status quo (especially in terms of gender and power), even when they are supposed to interrogate it.

Influence on Culture

(1) Jung had a 16-year long friendship with author Laurens van der post from which a number of books and film were created about Jung's life.

(2) The concept of the collective unconscious is one of the main topics in the Dune novel series.

(3) Jung's influence on noted Canadian novelist Robertson Davies is apparent in many of Davies's fictional works. In

Particular, The Cornish Trilogy and his novel The *Manticore* each base their design on Jungian concepts.

(4) The Progressive Metal band, Tool have incorporated Jung's work into their album, Aenima. Additionally, The Police made references to Carl Jung in their album *synchronicity.*

(5) J. Michael Stranczynski's "Badylon 5" television series used many of Jung's concepts throughout the series.

(6) The video game Xenogears and Xenosaga utilize many of the ideas proposed by Carl Jung as mayor storyline components of the game, and even create physical manifestations of his nations within actual characters, Albedo, Nigredo, Rubedo, etc.

(7) Jung's writing was introduced to Italian film maker, Federico Fellini in the 1950s and had an effect on the way Fellini incorporated dreams into films after La Dolce Vita.

Melanie Klein

Klein theories have their starting point in the maternal body. Rather than regarding the mother as the embodiment of castration and, therefore, as a mere reminder of the father's phallic power, as in Freud, or as the symbol of archetypal feminity, as in Jung, Klein reassesses the relation of mother and child from an empirical perspective: The fact that the mother provides protection and emotional stimulus as well as nourishment for the infant. Klein's move can be seen as a rejection of both masculine views of infantile psychological development and the restricted role allocated to women in the male-oriented theories of Freud and Jung,. Yet Klein refuses to create an idealised alternative model. The relationship between infant and mother is troubled. The maternal body is simultaneously the provider and guarantee of all things positive for the infant (a function summed up in the concept of the 'good breast') and the potential source of all frustration (the 'bad breast'). The split into ideal and its opposite is not the effect of the law of the father (as in Freud), or of the alienation from a mystical nature (as in Jung), but the result of the actual presence of the mother.

The effect of this ambivalence towards the original source of fulfilment is a first awareness of separateness that becomes the prerequisite of individuation. It confronts the emerging self with a crucial libidinal ambivalence: the combined love and hate for the maternal body. This body is the goal of the infant's first attempts at exerting power, but also the stumbling block that makes that child realise that it is far from omnipotent. But more than merely providing yet another model of the self in competition with chose of Freud and Jung. Klein's thinking also, encompasses the 'Other', the 'object' in Freud's object cathexes or the obstacle in Jung's quest for harmony. Object relations remain forever tainted by the ambivalence first experienced with and through the mother: the self remembers its union with her and wishes alternately to be part of hers and to make her part of itself. Klein calls the effects of these desire *projection* and introjection. Their consequence is the placing of the problematic aspects of the self (its frustrated desires as well as its idolised body) and the desired objects (the mother and those objects that eventually replace her) in an intermediate realm where they are neither subject nor object. Klein calls their status that of 'part-objects'. The self eventually learns to reject and even hate the frustrating other in what has become known as abjection. Abjection links the suppression of desire not with neuroses, as does Freud, but with aggression, an aggression that is always partly directed against the subject itself. This objection of the same as the alien and the desired as the detested has become an influential model for rethinking binary opposites in literary and cultural criticism.

Jacques Lacan

Psychoanalyst Jacques Lacan was one of the most influential thinkers of his time. The linguistic philosophical and political scope of his *theory of the subject* stirred intellectuals and artists in his native France and all over the world. He was a faithful interpreter of Freud, but he freely incorporated artistic, mathematical and philosophical insights into his own psychoanalysis without subordinating the Freudian field to any of them. It has been said with reason that Freud took root in France mainly through Lacan. Though he published relatively little in his lifetime, Lacan drew fascinated critical attention whenever his writing made its rare appearance. His impact has been felt across a broad range of disciplines, from feminist philosophy and film theory to the spheres of literature, politics and cultural studies. A dramatic personage with enormous intellectual energy, Lacan maintained friendships and theoretical engagements with a wide variety of people, from the artist Andre Breton and Salvador Dale, to the philosophers Georges Bataille, Raymond Queneau, and Maurice Merleau-Ponty, and such historians of thought as Alexandre Kojeve and Alexandre Koyre who transformed the intellectual landscape in France in the 1930s.

Apart from Freud, the main influences on Lacan's work were Saussure, Roman Jokobson, and Hegel. Lacan's reputation was established by his publication of *Ecrits* (1966), a large collection of essays and papers, which were translated into English in a much abbreviated format in 1977. Lacan's influence not only has extended over the field of psychoanalysis but also reaches into the work of Masxists such as Louis Althusser and feminists such as Julia Kristeva and Jane Gallop, as well as deconstructive thinkers such as Barbara Johnson. Other feminists have reacted strongly against the phallocentric thrust (a not altogether inapt expression) of Lacan's own work.

Lacan's notoriously complex thinking is best approached by its obvious link with literary analysis: his re-readings of Freud through the linguistic theories of Ferdinand de Saussure. He takes from Saussure the notion of language as a system of signs determined by their difference from each other. But where Saussure sees the sign as a bonding of signifier (sound-image) and signified (concept), Lacan sees each signifier as invested with unconscious desire. A gap opens between the inner private experience of bodily need and the outer public interpretation of it. Neither the subject nor others recognize this gap. Lacan's theory of the subject stresses this gap coming into being with the unconscious by the imposition of signifiers upon need. Through language, need is addressed to the Other (other subjects in the sign system) in the form of a demand for absolute love which the Other has not got to give. What is left over is unassuaged desire, desire for recognition of the Other's desire. The discourse of psychoanalysis is here taken as a model for any kind of speech or writing: there is no fixed meaning, either latent or manifest, to which Lacan's notorious style bears witness.

Whereas classical psychoanalytic criticism operated with a firm distinction between conscious and unconscious meaning, in

Lacan's theory conscious and unconscious cannot be separated. The unconscious bears the marks of the signifiers impressed upon it. The text no longer harbours regressive wishes but engages with current desires encompassing both past and future experience. As a child once lured by its mirror-image (Lacan's 'Imaginary order'), which promised it a wholeness which it lacked, so the text lures the reader by the force of its representation. But at the same time the text is also Law (Lacan's 'Symbolic order' of language) shattering the mirror, illusions and dispersing the reader. The lure of the Imaginary is a prelude to the capture of the subject in the signifying chain, as both the reading subjects in the text (the characters) and the reading subject of the text (the empirical reader) are caught in a structure of repetition. The text is a trap for the unwary readar character who chases his/her image, only to become trapped in the signifying chain. The reader can hence be seen as at the mercy of the text, since she or he will not know what referential effects will be brought into play in the cause of reading; but the text is also at the mercy of the reader, because of the mediating effects of her or his own unconscious.

Language is the place where personal and the cultural intersect, where there is a constant displacement of meaning. One of the difficulties of psychoanalytic reader-theory has been the problem of assigning an unconscious to the text: for Lacan transference is a process that goes on in language, but because the unconscious is that residue or excess that cannot be defined, there will always be gaps that neither author nor reader will finally be able to fill in. Both author and reader are controlled by the strategies of language. In his reading of Poe's *The Purloined Letter*, Lacan (1972) offers an allegory of the displacement of the signifier: the characters in the text are determined by the position of the master-signifier, which for Lacan is the phallus, Lacan's reading of this story is not a literary interpretation, but a study of discourse in the light of psychoanalytic theory. Lacan reveals a structure of desire which assigns a set of characters their places in a predetermined power-system.

The ego, the central concept in Freud's theories of tension and the ideal in Jung's concept of individuation, is consequently a painful delusion for Lacan. His radical attack on Freud's formula 'where the id was there ego shall be' is its reformulation as a cultural (rather than an individual) imperative in the paradoxical phrase 'it is my duty that I should come into being'. Maud Ellmann reads this rejection of the ideal ego (which is also a rejection of popular ego psychology) as an attack on 'the fiasco of the humanist tradition based on the Socratic dictum-*known thyself.*'

Stephen Dedalus, the protagonist of James Joyce's novel *A Potrait of the Artist as a Young Man* helps us to make better sense of how a boy's identity emerges in Lacan's re-reading. A sense of separation and loss expands Stephen's language at the end of each cycle of the linguistic flow. His mind moves back and forth between an attractive maternal image and a threatening paternal one. There are 'sunderings' from both parents and these contribute to his growth when the sets off in a new direction to find another world after one of his worlds has been threatened.

It involves a transformed maternity, a shifting of language. The sundering's in Stephen's case are tied up with Lacanian notions about lack, desire and movement from the Imaginary to the symbolic order.

In the same way it is possible to make better sense of the predicament of Prufrock in T.S. Eliots' poem "The Love Song of J. Alfred Prufrock" in the light of the Lacanian formulation's on lack and desire. Prufrock's basic problem is that he is enmeshed in divergent pulls of desire had his awareness of various kinds of lack. These go into the making of his otherness and a general unease of otherness always surrounds him. A line like: "It is impossible to say just what I mean" points to the lack of a neat fit between the signified and the signifier.

Feminist Psychoanalytic Criticism

To find a way out of the given representation is precisely the project of a feminist psychoanalytic criticism, through this is not where it would want to stop. Freud's several attempts to construct a narrative adequate to female sexuality end up with same bleak theme: the girl is a little man until the advent of the castration complex. Feminist psychoanalysis evolved out of two different narratives, two re-readings, one made by object-relations theory in England and America, the other by Lacanian theory in France.

Object-relations theory concentrates on the pre-oedipal relations between mother and child as a moment before the realization of the father's place in the social disrupts the symbotic relation between mother and child. Whereas in England and American this attempt to re-centre the mother-child relation has tended to ignore the question of sexual difference (sexual identity is not in question), in France the pre-oedipal relation has acquired a more radical potential. This is owing to a difference in theory: while the self in object-relations theory is regarded as rudimentarily present from the beginning, for Lacan the self, constituted via an illusory mirror-image of wholeness, remains fictional throughout life, acquiring a provisional identiy by giving up the (maternal) phallus. Castration is here seen as a symbolic event suffered by both sexes, irrespective of their biological sex. While some feminists accept Lacan's 'phallocentrism', arguing that he develops Freud's non-biologistic thinking to its logical conclusion by showing how men and women are constructed in a patriarchal system, others take the argument further by maintaining that Lacan does not merely lay down the phallic law, but reveals the frialty of psychic identity and the mobility of desire, both of which point to the fictionality of gender definations. French theorists, too, have returned to the pre-oedipal relation between mother and child and have constructed new narratives of this relation. Julia Kristeva (1984) sees the pre-oedipal as a play of bodily rhythm's and pre-liguistic exchanges between infant and mother, but displaces the Lacanian Imaginary as a site of illusion with the 'Semiotic' as a zone of resistance within the margins of the symbolic, producing effects before language has introduced psychic repression and continuing to do so throughout life. The semiotic is involved in the production of a poetic text that disrupts and subverts the conventional language system. Kristeva takes her examples from male avant grade poets, which illustrates her position regarding a gender-free marginality but does not please feminists.

The problem facing a feminist psychoanalytic criticism is how to give women access to discourse: the choice for her has been either submitting to the public language of patriarchy or of inventing a private language which keeps her marginalized and/ or involves the risk of making her sound mystical. The worlds that have encircled projections of women are to be subjected to decipherment with the help of a re-reading of psychoanalysis. The feminine, like any other term, is to be regarded, not as a natural given, but as a construction. What the various books of feminist criticism show is that discourses are not merely about producing definations but that they determine the 'nature' of the body and the mind of the subjects they govern. In the past this has been done by a process of hysterization', the turning of women's bodies into wombs; Freud 'discovered' psychoanalysis in the course of his researches into the bodily symptoms of hysteria. The most discussed case history in the anals of feminism must be the case of the girl hysteric given the name of 'Dora', who walked out on Freud because he mis-recognised her desire. Feminist critics examine the relation between psychoanalysis and feminism in order to produce subversive readings of psychoanalytic theory or of traditional literary texts. Taking psychonalysis as a form of narrative as well as a method of interpretation, they re-read Freud and Lacan, patriarchal texts, and texts by women writers re-writing woman. The common ground of their readings is the attempt to revise the maternal narrative, the disadvantageous way the mother has been constructed by psychoanalysts, from Freud to Klein to Winnicott, as always seen from the viewpoint of the child.

The writings and readings of feminist psychoanalytic critics are concerned with the interaction of literature, cultural and sexual identity, emphasizing the way that configurations of gender are located in history. The feminist psychoanalytic enquiry has perhaps the potential for becoming the most radical form of psychoanalytic criticism, since it is crucially concerned with the very construction of subjectivity. Science is a long way from providing a theory. Meanwhile psychoanalytic criticism can confront the issue because it addresses the question of genesis of the self as revealed in literature and the arts, and in all writing, including that of psychoanalysis itself, in all of which there is the attempt to insert the subject into the social.

12

Feminist Criticism

The emergence of feminist literary criticism is one of the major developments in literary studies in the past thirty years or so. The term 'feminism' first emerged in the English language in the 1890s a significant historical moment when there was an urgent need to name the activities of the women's movement, which was vibrant and popular as never before. Late nineteenth-century feminism joined together women from different classes and social backgrounds. Although the initial enthusiasm was to be dampened and many found their interests ignored by the political adopted by the leading figures, it achieved the status of a social movement. While more recent feminist criticism warns against understanding 'women' as a homogenous category and emphasizes the mistake of eradicating the unique characteristics of different groupings, in the late nineteenth century the emergence of a solidarity across national and class barriers was perceived and so novel that the common factor of being a woman was perceived as outweighing the differences. Among other things, the working conditions of female labourers were so appalling that the primary objective was to strive for some improvement for instance pregnant women were not infrequently fore a to work right up to the delivery of the baby and indeed sometimes gave birth in the factory itself. Like any politically oriented movement, the women's movements which formed in different national settings had to deal with the grossest social injustices of their daily experience, only then could it begin to think about equal rights among its members.

A theoretical engagement with the claims and rights of women concentrated on representations both in the sense of protesting against political disenfranchisement and challenging the insidious power of literature to propagate views about women's inferiority.

Feminist criticism is concerned with the impact of gender critique on writing and reading. It usually begins with a patriarchal culture. It is concerned with the place of female writers in the cannon. Finally, it includes a search for a feminine theory or approach to texts. Feminist criticism is political and often revisionist. Feminists often argue that male fears are portrayed through female characters. They may argue that gender determines everything, or just the opposite: that all gender difference are imposed by society, and gender determines nothing.

Women Writers: A Historical Perspective

To understand the nature of feminist literary criticism and its alternative approach to literatures, we must first understand its long history. Although critics like Simone de Beauvoir, Mary Elleman and Kate Millet were among the first to reveal the literary history of women's images and to discuss the dominant stereotyped images of female fictional characters, the history of feminist criticism goes back hundreds of years in time. It can even be traced back to Aristotle's declaration that "The female is female by virtue of a certain lack of qualities," and St. Thomas Aquina's belief that woman is an "imperfect man". Texts going back as far as Aristophane's comedy Lysistrata, "which is about how women achieved social change by withholding sexual favours from their men"; and Aeschylus's trilogy, The Oresteia, where Athena wins over Apollo's argument that the mother is no parent to her child, are among the earliest examples of feminist criticism. Also Raman Selden mentions John Donne's "Air and Angels" where Donne alludes to Aquina's theory that form is masculine and matter feminine: "the superior, godlike, male intellect impresses its form upon the malle-able, inert, female matter." Christine de Pisan's work as the "first major work of feminist criticism". Pisan's *Epistre au dieu d'amours* (1399) was written against the biased representations of women in de Meun's Work. In her *La cite des Dames* (1405), Pisan also argued that God created man and woman as equal beings. But, it is Mary Wollstonecraft's *A Vindication of the Rights of Woman* (1792) which marks the first modem awareness of women's struggle for equal rights, and therefore it is the first milestone for the equality of the sexes. Wollstonecraft was influenced by the ideas of the French revolution concerning the equal rights of individuals, K.K. Ruthven observes that "the anology with slavery, which is present in Wollstonecrafts book, "becomes the dominant trope in nineteenth-century feminist writing, doubtless because of feminist involvement in the abolitionist movement". Seventy seven years later in *The Subjection of Women* (1869), John Stuart Mill expressed it very powerfully: "All men, except the most brutish, desire to have in the woman most nearly connected with them, not a forced slave but a willing one, not a slave merely, but a favourite. They have therefore put everything in practice to enslave their minds". Sixty years later Virginia Woolf's *A Room of One's Own* (1929) developed and enhanced these views with a strong female sensibility and criticism. *A Room of One's Own* became an important precursor of feminist literary criticism. Here, Virginia Wolf argues that the male dominated ideas of the patriarchal society prevented women from realizing their creativity and true potential:

> In the first place, to have a room of her own, let alone a quiet room or a sound-proof room, was a out of the question, unless her parents were exceptionally rich or very noble, even up to the beginning of the nineteenth century—Such material difficulties were formidable; but much worse were the immaterial. The difference of the world which Keats and Flaubert and other men of genius have found so hard to bear was in her case not indifference but hostility.

As Virginia Woolf was especially emphasizing, women writers had to work against the grain in order to write. Yet writing was the only was left to women to assert individuality and autonomy. Excluded from many social, political and economic activities, women turned to writing. But it was not easy. In her essay, "Professions for Women" Virginia Woolf states that she had to kill "the Angel in the House" in order to write her novels and critical works:

> Had I not killed her she would have killed me. She would have plucked the heart out of my writing. For, as I found, directly I put pen to paper, you cannot review even a novel without having a mind of your own, without expressing what you think to be the truth about human relations, morality, sex. And all these questions, according to the Angel of the House, cannot be dealt with freely and openly by women. Killing the

Angel to the House was part of the occupation of a woman writer.

Reading this passage we can understand the difficulties involved in being a female writer. The idea is clear; it is dangerous for any woman who writes to think of herself as a passive, subordinate being in the house. To be a writer one has to destroy the stereotyped image of house-wife and mother. In other words, women writers had before them the enormous task of defying their marginality and subversion, not only in the house, but in society as well. Mrs. Gaskell's letter of 25 August 1850, concerning the deplorable conditions of charlotte Bronte's life provides an excellent example of such struggles of female writers as wolf was underlining Mrs. Gaskell writes that the Bronte girls were not taught anything by their father; it was the servant who taught them to read and write, and that they lived in extremely miserable conditions. Despite the unfortunate background of her education and unfavourable circumstances of her life, Charlotte, writes Mrs. Gaskell, "possesses a charming union of simplicity and power, and a strong feeling of responsibility for the gift—"Mrs. Gaskell continues her letter thus:

> Indeed I never heard of so hard, and dreary a life –extreme poverty is added to their trials-it (poverty) was no trial till her sisters had long lingering illnesses. She is truth itself; and of a very noble sterling nature-which has never been called out by anything kind or genial—She is very silent and very shy: and when she speaks chiefly remarkable for the admirable use she makes of simple words, and the way in which she makes language express her ideas.

Of course Charlotte Bronte is not the only exemplary figure who could defy her conditions and express herself in brilliantly written novels like Jane Eyre, Shirley, and Villette. She is just one among the multitude of women who had something of importance to say in fiction. There were many writers like her who had to endure extreme difficulties and yet could produce lasting literary works. It is not surprising that most of the 19th century female writers foregrounded woman as the subject of their novels, or expressed female experience in their literary rebellion against their deliberate marginalisation both as women and as writers. In the 19th century women writers usually invoked a centralized object of power although it contradicted their aim of creating a resistance discourse. The centralized object of power was the male authorial discourse. Yet, they had to identify one way or the other, with power and culture in order to be accepted for publication. But, the possibilities of transgressive potential were always there in their writing. Anne Bronte's "The Tenant of Wildfell Hall" (1848) is a striking example, which is regarded as the first manifesto for women's liberation. Here, Helen Huntingdon is driven to leave her atrocious husband for an independent existence. Her defying the current laws of the times came as a shock to the social convention of the day. In 1848 the wife and the children were under the husband's control, and it was impossible to leave a husband without causing legal problems and social scandal. Yet Anne Bronte's heroine after so many attempts at reforming her husband, walks out on him taking her son with her. Here is how Arthur Hunting-don gives voice to the commonly held ideas about wives: no matter how badly the husbands may behave, the wife is expected to obey and entertain him without complaint: "Are the marriage vows a jest: and is it nothing to make it your sport to break them—?" asks Helen after she encounters her husband flirting with the wife of his friend. Huntingdon gives a typical answer to her "You are breaking your marriage vows yourself said he, indignantly rising and facing to and fro. You promised to honour and obey me, and now you attempt to hector over me, and threaten and accuse me and call me worse than a highwayman—I won't be dictated to by a woman, though she be my wife". Yet Helen persists in showing the injustice in his behaviour, and asks him to imagine himself in her place : would he then honour and trust her under such circumstances? Again the answer is loaded with the double standards of the day: "The cases are different, he replied. It is a woman's nature to be constant-to love one and one only, blindly, tenderly, and for ever—". It is this double-sided reality that drives Helen Huntingdon to seek her independence. This double standard—especially in education—is evident in most of the 19th century female writing. For example, in Mrs. Gaskell's last novel, *Wives and Daughters,* the highly affectionate and protective father, Mr. Gibson, who is an intellectual man of medicine himself, is against his daughter gaining too much learning. Here is his instruction to his daughter's Molly's governess concerning her education:

> Don't teach Molly too much: she must sew, and read and write, and do her sums; but I want to keep her a child, and if I find more learning desirable for her, I'll see about giving it to her myself. After all, I'm not sure that reading or writing is necessary. Many a good women gets married with only a cross instead of her name; its rather a diluting of mother-wit; to my fancy; but, however, we must yield to the prejudices of society, Miss Eyre, and so you may teach the child to read.

Although Molly loves her father and obeys all his orders and fulfills all his demands, she instinctively realizes that it is unjust for him to withhold rich world of learning from her. So, "It was only by fighting and struggling hard, that bib by bit Molly persuaded her father to let her have French and drawing lessons". But Mrs. Gaskell writes that, "He was always afraid of her becoming too much educated". This attitude on the part of the male character is exemplary of the generally acknowledged patriarchal perception of women in society in order to control and to limit their power. It also indicates the masculine resistance to the development of the feminine identity, because possessing a strong identity means possessing power as well.

Most of the novels written in the 19th century by women used the house as the central image, because, like their heroines, female writers were almost exclusively confined to the house. Their experiences were not as broad as their male counterparts, because they were isolated especially from business life. Therefore, the novels display a highly static way of life. Although the female writers favoured the subjective voice in their fiction due to their limited experience of the world, they were aware of its disadvantages. First of all, in a world where the woman is regarded as the object, and not the subject who could participate in its affairs, the subjective voice was suggestive of a reaction against standard morality. He female writer had to conform to this morality in order to be accepted for publication. Yet, despite these difficulties the women novelists developed the subjective voice in their fiction as the only viable form of expression of the subject in process. Eva Figes states that, "the position of women, isolated within individual households, favoured the development of the subjective voice in afiction which concentrated on the domestic setting". The significance of their contribution to the literary establishment lies in the fact that the women writers have seen the female identity as a continuous process of becoming and thus have reflected its flexibility. This can be considered as an alternative method of character portrayal, and it had been initiated by the forgotten originators of the novel genre in the 18th century.

The literary achievements of Eliza Haywood, Aphra Behn, Delari-viere Manley, Sarah Fielding, Fanng Burney, Elizabeth Inchbald and Maria Edgeworth, to name only a few, established a tradition of 'subject in process' which later novelists like Jane Austen, the Bronte's, and George Eliot were to pursue. Charlotte Bronte's dialectical approach to the experiences of women provides an excellent example of the tradition of subject in process. The tension between personal powerlessness and desire for power and control in her female characters produces a process that enables the characters to review the dominant ideologies of the times. In *Jane Eyre* (1847), and *Villette* (1853) the heroine is able to resist social confinement and social limitations by her independent mind which combines strong will and moral integrity. Bronte's strong minded heroine displays as integrated female subjectivity. Lucy Snowe in *Villette* expresses it quite sharply: "I would deliberately have taken a housemaid's place, bought a strong pair of gloves, swept bedrooms and staircases, and cleaned stoves and locks, in peace and independence". Less strong heroines, like Caroline in *Shirley* (1849) too, are aware of this self in formation. This is evident in Caroline's inner search for a meaningful identity and existence: "What was I created for, I wonder? Where is my place in the world?" To ask such questions usually assumes a belief in the unity of self, a search of a coherent self that wants to know itself and control itself. This is also the rebellion of the female consciousness against the male images of female identity and experience. As Judith Kegan Gardiner points out, "The concept of female identity shows as how female experience is transformed into female consciousness, often in reaction to male paradigms for female experience". Elizabeth Bennet's wish for self-integration, control and affection in Jane Austen's *Pride and Prejudice* (1813) also points to the subject in process: "Elizabeth, on her side, had much to do. She wanted to ascertain the feelings of each of her visitors, she wanted to compose her own, and to make herself agreeable to all". Juliet Mitchell argues that especially the early women writers emphasized the process of becoming women within a new bourgeois society:

> They wrote novels to describe that process-novels which said: 'Here we are: women. What are our lives to be about? Who are we? Domesticity, personal relations, personal intimacies, stories' The novel is that creation by the woman of the woman, or by the subject who is in the process of becoming woman, of woman, under capitalism.

In the 19th century the awareness of the defects of the social system under capitalism is quite visible in the works of the female writers. The women novelists, like Mrs. Gaskell, began to question and comment on the social system in their fiction. Their position is essentially humanist. Eva Figes argues that the solution the female novelists offered was the "femenisation of society".

> When women did begin to comment on the social system in fiction their outlook was essentially humanist. Leaving aside isolated statements on the position of their own sex, which occur in the writings of all women, from Jane Austen to Mary Wollstonecraft, they tended to stand aside from and indeed, distrust political systems and solutions and view the problems they described in terms of human relations. In attempting to analyse the breakdown and failure of human relations they tended to blame male behaviour, and see the solution in terms of the feminization of society.

The contribution of women writers to humanist values is represented by a female identity that counterbalanced what they saw as the essentially destructive and anti-humanist male attitude and position in society. Therefore, female identity is represented as subject in process—a subject that is always in progressivist motion.

Although the women writers have seen female identity as a process and have emphasized its flexibility, they could not avoid being subjected to the unjustified claims on their intellectual powers. Thus, they have always been alienated from the mainstream of literature and society. Especially in the 19th century, women were debased for their so-called intellectual inferiority. Female artists were not believed to have an intellectual and creative capacity equal to that of "great men" like, among many others, Mozart, Michaelangelo and Milton, they could achieve equality only in one sense: that they could "die 'grandly' with an art comparable to a Milton's." This is the great talent that is freely acknowledged in women, the ability to lie like a man, that is cheerfully applauded by De Quincey, as Angela Leighton has pointed out. De Quincey's essay. "Joan of Arc" is typical evidence as to the barised male perception and deliberate attempts at constructing and establishing the binary oppositions of male/ female hierarchy in the social system:

> Women, a sister, there are some things which you do not execute as well as your brother, men; no, nor ever will. Pardon me if I doubt whether you will ever produce a great poet from your choirs, or a Mozart, or a great philosopher, or a great scholar—Yet, sister woman—I acknowledge that you can do one thing as well as the best of us men—a greater thing than ever Milton is known to have done, or Michaeangelo: you can die grandly.

Despite all these attacks and underrating of their creativity, intelligence and potential, women writers felt pressured to prove both their reliability and their physical endurance", and they established the pre-eminent form of literary narrative, the novel. The novel genre emerged with women's literary experiments in the 17th century, which was an age of transformation into a capitalist society full of un-certainties. Yet the female novelists have been deliberately kept out of critical consideration. A renowed critic like Walter Allen starts *The English Novel* (1954) with the following statement: "The comparatively sudden appearance at the turn of the seventeenth century of the novel as we know it was a manifestation of a marked change in the direction of men's interests". Why Allen overtly accords primacy to men and their interests is quite significant. Since the "vast majority of early novels" writes Juliet Mitchell, "were written by large number of women" how can a critic be so ignorant of their existence? It is quite clear that Allen deliberately excludes them from the canon by making no reference to their contribution to the formation of the novel genre. Women writers like Lady Mary Wroath, Anne Wearnys Margaret Cavendish (Duchess of Newcastle) are excluded from many critical works written on the emergence of the novel genre. Dale Spender argues that only the determinedly partisan would produce such a double standard in our literary heritage:

> 'Men of letters' have excluded women and women's writing from both participation and consideration within the literary circle, and they have compounded their errors of judgment with their failure to mention that there are different rules for the women, whom they have not included. Only individuals who are determinedly partisan could have for centuries practiced a double standard which judged the women writer as a true woman and the man writer was a true writer; only individuals who are in control and who wish to stay that way could have consistently refused to admit the part they were playing in keeping women out of the world of letters.

Since the novel is the creation of female writers, the exclusion of so many women novelists from the canon has caused an enormous degree of reaction from the feminist critics.

Therefore, reconstruction and re-evaluation of the canon as regards the novel genre has become one of the major tasks of feminist criticism.

From the 17th century onwards there were a significant numbers of women who took to writing despite the severe disadvantages, "because selling their literary wares were treated with much the same ribaldry and contempt as prostitutes". Therefore, the idea of writing and publications was regarded as a seriously dangerous issue for moral reasons. Yet, in spite of all the hindrances, women writers attempted to participate in the literary tradition, and created a new genre, the novel. The first major writer of importance is Lady Mary Wroath, niece of Sir Philip Sidney. Until the death of her husband and son in 1644, Lady Mary acted as a literary patron. For example, Dale Spender states that Ben Jonson dedicated much of his work to her, including in 1610 *The Alchemist.* Then, in order to pay her debts and to earn her living, she wrote *Urania,* a pastoral romance which is a new version of Sidney's *Arcadia. Urania* is significant because of its innovative technique. That is, for the first time a writer is using a direct reference to reality for a realistic representation as regards the similarities between her characters and the social figures of her time. Although this text is a variation on the conventions of the pastoral code, it has a bearing in the development of the novel genre. Despite its pastoral fantasy and flowery style, *Urania* actually moves away from the fantastic conventions of the pastoral romance with its realism of context and with its realistic portrayal of characters. In this respect, its realistic content. And its introduction of realistic dialogue separate *Urania* from fantasy fiction and make it a precursor of the realistic conventions. *Urania* is the first example to narrow the gap between fact and fiction.

Lady Mary Wroath was not the only woman writer who broke the line between fantasy and reality. Many more followed her. Although the literary field was occupied by 'men of letters' in the 17th century, the women, especially during the second half of the century, embarked on new forms of writing that brought fiction closer to reality. They initiated the emergence of the forms of biography, autobiography and letters by writing exclusively within these forms. Among these women the most notable ones included Anne Clifford, Lucy Hutchinson, Anne Fan-shawe and Margaret Cavendish. These women wrote autobiographical sketches that are notable for their realistic details concerning their times. Especially Margaret Cavendish's, Duches of Newcastle, introduced realism to the literary conventions. Moreover, she boldly expressed her opinions about the situation of women. In the "Preface to the Reader" part of her book *The World's Olio,* Cavendish claimed that women would not be victims if they were given the same education as men. Then, she argued, they would be intellectually equal to men: "if we were bred in schools to mature our brains and to manure our understandings, that we might bring forth the fruits of knowledge." In the Preface to another work-*Observations on Experimental Philosophy,* she continued the argument: "I will not say but many of our Sex may have as much wit, and are capable of learning as well as Men: but since they want instructions, it is not possible, they should attain to it: for learning is Artificial, but wit is natural". In her autobiography, *The True Relation of My Birth, Breeding and Life,* (1656), she documented, with intensity of detail, the difficulties she and her husband Cavendish, experienced while in exile. This autobiography constitutes only one part of her *Nature's Pictures Drawn by Fancie's Pencil to the Life* (1656) which is a collection of tales, fables and dialogues. Here is an example of her use of realistic dialogue and the expression of her own opinions on women's situation:

> There was a grave Matron, who came to visit a young virgin, whom she asked why she did not marry, since she was of marriageable years. 'Truly', said she, 'I am best pleased with a single life'. 'What, answered the Matron, 'will you lead Apes in Hell?' The young lady said, it was better to lead Apes in Hell, than to live like Devils on Earth, for, said she, 'I have heard that a married couple seldom or never agree, the Husband roars in his drink, and the wife scolds in her choler, the Servants quarrel, the Children cry, and all is disorder, than 'Us thought Hell is, and a more confused noise'. Said the Matron, 'Such are only the poor, meaner sort of people that live so: but the noble and rich, when they are drunk are carried straight to bed and laid to sleep, and their wives dance until their husbands are sober'. Said the Lady, 'If they dance until their husbands are sober, they will dance until they are weary'; 'So they do,' replied the Matron.

During the Restoration period in England one woman writer precedes all others in time with her authentic realism: Aphra Ben (1640-1689). Virginia Woolf hails her by claiming: "All women together ought to let flowers fall upon the tomb of Aphra Ben—for it was she who earned them the right to speak their minds." After Aphra Ben, came a number of female writers who took fiction, one step further. Delariviere Manley (1663-1724) and Eliza Haywood (1693-1756) should have their proper place in the history of the novel's development. Manley introduced the epistolary form, and made use of political satire, as well as bringing into use, "fantastical rendition of real life happenings Haywood established the epistolary novel, and she is, therefore the forerunner of Richardson. Eliza Haywood also wrote sentimental and realistic novels. Her, *History of Bessy Thoughtless* (1751) marks the true emergence of the novel with its plot, character and dialogue. Haywood presented the world through women's eyes and gave expression to women's experiences. Bessy Thoughtless became the source of inspiration for later novelists like Fanny Burney and Jane Austen. Burney's Evelina and Jane Austen's Elizabeth Bennet are modeled after Bessy. Bessy is the pioneer in the history of fictional characters who learn from their errors. Eliza Haywood "was as much an active force (and arguably the greater force)" writes Spenders, "in shaping the novel as were Daniel Defoe and Henry Fielding."

Thus, the Duchees of Newcastle, Aphra Ben, and Delariviere Manley were actually the very first writers to initiate the emergence of the realistic techniques, and Eliza Haywood became not only an active force in establishing conventions, but also the model to be followed in the new genre. They are the first representative figures for the 18th century women novelists who gave fiction its popular form. Elizabeth Inchbald, Charlotte Lennox, Charlotte Smith, Fanny Burney, Maria Edgeworth, Amelia Opie, Mary Burton, Sarah Fielding, Mary Wollstonecraft and Mary Hays, all had a share in furthering the novel and ensuring that it had popular appeal and recognition. As Showalter notes, "From about 1750 on, English women made steady inroads into the literary marketplace, mainly as novelists." It is owing to the systematic and extensive research devoted to bringing these women novelists to light that these early founders of the novel genre have taken their place in the literary canon of today. This is one of the most significant contributions of feminist literary criticism. The literary evaluations of the early texts from the view-points of many different methods brought a refreshing light to literary studies in general.

Feminist Literary Criticism: A Theoretical Perspective

Feminist literary criticism became a theoretical issue with the advent of the new women's movement initiated in the early 1960s. In fact, feminist criticism started as part of the international women's liberation movement. The first major book of particular significance, in this respect was Betty Friedan's *The Feminine Mystique* (1963) which contributed to the emergence of the new women's movement. In her book Friedan criticized "the dominant cultural image of the successful and happy American woman as a housewife and mother". According to Friedan, in the 1950s women had gone back to the house abandoning their jobs to men who came back from the war to claim their positions, and a feminine mystique was created in the media making the housewife and mother the ideal models for all women. Promoting women's ideal reality within the domestic realm, this mystique had reduced the identity of women to sexual and social passivity. Betty Friedan attempted to demystify this false feminine, mystique, which she described as "a world confined to her own body and beauty, the charming of man, the bearing of babies, and the physical care and serving of husband, children and home", in order to renew the women's fight for equal rights. She had started a new consciousness-raising movement, and played a central role in developing the new discipline of women's studies.

With the publication of Kate Millet's *Sexual Politics* (1969), feminist criticism became a challenge to the traditional norms of English studies in the 1970s. With this book Millet initiated the first modern principles of feminist criticism by embarking upon a critique of sexist assumptions in male-authored texts and introducing some of the fundamental terms, such as "patriarchal," which gained considerable significance in feminist literary studies *Sexual Politics* soon became a cult book among feminist critics, especially with its politics of female representations in literature. By "politics" Millet means the operations of power relations in society. She argues that Western institutions have manipulated power to establish the dominance of men and subordination of women in society. She also criticises Freud's psychoanalytical theory for its male bias. With her readings of passages from established writers like D.H. Lawrence, Henry Miller, Norman Mailer and Jean Gen-et, Millet shows the perspectives of a female reader. Obviously she uncovers negative images of women both in society and in literature had produced equally provocative but more cautious responses, such as Mary Ellman's *Thinking About Women* (1965). It was with Ellman that modern feminist criticism was initiated in the United States. Her somewhat humorous treatment of the stereotypes of women in literature written by men makes Ellman one of the pioneers in the development of contemporary feminist criticism. With Ellman, and more forcefully with Millet, feminist criticism has generated much public debate in women's rights, and in their search for equality in society.

However, in a 1929 essay titled 'Women and Fiction', published in the same year as *A Room of One's Own,* Virginia Woolf speculated on the 'new colours and shadow' in women's writing which would inevitably appear now that the 'English woman' was transformed from a nondescript influence, fluctuating and vague, to voter, a wage-earner, a responsible citizen.' As women took up their place as full civic subjects in the public sphere, Woolf considered that their 'relations' would become 'not only emotional' but also 'intellectual' and 'political'. Their novels would become more engaged with the 'impersonal', more 'critical of society and less analytical of individual lives'. No longer the 'dumping ground for personal emotions' women's fiction would observe men and women 'as they cohere and clash in groups and classes and races'. This political transformation of imaginative writing would, she hoped, be but a first short step to the practice of the sophisticated art—to the writing of essays and criticism, of history and biography'. More important still, for Woolf, the 'greater impersonality of women's lives will encourage the poetic spirit' that will lead them even further, 'beyond the personal and political relationships to the wider questions which the poet tries to solve-of our destiny and the meaning of life'. Lest this hope resonate as pure idealism, Woolf reminds the reader that 'the poetic attitude is largely founded upon material things,' 'upon leisure, and a little money' which provide 'the chance—to observe impersonally and dispassionately.' With all the advantages of middle-class men—a professional job, a vote, economic independence, leisure and a legitimate public presence-women, Woolf prophesied, 'will make a fuller and more subtle use of the instrument of writing'.

Moreover, the continuing critique or woman' cultural, social and literary identity as the "other still sparks off a great deal of controversy and interest, not only among feminist critics, but also in literary studies in general. So consequently, as Elaine Showalter has stated in her article, "The Feminist Critical Revolution," feminist criticism has altered the traditional norm of literary study "Since the late 1960s, when feminist criticism developed as part of the international women's movement, the assumptions of literary study have been profoundly altered". The study of a female tradition in literature has transgressed the boundaries of the traditional canon both in its theoretical, political and literary assumptions. Hence, feminist literary criticism has become, to put it in Toril Moi's words, "an urgent political necessity". The over-riding problem is now, "how to avoid bringing patriarchal notions of aesthetics, history and tradition to bear on the female tradition". In this respect, Moi criticises Showalter who did not avoid these pitfalls and other feminist critics, like Myra Jehien, who, she thinks, are not even aware of the problem. In view of the arguments presented above, one can, as far as I am concerned, point out that to write outside the dominant discources, aesthetics and literary theory is already to accept the fact of being an outsider and posing willingly as "the other". Obviously, the problem of the relationship between politics or ideological criticism and aesthetics is already a higly complex one.

Feminist criticism today is as much concerned with women as reader as with women as writer-what Elaine Showalter usefully defined in 'Towards a Feminist Poetics' (1979) as the twin projects of 'feminist critique' and in a word she coined-'gynocritics'. Showalter originally thought of 'feminist critique' as a somewhat negative enterprise, teaching us 'only what men have thought women should be', and, in its theoretical register, requiring 'a long apprenticeship to the male theoretician'. In practice, however, it has seemed more liberating and less depressive than that, generating a wide variety of work that does much more than confirm the burden of our oppression, from Kate Millet's *Sexual Politics* (1969), which made it impossible to read the sexual scenarios of modern literature as innocently liberatory, to such different kinds of studies as Alice Jardine's *Gynesis: Configuration of Women and Modernity* (1985), Naomi Schor's *Reading in Detail: Aesthetics and the Feminine* (1987) and Tania Modleski's study of Hitchcock, *The Women Who Knew Too Much* (1988).

In *A Literature of Their Own* Showalter argued that literary subcultures all go through three major phases of development. For literature by or about women, she labels these stages the Feminine, Feminist, and Female:

1. Stage - involves "*imitation* of the prevailing modes of the dominant tradition" and "*internalization* of its standards."
2. Stage- involves "*protest* against these standards and values and *advocacy* of minority rights—"
3. Stage- this is the "phase of *self-discovery,* a turning inwards freed from some of the dependency of opposition, a search for identity."

Showalter's three stages of feminine, feminist, and female are identifiable in the life of Cleofilas in Sandra Cisneros's "Women Hollering Creek."

Modern critical theory states that reading a text with the intention of decoding its meaning (s) is a reductive act, and it imposes some kind of limitation (in the sense of closure) on the text. That is what feminist literary criticism should try to avoid if it claims a serious place within the theoretical field of literature. Toril Moi's argument that "without an aesthetic effect there will be no political effect" is right in as so far as feminist criticism deconstructs the binary opposition between politics and aesthetics and takes them as relational concepts and as value-free categories. If feminist criticism wants to generate new analytical methods in its reading of literary texts, it can only achieve its aim by challenging and disrupting the patriarchal tradition within its dominant discourses, that is, by working from within that tradition. Besides, feminist critics can no longer claim that they work from marginalized positions. They now constitute the majority of scholars in a great number of women's studies departments at the universities both in Europe and in the United States.

A reading of critical theories and methods of the literary tradition is possible only if those theories and methods are challenged from within their own assumptions. That is what French feminist criticism aimed at starting with Helene Cixous who has challenged the binary opposition of man/women in the value system. Cixous has subverted the logocentric logic behind the underlying paradigms of male/female opposition in culture and literature. Binary systems validate logocentricism so convincingly that "to decentre logocentricism would invoke reversing the values placed on each component in the binary terms which constitute it". Once the binary opposition of male/female is reversed, as the first step to construct a new methodological basis for literary analysis, the signifying supremacy passes on to the once - secondary term in the hierarchy: "female". The second step is to avoid the temptation of forcing this terms dominance over the now-secondary term: "male". In other words, the second step is to avoid the elatic closure of the binary opposition. The supremacy of the privileged term, female, cannot remain in its privileged position to create a new values and meanings.

As Barbara Johnson notes, the deconstruction "of a binary opposition is—not an annihilation of all values or difference: it is an attempt to follow the subtle, powerful effects of differences already at work with-in the illusion of a binary opposition". The meanings are achieved through a free play between presence and absence of the signifier (that produces meaning). The deconstruction of a text aims to undo "the domination of one mode of signifying over another. The problem is that, meaning is never truly present, because it is endlessly deferred. It is created in an infinite process of referring to other signifiers, which, in fact give meaning to the previous signifier. This goes on infinitely. Thus, one can never reach a transcendental signified where the process of postponing meaning comes to an end. It is because "Writing is the endless displacement of meaning which both governs language and places it for ever beyond the reach of a stable self-authenticating knowledge."

There is no origin of meaning and an end to the signification process. As Jonathan Culler notes: "If either cause or effect can occupy the position of origin, then origin is no longer originary: it loses its meta-physical privilege. A non-originary origin is a "concept" that cannot be comprehended by the former system and thus disrupts it." In short, the feminist literary tradition cannot claim to work outside this freeplay and assert any presence of origins in its analysis and evaluations of literary texts by privileging the term "female". The terms female and male can be studied, however, as a relational and differential process. They are related to each other as signifiers in an endless signification process. It is not possible to stop this process as Derrida has brilliantly demonstrated in his theory of deconstruction. Therefore, it is necessary to study the female literary tradition in relation to its male counterpart, and to deconstruct all the binary oppositions that have been falsely created and accepted over the centuries as universal and privileged value systems, or meta-narratives.

So, no matter how strongly the Western logocentricism has claimed the supremacy of meta-narratives (such as history, logic, reason, or truth), they have been challenged since all "origins" have been shattered and all illusions broken. Now, these meta-narratives all split into multiple discources. Feminist literary criticism has played a crucial part in breaking the logocentric tradition and challenging the supremacy of the privileged concepts and values in the patriarchal systems. This is its alternative approach to literary as well as cultural studies.

Today recent critical theories of literature claim that there is no one single reality or any dominant narrative that can find the individual writer in any way. Since the shattering of all meta-narratives there flourished a plurality of diversified narratives. Therefore, the ideologies of feminity and female writing, or the male literary tradition, should no longer be thought of in terms of universal origins or frameworks. Today no literary critic can claim to mobilise the innumerable discources that are produced to deconstruct each other. Like any other literary discourse, feminist discourses, too should be read intertextually, not only in terms of writer against other writers, but also in terms of the literary against itself. With the advent of deconstructive criticism, there is now a way to question and to challenge the ideologies by which the female writers had written and under-written fiction, and also against which they had encouraged a sustained reading of that fiction.

Feminist criticism is especially notable as regards its diversity of aims and methods. As Elizabeth Abel notes in her "Introduction" to *Writing and Sexual Difference* (1982), deciphering the interplay of writing and sexual difference requires a variety of critical approaches. Feminist critics are pluralistic in their literary methods and theorises. Annette Kolodny also states that only by employing a plurality of methods will be protect ourselves from the temptations of oversimplifying any text." But, as Kolodny also points out, there is a basic principle that unites feminist literary critics under one roof dispute their plurality of methods :

> What unites and repeatedly invigorates feminist literary criticism.......is neither dogma nor method but an acute and impassioned attentiveness to the ways in which primarily male structures of power are inscribed (or encoded) within our literary inheritance : the consequences of that encoding for women—as characters, as readers, and as writers; and, with that, a shared analytic concern for the implications of that encoding not only for a better understanding of the past but also for an improved reordering of the present and future.

Feminist literary criticism has been very successful especially in reclaiming the lost literary women and in documenting the sources. In this respect, feminist criticism has successfully directed attention to the female intellectual tradition. Many early works on women writers before the 1960s usually focus on the female literary tradition. Here it is necessary to point out the difference between "female" and "feminist" positions in literary studies. According to Toril Moi in *Feminist Literary Criticism* : "Feminist criticism.. is a specific kind of political discourse, a critical and theoretical practice committed to the struggle against patriarchy and sexism......". Thus the term "feminist" implies a political position. As Sharon Spencer argues, feminist criticism "attempts to set standards for a literature that is as free as possible from biased portraits of individuals because of their class, race or sex." The term "female" on the other hand, does not imply a political or feminist position it implies a gender difference. Female writing can be taken as the special female expression of women's perspectives on a variety of social, cultural and political issues without being committed to the feminist position. Patricia Meyer Spacks points out that "the difference between traditional female preoccupations and roles and male ones make a difference in female writing". Not all women writing have a feminist approach in the sense that they attempt to raise the consciousness of women, or in the sense of expanding women's culture-bound images. Female writing, then, can be explained in terms of gender, not in terms of a collective experience of women or their political perspectives. Hence, male writers can be feminists but they cannot be female writers. The same holds true for male critics. The male feminist critic K.K. Ruthven in his *Feminist Literary Studies* (1984), for example, has stated that "the aim of a feminist criticism as of any revolutionary criticism should be to subvert the dominant discourses, not to make compromises with them". He rejects the idea that Toril Moi for its "divisiveness, aggression and patronising gestures." This kind of critique shows the female critic's keen observation of the male vision, and indicates the fact that feminist literary criticism is the only alternative critical field where women wish to be dominant in practice.

Since the 1970's feminist criticism also engaged itself in extensive discussions about the representations of women in literary tradition and the discovery of the impressive tradition of female writing, because the novel was actually represented almost wholly by women. Many critics like Dale Spender, Elaine Showalter, Juliet Mitchell, among others, have investigated the reason why "To be seen as a woman writer" was "to be seen in a subcategory". Thus women began to resent the imposed literary categories and judgements by openly challenging and disrupting the logocentric tradition. This disruption of the dominant discourses of the literary establishment actually started with a number of notable books in the 1970s. These include, Patricia Meyer Spack's *The Female Imagination* (1975) which dealt with English and Americal novels of the past three hundred years; Ellen Moer's *Literary Women* (1976) which discusses the history of women's writing and which is considered a landmark book; Elaine Showalter's *A Literature of their Own* (1977) which describes the female tradition in the English novel from the Brontes onward as a development of subculture; and Sandra Gilbert and Susan Gubarts *The Madwoman in the Attic* (1979) which studies the major female writers of the 19th century. All these notable books have paved the path for further and more detailed studies of gender and sexism in literature.

Sandra Gilbert and Susan Gubar's *The Mad-woman in the Attic* is brilliantly written massive book on the major female writers of the 19th century. It presents the nature of the "distinctively female tradition" of the 19th century. Gilbert and Gubar's main argument is that artistic creativity, which is perceived within the dominant 19th century tradition basically as a male quality, is in fact a patriarchal superimposition upon the women writers who are imprisoned within it. They write that in the image of the Divine Creator the male author fathers this text. Since women take the same masculine cosmic author as their model too, they end up copying or identifying with the dominant literary images of feminity which come out of the Phallocentric myth of creativity." Authored by a male God and by a godlike male, killed into a "perfect" image of herself, the woman writer's self-contemplation may be said to have begun with a searching glance into the mirror of the male-inscribed literary text. Sandra M. Gilbert and Susan Gubar especially emphasise the metaphor of paternity" in reference to the notion of authority as the legitimised masculine concept in the ownership of texts. Associating author with the father image. Gilbert and Gubar argue that, "if the author/father is owner of his text, and of his reader's attention, he is also, of course owner/possessor of the subject of his text, that is to say of those figures, scenes, and events." From the male perspective, then, since the owner of the text is the author, he is entitled to the control of all his images. Women, thus, had to conform to the male standards of the images of femalenes in their own writing. According to Judith Fetterley, "that is the consequence of the patriarchal prediction that to be human is to be male." Literary women, then, are forced to identify with men and male standards of writing, and yet they are, at the same time, constantly reminded of being female writers. So, deprived of the power of discourse that is given universal parameters in the hands of male writers, the female writers fought against being the "other" and the outsider in the literary tradition : "When only one reality is encouraged, legitimised, and transmitted, and when that limited vision endlessly insists on its comprehensiveness, then we have the conditions necessary for that confusion of consciousness in which impalpability flourishes."

Feminism and Marxism

Feminist criticism has in its discussions the problems of patriarchy and inequality created by the male dominance. Feminism shows that women are conditioned to help their own subordination. They say that the language too is not a neutral medium and is gender biased. The general grievances of feminist critics are inequality, neglect, dominance of women and their derogatory stereotypes in literature mainly written by male authors implicitly for male readers. All these statements and claims of feminism suggest that the feminist criticism is concerned with the conflict with patriarchy and the social structures and conventions made by male oriented society. This brings it closer to Marxist Approach.

According to Marxism, there has been a struggle between powerful and the powerless. The powerful part of society ultimately acquiring the economic base for its ideology, creates super-structures which forms power relations and social structures along with conventions in the society. All this is formed to benefit the power structure. The conflicts of class, race and gender come up. Here the gender conflict in the Marxist theory is directly related to Feminist criticism. Hence, as the feminist criticism acquiring the ground of 'powerful' in the form of patriarchy and the 'powerless' in the form of feminine, considers for its purpose the subsequent part of Marxist approach, is very likely to be called Marxist in origin.

Feminism and Psychoanalysis

In some surprising ways, literary critics have shown that Freudian criticism does not exist in a vacuum. We might expect feminists to ignore Freud; but in fact several feminist critics have taken an interest in Freud's theories. Luce Irigaray, for example, examines Freud's belief that the female sexual identity results from a 'castration complex." According to Freud when a girl realizes that she lacks a penis, the emotions which result from her lack of and desire for a penis will lead her to submit to the social patriarchy. Irigaray takes issue with Freud and his method of defining female sexuality in terms of lack of having "nothing". Irigaray suggests that having "nothing" means "having no thing, no being and no truth". Irigaray's argument leads us to wonder if it is not the "castration complex" which determines a woman's role in the patriarchal system, but rather the defination of a woman as "nothing" which is reinforced by the roles and portrayals of women in society.

Feminism and Poststructuralism

Poststructuralism is a composite term drawing on a number of influential theoretical methodologies developed in the late 1960s and 1970s France. Poststructuralist feminists are influenced by Derrida, Foucault and Lacan (Poststructuralists). The most influential French feminist-poststructuralists (Cixous, Irigaray, Kristeva, et al.) have been drawn on in a variety of ways in the development of what has come to be called 'Sexual Difference' feminism, active mostly outside the UK in the work of Moira Gatens, Rosi Braidotti, Michelle Boulous Walker, Elizabeth Grosz as well as current in Italian feminist theory more generally. British feminism, on the other hand, with its history of engagement with a tradition of British socialism, tends to be turned off by ideas of 'Sexual Difference', but has taken up aspects of poststructuralist methodologies—as conducive to an extended materialist analysis of gender, power and representation. However, the British feminist encounter with poststructuralism is largely—if not exclusively—the result of an ongoing feminist critique of the implications and pitfalls of poststructuralist methodologies for women inside and outside the academy, a response to poststructuralism that is a direct result of British feminism's largely socalist roots. At one extreme of the range of views in play poststructuralism is considered to be a threat to the very terms in which a feminist politics is grounded characterized by Kate Soper's announcement that feminism as theory has pulled the rug from under 'feminism as politics.'

The most compelling and distinctive aspect of British feminist-poststructuralist work derives from British feminism's long history of and investment in a committed socialism and a related cultural materialism. Mitchell's work was steeped in a British Marxist tradition, and her argument was challenging in its appropriation of psychoanalytic critical tools in this context. Hence poststructuralist critical apparatus tends to have been subjected to a rigorous and highly critical scepticism in British academic feminism, rather than ingested whole and unaltered. The resulting arguments have a refreshing absence of jargonese, tend towards a careful self-examination of concepts and positions, and are usually successful in avoiding narcissistic theoretical loops. The British encounter between feminist and poststructuralism, then, has resulted in recent years in an internalization by feminist theorists and practitioners of the serious questions raised by post-structuralist methodologies, and these questions in themselves have become integral to rather than under mining of—the larger feminist academic project. So while Radstone identifies 'insecurities and doubts which currently shake feminist theory to its core, producing a range of questions concerning the status of the category "woman" leading to the fundamental question 'is a politics grounded in women's *collective* experience still desirable, given poststructuralism's deconstruction of binary oppositions?', feminist theory continues to produce a range of committed feminist theoretical and pedagogic practices which incoporate poststructuralist questions and methodologies without conceding the political efficacy and importance of notional 'woman' in whose name the feminist project acts. Elizabeth Grosz understands this process well at the level of political intervention when she notes that some anti-poststructuralist critics radically miss the point when they assume that 'feminists take on essentialist or universalist assumptions....... in the same way as patriarchs, instead of attempting to understand the ways in which essentialism and its cognates function as unavoidable and therefore possibly strategically useful terms.' For Grosz, the anti-poststructuralist-feminist position 'silences and neutralises the most powerful of feminist theoretical weapons, the ability to use patriarchy and phallocratism against themselves, to take up positions ostensibly opposed 'to feminism and to use them for feminist goals'. Feminism remains undeniably—and some might say gloriously—parasitic on the academy in British universities, surviving and in some areas flourishing by its radical and unsettling mimeticism, a transmuting ability to reproduce itself in forms ostensibly designed or appropriated to undermine it (poststructuralism included).

Feminism and Deconstruction

Feminism and deconstruction have influenced literary criticism by rethinking the terms of sexual difference, politics and ethics. Emphasising indeterminacy, the openness of interpretation and the importance of difference, their alliance has given rise to powerful interrogation of representations of women across a range of literary fields.

While the alliance between feminism and deconstruction is acknowledged by literary criticism, there is not a simple formula for how they work together. Their relationship takes a variety of shapes, partially because feminism and deconstruction continuously redefine one another. The resulting instability produces a fluid relationship, in which neither term is subordinated.

Jacques Derrida claims that 'deconstruction is *certainly* not feminist....... if there is one thing that it must not come to, it's feminism'. For Derrida, feminism is the operation through which a woman desires to be like a man, like a dogmatic philosopher, demanding truth, science, objectivity'. Feminism is therefore accused of eliding difference and judged to be just another form of western metaphysics, pinning its hopes on truth and objectivity.

To begin with, feminism and deconstruction stress that there is no thematic identity to the categories 'women'. What deconstruction does, is that, it provide feminism with more than a simple anti-essentialism. By offering a radical account of meaning as *deferral,* deconstruction suggests that 'women' as a category would be indeterminate. While 'women' would not be determinable as purely a question of either ontology or meaning, neither would they be determinable *within* the category of meaning because meaning itself is ultimately indeterminate, always subject to deferral. Deconstructions terms of deferral and indeterminacy thus help to articulate the claim that feminism's struggle can perhaps best be understood not simply as a struggle to assert identity but as a struggle to assert difference. And feminism cannot get to the end of that struggle by just being mere careful about listing a number of qualifiers every time it mentions women. Women may exist in relation to a complex matrix of difference, but as Judith Butler points out, 'it would be wrong to assume in advance that there is a category of "women" that simply needs to be filled it with various components of race, class, age, ethnicity, and sexuality in order to become complete.' More differences more meanings, will always remain to be articulated and contested. 'Women' is a permanently contested site of meaning, where meaning is always deferred, ultimately indeterminate.

It could be said, then, that women pose questions *for* feminism as much as they provide the basis *of* feminism. And one such crucial question involves the framework of gender and sex : how do 'women' stands in relation to gender and sex ? A deconstructionist feminist analysis responds by interrogating the very distinction between sex and gender, suggesting that it is time to rethink the position that sex is a biological, natural attribute into which cultural notions of gender are grafted. Making a crucial move, Joan Scott calls for 'a genuine historicization and deconstruction of the terms of sexual difference', shifting the emphasis away from sex so that gender could be 'redefined and restructed in conjunction with a vision of political and social equality that includes not only sex but class and race'.

The radicality of questioning the sex/gender divide leads on to a rethinking of the opposition between language and materiality. Derrida begins this work by attempting to denaturalise the rhetoric of the female body. Concentrating on the hymen and the process of invagination as graphic entities, he argues against assigning any natural or essential feminity to them. The hymen has no proper meaning, belongs to no woman in particular; invagination and the hymen exist outside the discourse of biology. As such, they may mark a space of material difference, but there is no real space of difference to mark. For Derrida, bodies are always discursive, always both inscribed and inscribing.

Luce Irigaray, while not always strictly a deconstructionist thinker, also makes use of morphological language in her search for new linguistic avenues that can begin to speak about women's unspeakable pleasure, pleasure that exists but is not able to be articulated within the terms of patriarchal discourse. For Irigaray, woman is never a sex that in one-singular or divisible into one. Her pleasures are always multiple, occuring in multiple places on the body. She is not limited to a single pleasure in a single place on her body; her pleasures are not even limited to individual bodies which clearly draw divisions : 'the passage from the inside out, from the outside in, the passage between us, is limitless. Without end. No knot or loop, no mouth ever stops our exchanges.' Moving away from hypostatisations of the female body, Irigaray's use of the rhetoric of bilogical discourse reconfigures anatomy in terms of which refuse to situate the body as a substance or essence. Irigaray is effectively 'writing the body'; to use Helene Cixous's phrase, by writing *through* and *with* the body rather than simply writing *about* the body. What becomes evident in both Derrida's and Irigaray's work is that language and materiality always entail one another.

Approaches to Feminism/Types of Feminism

(1) Liberal Feminism : Liberal feminism has its roots in 18th century philosophy called Enlightment period. It was the time when two strong values developed viz. rationalities and individuality. It is also called as age of reason. It was against religious dogmas and autocratic government. One of the main issue was the role of woman. Mary Wollstonecraft's "Vindication of the rights of women" deals with the critical theme as"—women are first and foremost human being, rational creatures and not sexual being. They are capable of governing themselves by reason. Hence, if women are to be denied natural rights, then it must be, proved that they are not rational creature.

In America, liberal feminist believe, American constitution has given rights and freedom to women which is more than many other countries. Equal opportunities recognized by the constitution, is not practiced because of sexist attitudes. Hence, the contemporary society and attitudes of people must change. Three major themes came up like equal pay for similar work, equal distribution of household work and reproductive choice. Liberal feminism is widely diffused approach in contemporary women's movements. There are many issues taken up by women activists such as careers for women, equal parenting, gender-free education etc.

Liberal feminism dominated till 1960s. Yet did not provide any explanation for roots of women's inferior status. Liberal feminists argued for equal rights for women, but accepted the existing social order as valid. The advocated for improvement of social customs, institutions, laws, attitudes without altering social structure. They strongly believed that progressive reforms will lead to real and substantial equality for women as individuals. There is no need for revolutionary changes in economic, political or cultural areas. Liberal feminists state that democracy and democratic structure constitute essential condition for successful reform. Radical change could only diminish the available freedom and justice for both men and women.

(2) Socialist Feminism : This is a very broad term and includes different shades. It is a diverse cluster of writings, referring to different cultural situations. All these types of socialist feminisms share theoretical background though there conclusions, strategies may differ. Socialist feminism combines three different ideologies viz. Marxian, radical and phenomenological. Socialist feminism has its roots in Marxian thoughts and it is linked with radical feminism. Like any other type of feminism, socialist feminism also stresses women's perspective. Hence, it is close to phenomenology stating women's subjective construction of social reality.

Socialist feminists set three main goals for themselves. Those are :

(*a*) To achieve a combination of breadth and precision, so that all forms of oppression are explored and that exploration is anchord in women's experiences. Here the stress is on finding out different forms of oppression of women; either within the family or outside. Then to develop a common agenda for women's movements.

(*b*) To develop explicit and adequate methods for social analysis by standing in on expanded rotion of historical materialism. All types of socialist feminisms rely on historical materialism. Throughout history material culture, system of production are owned by one class (capitalist) are used it as a weapon to exploit labour class. This labour also include labour class women. Hence, socialist feminists aim to find out different methods to gain information and to use it.

(*c*) To treat ideas as equal to material production in determining human affairs. This is specially with reference to women.

According to socialist feminist, the powerlessness of women in society is rooted in four basic structures: production, reproduction, sexuality and socialization of children. Family re-enforces women's oppressive conditions. Family and economy should not be looked upon as separate systems, but as vitally interacting systems. Socialist feminist have raised debate over household work. Women's oppression is based on unpaid work, child bearing, child care, house-work are material activities resulting in products. Such products have use value but not exchange value.

The important criticism of socialist feminism and indeed all varieties of feminism is that despite their emancipatory claims, they tend to be located in the assumption and aspiration at urban middle class women. There is growing concern within feminist theory over practical and theoretical problems posed by the exploitation of women of one class, race, ethnic group and religious community by another group. Using Marx and Engel's frame-work they have observed and analyzed women's problems. Oppressed women's involvement in the struggle, is achieved by socialist feminist.

(3) Radical Feminism : Radical feminism is the breeding ground for many of the ideas arising from feminism. Radical feminism was the cutting edge of feminist theory from approximately 1967-1975. It is no longer as universally accepted as it was then, and no longer serves to solely define the term, "feminism".

This group views the oppression of women is the most fundamental form of oppression, one that cuts across boundaries of race, culture, and economic class. This is a movement intent on social change, change of rather revolutionary proportions. Radical feminism questions why women must adopt certain roles based on their biology, just as it questions why men adopt certain other roles based on theirs. Radical feminism attempts to draw lines between biologically-determined behaviour and culturally-determined behaviour in order to free both men and women as much as possible from their previous narrow gender roles.

(4) Amazon Feminism : Amazon feminism is dedicated to the image of the female hero in Greek mythology, as it is expresed in art and literature, in the physiques and fears of female athletes, and in sexual values and practices.

Amazon feminisms focuses on physical equality and is opposed to gender role stereotype and discrimination against women based on assumptions that women are supposed to be, look or behave as if they are passive, weak and physically helpless. Amazon feminism rejects the idea that certain characteristics or interest are inherently masculine (or feminine), and upholds and explores a vision of heroic womanhood.

(5) Cultural Feminism : The theory that there are fundamental personality differences between men and women, and that women's differences are special are should be celebrated. This theory of feminism supports the notion that there are biological differences between men and women. For example, "Women are kinder and more gentle the men", leading to the mentality that if women ruled the world there would be no wars. Cultural feminism is the theory that wants to overcome sexism by celebrating women's special qualities, women's ways, and women's experiences, often believing that the "woman's way" is the better way.

(6) Ecofeminism : Ecofeminism is a theory that rests on the basic principal that patriarchal philosophies are harmful to women, children, and other living things. Parallels are drawn between society's treatment of the environment, animals, or resources and its treatment of women. In resisting patriarchal culture, ecofeminists believe they are also resisting plundering and destroying of the Earth. They feel that the patriarchal philosophy emphasizes the need to dominate and control unruly females and the unruly wilderness.

Ecofeminism states that the patriarchal society is relatively new, something developed over the last 5,000 years or so and that the matriarchial society was the first society. In the matriarchal society, women were the center of society and people worshipped goddesses. This is known as the *Feminist Eden.*

Characteristics of Feminism and Feminist Approach

1. Feminism is not just an acedemic exercise but action oriented.
2. It is an ideology, belief system, an ideology against oppression and exploitation of women. It is a doctrine advocating social, political, economic rights for women.
3. It is a body of knowledge, thoughts, theories, perspective, way of looking at present available knowledge from women's point of view.
4. It is women's search for self-identity.
5. Feminism as a Philosophy shares with all traditions of progressive thoughts and principle of equal worth of all human beings.
6. Feminism is a movement. It is a struggle against women's exploitation and opression.
7. It is an inner-struggle both for men and women.
8. Feminist scholars differentiate sex from gender and view the latter as a socially/culturally constructed category. Gender is learned and performed; it involves the myriad and often normative *meanings* given to sexual difference by various cultures. Feminists may differ in the importance they assign to sex, which is a biologically

based category, but the idea that gender norms can be changed is central to feminist theory.

9. Although sex/gender systems differ cross-culturally, most known societies have used and still use sex/gender as a key structural principle organizing their actual and conceptual worlds, usually to the disadvantage of women. Hence, feminist scholars argue that gender is a crucial cateogry of analysis and that modes of knowledge which do not take gender into account are partial and incomplete.
10. Feminist scholars also seek to question and transform androcentric systems of thought which posit the male as the norm. In practice this means not only revealing and critiquing androcentric biases, but also attempting to examine beliefs and practices from the viewpoint of the "other", treating women and other marginalized groups as subjects, not merely objects.
11. Feminists believe that existing inequalities between dominant and marginalized groups can and should be removed. Therefore, feminist scholarship has an acknowledged and accepted political dimension, as opposed to be hidden political dimension of scholarship that claims to be "neutral" and "objective". Although the commitment to feminist politics and organized feminist movements will not be equally stressed in all pieces of scholarship, it will never be denied or criticized. With regard to scholarship, the political goal of feminist work is broader than simply a stronger emphasis on women, though that is an important part of it; the goal is to revise our way of considering history, society, literature etc. so that neither male nor female is taken as normative, but both are seen as equally conditioned by the gender constructions of their culture.

13

Marxist Criticism

Marxism is the political philosophy and practice derived from the work of Karl Marx and Friedrich Engels. Any political practice or theory that is based on an interpretation of the works of Marx and Engels may be called Marxism; this includes different forms of politics and thought such as those of Communist Parties and Communist states, as well as academic research across many fields. While there are many theoretical and practical differences among the various forms of Marxism, most forms of Marxism share :

(1) a belief that capitalism is based on the exploitation of workers by the owners of capital

(2) a belief that people's consciousness of the conditions of their lives reflects material conditions and relations

(3) an understanding of class in terms of differing relations of production, and as a particular position within such relations

(4) an understanding of material conditions and social relations as historically malleable

(5) a view of history according to which class struggle, the evolving conflict between classes with opposing interests, structures each historical period and drives historical change.

The main points of contention among Marxists are the degree to which they are committed to a worker's revolution as the means of achieving human emancipation and enlightment, and the actual mechanism through which such a revolution might occur and succeed. Marxism is correctly but not exhaustively described as a variety of Socialism being by far the variety for which there is the most historical experiences both as a revolutionary movement and as the basis of actual governments. Some Marxists, however, such as Trotskyists, argue that no actual state has ever fully realized Marxist principles; other Marxists, such as Antonomists claim Marxist principles cannot be realized in any state construct seen through the 20th century, and would necessitate a reconceptualization of the notion of state itself.

Marxist criticism which sprang up out of the nineteenth century realist criticism is a syntematic doctrine, finds its echoes in Russian, English and American writing in the later 1920's and 1930's. Marxist criticism is based on the doctrine of socialism realism. The term covers a theory which asks the writer to reproduce reality accurately and to use his art for spreading socialism, the party spirit and the party line as Lenin said "Literature must become a component part of the organised, planned, unified socialist party work."

Marxism sees different phenomena in the environment as a part of the larger social reality. From this we infer that since we live in a society, whatever we think, feel or believe in, would necessarily be a part of our society and therefore, reflect upon the social reality surrounding us. Organised under a specific system of production and distribution, a society exerts immense amount of pressure on its members. At the same time, according to Marxism, individuals or groups in a society, moulded as they are by the forces of production and distribution, are not totally helpless in the environment. In fact, classes of people, the haves and have-nots, remain in constant clash with one another and strive to establish or retain their supremacy in the structure they operate in Marxism tell us that class struggle is the essence of a society and nothing happening in society can be adequately explained without reference to this fact. At the philosophical level, Marxism provides investigative-analytical methods, superior, objective and scientific, to study and assess the phenomena of history. Through an application of these methods, various historical phenomena can be probed and comprehended in their fulness and interconnection. The Marxist method of enquiry and analysis is called the dialectical method under which the contending and opposing elements of a phenomenon are seen as linked to each other in an ever-changing process. This means that when two elements clash, they should be studied and judged with reference to the structure that produced them. At the same time, the clash is a positive and productive clash in which a struggle for resolving the conflict may also be noticed. The dialectical method shows how the very survival of a structure rests on its different conflicting elements. Seen dialectically, a historical phenomenon is both a product of one particular phenomenon and the producer of the other. For this reason, Marxism assigns a deeper significance to terms such as "society" and "social reality" and makes us aware of the fact that society is aliving and changing reality subject to the laws of history, such as the class struggle, the role and function of the state and radical restructuring of society by actual political formations. Growth and development are the outcome of important conflicts taking place between groups, sections and classes of people.

Since Marxism lays stress upon the importance of history within which various social and cultural trends emerge, it gives new dimension to the study of literature. It is with the help of Marxism that we comprehend the relationship between a writer and his/her society. This relationship is that of a sensitive individual with his/her environment. This individual is deeply concerned with the conditions of people around him/her. She/he recognises the existence of not merely pain and anguish but also anger and a sense of resistance in their lives. At the same time, the writer notices among people the great urge to enjoy, celebrate and be happy. This makes him/her combine within their writing the different human emotions of melancholy, disquiet as well as anger and joy. On the surface, these appear to be expressions of an individuals response. However, the writer's response has its roots in the society to which she belongs and, therefore, reflects upon the nature of his/her surroundings. Marxisms does not stop at this point but takes the consideration further to the specific mode of production, the governing economic structure, which regulates the activity of men and women in a decisive way. Marxism also pinpoints the role of human beings in shaping their society through sharp questioning and active mobilisation.

Classical Marxism

Classical Marxism refers to the body of theory directly expounded by Karl Marx and Friedrich Engels. The term

"Classical Marxism" is often used to distinguish between "Marxism" as it is broadly understood and "what Marx believed", which is not necessarily the same thing. For example, shortly before he died in 1883, Marx wrote a letter to the French worker's leader Jules Guesde and to his own son-in-law Paul Lafarque, both of whom claimed to represent Marxist principles, in which he accused them of "revolutionary phrase-mongering" and of denying the value of reformist struggles. Paraphasing Marx : "If that is Marxism, then I am not a Marxist". As the American Marx scholar Hal Draper remarked, "there are few thinkers in modern history whose thought has been so bodly misrepresented, by Marxists and anti-Marxist's alike."

Karl Marx and Friedrich Engels

Karl Heinrich Marx (May 5, 1818, Trier, then part of Prussian Rhineland—March 14, 1883, London) was an immensely influential German Philosopher, political, economist, and socialist revolutionary. Marx addressed a wide variety of issues, including alienation and exploitation of the worker, the capitalist mode of production, and historical materialism. He is most famous, however, for his analysis of history in terms of class struggles, as summed up in the opening line of the introduction to the "Communist Manifesto": "The history of all hitherto existing society is the history of class struggles." The influence of his ideas, already popular during his life, was greatly broadened by the victory of the Russian Bolsheviks in the October Revolution of 1917. Indeed, there are few parts of the world which were not significantly touched by Marxian ideas in the course of the 20th century.

Friedrich Engels (November 28, 1820, Wuppertal-August 5, 1895, London) was a 19th century German political Philosopher. He developed communist theory alongside Marx.

The two first met in person in September 1844. They discovered that they had similar views on Philosophy and on capitalism and decided to work together, producing a number of works including *Die hellige Familie (The Holy Family).* After the French authorities deported Marx from France in January 1845, Engels and Marx decided to move to Belgium, which then permitted greater freedom of expression than other countries in

Europe. Engels and Marx returned to Brussels in January 1846, where they set up the Communist Correspondence Committee.

In 1847 Engels and Marx began writing a pamphlet together, based on Engel's *The Principles of Communism.* They completed the 12,000–word pamphlet in six weeks, writing it in such a manner as to make communism understandable to a wide audience, and published it as *The Communist Manifesto* in February 1848. In March, Belgium expelled both Engels and Marx. They moved to Cologne, where they began to publish a radical newspaper, the *Neue Rheinische Zeitung.* By 1849, both Engels and Marx had to leave Germany and moved to London. The Prussian authorities applied pressure on the British government to expel the two men, but Prime Minister Lord John Russell refused. With only the money that Engels could raise, the Marx family lived in extreme poverty.

After Marx's death in 1883, Engels devoted much of the rest of his life to editing and translating Marx's writing. He also contributed significantly to feminist theory and Marxist feminism in *Origins of the Family, Private Property, and the State,* conceiving, for instance, the concept of monogamous marriage as having arisen because of the domination of men over women. In this sense, he ties communist theory to the family, arguing that men have dominated women just as the capitalist class has dominated workers. Engels died in London in 1895.

Classical Marxism was influenced by a number of different thinkers. These thinkers can be divided roughly into 3 groups :

1. German Philosophers including : Immanuel Kant, Georg Hegel, Ludwig Feuerbach.
2. English and Scottish Political Economist including : Adam Smith and David Ricardo.
3. French Social Theorists including : Jean-Jacques Rousseau, Charles Fourier, Henri de Saint-Simon, Pierre-Joseph Proudhon, Flora Tristan and Louis Blank?

Other influences include :

1. Antique materialism, e.g. Epicurus, Lucretius
2. Giambattista Vico
3. Lewis Morgan

Main Ideas

The main ideas to come out of Marx and Engel's collective works include :

(1) ***Exploitation :*** Marx refers to the exploitation of an entire segment or class of society by another. He sees it as being an inherent feature and key element of capitalism and free markets. The profit gained by the capitalist is the difference between the value of the product made by the worker and the actual wage that the worker receives in other words, capitalism functions on the basis of paying workers less than the full value of their labour, in order to enable the capitalist class to turn a profit. This profit is not however moderated in terms of risk vs. return.

(2) ***Alienation :*** Marx refers to the alienation of people from aspects of their "human nature" ("*Gattungswesen*", usually translated as 'species essence' or 'species-being'). He believes that alienation is a systematic result of capitalism. Under capitalism, the fruits of production belong to the employers, who expropriate the surplus created by others and in so doing generate alienated labour. Alienation describes objective features of a person's situation in capitalism—it isn't necessary for them to believe or feel that they are alienated.

(3) ***Base and Superstructure :*** Marx and Engels use the "base-structure" metaphor to explain the idea that the totality of relations among people with regard to "the social production of their existence" forms the economic basis, on which arises a superstructure of political and legal institutions. To the base corresponds the social consciousness which includes religious, philosophical, and other main ideas. The base conditions both, the superstructure and the social consciousness. A conflict between the development of material productive forces and the relations of production causes social revolutions, and the resulting change in the economic basis will sooner or later lead to the transformation of the superstructure. For Marx, through, this relationship is not a one way

process—it is reflexive; the base determines the superstructure in the first instance and remains the foundation of a form of social organization which then can act again upon both parts of the base-structure metaphor. The relationship between superstructure and base is considered to be a dialectical one, not a distinction between actual entities "in the world".

(4) ***Class Consciousness :*** Class consciousness refers to the awareness, both of itself and of the social world around it, that a social class possess, and its capacity to act in its own rational interests based on this awareness. Thus class consciousness must be attained before the class may mount a successful revolution. Other methods of revolutionary action have been developed however, such as vanguardism.

(5) ***Ideology :*** Without offering a general defination for *ideology*, Marx on several instances has used the term to designate the production of image of social reality. According to Engles, "ideology is a process accomplished by the so-called thinker consciously, it is true, but with a false consciousness. The real motive forces impelling him remain unknown to him, otherwise it simply would not be an ideological process. Hence he imagines false or seeming motive forces". Because the ruling class controls the society's means of production, the superstructure of society, as well as its ruling ideas, will be determined according to what is in the ruling class's best interests....As Marx said famously in *The German Ideology* "the ideas of the ruling class are in every epoch the ruling ideas, *i.e.* the class which is the ruling material force of society, is at the same time its ruling intellectual force". Therefore the ideology of enormous importance since its confuses the alienated groups and can create false consciousness such as commodity fetishism (perceiving labor as capitals~a degration of human life).

(6) ***Historical Materialism :*** Historical materialism was first articulated by Marx, although he himself never used the term. It looks for the cause of developments and changes

in human societies in the way in which humans collectively make the means to life, thus giving an emphasis, through economic analysis, to everything that co-exists with the economic base of society (e.g. social classes, political structures, ideologies).

(7) ***Political Economy* :** The term "political economy" originally meant the study of the conditions under which production was organized in the nation-states of the new-born capitalist system. Political economy, then, studies the mechanism of human activity in organizing material, and the mechanism of distributing the surplus or deficit that is the result of that activity. Political economy studies the means of production, specifically capital, and how this manifests itself in economic activity.

Class

Marx believed that the identity of a social class is derived from its relationship to the means of production (as opposed to the notion that class is determined by wealth alone, *i.e.,* lower class, middle class, upper class).

Marx describes several social classes in capitalist societies, including primarily :

- **The Proletariat :** "those individuals who sell their labour power, (and therefore add value to the products), and who, in the capitalist mode of production, do not own the means of production". According to Marx, the capitalist mode of production establishes the conditions that enable the bourgeoisie to exploit the proletariat due to the fact that the worker's labour power generates a surplus value greater, than the worker's wages.
- **The Bourgeoisie :** Those who "own the means of production" and buy labour power from the proletariat, thus exploiting the proletariat. The bourgeoisie may be further subdivided into the very wealthy bourgeoisie and petit bourgeoisie.

The petit burgeoisie are those who employ labour, but may also work themselves. These may be small proprietors, land-holding peasants, or trade workers. Marx predicted that the petit bourgeoisie would eventually be destroyed by the constant reinvention of the means of production and result of this would be the forced movement of the vast majority of the petit burgeoisie to the proletariat.

Marx also identified various other classes such as :

- **The Lumpen Proletariat :** criminals, vagabonds, beggars etc. People that have no stake in the economic system and will sell themselves to the highest bidder.
- **The Landlords :** a class of people that were historically important, of which some still retain some of their wealth and power.
- **The peasantry and farmers :** this class he saw as disorganized and incapable of carrying out change. He also believed that this class would disappear, with most becoming proletariat but some becoming landowners.

Marx's Theory of History

The Marxist theory of historical materialism understands society as fundamentally determined by the *material conditions* at any given time—this means the relationship which people enter into with one another in order to fulfill their basic needs, for instance to feed and clothe themselves and their families. In general Marx and Engels identified five (and one transitional) successive stages of the development of these material conditions in Western Europe.

1. *Primitive Communism :* as seen in cooperative tribal societies.
2. *Slave Society :* which develops when the tribe becomes a city-state. Aristocracy is born.
3. *Feudalism :* aristocracy is the ruling class. Merchants develop into capitalists.
4. *Capitalism :* capitalists are the ruling class, who create and employ the true working class.
5. *Socialism (Dictatorship of the Proletariat) :* workers gain class consciousness, overthrow the capitalists and take control over the state.
6. *Communism :* A classless and stateless society.

MARXIST SCHOOL OF THOUGHT

Western Marxism

Western Marxism is a term used to describe a wide variety of Marxist theoreticians based in Western and Central Europe (and more recently North America), in contrast with philosophy in the Soviet Union, the Socialist Federal Republic of Yugoslavia or the People's Republic of China.

Structural Marxism

Structural Marxism is an approach to Marxism based on structuralism, primarily associated with the work of the French theorist Louis Althusser and his students. It was influential in France during the late 1960s and 1970s, and also came to influence philosophers, political theorist and sociologist outside of France during the 1970s.

Neo-Marxism

Neo-Marxism is a school of Marxism that began in the 20th century and hearkened back to the early writings of Marx, before the influence of Engels, which focussed on dialectical idealism rather than dialectical materialism. It thus rejected economic determinism being instead far more libertarian. Neo-Marxism adds Max Weber's broader undersanding of social inequality, such as status and power, to orthodox Marxist thought ......

The Frankfurt School

The Frankfurt school is a school of neo-Marxist social theory, social research, and philosophy. The grouping emerged at the Institute for Social Research *(Institut fur Sozialforschung)* of the University of Frankfurt am Main in Germany. The term "Frankfurt School" is an informal term used to designate the thinkers affiliated with the Institute for Social Research or influenced by them : it is not the title of any institution, and the main thinkers of the Frankfurt School did not use the term to describe themselves.

The Frankfurt School gathered together dissident Marxists, severe critics of capitalism who believed that some of Marx's alleged follower has come to parrot a narrow selection of Marx ideas, usually in defense of orthodox Communist or Social-

Democratic parties. Influenced especially by the failure of working-class revolutions in Western Europe after World War I and by the rise of Nazism in an economically, technologically and culturally advanced nation (Germany), they took up the task of choosing what parts of Marx's thought might serve to clarify social conditions which Marx himself had never seen. They drew on other schools of thought to fill in Marx's perceived omissions.

Max Weber exerted a major influence, as did Sigmund Freud (as in Herbert Marcuse's Freudo-Marxist synthesis in the 1954 work *Eros and Civilization).* Their emphasis on the "critical" component of theory was derived significantly from their attempt to overcome the limits of positivism, crude materialism, and phenomenology by returning to Kant's critical Philosophy and its successors in German idealism principally Hegel's Philosophy, with its emphasis on negation and contradiction as inherent properties of reality.

Cultural Marxism

Cultural Marxism is a form of Marxism that adds on analysis of the role of the media, art, theatre, film and other cultural institution in society, often with an added emphasis on race and gender in addition to class. As a form of political analysis, Cultural Marxism gained strength in the 1920s, and was the model used by the Frankfurt School; and later by another group of intellectuals at the Centre for Contemporary Cultural Studies in Birmingham, England.

Autonomist Marxism

Autonomism is a term applied to a variety of social movements around the world, which the ability to organize in autonomous and horizontal networks, as opposed to hierarchial structures such as unions or parties. Autonomist Marxist, including Hary Cleaver, broaden the defination of the working-class to include salaried and unpaid labor, such as skilled professions and housework; it focuses on the working class in advanced capitalist states as the primary force of change in the construct of capital. Modern autonomist theorists such as Antonio Negri and Michael Hardt argue that network power constructs are the most effective methods of organization against the neoliberal regime of accumulation, and predict a massive shift in the dynamics of capital into a 21st Century Empire.

Analytical Marxism

Analytical Marxism refers to a style of thinking about Marxism that was prominent amongst English-speaking philosophers and social scientists during the 1980s. It was mainly associated with the September Group of Academics, so called because they have biennial meetings in varying locations every other September to discuss common interests. The group also dubbed itself "Non-Bullshit Marxism". It was characterized, in the words of David Miller, by "clear and rigorous thinking about questions that are usually blanketed by ideological fog."

Marxist Humanism

Marxist humanism is a branch of Marxism that primarily focuses on Marx's earlier writings especially the *Economic and Philosophical Manuscripts of 1844* in which Marx develops his theory of alienation, as opposed to his later works, which are considered to be concerned more with his structural conception of capitalist society. It was opposed by Louis Althusser's "antihumanism", who qualified it as a revisionist movement.

Marxist humanists contend that 'Marxism' developed lopsided because Marx's early works were unknown until after the orthodox ideas were in vogue—the Manuscripts of 1844 were published only in 1922—and it is necessary to understand Marx's philosophical foundations to understand his latter works properly.

Western and Russian Marxists

As Europe witnessed a widespread nascence of socialist political parties in the later nineteenth century, together with the impact of Marxism on sociology, anthropology, history and political science, the first generation of Marxist intellectuals included the influential Italian Antonio Labriola, who emphasized the highly mediated connection between economic conditions and artistic products and the casual potential of such products in subsequent economic and superstructural developments. Another star in the firmament of early Marxist theory was Franz Mehring, who, along with Rosa Luxemburg and others, founded the German Communist Party in 1918. His writings included the first authoritative biography of Marx, *Karl Marx: The Story of His Life* (1918) and *The Lessing-Legend* (1892-93), which both applied

Marxist categories to the analysis of major German literary figures and brought these within the reach of working-class readers. Mehring attempted to situate Marxist thought and aesthetics in necessary relation to the preceding classical German tradition. Another German, Karl Kautsky, was a propagandist for the Social Democratic party and founded in 1883 the prestigious Marxist journal *Die neue Zeit,* a forum for the elaboration of Marx's economic and political thought. In his *Foundations of Christianity (1908)* Kautsky showed how religious ideas are tied to the levels of artistic and industrial maturity allowed by a particular economic structure.

Georgi Plekhanov (1856-1918), the "father of Russian Marxism," was a founder of the Russian Social Democratic Party. His writings include *Fundamental Problems of Marxism (1908), Art and Social Life* (1912), and some shorter pieces, such as *The Role of the Individual in History* (1898). In the last of these he argues that gifted individuals in history, such as Napoleon, appear only wherever social conditions facilitate their development: every talent that acts as a social force is the product of social relations. In *Art and Social Life* Plekhanov notes that an "art for arts, sake" tendency arises "where the artist is in disaccord with his social environment." A "utilitarian" attitude, viewing art as promoting social betterment, "arises—wherever a mutual sympathy exists between the individuals more or less actively interested in artistic creation and some considerable part of society." Another area in which Plekhanov pioneered a Marxist standpoint was the significance of "play", whereby human beings pursue an activity not for its usefulness but simply for pleasure. This subject was later taken up by Herbert Marcuse. A striking figure in the Marxist canon was Rosa Luxemburg (1871-1919), whose contributions to Marxist economics was profound. However, she was anxious to preserve an aesthetic dimension of art, a recalcitrance to what she saw as reductive theoretical analysis.

Marx and Engels had the time and opportunity to formulate a systematic theory of art and literature. From the relevant titbits of their writings and *obiter dicia,* however, their approaches to literature are discernible. There was nothing pontifical about Marx, and he never spoke ex-cathedra. A widely read person, Marx had classically orthodox literary tastes. He read Aeschylus, Shakespeare, Dickens and Balzac with profit and pleasure. Balzac produce a more valid knowledge of Restoration French Society that do more 'progressive' writers free of Balzac's ruling class sympathies. On the other hand, the concepts of ideology and class interest have forced attention to the possible role of writers and intellectuals in the revolutionary process such as Brecht and Trotsky. Though not exactly a bardolator, Marx read Shakespeare, with particular interest, and his monumental work, The Capital abounds in numerous quotations from the plays of Shakespeare. He did not ignore Shakespeare, because the latter was the chronicler of an age of monarchy and feudalism. All that he emphasized was that art and literature were the products of socio-economic forces. Bourgeois literature is the reflection of the bourgeois ideology, philosophy, and outlook. Literature became the hand-maiden of the ruling class, be it feudal or capitalist.

Vladimir Ilyich Lenin (1870-1924) occupied a central role not only in the revolution of 1917 but also in the unfolding of Marxist aesthetics toward a more politically interventionist stance. Linin's most controversial piece in his "Party Organization and Party Literature" (1905), which, along with certain comments of Marx and Engels, was later misleading claimed to authorize socialist realism. But hostile, non-Marxist critics have also misinterpreted Lenin's essay, viewing it as an attempt to repress free creativity in literature. This interpretation overlooks both the context of the essay and its arguments. Written shortly after the general strike of October 1905, it belongs to a politically volatile period in which the work of revolution was far from complete, as Lenin emphasizes: "While tsarism is *no longer* strong enough to defeat the revolution, the revolution is *not yet* strong enough to defeat tsarism" (*On Literature and Art* 23). Lenin is well aware that art cannot be "subject to mechanical adjustment or levelling, to the rule of the majority over the minority." But he is not prescribing partisanship (*partypost*) for all literature : only for literature that claims to be party literature. He grants that freedom "of speech and the press must be complete".

Lenin's articles on Tolstoy (1908-11) exemplify through their detailed analyses both the political urgency informing Lenin's aesthetics approach and his ability ot explain the circumstances limiting the potential partisanship of great writers. According to Lenin, the contradictions in Tolstoys works—for example, his "merciless criticism of capitalist exploitation," his denunciation of "poverty, degradation and misery among the working masses" as against his "Crackpot preaching of—'resist not evil' with violence," "and his preaching of a reformed religion-mirror the contradictory conditions of the revolutionary peasantry. Tolstoy's misguided renunciation of politics reflect the "pent-up hatred, the ripened striving for a better lot, the desire to get rid of the past—and also the immature dreaming, the political inexperience, and the revolutionary flabbiness characterzing the peasantry. But while Tolstoy's doctrines are "certainly utopian", Lenin is able to call them "socialistic" and to hail Tolstoy's portrayal of the epoch of revolution as "a step forward in the artistic development of humanity as a whole". Lenin's methodological insights are equally interesting: the contradictions in Tolstoy can only be apprehended from the standpoint of the class that led the struggle for freedom during the revolution. This point helps to put into perspective some of Lenin's earlier comments on "Party literature": not only is it impossible to write as an individual, but equally, "individual" acts of reading and interpreting are conducted within parameters dictated by class interests. At a deeper level, Lenin's approach to aesthetic value, embracing as it does the totality of historical circumstances including class, preceding literary traditions and relation to political exigency, can be seen to derive from his acknowledgement in his *Philosophical Notebooks,* of the dialectical character of Marxism, which insists on viewing any "individual" entity in its necessary historical connection with what is universal.

The early debates on art during and after the revolutionary period in Russia focused on questions such as the degree of Party control over the arts, the appropriate stance toward the bourgeois cultural legacy, and the imperative to clarify the connections between the political and the aesthetic. A related question was the possibility of creating a proletarian culture. The other major protagonist in the Russian Revolution, Leon Trotsky (1879-1940), played a crucial role in these debates. His works include *Lenin* (1924), *History of the Russian Revolution* (1932), and *The Revolution Betrayed* (1937), as well as his renowned *Literature and Revolution*

(1924). Trotsky, already exiled in 1900 and 1905 for his revolutionary activities, was finally ousted by Joseph Stalin in the struggle for leadership following Lenin's death in 1924. He continued, in exile, to oppose death in 1924. He continued, in exile, to oppose Stalin's regime until his murder in 1940. In *Literature and Revolution* (1924) Trotsky stressed that only in some domains can the Party offer direct leadership, the "domian of art is not one in which Party is called upon to command. It can and must protect and help it, but it can only lead it indirectly". But just as Lenin's views on this topic have been misread, so Trotsky's claims for freedom of art have been subject to misprison. He states quite clearly that what is needed is "a watchful revolutionary censorship, and a broad and flexible policy in the field of art." What is important for Trotsky is that the limits of such censorship be defined very clearly: he is against "the liberal principle of *laissez faire* and *laissez passer*, even in the field of art." Hence Trotsky cannot be accused of indifference to the iedological threats posed by reactionary literature and ideas, although in a 1938 manifesto, Trotsky urges a "complete freedom for art", while acknowledging that all true art is revolutionary in nature. The latter position evolved in reaction to what Trotsky calls Stalins "police patrol spirit". Trotsky's affirmation of 'the law of art' and his application of the discrepancy theory to authors such as Celine served to legitimise a positive reception of modernism, and indeed (almost certainly contrary to Trotsky's own views) to license Clement Greenbergs declaration of the autonomy of form in modern art.

Modernism in any case represented a major test of the Marxist approach to art and literature. Here Lukacs made a decisive, albeit contradictory contribution. In the first place, *History and Class consciousness* (1923) offered a theoretical framework in which to address far more rigorously than before the relationship between literary form and social context. In effect Lukacs displaced the base superstructure model by affirming the methodological priority of the Marxist conception of social totality: *The primacy of the category of totality is the bearer of the principle of revolution in science*. This move, which took its inspiration from Hegel, focussed on the relationship between part and whole. To conceptualise this relationship Lukacs invoked the theory of commodity fetishism which Marx had developed in *Capital*. Marx had argued that the fact that under capitalism the products of human labour were exchanged on the market led to the transformation of social relations into relations between things. What were in fact features of historically specific social arrangements appeared to be the consequences of universal natural laws operating outside human control.

Lukac's *History and Class Consciousness* is notable for contributing to debates concerning Marxism and its relation to sociology, politics and philosophy, and for reconstructing Marx's theory of alienation before many of the works, of the young Marx had been published: Lukac's work elaborates and expands upon Marxist theories such as ideology, false consciousness, reification and class consciousness. Luckac's developed an aesthetic theory systematically hostile to modernism. For him, the great nineteenth century realist writers represented a period when the bourgeoisie had been a revolutionary class, striving to understand, within the limits allowed by its interest in entrenching a new form of exploitation, the nature of the social world. After 1848, however, the capitalist class is increasingly in the saddle. Objective insight is now a positive disadvantage to a class that needs to conceal, even from itself, its dependence on the extraction of surplus value. And so bourgeois literature becomes, even in its most skilled practitioners such as Flaubert, obsessed with surface sensation rather than underlying structures. Modernism is merely the transformation of this obsession into a self-conscious style. Writers such as Joyce are 'frozen in their own immediacy'. What for Trotsky was a strength in Celine is, according to Lukacs, the modernist's chief weakness; 'they all develop their own artistic style—as a spontaneous expression of their immediate experience'. Modernism is thus largely a symptom of bourgeois decline.

Karl Korsch in his later work, rejected orthodox (classical) Marxism as historically outmoded, wanting to adapt Marxism to a new historical situation. He wrote in his *Ten Theses* (1950) that "the first step in re-establishing a revolutionary theory and practice consists in breaking with that Marxism which claims to monopolize revolutionary initiative as well as theoretical and practical direction" and that "today, all attempts to re-establish the Marxist doctrine as a whole in its original function as a theory of the working classes social revolution are reactionary utopias. Korsch was especially concerned that Marxist theory was losing its precision and validity—in the words of the day, becoming "vulgarized"—within the upper echelons of the various socialist organizations. His masterwork, *Marxism* and *Philosophy* is an attempt to re-establish the historic character of Marxism as the heir to Hegel.

Antonio Gramsci was an Italian writer, politician and political theorist. He was a founding member and one time leader of the Communist Party of Italy. Gramsci can be seen as one of the most important Marxist thinkers of the twentieth century, and in particular a key thinker in the development of Western Marxism. He wrote more than 30 notebooks and 3000 pages of history and analysis during his imprisonment. These writings known as the *Prison Notebooks,* contain Gramsci's tracing of Italian history and nationalism, as well as some ideas in Marxist theory, critical theory and educational theory associated with his name, such as:

- Cultural hegemony as a means of maintaining the state in a capitalist society.
- The need for popular worker's education to encourage development of intellectuals from the working class.
- The distinction between political society (the police, the army, legal system, etc.) which dominates directly and coercively, and civil society (the family, the education system, trade unions, etc.) where leadership is constituted through ideology or by means of consent.
- 'Absolute historicism'.
- The critique of economic determinism.
- The critique of philosophical materialism

Theodar Adorno's criticism is in many ways, and particularly in its commited defence of modernism and its concern with the irreducibility of formal structure diametrically opposed to that of Lukacs', but Adorno shares with him much of Hegelian Luckacs conceptual framework. Where Lukacs thinks of the literary text in terms of its representational potential, Adorno tends to think of it as a closed monad whose historicity is internal and formal rather than a function of its content. The development of artistic material corresponds (as the 'answer' to a 'problem') to the necessary stages of the self-realization of spirit, and so bears a direct by concealed testimony to the historical dialectical. The immanent determination of the truth of the work through this relation to an autonomous history of forms thus demands and uncompromising rejection of extra-aesthetic considerations. Social categories cannot be externally applied but only deduced from the work's formal structure, and 'it is only in the crystallization of its own law of form, not in the passive registration of objects, that art converges with the real'. Through its formal structure the work negates the empirical, and *thereby* hides empirical substance in itself. The degree of its 'negation of' identity becomes the criterion for the real and paradoxical identity of the work with social being, communication takes place. Precisely through the denial referentiality implicit in the work's closure.

The German critic Walter Benjamin introduced certain revolutionary ideas related with art and literature. According to Benjamin, the modern technological revolution such as film, photography, radio, T.V. etc. had brought a revolution in the field of art and literature. In his essay, "The Work of Art in the Age of Mechanical Reproduction" Benjamin says that these technological innovations "transformed the very concept and status of a work of art". It revolutionalized and democratized art. Art for Benjamin was not so much a question of individual talent but the material problem of gaining access to means of communication. Thus when the working class have access to art and literature it democratizes art, this is achieved through these technologies. In such a system, everybody becomes potentially an artist. For example, a novel is filmed and viewed by so many people. It also destroys the autonomy of the writer in the society and his isolation from the masses.

Benjamin's work depends upon the ability to move freely from one domain of being to another, to read any one moment of the social as possessing a kind of expressive radiance such that it can be used to illuminate other moments informed by the historical meaning. Take the theme of the experience of shock, which Benjamin elaborates in his essay. On Some Motifs in Baudelaire'. Beginning as part of a general meditation on the quality of modern urban and capitalist experience, especially in its organization by different modes of communication (narration, information, journalistic sensation), the concept of shock is then developed in relation to Freud's account in *Beyond the Pleasure Principle* (1920) of the link between the psyche's defence against external stimuli and the formation of unconscious memory traces.

Bretott Brecht a dramatist, introduced ideas of Marxism and class struggle through his experimental theatre called 'The Epic Theatre'. Through this theatre and its technique, Brecht rejected the conventional aesthetic theories on drama. He rejected the Aristotelian concept of tragedy which sees drama as a imitation of reality that has a unified plot and a universal theme. He attacked the Aristotelian concept of "catharsis" which is the result of the audience identifying themselves with the hero and the arousal of emotion due to it. What Brecht propogated was a type of drama with defamiliarization by breaking with the conventions of theatrical realism. Brecht encouraged the audience to reflect critically on the action presented, which he termed as the "alienation effect". Brecht's aim was to create reality on the stage, but to shatter the illusion of reality in the mind of the audience. He used various radical, experimental dramatic devices to achieve this by using an *episode plot,* by employing characters who do not attract the audience sympathy, by emphasizing theatricality in staging and acting. The ultimate aim of these new techniques was to produce *estrangement effects* and obtain defamiliarization in the mind of the audience. Literature according could become an active agent or catalyst for social change. Brecht showed that aesthetics and ideology are inextricably linked, and that to change the prevailing ideology the dominant aesthetic has to be fractured and reconstructed.

The other major Marxist school of critical theory to offer a positive appreciation of modernism was, by contrast, unambiguously hostile to the Hegelian influence on Marxism. For Louis Althusser and his followers, Lukacs' conception of totality was an instance of what they called 'expressive totality'. Here all the different aspects of the social whole are conceived as expressions of a singular essence. Thus in Hegel himself, the whole movement of human history is the coming to self-consciousness of Absolute Spirit. In Luckacs' apparently more materialist version, all the different phenomenona of capitalist society replicate the basic structure of commodity fetishism. The result is an economic reductionism as complete as any to be found in social International Marxism.

The authentic Marxist totality, Althusser argues, is a complex, structured whole, a plurality of different structures and practices. Within this whole, economic determination operates only 'in the last instance'. But while Althusser thus adopts Engel's formula, he gives it a different meaning. Every society has a 'structure in dominance', a set of hierarchial relationships in which one practice has primary over the others. The economy plays its ultimately determining role by selecting whichever practice is dominant. Economic causality thus operates indirectly through the structure in dominance, rather than a direct influence on the superstructure. Individual practices develop according to the differential logic, within the limits laid down by the structure in dominance. The superstructure is thus 'relatively autonomous' of the economy.

Being a philosopher, Althusser's arguments were a response to multiple threats to the ideological foundations of orthodox Communism. These included both the influence of empiricism which was beginning to influence Marxist sociology and economics, and growing interest in humanistic and democratic socialist orientations which were beginning to cause division in the European Communist Parties. Althusser is commonly referred to as a structural Marxist, although his relationship to other schools of French structuralism is not a simple affiliation.

His essay *Marxism and Humanism* is a strong statement of anti-humanism in Marxist theory, condemning ideas like "human potential" and "species-being", which are often put forth by Marxist, as outgrowths of a bourgeois ideology of "humanity". His essay *Contradiction and Overdetermination* borrows the concept of overdetermination from psychoanalysis, in order to replace the idea of "contradiction" with a more complex model of multiple casuality in political situations (an idea closely related to Antonio Gransci's concept of hegemony). Althusser is also widely known as a theorist of ideology, and his best known essay is *Ideology and Ideological State Appartuses : Notes Toward an Investigation.* The essay establishes the concept of ideology, also based on Gramsci's theory of hegemony. Whereas hegemony is ultimately determined entirely, by political forces, ideology draws on Freud's and Lacan's concept of the unconscious and mirror phase respectively, and describes the structures and systems that allow us to meaningfully have a concept of the self.

Althusser's follower Machery, in *A Theory of Literary Production* (1966) developed Althusser's concept of the relationship between literature and ideology. A realist novelist, he argues, attempts to produce a unified, coherent text, but instead ends up producing a work containing lapses, missions, and gaps. Why? Because within an ideology there are subjects that cannot be covered, things that cannot be said, contradictory views, that aren't recognized as contradictory. (The critic's challenge in this case is to supply what the text cannot say, thereby making sense of gaps and contradictions). Furthermore, works don't simply reflect ideology (which Goldmann referred to as "myth" and which Macherey refers to a system of "illusory social beliefs"); they are also "fictions", works of art, products of ideology that offer what Goldmann would call a "world-view." What kind of product, Macherey implicity asks, is identical to the thing that produced it ?

A follower of Alhusser, Macherey is sometimes called a *post-Althusserian Marxist.* Eagleton, too, is often described that way, as in his American contemporary, Fredric Jameson. Jameson and Eagleton, both post-Althusserian are also among the few contemporary Anglo-American critics who have closely followed and significantly developed Marxist thought.

Eagleton's *Criticism and Ideology* (1978) is in many ways a response to the work of Williams Eagleton proposes an elaborate theory about how history—in the form of "general", "authorial", and "aesthetic" ideology-enters texts, which in turn may revivify, open up, or critique those same ideologies, setting in motion a process that may alter history. He shows how texts by Jane Austen, Matthew Arnold, Charles Dickens, George Eliot, Joseph Conard, and T.S. Eliot address conflicts at the heart of the ideologies behind them : conflicts between morality and individualism, individualism and social organicism and utilitarianism.

In *Marxism and Literature* (1977) Raymond Williams had argued for a version of Marxism that would give up its determinism, the whole assumption that literature reflects reality passively in favour of an emphasis on human creativity and self-creation. Williams felt that the Marxist Critics unduly separated economics from culture and overlooked individualism. So he moved away from them by preferring culture to ideology. He coined the term 'cultural materialism' and modified Marxist thinking', by utilising the ideas of neo-Marxian theorists, notably Gramsci.

In *The Political Unconscious : Narrative as a Socially Symbolic Act* (1981), Jameson expressely adapts to his synthetic critical enterprise such seemingly incompatible veiwpoints as the medieval theory of fourfold levels of meaning in the allegorical interpretation of the Bible, the archetypal criticism of Northrop Frye, Structuralist Criticism, Lacan's reinterpretation of Freud, semiotics and deconstruction. In *Marxism and Form,* Jameson takes up the question of form and content, arguing that the former is "but the working out" of the latter "in the realm of super-structure."

British Marxism deviated sharply from French (especially Althusserian) Marxism and, like the Frankfurt School, developed an attention to cultural experience and an emphasis on human agency while growing increasingly distant from determinist views of materialism. A circle of historians inside the Communist Party of Great Britain (CPGB) formed the Communist Party Historians Group in 1946. They shared a common interest in 'history from below and class structure in early capitalist society. Important members of the group included E.P. Thompson, Eric Hopsbawn, Christopher Hill and Raphael Samuel.

While some members of the group (most notably E.P. Thompson) left the CPGB after the 1956 Hungarian Revolution, the common points of British Marxist historiography continued in their works. They placed a great emphasis on the subjective determination of history E.P. Thompson famously, engaged Althusser in 'The Poverty of Theory' arguing that Althusser's theory overdetermined history, and left no space for historical revolt by the oppressed.

Post Marxism

Post-Marxism represents the theoretical work of philosophers and social theorists who have built their theories upon those of Marx and Marxists but exceeded the limits of those theories in ways that puts them outside of Marxism. It begins with the basic tenets of Marxism but moves away from the Mode of Production as the starting point for analysis and includes factors others than class, such as gender, ethnicity etc., and a reflexive relationship between the base and superstructure.

Marxism remains a powerful theory in some unexpected and relatively obscure places, and is not always properly labeled as "Marxism". For example, many Mexican and some American archeologists still cling to Marxist model to explain the Classic Maya Collapse (c. 900 A.D.) without mentioning Marxism by name.

Marxist Feminism

Marxist feminism is a sub-type of feminist theory which focuses on the dismantling of capitalism as a way to liberate women. Marxist feminism states that capitalism, which gives rise to economic inequality, dependence, political confusion and ultimately unhealthy social relations between men and women, is the root of women's oppression.

According to Marxist theory, in capitalist societies the individual is shaped by class relations; that is, people's capacities, needs and interests are seen to be determined by the mode of production that characterises the society they inhabit. Marxist feminists see gender inequality as determined ultimately by the capitalist mode of production. Gender oppression is class oppression and women's subordination is seen as a form of class oppression which is maintained (like racism) because it serves the interests of capital and the ruling class. Marxist feminists have extended traditional Marxist analysis by looking a domestic labour as well as wage work in order to support their position.

Marxism and Postcolonialism

Marxism is also linked with post-colonialism. Aijaz Ahmend's *In Theory* (1992) is a systematic study of post-colonialism from Marxist perspective. In the words of Bart Moore-Gilbert, "Marxism is already 'inside' post-colonialism, even with post-colonial theory to a much greater degree than some Marxist critics have acknowledged.....Post-colonialism has infact been just as harsh at times as Marxism about both post-structuralism and post-modernism, consistently critiquing their tendency to Eurocentrism, even ethnocentricism, while holding onto what is valuable in both approaches for its own project."

Literature and Ideology

Ideology is a more or less coherent set of beliefs and has roots in a class or group of people at a particular time. A socio-economic system with its neutral-looking structures (parts and segments of the state) appropriates old beliefs and views and also generates new ones to perpetuate its strangehold on people's minds. Religion, morality and ethical principles form the core of many a ruling class ideology. It is important for the owners of the means of production to mould as well as forge people's consciousness with a view to getting their uncritical approbation of the existing social relationships. A discussion of ideology is greatly helpful in understanding the meaning and message of a literary work as well as its aesthetic appeal. One can see a particular ideology influencing and determining a writer's consciousness and also the way in which that consciousness shapes characters, voices, responses and situations in a literary work. An alert reading of literature is sure to grasp the broadly political function of an ideology.

The Marxists see "Literature, along with other cultural products—primarily as a form of ideology." The ideology too takes care of the interests of the dominant and bourgeoisie class. It legitimizes the power of the ruling class. Most theories of ideologies create an illusory or "false consciousness" which distorts actual historical conditions and inverts reality and events.

Based on the Marxian theories stated above, the following points can be listed as the manifestation of Marxian theory when it is applied to literature :

1. A good literary work will have correlation with the social reality of its contemporary study.
2. Emphasis on realistic protrayal of life and society.
3. Literary work is not timeless but product of the said economic factors specific to era.

Take the Marxist approach to Shakespeare's *The Tempest* for example. The standard Marxist party line would be to interpret Prospero as the representative of European imperialism. Prospero has come to the island from Italy. He has used his magic (perhaps a symbol of technology) to enslave Caliban, a native of the island. Caliban resents being the servant of Prospero and attempts to rebel against his authority. Since Prospero is presented in a favourable light, the Marxist critic might condemn Shakespeare as being a supporter of European capitalist ideology. A more subtle Marxist critic might see that the play has far more complexity, and that Caliban has been invested with a vitality that makes it possible for audience to sympathize with him. Certainly, the Marxist view of the play brings out ideas that might be overlooked by other kinds of critics and, thus, contributes to the understanding of the play.

E.M. Forster's *A Passage to India* is another example of ideology in a literary work. Here the ideology of liberal-humanism is been used. Humanism is broadly understood as the doctrine that not only recognises and support humanist cause in the modern world—equality between man and man, justice, peaceful coexistence, unprejudiced treatment of communities, nationalities and races other than one's own, etc.—but also stands in clear opposition to those tendencies that work against these causes. The word 'liberal' in modern discourse stands for courtesy, integrity, deep and sensitive understanding of issues, dignity and a respect for the person who may disagree with us. Fielding in *A Passage to India* is such a person. A liberal humanist to the core, Fielding makes no distinction between an Indian and a European and relates to people on the strength of personal appeal.

Coming to the protrayal of mass protest by Indians in *A Passage to India,* one cannot fail to notice the rather curious equating of the British Masters with the Indian educated and lower classes. The text also covers the awareness of the political movement in India led by Gandhi.

14

Formalism

Literary critics and thinkers of various historical periods have placed emphasis on the formal aspects of art and literature. Aristotle, ancient and medieval rhetoricians, Kant, many of the Romantics, and writers in the nineteenth-century movements of symbolism and aestheticism all placed a high priority on literary forms. This emphasis reached a new intensity and self-consciousness in the literatures and critical theories of the early twentieth century, beginning with the Formalist movement in Russia and Europe modernism, extending subsequently to the New Criticism in England and America and later schools such as the New-Aristotelians. In general, an emphasis on form parenthesizes concern for the representation, initiative, and cognitive aspects of literature. Literature is no longer viewed as aiming to represent reality or character or to impart moral or intellectual lessons, but is considered to be an object in its own right, autonomous (possessing it own laws) and autotelic (having its aims internal to itself). Moreover, in this formalist view, literature does not convey any clear or paraphrasable message; rather it communicates what is otherwise ineffable. Literature is regarded as a unique mode of expression, not an extension of rhetoric or philosophy or history or social or physiological documentary. Critics have variously theorized that preoccupation with form betokens social alienation, a withdrawal from the world, an acknowledgement of political helplessness, and a retreat into the aesthetic as a refuge of sensibility and humanistic values. Such an insular disposition also betokens a retreat from history and biography, effectively isolating the literary artifact from both broad social forces and the more localized and personal circumstances of its author.

The formalistic approach began with Aristotle (384-322 B.C.), a philosopher of ancient Greece, who in his book *The Poetics* attempted to define the form of tragedy. Aristotle wrote that the tragic hero was an essentially noble individual who, nevertheless, manifested a flaw in character that caused him or her to fall from a high position to a low position. The flaw in character (hamartia) was a kind of blindness or lack of insight that resulted from an arrogant pride (habris). During the course of the tragic action, the hero came to a moment of insight—today it might be seen as an epiphany—that Aristotle called *anagnorsis*. Thus the tragic plot moves from blindness to insight. As an imitation (mimesis) of a serious action, the tragic plot had to be written in a dignified style. The effect of the tragedy was supposed to be catharsis or the purging of the emotions of pity and fear. All the elements of tragedy went together to produce a formal unity: this is the essence of the formalistic approach.

The twentieth century formalistic approach, often referred to as the New Criticism, also assumes that a work of literary art is an organic unity in which every element contributes to the total meaning of the work. This approach is as old as literary criticism itself, but it was developed in the twentieth century by John Crowe Ransom (1884-1974), Allen Tate (1899-1979). T.S. Eliot (1888-1965) and others. 20th century literature and literary criticism particularly the early decades saw different literary trends. The New Criticism as the term was applied to describe literary theories produced both in England and America insisted on the outer accomplishment rather than on the inner content. Form became more important than any other aspect of creative art. Context or meaning held secondary position. A famous statement by an American poet-critic became the key phase of New Criticism—"A poem should not mean, but be." Meaning is to be sought within the form itself. It means, the form itself should be so effective as to bring out the entire meaning. The form of literary art depends on the effective use of language which is its medium as colours are the medium of painting. The effective use of medium produces perfect form and the form itself brings a exact meaning. This belief, in the literary term, was called *Formalism*. The main exponent of Formalism in England were T.S. Eliot, I.A. Richards, Sir Herbert Read, F.R. Leavis and a host of others. While in America they included Cleanth Brooks, John Crowe Ransom, William Empson etc. All these critics together formed a movement of New

Criticism. It was called so because their theories were different from the earlier trends in criticism particularly Nineteenth century criticism of S.T. Coleridge, Matthew Arnold and other Victorians. All these critics were deeply influenced by what is called 'Russian Formalism' which became easily identifiable immediately after the Russian Revolution of 1917. These Russian Formalists were a group of like minded scholars, though they never belonged to any one particular *School of Thought*. Most of them were linguists and upheld the prominent role language plays in the creation of literary creation. They included—Victor Shklovsky, Boris Fichenbaum, Jurij Tynyanov and Roman Jakobson. They were united in their wish to establish the study of literature on a scientific footing, to constitute it as an autonomous science using methods and procedures of its own. This raised the question of 'literariness' which could specify those formal and linguistic properties which could be said to distinguish literature and poetry from other forms of discourse, particularly from prosaic and ordinary language. The question of 'literariness', the Formalists believed, could be solved solely with reference to the formal properties of literary text. It was not necessary, they argued, to take into account the historical forces operative in the creation of such texts. This belief brought them in sharp contrast with the Marxist critics who believed in the Marxist doctrine of dilectical materialism and asserted the belief that historical forces and background play a definity and definite role in the creation of literature. Marxist criticism a part of sociological approach to literature which stated that the writer's socio-historical background is a determining factor in the area of his artistic work. A sociological critic values the writers' origin, his social and cultural background and his entire biography, because he thinks, this approach helps to understand the writers work better than any other approach. Formalists opposed this critical notion and developed a different notion of literatriness. They approached a particular literary text not just to understand it, but as a vehicle to exemplify their notion of literariness.

The formalist critic embraces an objective theory of art and examines plot, characterisation, dialogue and style to show how these elements contribute to the theme or unity of the literary work. Moral, historical, psychological, and sociological concerns are considered extrinsic to criticism and of secondary importance to the examination of craftsmanship and form. Content and form in a work constitute a unity, and it is the task of the critic to examine and evaluate the integrity of the work. Paradox, irony, dynamic tension, and unity are the primary values of formalist criticism.

Because it posits on objective theory of art, there are two axioms central to formalist criticism. One of these is *The Intentional Fallacy* which states that an author's intention (plan or purpose) in creating a work of literature is irrelevant in analyzing or evaluating that work of literature because the meaning and value of a literary work must reside in the text itself, independent of authorial intent. Another axiom of formalist criticism is *The Affective Fallary* which states that the evaluation of a work of art cannot be based solely on its emotional effects on the audience. Instead, criticism must concentrate upon the qualities of the work itself that produce such effects. The formalistic approach stresses the close reading of the text and insists that all statements about the work be supported by references to the text. Although it has been challenged by other approaches recently, the New Criticism is the most influential form of criticism in this century.

Formalism is intrinsic literary criticism because it does not require mastery of anybody of knowledge besides literature. As an example of how formalistic criticism approaches literary work consider Shakespeare's *Macbeth*. All the elements of the play form an organic whole. The imagery of the gradual growth of plants is contrasted with the imagery of leaping over obstacles : Macbeth is an ambitious character who cannot wait to grow gradually into the full stature of power, but, instead, must grasp everything immediately. A related series of clothing images reinforces this point : because Macbeth does not grow gradually, his clothing does not fit. At the end of the play, his, "Tomorrow and tomorrow and tomorrow" soliloquy drives home the point as we see, and pity, a man trapped in the lock-step pace of gradual time. Formalistic critic would immediately see that the repitition of the word "tomorrow" and the natural iambic stress on "and" enhance the meaningless and frustration that the character feels. References to blood and water pervade the play, and blood comes to symbolize the guilt Macbeth feels for murdering Duncan. Even the drunken porter's speech provides more than *comic* relief, for his characterization of alcohal as "as equivocator" is linked to the equivocation of the witches. Shakespeare's craftsmanship has formed an aesthetic unity in which every part is connected and in which the whole is greater than the sum of the parts.

Russian Formalism

Russian formalism represents one of the earliest systematic attempt to put literary studies on an independent footing, and to make the study of literature an autonomous and specific discipline. Formalist theory systematically excludes the non-literary—The Anglo-American tradition often sees life and art as interrelated, the Russian formalists see the two as opposites. Literary studies till the end of 19th century devoted much of their times and energies to uncover the source and genesis of a particular work of art, and to the role of biography, history, and the history of ideas. It obviously reduced the importance of literature itself. The study of literature became little more than a loose aggregate of philosophy, history, ethnography, social science and so on. Jakobson calls thus study as 'homespun' discipline based on subjects other than literature, for example, which studying and analysing a poem by Pushkin—a great 19th century Russian poet, a critic would brood over a question—"did Pushkin Smoke?"

The Russian formalists wanted to create an independent science of literature. They were not interested in the question—"how to study literature?"—but in "what really is the subject matter of literary study and literature?" The 'homespun' view of literature had tended to see literature either as an expression of the author's personality or his world-vision, or as a mimetic (realistic) representation of the world in which he lives or the combination of the two, which Catherine Belsey has described as "expressive realism". To see a literary work as an expression of the author's personality leads to his biography and psychology. To regard it as a literature of given society leads in turn to history, politics or sociology. Even the symbolist view that "art is thinking in images" is not admitted, because in the end, it leads to the study of thought, mind, feeling etc. something which is not literature. The formalist defination of literature is based simply on its differences from other order of facts. Formalism concentrates on those factors in a literary text which differentiate it from other discipline. The formalist were influenced deeply by the new linguistics, particularly by the linguistic theories of Ferdinand saussure—the Swiss linguist, who pioneered structuralism and the separation of scientific language description from historical philology.

Along with movements in futurism and symbolism, the Russian Formalist were a group of writers who flourished during the period of the Russian Revolution of 1917. The Formalists and the futurists were active in the fierce debates of this era concerning art and its connections with ideology. The Formalists and futurists found a common platform in the journal LEF (Left Front of Art). The Formalists, focusing on artistic forms and techniques on the basis of linguistic studies, had arisen in pre-revolutionary Russia but now saw their opposition to traditional art as a political gesture, allying them somewhat with the revolution. However, all of these groups were attacked by the most prominent Soviet theoreticians, such as Trotsky, Nikolai Bukharin, Anatoly Lunacharsky, and Voronsky, who decried the attempt to break completely with the past and what they saw a reductive denial of the social and cognitive aspects of art. V.N. Volosinov and Bakhtin later attempted to harmonize the two sides of the debate, viz., formal linguistic analysis and sociological emphasis, by teating language itself as the supreme ideological phenomenon, as the very site of ideological struggle. Other groups, called "Bakhtin Circles", formed around this enterprise.

There were two schools of Russian Formalism. The Moscow Linguistic Circle, led by Roman Jakobson, was formed in 1915; this group also included Osip Brik and Boris Tomashevsky. The second group, the Society for the Study of Poetic Language (*Opoyaz*), was founded in 1916, and its leading figures included Victor Shklovsky, Boris Eichenbaum, and Yuri Tynyanov. Other important critics associated with these movements included Leo Jakubinsky and the folklorist Valdimir Propp.

It should be said that the Russian Formalists emphasis on form and technique was different in nature from that of the later New Critics. The Formalists' analyses were far more theoretical, seeking to understand the general nature of literature and literary devices, as well as the historical evolution of literary techniques, the New Critics were more concerned with the practice (rather than the theory) of close reading of individual texts. Though Russian Formalism as a shcool was lipsed with the rise of Stalin and the official Soviet aesthetic of socialist realism, its influence was transmitted through figures such as Jakobson and Tzvetan Todorov to their own structuralist analyses and those of writers such as Ronald Barthes and Gerard Genette. Even reception theorists such as Hans Robert Jauss have drawn upon Shklovsky's notion of defamiliarization.

The Russian Formalist consider 'Form' as the result of two operations : *deformation* and *organization*. The term deformation has no derogatory implication, it means simply 'the changes imposed on the material' and the effect achieved, for instance, by poetic language in contrast with the language of prose, the patterning by sound repititions and figures, the nods and turns of a novelistic plot—in short, all the 'devices', procedures or 'instruments' of arts. But these devices must be employed in a systematic manner, must be organized, must harmonize with each other to achieve the totality of a work of a genuine art, its specific shape or structure. Thus, the Russian formalists, studied not only devices such as sound-pattern, meters, compotional forms, and genre conventions, but also the aesthetic function of themes, motifs and plot. In doïng so, the formalists restored merit to its necessary contact with linguistics and semantics.

Victor Shklovsky

Victor Shklovsky was a leading figure in the school of literary and linguistic theory known as Russian Formalism. His essay "Art as Technique" (1917) was one of the central statements of formalist theory. Like others in his group, he was denounced by Leon Trotsky for his formalist views.

It is in "Art as Technique" that Shklovsky introduces one of the central concepts of Russian Formalism : that of defamiliarization. As our normal perceptions become habitual, they become automatic and unconscious : in everyday speech, for example, we leave phrases unfinished and words half-expressed. Shklovsky sees this as symptomatic of a process of "algebraization" which infects our ordinary perceptions : "Things are replaced by symbols"; we fail to apprehend the object, which "fades and does not leave even a first impression; ultimately even the essence of what it was is forgotten." It is this process of algebraization or over-automatization of an object which permits the greatest economy of perceptive effort whereby objects are reduced to one salient feature or function as though by formula.

The essay begins with an argument disputing the validity of the symbolist movement in Russian poetry. Russian symbolism was different from the French symbolism of late 19th century. Its main spokesman, Potebnya believed that "Art is thinking in images" particularly poetry. So it is the first and foremost way of 'thinking and 'knowing'. Shklovsky points out that this argument leads us to believe that thinking in image is the chief characteristic of poetry wich is not true. There is hardly any difference between the images poets use in different ages. Poets are concerned not really with creating images rather with arranging the already existing images in the work of earlier poets. Aesthetic pleasure which is the main aim of poetry can be created without its awareness—a change in images is not essential for that certain language, like *slavic* are said to be poetic and then there are certain poetic works gone almost flat and prosaic. This suggests that the artistry attributed to a given work is the result of our own perception. By 'works of art' we mean a work created by certain techniques. Potebnya's conclusion that poetry equals imagery is the result of his misunderstanding between the language of prose and that of poetry. These is a basic difference between the language of poetry and that of prose. Poetic language means 'precision' whereas prose language is 'abstraction'.

Shklovsky quotes Tolstoy as saying that "the whole complex of lives of many lives of many people go on unconsciously ..... such lives are as if they had never been." Hence habituation can devour work, clothes, furniture, one's wife, and the fear of war. It is against this background of ordinary perception in general that art assumes its significance : "art exists that one may recover the sensation of life; it exists to make one feel things, to make the stone *stony*. ..... The technique of art is to make objects 'unfamiliar', to make forms difficult, to increase the difficulty and length of perception because the process of perception is an aesthetic end in itself and must be prolonged. *Art is a way of experiencing the artfulness of an object; the object is not important."*

Shklovsky offers examples from two of the short stories of Tolstoy. *Shame* in which the act of 'flogging' (beat severely with rod or whip) is presented in defamiliar images—'to strip people who have broken the law, to hurl them to the floor, and to rap on their bottom with switches' and 'to lash about on the naked buttocks'. Another example provided by Shklovsky is of 'Kholstomer' in which the narrator is the horse and the whole narration comes from the horse's point of view. In *War and Peace* Tolstoy uses the same technique in describing battles as if battles were something new. Even the drawing rooms and theatres are described in the same defamiliar way. Tolstoy, described the customs and dogmas and rituals and attacked as if they were unfamiliar. Many people were painfully wounded because they considered it blasphemous to present as strange and mostrous what they consider sacred. Their reaction was due mainly to the technique Tolstoy adopted.

This technique of defamiliarization is to be found in almost all arts. Its purpose is not to make us perceive meaning, but to create special perception of it, to create a vision of the object instead of serving as a means for knowing it. This perception of things is evoked more accurately in erotic art than anywhere else, obviously because a writer there cannot be thoroughly explicit and Shklovsky offers several passages from erotic writings.

Shklovsky concludes his essay with a brief comment on rhythm. The rhythm of prose is an important automatizing element : the rhythm of poetry is not. There is 'order' in art yet not a single column of Greek temple stands exactly in its proper order, poetic rhythm is similarly disordered rhythm. Disordering rhythm is what brings out 'defamiliarization' on which Shklovsky stressed throughout the essay.

Boris Eichenbaum

Like Shklovsky, Eichenbaum was one of the leaders of the Russian Formalist group known as the society for the study of Poetic Language. Like others of his school, Eichenbaum was denounced by Trotsky, and wrote an important essay, "The Theory of the 'Formal Method'", expounding the evolution of the certain principles of the formalist method.

1. Origins of Formalism and the Science of Literature

Eichenbaum begins by stating that formalism is "Characterized only by the attempt to create an independent science of literature which studies specifically literary material." And it is formalism's insistence on "empirical study" which comprised its must significant "quarrel with the old traditions." The chief characteristics of the Formalists, says Eichenbaum was their rejection of all "ready-made raesthetics and general theories."

Russian Formalists entered the debate and opposed the symbolists "in order to wrest poetics from their hands – to free it from its ties with their subjective philosophical and aesthetic theories and to direct it toward the scientific investigation of facts." According to Eichenbaum, the Formalists were aware that "history demanded ..... a really revolutionary attitude. ..... Hence our Formalist movement was characterized by a new passion for scientific positivism—a rejection of philosophical assumptions, of psychological and esthetic interpretations, etc." In the context of early twentieth century Russian, Eichenbaum evidently sees this strategy is revolutionary, as attempting to free art from serving ideological and political ends.

2. The Independent Value of Poetic Sound

In impunging previous approaches to literature, says Eichenbaum, the Formalists sought to isolate the study of literature from "secondary, incidental features" that might belong to philosophy, phychology, or history. And it is this isolation that makes the study of literature scientific. Eichenbaum quotes Roman Jakobson's affirmation that the "object of the science of literature is not literature, but literariness—that is, that which makes a given work a work of literature." Hence, says Eichenbaum, instead of looking to these other disciplines, the Formalists focused on linguistics, a science which borders on poetics and shares material with it. Eichenbaum cites Osip Brik's essay "Sound Repititions", which had argued that sound "are not only euphonious accessories to meaning; they are also the result of an independent poetic purpose."

3. The Formalist's Redefination of Form

Eichenbaum points out that the fundamental formalist distinction between poetic and practical language led to the formulation of a whole group of basic questions. Potebnya and others has presupposed the conventional notion of the harmony of form and content; the Formalist rejected this notion, whereby form was viewed as an "envelope" or vessel into which a liquid (the content) is poured. The new, formalist notion of form required no correlative content; instead of being an envelope, form is viewed as " a complete thing, something concrete, dynamic, self-contained". Eichenbaum cites Shklovsky's defination of artistic or poetic perception as "that perception in which we experience form." This view represented a break from both symbolism, which saw content as somehow shining through the form, and aestheticism, which isolated certain elements of form from content. In the formalist view, form is itself understood as content. The principle of perceptible form, the heightened perception of form, results from "special artistic techniques which force the reader to experience the form."

4. Plot and Literary Evolution

The next phase of formalist studies, as Eichenbaum explains, attempted to move toward a general theory of verse and the study of narrative plot and specific techniques. He cites Shklovsky's theory of plot and fiction which identified special devices of plot construction. Most importantly, Shklovsky rejected the traditional notion of plot as a combination of *motifs* (the smallest units of narrative); plot was no longer viewed as synonymous with "story"; rather, it was viewed as a compositional device rather than a thematic concept. In other words, plot comprised the distinguishing features of narrative art, and as such became an important focus of formalist inquiry. The idea of "motivation" (the rotational behind the use and function of a given device) enabled Shklovsky to distinguish between "story", which was merely a "description of events", and "plot", which was a structure. Techniques of plot construction, according to the Formalists, included parallelism, framing, and the weaving of motifs. The story, on the other hand, was merely "material for plot formulation", material which also included choice of motifs, characters, and themes.

Further he argued that literature has its own, relatively independent, history, and it is this history – comprised by the interaction and influence between literary works themselves, rather than "external" influences of society, morals, or manners—that is the appropriate object of formalist analysis. Clearly, such a model of literary history anticipates later theories such as those of Pound and T.S. Eliot; the latter saw works of literature as forming an "ideal order" among themselves, an order that both influenced new works and was in turn slightly modified by these new additions. As Eichenbaum sees it, the Formalists realized that their study of theoretical poetics had to broaden to include a study of literary history.

5. Formalists Conceptions of Poetry

Eichenbaum observes that the Formalists insisted upon a clear demarcation between poetry and prose, as opposed to the symbolists, who were attempting to erase this boundary. The formalist position was first stated in Osip Brik's "On Rhythmic Syntactic Figures", which argued that rhythm was not merely a "superficial appendage" but rather the "structural basis" of verse; rhythmic patterns were indissolubly connected with syntactical and grammatical patterns. In his own book *Verse Melody*, Eichenbaum had maintained that stylistic features were mainly lexical; he also formulated the idea of the *dominant*, the chief element in a hierarchy of compositional factors. On the basis of certain dominant elements, he distinguished three styles of lyric poetry : declamatory (oratorical), melodic, and conversational. The most fundamental point here is that poetic form was not understood as an outer expression of a given content; rather, form itself was viewed as the "genuine content of poetic speech". Eichenbaum puts this another way : form is not dependent upon content; it is self-sufficient and must be considered "in relation to its purpose."

Again Eichenbaum stresses that formalist advances in the study of poetry were enabled not by some rigid "formal method" but by close attention to an appropriately isolated object of inquiry, by a "study of the specific peculiarities of verbal art." He reiterates his position that the "ability to see facts" as "far more important than the construction of a system. Theories are necessary to clarify facts; in reality, theories are made of facts. Theories perish and change, but the facts they help discover and support remain." Such statements, one imagines, might tempt Hegel to rise from the grave.

6. Historical Criticism and Literary Evolution

As against the broad histories of the Russian academics and the effective rejection of history by the symbolists, the Formalists adopted a new understanding of literary history which rejected the idea of some overall unity, coherence, and purpose, as well as the idea of historical "progress" and "peaceful" linear succession in some directly continuing line. Rather, the Formalists saw literary tradition as involving struggle, a destruction of old values, competition between various schools in a given epoch, and persistence of vanquished movements alongside the newly dominant groups. The Formalists insisted that literary evolution had a distinctive character and that it "stood alone, quite independent of other aspects of culture." This, evolution, moreover, they held to be independent of biography and psychology.

At the end of his essay, Eichenbaum provides a useful and prevocative summary of the evolution of the Formalists method. Their initial distinction between poetic and practical language led them to differentiate these in terms of their various functions. Their new conception of "form" as dynamic, self-contained, and as not dependent upon some external content led them to stress first the notion of technique, and then the notion of function. Taking rhythm as an integral element is the construction of a poem – as an element not extraneous to but intrinsically connected with syntax – the Formalists viewed poetry as a special form of speech having its own linguistic (syntactical, lexical, semantic) features.

Mikhail M. Bakhtin

Mikhail Bakhtin is increasingly being recognised as one of the major literary theorists of the twentieth century. His is perhaps best known for his radical philosophy of language, as well as his theory of the novel, underpinned by concepts such as "dialogism", "polyphony", and "carnival", themselves resting on the more fundamental concept of "heteroglossia." Despite his critique of formalism, he has also been claimed as a member of the

Jokabsonian formalist school, as a post structuralist, and even as a religious thinker.

Bhakhtins major works as translated include *Art and Answerability : Early Philosophical Essays, Problems of Dostoevsky's Poetics, The Dialogical Imagination : Four Essays* etc. Bakhtins major achievements include the formulation of an innovative and radical philosophy of language as well as a comprehensive "theory" of the novel (though Bakhtin's work eschews systematic theory that attempts to explain particular phenomena through generalizing and static schemes). Bakhtin's essay "Discourse in the Novel", furnishes an integrated statement of both endeavors. Indedd, what purports to be a theory of the novel entails not only a radical account of the nature of language but also a radical critique of the history of philosophy and an innovative explanation of the nature of subjectivity, objectivity, and the very process of understanding. At the outset, Bakhtin states that his principal object in this essay is to overcome the divorce between on abstract "formal" approach and an equally abstract "ideological" approach to the study of "verbal art" (here referring to the language of poetry and the novel). He insists that form and content in discourse "are one", and that "verbal discourse is a social phenomenon." Bakhtins point is that traditional stylistics have ignored the social dimensions of artistic discourse, which has been treated as a self-subsistent phenomenon, cut off from broader historical movements and immersion in braod ideological struggles. Moreover, traditional stylistics have not found a place for the novel, which, like other "prosaic" discourses, has been viewed as an "extra artistic medium", an artistically "neutral" means of communication on the same level as practical speech. Bakhtin lists the stylistic feature into which the "unity" of the novel is usually divided : (1) direct authorial narration, (2) stylization of everyday speech, (3) stylization of semiliterary discourse such as letters and diaries, (4) various types of extra-artistic speech, such as moral, philosophical, and scientific statements, and (5) the individualized speech of characters. This point is that each of these "heterogeneous stylistic unities" combines in the novel to "form a structured artistic system" and that the "stylistic uniqueness of the novel as a genre consists precisely in the combination of these subordinated, yet still relatively autonomous unities ..... into the higher unity of a work as a whole." Hence the novel can be "defined as a diversity a social speech types (sometimes even diversity of languages) and a diversity of individual voices, artistically organized."

Bakhtin's "Dialogism" is difficult to explain. On the most basic level, it refers to the fact that the various langauges that stratify any "single" language are in dialogue with one another; Bakhtin calls this "the primordial dialogism of discourse", whereby all discourse has a dialogic orientation. Bakhtin has a further, profounder, explanation of the concept of dialogism. He explains that there is no direct, unmediated relation between a word and its object : "no living word relates to its object in a *singular way*." In its path toward the object, the word encounters "the fundamental and richly varied opposition of ..... other, alien words about the same object."

Bakhtin's account of language as constitutively underlying the interactions of human subjects bears a certain resemblance of Hegel's account of the formation of the human subject in interaction with others; whereas Hegel sees subjectivity as a reciprocal effect, arising from the mutual acknowledgement between the consciousness of two people, Bakhtin's exposition explicitly posits language as the medium of such interaction, and hence sees subjectivity as a linguistic effect, though no less reciprocal and dialogic. As Bakhtin puts it, consciousness is faced with "the necessity of *having to chose a language*. With each literary – verbal performance, consciousness must actively orient itself amidst heteroglossia." From these political and metaphysical implications of Bakhtins views of language, it is clear that for him, the study of works of literature cannot be reduced to the examination of a localized and self-enclosed verbal construct. Even literary language as Bakhtin points out, is stratified in its own ways, according to genre and profession. The various dialect and perspectives entering literature form "a dialogue of languages". It is precisely this fact which, for Bakhtin, marks the characteristic difference between poetry and the novel.

Roman Jakobson

The work of Roman Jakobson occupies a central and seminal place in the development of formalism and structuralism. Essentially a linguist, Jakobson was born in Moscow, where he co-founded the Moscow Linguistic Circle in 1915, which also included Osip Brik and Boris Tomashevsky. Along with Victor shklovsky and Boris Eichenbaum, he was involved in a second Russian Formalist group. The society for the study of Poetic Language formed in 1916. The Formalists were in some ways precursors of structuralism : in 1926 Jakobson founded the Prag Linguistic Circle, which engaged critically with the work of Saussure.

In his paper "Linguistics and Poetics" (1958) Jakobson argues that, since poetics concerns the artistic features of a "verbal message", and linguistics is the "global science of verbal structure", poetics is an integral part of linguistics. His point here is that poetic elements belong to the science of language as a whole; indeed, they belong to the yet broader field of semiotics or theory of signs since they are not confined to verbal art. Jakobson insists that "literary criticism", which often evaluates literature in subjective terms, must be distinguished from "literary studies" proper, which engage in "objective scholarly analysis of verbal art." Like linguistics, literary studies, whose focal point is poetics, are concerned with problems of synchrony and diachrony. Synchronic description views the various elements of a literary tradition as they occur at a given point in time; these elements will include, however, literary values and figures whose influence has persisted. A diachronic study would analyze the various changes in a given tradition or system over a period of time.

The three functions of language mentioned by Jakobson – referential, emotive, and conative—belong to the traditional model of language as fomulated by the German psychologist Karl Buhler. Jakobson suggests that this model can be augmented to include additional verbal functions. One of these might be a "magic, incantatory" function, where the person addressed in a conative message would be an absent or inanimate third person, as in prayers or supplications to various forces considered to be divine. There are also messages whose main function is to establish or prolong communication ("Hello, do you hear me?"), this is the "phatic" function, which might involve an exchange of "ritualized formulas." This, says Jakobson, is the first verbal function acquired by infants. The third additional function is metalinguistic.

Jakobson notes the distinction made by modern logicians between two levels of language ; "object language", which speaks of objects and events, and "metalanguage", which speaks about language itself.

Jakobson's essay "Two Aspects of Language and Two Types of Aphasic Disturbances" suggest that language has a bipolar structure, oscillating between the poles of metaphor and metonymy. This dichotomy, he urges, "appears to be of primal significance and consequence for all verbal behavior and for human behaviour in general." The development of any discourse takes place along two different semantic lines. One is metamorphic, where one topic leads to another through similarity or sub-situation. The other is metonymic, where one topic suggests another via contiguity (closeness in space, time, or psychological association). In normal behavior, says Jakobson, both processes operate, but one is usually preferred, according to cultural and personal conditions. In verbal art, also, while the two processes richly interact, one is often given predominance. Jakobson notes that the primary of metaphor in literary Romanticism and symbolism has been widely acknowledged. What has been neglected, he thinks, is the predominance of metonymy in realism : the realist author often "metonymically digresses from the plot to the atmosphere and from the characters to the setting in space and time." He is also fond of synecdocic details such as "hair on the upper lip" and "bare shoulders" that are used to express character.

The New Criticism

Around the beginning of the twentieth century the predominant critical modes were biographicals, historical, psychological, romantic, and impressionistic. Liberal critics such as Parrington and F.O. Matthiessen employed a historical approach to literature but Mathiessen insisted on addressing its aesthetic dimensions. This formalist disposition became intensified in both the New Criticism and the Chicago School. The term "The New Criticism" was coined as early as 1910 in a lecture of that title by Joel Spingarn who, influenced by Croce's expressionist theory of art, advocated a creative and imaginative criticism which gave primacy to the aesthetic qualities of literature over historical, psychological, and moral considerations. Spingarn, however, was not directly related to the New Criticism that developed in subsequent decades. Some of the important features of the New Criticism originated in England during the 1920s in the work of T.S. Eliot and Ezra Pound, as well as in seminal studies by I.A. Richards and William Empson. Richard's *Principles of Literary Criticism* (1924) advanced literary – critical notions such as irony, tension, and balance, as well as distinguishing between poetic and other uses of language. His *Practical Criticism* (1929), based on student analyses of poetry, emphasized the importance of "Objectivity" and balanced close reading which was sensitive to the figurative language of literature. Richard's student William Empson produced an influential work, *Seven Types of Ambiguity* (1930), which was held up as a model of New Critical close reading.

During the 1940s the New Criticism became institutionalized as the mainstream approach in academia, and its influence, while pervasively undermined since the 1950s, still persists. Some of the central documents of New Criticism were written by relatively late adherents : W.K. Wimsatt and Monroe Beardsley's essays "The International Fallacy" (1946) and "The Affective Fallacy" (1949) and Murray Krieger's *The New Apologists for Poetry* (1956).

There are several similarities between the operational procedures of Russian formalism and American New Criticism. Like Russian formalism, New Criticism tried to displace content in literary analysis. Also New Criticism tried to organize the larger generic in accordance with the inner ordering of works as revealed in specific analyses or "close reading." But the New Criticism departed from Russian formalism on the key issue of the function of forms. Russian formalism considered the formal properties of literature as a means of achieving particular effects. But the New Critics considered literature to be a self-sustaining "artifact", a "spatial form" or an "autonomous entity." Perhaps this was a very serious limitation of New Criticism. New Critics like Cleanth Brooks made the literary image the primary material or constituent of form itself. While the Russian formalists successfully avoided any focus on literary content, the New Critics posited paradox and irony as controlling figures and, in effect turned them into content.

John Crowe Ransom

The seminal manifestos of the New Criticism however, had been proclaimed earlier by Ransom, who published a series of essays entitled *The New Criticism* (1941) and an influential essay, "Criticism, Inc., " published in *The World's Body* (1938). This essay succintly expresses a core of New Critical principles underlying the practice of most "New Critics", whose views often differed in other respects. As Ransom acknowledges, his essay is motivated by the desire to make literary criticism "more scientific, or precise and systematic"; it must, says Ransom, become a "serious business." He urges that the emphasis of criticism must move from historical scholarship to aesthetic appreciation and understanding. Ransom characterizes both the conservative New Humanism and left-wing criticism as focusing on morality rather than aesthetics. While he accepts the value of historical and biographical information, Ransom insists that these are not ends in themselves but instrumental to the real aim of criticism, which is "to define and enjoy the aesthetic or characteristic values of literature." In short, Ransom's position is that the critic must study literature, not *about* literature. Hence criticism should exclude : (1) personal impressions, because the critical activity should "cite the nature of the object rather than its effects upon the subject", (2) synopsis and paraphrase, since the plot or story is an abstraction from the real content of the texts; (3) historical studies, which might include literary backgrounds, biography, literary sources, and analogues; (4) linguistic studies which include identifying allusions and meanings of words; (5) moral content, since this is not the whole content of the text; (6) "Any other special studies which deal with some obstract or prose content taken out of the work." Ransom demands that criticism, whose proper province includes technical studies of poetry, metrics, tropes, and fictiveness, should "receive its own charter of rights and function independently." Finally, in this essay and other works, Ransom insists on the ontological uniqueness of poetry, as distinct from prose and other uses of language, as in prose. "The critic should", he urges, "regard the poem as nothing short of a desperate ontological or metaphysical manoeuvre, "which cannot be reduced to prose. All in all, he urges that literature and literary criticism should enjoy autonomy both ontologically and institutionally. His arguments have often been abbreviated into a characterization of New Criticism as focusing on "the text itself" or "the words on the page."

I.A. Richards

Richards was a scholar of semantics, and along with C.K. Ogden, formulated Basic English. *The Meaning of Meaning* (1923) written by C.K. Ogden, is an important contribution to linguistics. Richards *Principles of Literary Criticism* (1924), was followed by *Science and Poetry* (1926), *Practical Criticism* (1929), and *Coleridge on Imagination* (1934). Richards believed that literary criticism should be objective. He was fascinated by the newly developing science of psychology, and wanted to evaluate art in terms of the state of mind induced by it. He promoted a psychological theory of value. This theory has become outdated due to later researchers in psychology. But his comments on language and on the practical analysis of poetry, are still valid, and have an enormous influence on Anglo-American literary criticism in the twentieth century.

In *Principles of Literary Criticism,* I.A. Richards set out to establish a theoretical framework for criticism which would free it from subjectivity and emotionalism. In the second chapter, "The Phantom Aesthetic State", he dismisses the concept of a special aesthetic state. Richards believes that aesthetic experiences are not sui generis, that is, they do not merely have intrinsic value. It is possible to analyze art experience, and examine its value in terms of ordinary life, because it is not a special state cut off from ordinary life. Chapter Thirtyfour is devoted to "The Two Uses of Language." Richard observes that the terms we use to discuss poetry are ambiguous and fail to record distinctions. In this book, he has used words like causes, characters and consequences when analyzing mental activity, in place of *thought, feeling,* and *will.* Richards distinguishes between two kinds of causation for "mental events."

William K. Wimsatt and Monroe C. Beardsley

Critic Wimsatt and the philosopher Beardsley is known for their two influential and controversial papers that propounded central positions of New Criticism, "The International Fallacy" (1946) and "The Affective Fallacy" (1949). In the first of these, they lay down certain propositions that they take to be axiomatic : while acknowledging that the cause of a poem is a designing intellect, "They refuse to accept the notion of design or intention as a standard of literary-critical interpretation. In stating their second "axiom", they raise the question of how critic might find on what a poet's intention was and state what is effectively their central claim : "If the poet succeeded in doing it, then the poem itself shows what he was trying to do. And if the poet did not succeed, then the poem is not adequate evidence, and the critic must go outside the peom – for evidence of an intention that did not become effective in the poem." The third axiom is the American poet Archibald's MacLeish's statement that a "poem should not mean but be." Wimsatt and Beardsley explain this statement as follows : "A peom can *be* only through its *meaning* – since its medium is words – yet it *is,* simply *is,* in the sense that we have no excuse for inquiring what part is intended or meant. ..... In this respect poetry differs from practical messages, which are successful if and only if we correctly infer the intentions." This is an effective restatement of a New Critical position that the poem is an autonomous verbal structure which has its end in itself, which has no purpose beyond its own existence as an aesthetic object. It is not answerable to criteria of truth, accuracy of representation or imitation, or morality. Finally, Wimsatt and Beardsley insist that the thoughts and attitudes of a poem can be imputed only to the dramatic speaker or person of the poem, not directly to the author.

Like Ransom, Wimsatt and Beardsley are concerned to exclude from criticism certain related studies such as author psychology, biography and history. They in fact make a distinction between "internal" and "external" evidence for the meaning of a poem. Usually author allows only internal evidence. They give examples of how resort to evidence of the other types can distort a poem's meaning : if we approach John Donne's poem "A Valediction Forbidding Mourning" through our prior knowledge of this interest in astronomy, we might interpret the following stanza in the poem as centered on a metaphor involving geocentric and heliocentric views of the world.

Moving of th' earth brings harmes and feares,

  Men reckon what it did and meant,

But trepidation of the spheares,

Though greater farre, is innocent. But to advance such an interpretation, the author warn, is "to disregard the English language, to prefer private evidence to public, external to internal." In other words, we are reading the poem through our knowledge of Donne's "private" interests, rather than attending to what the words themselves might signify.

One of the major problems arising in literary scholarship from the intentional fallacy, according to the authors, concerns the poetic use of allusion by writers such as T.S. Eliot and Ezra Pound, whose verse extensively alludes or refers to lines and phrases of earlier poets.

Wimsatt and Beardsley's later essay "The Affective Fallacy" is motivated by the same pre-supposition, namely, that literature or poetry is an autonomous object, independent not only of author psychology, biography and history but also of the reader or audience that consumes it. The word "affection" is used by philosophers to refer to emotion, mental state, or disposition. Hence, the "affective fallacy" occurs according to Wimsatt and Beardsley, when we attempt to explicate or interpret a poem through recourse to the emotions or mental state produced in the reader or hearer. As these, authors put it, just as the intentional fallacy "is a confusion between the poem and its origins", so the affective fallacy "is a confusion between the poem and its *results* (what it *is* and what it *does*)." Again, part of their problem with using the reader's response as a criterion of interpretation is that it makes criticism a subjective rather than objective activity, a discourse about the subject (the reader) rather than the object (the text). An affective reading of a poem "begins by trying to derive the standard of criticism from the psychology effects of the poem and ends in impressionism and relativism. The outcome of either Fallacy, the Intentional or the Affective, is that the poem itself as an object of specifically critical judgement, tends to disappear."

The Chicago School

Another group of critics, known as the Chicago School or the Neo-Aristotelians, began formulating their central ideas around the same time as the New Critics were voicing their manifestos. Six of the figures later known as the Chicago critics were involved in reviving radical transformation to scientific were — R.S. Crane, Richard McKeon, Elder Olson, W.R. Keast, Norman Maclean, and Bernard Weinberg. These critics later produced the central manifesto of the Chicago School. *Critics and Criticism Ancient and Modern* (1952), which both attacked some of the important tenets of the New Criticism and elaborated an alternative formalistic method of criticism derived in part from Aristotle's *Poetics*.

In an earlier essay of 1934, Crane had anticipated (and influenced) Ransom's call that professional criticism should move from a primarily historical toward an aesthetic focus. However, Crane and the Chicago School generally diverge from the New Criticism in their insistence that literary study should integrate both systematic theory of literature (being informed by the history of literary theory) and the practice of close reading and explication of literary texts. Moreover, the Chicago School drew from Aristotle *Poetics* a number of characteristic critical concern such as the emphasis on literary texts as "artistic wholes", the analytical importance of locating individual texts within given genres and the need to identify textual and generic (as opposed to authorial) intention. Whereas the New Critics had focussed attention on specifically poetic uses of langauge, irony, metaphor, tension, and balance, the Chicago School followed Aristotle in emphasizing plot, character, and thought. In general, the Neo-Aristotelians offered an alternative formalist poetics which acknowledged the mimetic, didactic, and affective functions of literature. The influence of this school, however, was over-shadowed by the widespread adoption of New Critical dispositions throughout the American education system.

Cleanth Brooks

Cleanth Brooks has been a prominent American critic from nineteen-thirties. He started his career as critic with the publication of *Modern Poetry and the Tradition* (1938) and *The Well Wrought Urn* (1947), both the books containing analyses of poem selected from the entire gramut of English poetry. His other books include *Understanding Poetry* (1938), *Understanding Fiction* (1943) and *Understanding Drama* (1945). Brooks is a practical critic as well as a theorist. He applies theory to a definite poem or a work of fiction, and illustrates in detail the result of the applied theory.

Some of the examples of such titles are *The Language of Paradox* (1942), *Irony as Principle of Structure* (1951), *Religion and Literature* (1974), *The Modern Writer and The Burden of History (1977), The New Criticism* (1979).

Brook's *The Well Wrought Urn* is a book which demonstrates Brook's formal approach to poetry. *The Well Wrought Urn* as the title suggests, (Keat's Urn) contains essays mostly on English, poetry. It deals with Milton's 'L. Allegro' —'I.L. Penseroso', Thomas Gray's — 'Elegy', Wordsworth's 'Intimation : An Immortality', Keat's Odes, Tennyson's 'In Memorian', and W.B. Yeats. The criteria and standard he applies to these poems are well stated in the first essay of the book — 'The Language of Paradox.' He says, "Paradox is the langauge appropriate and inevitable to poetry It is scientist whose truth requires a language purged of every trace of paradox; apparently the truth which the poet utters can be approached only in terms of paradox."

Another important article by Brooks is "The Formalist Critic." He presents the basic assumptions of the New Critics, "Literary criticism is a description and evaluation of its objects." It concerns itself with the work of art itself. In reply to those who argue that, the work should not be isolated from the author's life or the readers and their response, he replies that biography and history may be interesting, but "they should not be confused with an account of the work. Such studies describe the process of composition, not the structure of the thing composed, and they may be performed quite as validly for the poor work as the good one. They may be validly performed for any kind of experience ..... non-literary as well as literary." Brooks implies that it is the duty of the critic to be concerned with value judgements; he should examine the value of a literary work, and whether a work is literary or non-literary.

He observes that the formalist critic (by which he means the New Critic) makes two assumptions : (1) the author's intention as *realized* is the "intonation" that counts. And (2) the formalist critic assumes an ideal reader, that is, instead of focusing on a range of possible reading, he attempts to find a central point of reference from which he can focus on the work itself. In answer to the objection that there is no ideal reader, Cleanth Brooks grants that "there is no ideal reader, of course. But he defends the New Critic by saying that it is "a defensible strategy" adopted by all critics for the purpose of focusing on the poem instead of his own reactions. Laying stress on the reader means that "we move from literary criticism into socio-psychology." He sums up their avoidance of the intentional fallacy and the affective fallacy in these words : "The reduction of a work of literature to its causes does not constitute literary criticism, nor does an estimate of the effects."

The Poetics of Modernism : Ezra Pound and T.S. Eliot

Modernism comprised a broad series of movements in Europe and America that came to fruition roughly between 1910 and 1930. Its major exponents and practitioners included Marcel Proust, James Joye, Ezra Pound, T.S. Eliot, William Faulkner, Virginia Woolf, Lugi Pirandello and Franz Kafka. These various modernisms were the results of many complex economic, political, scientific, and religious developments over the nineteenth century which culminated in World War I (1914-1918). The vast devastation, psychological demoralization, and economic depression left by the war intensified the already existing reactions against bourgeois modes of thought and economic practice. Rationalism underwent renewed assaults from many directions : from philosophers such as Bergson, from the sphere of psychoanalysis, from neoclassicists such as T.E. Hulme, the New Humanists in America, and neo-Thomists such as Jacques Maritain. These reactions were often underlain by a new understanding of langauge, as a conventional and historical construct. The modernist writer occupied a world that was often perceived as fragmented, where the old bourgeois ideologies of rationality, science, progress, civilization, and imperialism had been somewhat discredited; where the artist was alienated from the social and political world, and where art and literature were marginalized; where populations had been subjected to process of mass standardization; where philosophy could no longer offer visions of unity, and where language itself was perceived to be an inadequate instrument for expression and understanding.

Literary modernism was marked by a number of features :

1. The affirmation of a continuity, rather than a separation, between the worlds of subject and object, the self and the

world. The human self is not viewed as a stable entity which simply engages with an already present external world of objects and other selves.

2. A perception of the complex roles of time, memory and history in the mutual construction of self and world. Time is not conceived in a static model which separates past, present, and future as discrete elements in linear relation; rather, it is viewed as dynamic, with these elements influencing and changing one another. Human history is thus not already written; even the past can be altered in accordance with present human interests, motives and viewpoints.
3. A breakdwon of any linear narrative structure following the conventional Aristotelian model which prescribes beginning, middle, and end. Modernist poetry tends to be fragmented, creating its own internal "logic" of emotion, image, sound, symbol, and mood.
4. An acknowledgement of the complexity of experience : any given experience is vastly more complex than can be rendered in literal langauge. For example, the experience of "love" could be quite different from one person to another, yet language coercively subsumes these differing experiences under the same word and concept. Modernist poetry tends to veer away from any purpoted literal use of language which might presume a one-to-one correspondence between words and things; it relies far more on suggestion and allusion rather than over statement.
5. A self-consciousness regarding the process of literary composition. This embraces both the awareness of how one's own work relates to the literary tradition as a whole, and also an ironic stance toward the content of one's own work.
6. Finally, and most importantly, an awareness of the problematic nature of language. This indeed underlies the other elements cited above. If there is no simple correspondence between langauge and reality, and if these

> realms are mutually constituted through patterns of coherence, then a large part of the poet's task lies in a more precise use of language which offers alternative definitions of reality. Eliot once said that the poet must "distort" language in order to create his meaning.

Of all the Western modernists, T.S. Eliot has been the most pervasively influential through both his poetry and his literary criticism. He was initially influenced by the American New Humanists such as Irving Babbitt and Paul Elmer, and his early ideas owed a great deal to their emphasis on tradition, classicism, and impersonality. Eliot was also indebted to later nineteenth century French poets and particularly to Ezra Pound and the imagist movement.

Eliot took his so-called theory of "tradition from both Babbit and Pound, though it had political precedents in conservation theories of tradition such as that of Edmund Burke. Eliot's theory claimed that the major works of art, both past and present, formed an "ideal order", which is continually modified by subsequent work of art. The central implication here was that contemporary writers should find common ground with that tradition even as they extended it. Eliot effectively succeeded in redefining the European, literary tradition, continuing the humanists onslaught against the Romantics, and bringing into prominence Dante, the Metaphysical poets, and the French symbolists. Eliot also advanced an "impersonal" notion of poetry, whereby the poet expresses not a personality but a precise formulation of thought and feeling such as is lacking in "ordinary" experience. The poet, according to Eliot, employs an "objective correlative", whereby objects and events in the external world are used to express complexes of thought and emotion.

In terms of literary history, Eliot held that a "dissociation of sensibility" had set in after the seventeenth century that entailed a disjunction of various human faculties such as reason and emotion which has previously been integrated within a unified sensibility. Eliot's ideas bore an ambivalent relationship with the claims of the New Criticism. On the one hand, he believed that the aesthetic dimensions of works of art is irreducible; on the other, he believed, with increasing insistence throughout his career, that art is irreducibly bound to its social, religious and literary context. The ideas of Pound and Eliot have had a lasting influence but their most forceful impact occured between the 1920s and the 1940s.

A formalistic approach (New Critic) to John Milton's *Paradise Lost* would take into account the physical description of the Garden of Eden and its prescribed location, the symbols of hands, seed, and flower, the characters of Adam, Eve, Satan, and God, the epic similies and metaphor, and the point of view from which the tale is being told (whether it be the narrator's God's, or Satan's). But such an approach would not discuss the work in terms of Milton's own blindness, or in terms of his Puritan beliefs. Therefore, when the narrator says "what in me is dark/Illumine, "a formalistic critic could not interpret that in light of Milton's blindness. He would have to find its meaning in the text itself, and therefore would have to overlook the potential double-meaning.

Thus, formalistic critics spend much time analyzing irony, paradox, imagery, and metaphor. They are also interested in the work's setting, characters, symbols, and point of view.

The text according to formalist is seen in isolation. Formalism ignores the context of the work. It cannot account for allusions. It tends to reduce literature to little more than a collection of rhetorical device.

15

Archetypal Criticism

Archetypal literary criticism is a type of critical theory that interprets a text by focusing on recurring myths and archetypes (from the Greek *archē*, or beginning, and *typos*, or imprint) in the narrative, symbols, images, and character types in a literary work. As a form of literary criticism, it dates back to 1934 when Maud Bodkin published *Archetypal Patterns Poetry*. Archetypal literary criticism's origins are rooted in two other academic disciplines, social anthropology and psychoanalysis; each contributed to the literary criticism in separate ways, with the latter being a sub-branch of the critical theory. Archetypal criticism was its most popular in the 1950's and 1960's, largely due to the work of Canadian literary critic Northrop Frye. Though archetypal literary criticism is no longer widely practised, nor have there been any major developments in the field, it still has a place in the tradition of literary studies. The advent of post modern theory initially dampened the interest and influence of archetype theory, but in recent years many writers and scholars have responded to the misconceptions and misrepresentation often found in post modern critiques of archetypal theory.

The popular saying "when they made you, they threw away the mold "hints that literally the stature or figuratively the person is singular, exceptional, unique. With no mold or pattern to follow, a duplicate is impossible. An archetype, however, is the mold that has not been discarded. The archetypal mold, flexible and long-lasting, provides many close copies of the original. Consider possibly the most popular archetype of all—the Hero. John Wayne as Rooster Coybarn and Harrison Ford as Indiana Jones are strikingly different actors, but as heroes who overcome the obstacles in their respective paths, they are undoubtedly from the same mold, an obviously flexible one given the birth of Wayne.

The hero archetype appears in every culture; its a favourite mold of humanity.

An archetype then is a pattern or prototype of character types, images, descriptive details, and plot patterns that find their way from our minds to our myths to our literature to our lives. The psychologist Carl Jung, a colleague of Sigmund Freud, first popularized the use of the term *archetype* when he postulated the theory that, similar to the instincts of animals, humans are born with a "collective unconscious", a level below the conscious and subconscious, wherein the source of the archetypes or the molds exist. He believed it was this collective unconscious that gave humans certain predispositions to specific stimuli. In other words, we all respond to archetypes in the same way because our minds are made the same way and "programmed" by thousands of years of human experience. Some texts refer to this idea as a "racial memory", as in human race. A fair analogy might be the mind reacts to an archetype in the same way that the body reacts when a doctor taps the knee with a hammer – reflexively and predictably. As a product of our collective unconscious, archetypes naturally found their way into our subconscious and our dreams. Jung believed he could analyze his patients by focusing on the archetypal elements of their dreams. From dreams archetypes migrated to myths, the stories we told to explain our world before science arrived to help, the stories that reveal our "deepest instinctual life", the stories that reveal to us our inner selves. Joseph Camphell, author of *The Hero with a Thousand Faces*, believed that there was really *just* one universal hero story. Anthropologists like James Frazer have reinforced the universality of archetypes by finding that peoples who could never have encountered each other have the same archetypes in their myths and rituals. From mythology archetypes made the short hop into literature. From our minds to our myths to our literature is a natural progression that shows us that the study of literature is the study of ourselves, archetypes included.

Character Archetypes

The Here	The protagonist on a literal or figurative journey often from childhood to adulthood, innocence to experience.

Death	The antagonist or character blocking the hero's path.
Shadow	The hero's inner evil, the dark side of his psyche that makes success difficult or impossible unless accepted.
Mother and Father	Yup, the parential units are near and dear to our hearts and especially our minds because of their nurturing or lack thereof.
The Wise Old	A mentor, a teacher, a Counselor Man.
The Friendly	This show that nature is pro-hero Beast.
The Devil	The bad, bad person who tempts the hero.
The Scapegoat	A person (or animal) whose death relieves others of a sin or wrong
The Outcast	A character banished because of his wrong doing; often a wonderer.
The Earth Mother	A female character, naturally, who offers spiritual and emotional comfort.
The Temptress or Terrible Mother	A femple who tempts the here and tries to bring about his end. Synonyms include femme fatale, witch, sorceress, and siren because these suggest the magical powers of a seductive woman.
The Platonic or Perfect Woman	The hero has primarily an intellectual love for this woman who inspires his best.
The Unfaithful Wife	Cheater, cheater
The Damsel in Distress	Help me! Help me, please!
Star-crossed Lovers	Lovers fated to suffer a tragic end.
The Trickster	This character has a negative nature, a character that might be a fraud, a prankster, a con man, a joker, etc. However, they might be helful to the hero at some point.

Plot Patterns/Elements	**Archetypes**
The Quest	The search for someone or something that will restore rightness to the hero's work that involves hardships, monsters, or riddles (literal or figurative in nature like all of these)
The Task	The hero must perform a deed beyond the norm
The Initiation or Transformation	The hero undergoes a hazing to pass from ignorance and immaturity to social and spiritual adulthood. It usually occurs in three stages : separation, transformation, and return and thusly may include the fall and death/rebirth.
The Journey	In search of Information, the hero passes into a real or figurative hell from which he may energy after he discovers the blackest truths of himself.
The Fall	The hero falls to a lower level from a comparative heaven after a loss of innocence and happiness because of a transgression, a wrong.
Death and Rebirth	Usually a metaphorical death, a spiritual or emotional death and reviving of the spirit and emotions.
Nature vs. the Mechanical World	Nature good, machines bad.
The Unheable Wound	A physical or psychological wound that indicates a loss of innocence.
The Ritual	Weddings, baptisms, coronations – real or figurative – that mark a rite of passage to another state or level.
The Magic Weapon	The Hero's weapon that no one else can use to its full potential if at all.
Garden	Paradise, innocence, unspoiled beauty, fertility.

Tree	Life of the cosmos, immortality.
Desert	Spiritual aridity, death, nihilism, hoplessness

Archetypal Images

Archetypal images are often just labeled as examples of symbolism, but they are able to symbolize because of their archetypal origin.

Water	Water has archetypal possibilities in every form it takes. It can represent purification, redemption, birth-death-resurrection, sadness, etc.	
The Sea	The mother of all life, spiritual mystery and infinity, death and rebirth, time-lessness, eternity, and often the unconscious mind.	
Rivers	Death/rebirth, the flowing of time, the life cycle, gods.	
Sun	Creative energy, natural law, the conscious mind, the father principle; the rising sun is birth, creation and enlightenment while the setting sun is death.	
Colors	Red	: blood, sacrifice, violent passion : disorder.
	Green	: growth, sensation, hope, fertility or negatively death/decay.
	Blue	: truth, religious feeling security, purity.
	Black	: chaos, mystery, the unknown, death, evil, melancholy (sadness), primal wisdom.
	White	: light, purity, innocence, time-lessness or death, terror, the supernatural or blinding truth.
Circle	A mandala, figure that represents the desire for spiritual unity and integration.	

The Egg	The mystery of life.
Yang-Yin	That funky Chinese symbol for a union of opposites : male-female, light-dark, activity-passivity, conscious-unconscious.
Segment	Symbol of energy, pure force, evil, corruption, sensuality, destruction, mystery, wisdom, the unconscious.
Numbers	Three : light, spiritual, awareness, and unity, the male principle.
	Four : associated with the circle, the life cycle (seasons) earth, nature (four elements).
	Seven : the sum of three and four, the completion of a cycle, perfect order.

Archetypal Narrative Patterns

Four archetypal narrative patterns, which sursive according to Frye, "because they are fundamental structures of the human imagination, perennially useful ways of perceiving the world we experience."

Romance	A world where goals are achieved and dreams fulfilled.
Irony	Goals are thwarted and nightmares become reality.
Tragedy	Moving from a desirable state to an undesirable one.
Comedy	From an undesirable state to a desirable one.

Literature was all these archetypes, but usually in comouflaged ways. No literal magic weapon or damsel in a tower waiting for aid or garden appears, but figuratively they do. A magic weapon can simply be a characters' education or skills; the damsel can be a woman with a flat tire on the roadside; the garden can be any peaceful, natural place like a park or a character's dream world. A journey can be a spiritual journey. When the archetypes are used literally, the stories can become more mythological and dated but no less enjoyable.

James G. Frazer

The anthropological origins of archetypal criticism can predate its psychoanalytic origins by over thirty years. *The Golden Bough,* written by the Scottich anthropologist James G. Frazer was the first influential text dealing with cultural mythologies. Frazer was part of a group of comperative anthropologists working out of Cambridge University who worked extensively on the topic. *The Golden Bough* is widely accepted as the seminal text on myth that spawned numerous studies on the same subject. Eventually, the momentum of Frazer's work carried over into literary studies.

In *The Golden Bough* Frazer identifies shared practices and mythological beliefs in almost all cultural mythologies, and is acted out in terms of growing seasons and vegetation. The myth is symbolized by the death (*i.e.,* final harvest) and rebirth (*i.e.,* spring) of the god of vegetation. As an example, Frazer cites the Greek myth of persephone, who was taken to the Underworld by Hades. Here mother Demeter, the goddess of the harvest, was so sad that she struck the world with fall and winter. White in the Underworld Persephone ate 6 of the 12 pomegrate seeds given to her by Hades. Because of what she ate, she was forced to spend half the year, from then on, in the underworld, representative of autumn and winter, or the death in the death-rebirth myth. The other half of the year Persephone was permitted to be in the mortal realm with Demeter, which represents spring and summer, or the rebirth in the death-rebirth myth.

Carl Gustav Jung

While Frazers work deals with mythology and archetypes in material terms, the work of Carl Gustav Jung, a Swiss born psychoanalyst, is, in contrast, immaterial in its focus. Jung's work theorizes about myths and archetypes in relation to the unconscious, an inaccessible part of the mind. From a Jungian perspective, myths are the "culturally elaborated representations of the contents of the deepest recess of the human psyche : the world of the archetypes.

Jung addresses the relevance of archetypal theory in literature and the arts most clearly in *The Spirit in Man, Art, and Literature* which contains two significant essays on literature and poetry. In Jung's archetypal theory, the unconscious mind plays a profound role, and it has a purpose, which is to assist individuals in maintaining a balanced psychological state. When one deviates from one's particular middle way, the unconscious mind sends signals, which try to get the attention of one's consciouness in order to alert one to alter one's behaviour. The language of the unconscious mind is symbolic. It uses images and symbols to convey its messages; its vocabulary and grammar are fundamentally different from rational, conscious thought. It is up to the conscious mind to notice, decode and implement the messages of the unconscious mind in order to more closer to a middle or balanced psychological state, particular for the individual.

The unconscious mind itself has two parts, the personal and the collective. The personal unconscious is specific to the individual, and it is the location of individual repressions and complexes, which are normal, and everyone has them. Jung also describes "the collective unconscious", about which there is much misunderstanding. The collective unconscious is not an otherworldly or supernatural phenomena; it does not exist on its own, and it has no content. It is distinguished by potential; it is a dimension of the psyche general to all humans and is characterized by instinctive, latent patterns of symbol-making.

Jungian psychoanalysis distinguishes between the personal and collective unconscious, the latter being particularly relevant to archetypal criticism. The collective unconscious, or the objective psyche as it is less frequently known, is a number of innate thoughts, feelings, instincts, and memories that reside in the unconsciousness of all people. Jung's definition of the term is inconsistent in his many writings. At one time he calls the collective unconscious the "a priori, inborn forms of intution", while in another instance it is a series of "experiences that come upon us like fate." Regardless of the many nuances between Jung's definations, the collective unconsciousness is a shared part of the unconscious.

To Jung, archetypes in the collective unconscious, as quoted from leitch *et. al.*, it "irrepresentable, but has effects which make visualizations of its possible, namely the archetypal images and ideas", due to the fact they are at an inaccessible part of the mind. The archetypes to which Jung refers are represented through primordial images, a term he coined. Primordial images originate from the initial stages of humanity and have been part of the collective unconscious ever since. It is through primordial images that universal archetypes are experienced, and more importantly, that the unconscious is revealed.

With the same death-rebirth myth that Frazer sees as being representative of the growing seasons and agriculture as a point of comparison, a Jungian analysis envisions the death-rebirth archetype as a "symbolic expression of a process taking place not in the world but in the mind. That process is the return of the ego to the unconscious – a kind of temporary death of the ego – and its re-emergence, or rebirth, from the unconscious.

By itself, Jung's theory of the collective unconscious accounts for a considerable share of writings in archetypal literary criticism; it also pre-dates the height of archetypal literary criticism by over a decade. The Jungian archetypal approach treats literary texts as an avenue in which primordial images are represented. It would be not be until the 1950's when the other branch of archetypal literary criticism developed.

Northrop Frye

Bodkin's *Archetypal Patterns in Poetry,* the first work on the subject or archetypal literary criticism, applies Jung's theories about the collective unconscious, archetypes, and primordial images to literature. It was not until the work of the Canadian literary critic Northrop Frye that archetypal criticism was theorized in purely literary terms. The major work of Frye's to deal with archetypes in *Anatomy of Criticism* but his essay. "The Archetypes of Literature" is a precursor to the book. Frye's Thesis in "The Archetypes of Literature" remains largely unchanged in *Anatomy of Criticism*. Frey's work helped displace New Criticism as the major mode of analyzing literary texts, before giving way to structuralism and semiotics.

Frye's work breaks from both Frazer and Jung in such a way that it is distinct from its anthropological and psychoanalytical precursors. For Frye, the death-rebirth myth that Frazer sees manifest in agriculture and the harvest is not ritualistic since it is involuntary, and therefore, must be done. As for Jung, Frye was uninterested about the collective unconscious on the grounds of feeling it was unnecessary : Since the unconscious is unknowable it cannot be studied. How archetypes came to be was also of no concern to Frye; rather the function and effect of archetypes is his interest. For Frye, literary archetypes "play an essential role in refashioning the material universe into an alternative verbal universe that is humanly intelligible and viable, because it is adopted to essential human needs and concerns."

There are two basic categories in Frye's framework, comedic and tragic. Each category is further subdivided into two categories : comedy and romance for the comedic; tragedy and satire (or ironic) for the tragic. Though he is dismissive of Frazer. Frye uses the seasons in his archetypal scheme. Each season is aligned with a literary genre : comedy with spring, romance with summer tragedy with autumn, and satire with winter.

Comedy is aligned with spring because the genre of comedy is characterized by the birth of the hero, revival and resurrection. Also, spring symbolizes the defeat of winter and darkness. Romance and summer are paired together because summer is the culmination of life in the seasonal calender, and the romance genre culminates with some sort of triumph, usually a marriage. Autumn is the dying stage of the seasonal calendar, which parallels the tragedy genre because it is, above all, known for the "fall" or demise of the protagonist. Satire is metonymized with winter on the grounds that satire is a "dark" genre; satire is a disillusioned and mocking form of the three other genres. It is noted for its darkness, dissolution, the return of chaos, and the defeat of the heroic figure.

The context of a genre determines how a symbol or image is to be interpreted. Frye outlines five different spheres in his schema : human, animal, vegetation, mineral, and water. The comedic human world is representative of wish-fulfillment and being community centred. In contrast, the tragic human world is of isolation, tyranny, and the fallen hero. Animals in the comedic genres are docile and pastoral (*e.g.*, sheep), while animals are predatory and hunters in the tragic (*e.g.*, wolves). For the realm of vegetation, the comedic is, again, pastoral but also represented by gardens, parks, roses and lotuses. As for the tragic, vegetation is of a wild forest, or as being barren. Cities, a temple, or precious stones represent the comedic mineral realm. The tragic mineral realm is noted for being a desert, ruins, or "of sinister geometrical images." Lastly, the water realm is represented by rivers in the comedic. With the tragic, the seas, and especially floods, signify the water sphere.

Frye admits that his schema in "The Archetypes of Literature" is simplistic, but makes room for exceptions by noting that there are neutral archetypes. The example he cities are islands such as Ciree's or Prospero's which cannot be categorized under the tragic or comedic.

The essay "The Archetypes of Literature" contains two sections. Frye begins his essay by saying that one cannot 'learn literature', 'one learns about it in a certain way', but 'what one learns, transitively, is the criticism of literature'. He proposes to take a scientific study of criticism. For him criticism is a kind of commentary. But the commentators lack scientific discipline. Frye laments the lack of principles by which one can 'distinguish a significant from a meaningless statement in criticism.' He disapproves of literary chit-chat and calls it pseudo-criticism. On the other hand, he goes with those critics who say that 'the foreground of criticism is the impact of literature on the reader' and pleads for 'the centripetal' study of literature. Frye considers the structural approach to criticism inadequate, for it 'brings rhetoric back to criticism.' He underlines the limitation of criticism in the following words :

> "I suggest that what is at present missing from literary criticism is a co-ordinating principle, a central hypothesis which, like the theory of evolution in biology, will see the phenomena it deals with as part of a whole. Such a principle, though it would retain the centripedal perspective of structural analysis, would try to give the same perspective to other kinds of criticism too."

Frye is of the opinion that every poet has his private mythology, 'his own spectroscopic band or peculiar formation of symbols, of much of which he is quite unconscious.' Frye refers to grave-digger scene in *Hamlet* to say how all the critics from Bradley, Wislon Kinght to Stall and Shaw have taken the archetype of the scene as 'the hero's Libestod' (*i.e.*, the convergence of love and death).

In the beginning of section III of the essay, Frye takes literature as an intermediary between music and painting — "its words form rhythms which approach a musical sequence of sounds at one of its boundaries, and form patterns which approach the hieroglyphic or pictorial image of the other." Further he says that "we may call the rhythm of literature the narrative and the pattern, the simultaneous mental grasp of the verbal structure, the meaning or significance. We fear or listen to a narrative but when we grasp a writer's total pattern we 'see' what he means".

According to Fyre, there is a unique opportunity to profoundly learn about ourselves while reading Tolstoy, Milton, or Shakespeare. This personal encounter with literature leads to the balancing and unfolding of the self, the awareness and transformation of individual repressions, neglects and one-sidedness. He writes :

> "Our sense experience our memories, our established habits and rituals, all acts as filters : they can screen out or accommodate whatever in our lives is disturbing or threatening ..... it is only the arts that allow this screened out emotion and experience to return in some bearable form, and make us realize that while we have been living our lives as 'normally' as we can, we have also been, all the time, citizens of the lunatic country of Don Quixote and Captain Ahab and King Lear. That is why their moods and behavior can be intelligible to us."

Their moods and behavior are not only intelligible to us, but more importantly serve as a bearable means of accessing, confronting and integrating screened out or unknown emotion and experience. In doing so, literature contributes to healthy development of not only societies but also of individuals.

The publication of his unpublished works lead to new insights into Frye's work and life. For instance, the publication of Northrop Frye's *Notebooks and Lectures on the Bible and Other Religious Texts* has revealed that, for Fyre, the discovery and articulation of archetypal unities is no mere intellectual exercise. Frye's analytical, intellectual, and Aristotelian classifying of literature according to patterns that unite seemingly disparate works is actually founded on and motivated by the belief that such unity is an aspect of spiritual experience. Frye considers the arts a spiritual discipline this effect is achieved through the unification of subject and object in metaphor. The embodied experience for the artist or the respondent can be felt as a spiritual one, and Frye turns to eastern texts and mystical revelations as barallels, allusions, and explanations for the phenomenon. The intimacy of the *Notebooks* reveals that, in Northrop Fyre's experience and theories, the arts serve as a font of profoundly human spiritual energy art has always been his yoga, and literature his secular monastery.

Critiques of Archetypal Criticism

It has been argued that Fyre's version of archetypal criticism strictly categorizes works based on their genres, which determines how and archetype is to be interpreted in a text. According to this eargument the dilemma Frye's archetypal criticism faces with more contemporary literature, and that of post-modernism in general, is that genres and categories are no longer distinctly separate and that the very concept of genres has become blurred, thus problematizing Frye's schema. For instance Beckett's *Waiting For Godot* is considered a tragicomedy, a play with elements of tragedy and satire, with the implication that interpreting textual elements in the play becomes difficult as the two opposing seasons and conventions that Frye associated with genres and pitted against each other. But in fact arguments about generic blends such as tragicomedy go back to the Renaissance, and Frye always conceived of genres as fluid. Frye thought literary forms were part of a great circle and were capable of shading into other generic forms.

16

Structuralism

Structuralism is a theory of humankind in which all elements of human culture, including literature, are thought to be parts of a system of signs. Critic Robert Scholes has described structuralism as a reaction "'modernist' alienation and despair."

European structuralists such as Roman Jakobson, Claude Levi-Strauss, and Ronald Barthes (before his shift toward post structuralism) attempted to develop a semiology, or semiotics (science or signs). Barthes, among others, sought to recover literature and even language from the isolation in which they has been studied and to show that the laws that govern them govern all sings, from road signs to articles of clothing.

Structuralism began in linguistics with the work of Ferdinand de Saussure. But many French intellectuals perceived it to have a wider application, and the model was soon modified and applied to other fields, such as anthropology, psychoanalysis and literary theory. This ushered in the dawn of structuralism as not just a method, but also an intellectual movement that came to take existentialism's pedestal in 1960s France.

As a method, the basics of structuralism consist of analyzing social events (speech, familial identity, and recounts of history, for example) to discover the synchronic structures that both underlie them and make them possible (language, kinship and narrative structure, respectively), which are then typically broken down into units, cades, rules of combination, etc. The essential theory underlying this method is that these structures are autonomous, and that their units are interdependent, because they are constituted through contrasts with one another. So how we discursively conceive of ourselves, or anything, for that matter, is dependent an contexts found within historically contingent systems.

Structuralism enjoyed much popularity, and its general stance of antihumanism was in sheer opposition to the sartrean existentialism that preceded it. But in the 1970s, it could under internal fire from critics who accused it of being too rigid and a historical. However, many of structuralism's theorists, from Michel Foucault to Jacques Lacan, continue to assert an influence on continental philosophy, and many of the fundamental assumptions of its critics, that is, of adherents of post structuralism, are but a continuation of structuralism.

Structuralism appeared in academia in the second half of the 20th century, and grew to become one of the most popular approaches in academic fields concerned with the analysis of language, culture and society. The work of Ferdinand Saussure concerning linguistics is generally considered to be a starting point of structuralism. The term "structuralism" itself appeared in the works of French anthropologist Claude Levi-Strauss, and gave rise, in France, to the "Structuralist movement," which spurred the work of such thinkers as Michel Foucault, Louis Althusser, the psychoanalyst Jacques Lacan, as well as the structural Marxism of Nicos Poulantzas. Almost all members of this so called movement denied that they were part of it. Structuralism is closely related to semiotics. Post-structuralism attempted to distinguish itself from the simple use of the structural method. Deconstruction was an attempt to break with structuralist thought. Some intellectuals like Julia Kristeva, for example, took structuralism (and Russian formalism) for a starting point to later become prominent post-structuralists. Structuralism had had varying degrees of influence in the social sciences: a great deal in the field of sociology.

Structuralism in Linguistics

Structuralism was heavily influenced by linguistics, especially by the pioneering work of Ferdinand de Saussure. Particularly useful to structuralists was Saussure's concept of the phoneme (the smallest basic speech sound or unit of pronunciation) and his idea that phonemes exist in two kinds of relationships: diachronic and synchronic. A phoneme has a diachronic or "horizontal," relationship with those other phoneme that precede and follow it (as the words appear left to right, on this page) in a particular usage. ulterance, or narrative-what Saussure, a linguist. called *Parole*

(French for "word"). A phoneme has a synchronic, or "vertical," relationship with the entire system of language within which individual usages, utterances, or narratives have means what Saussure called *langue* (French for "tongue" as in "native tongue," meaning language). *An* means what it means in English because those of us who speak the language are plugged into the same system (think of it as a computer network where different individuals can access the same information in the same way at a given time).

Ferdinand de saussure was the originator of the 20th century structuralism, and evidence of this can be found in course in General Linguistics, written by Saussures colleagues after his death and leased on students notes, where he focused not on the use of language (parole, or speech), but rather on the underlying system of language (langue) and called his theory *Semiology.* However, the discovery of the underlying system had to be done via examination of the parole (speech). As such, structural Linguistics are actually an early form of *corpus* linguistics (quantification). This approach focused on examining how the elements of language related to each other in the present, that is, 'synchronically' rather than 'diachronically'. Finally, he argued that linguistic signs were composed of two parts, a signifier *the round pattern* of a word, either in mental projection-as when we silently recite lines from a poem to ourselves-or in actual, physical realization as part of a speech act) and a *signified* (the concept of *meaning* of a word). This was quite different from previous approaches which focused on the on the relationship between words and things in the world that they designate.

Prior to Saussure, the predominant modes of analyzing language were historical and philological. As opposed to diachronic approach which studies changes in language over a period of time, Saussure undertook a synchronic approach which saw language as a structure that would be studied in its entirety at a given point in time. Saussure pioneered a number of further influential and radical insights. Firstly, he denied that there is some how a natural connection between words and things, urging that this connection is conventional. This view of language also challenges the view of reality as some how independent and existing outside of language, reducing language to merely a "name-given system." Saussures view implies that we build up an understanding of our world by means of language and view the world *through* language. Secondly, Saussure argued that language is a system in relation: no sign has meaning in isolation, rather, its signification depends on its difference from other signs and generally on its situation within the entire network of signs. Finally, Saussure made a distinction between two dimensions of language, which refers to language as a structural system, grounded on certain rules; and *parole,* the specific acts of speech or utterance which are based on those rules.

In his *Course in General Linguistics* Saussure explains that it is *langue,* not the acts of speech which must be the object of scientific investigations. Indeed, the "science of language" is possible only if many elements of speech are excluded. Understood in this sense, language (as opposed to speech) is "outside of the individual who can never create nor modify it by himself." It exists through an implicit contract between the members of a community, and it must be learned in order for a person to communicate through speech. Saussure goes so far as to say that the "distinguishing character of the sign.....is that in some way it always eludes the individual or social will". He points out other differences between language and speech. Whereas speech is homogenous, language is heterogenous: "It is a system of signs in which the only essential thing is the union of meanings and sound images, and in which both parts of the sign are psychological." Moreover, language is no less concrete than speech: language is constituted by linguistic signs which are collectively approved, and these signs "are realities that have their seat in the brain." Finally, unlike speech language can be classified among human phenomena: It is a social institution, with unique features that distinguish it from other, political and legal, institutions.

Saussure suggests that the study of language should be situated within a larger investigative province, which he names semiololgy, from the Greek word *semeion* meaning "sign". Semiology, he explains, "would show what constitutes signs, what laws govern them—linguistics is only a part of the general science of semiology; the laws discovered by semiology will be applicable to linguistics" Saussure proposes that semiology be "recognized as an independent science with its own object like all the other sciences." Language needs to be studied "in itself," rather than, as in the past, in its connection with other things. The task of linguistics is to discover what makes language a "special system," but to do this, the linguist must learn what language has in common with other semiological systems.

In part II of his *Course,* Saussure addresses the important connection between thought and language. Prior to language he suggests, our thought is "a shapeless and indistinct mass," and we "would be unable to make a clear-out, consistent distinction between two ideas." There are no ideas, he insists, before the appearance of language. Equally, however, sounds by themselves are not delimited or clear prior to their expression of thought and ideas. Saussure pictures what he calls the total "linguistic fact," i.e. the two elements involved in the functioning of language, as comprising two series: a series of "jumbled ideas" on one plane, and "the equally vague plane of sounds." The role of language is to "serve as a link between thought and sound" under conditions that bring about a "reciprocal delimitation" of the units of both thought and sound. It is not a question of thoughts being given material form or of sounds being transformed into mental entities. The reciprocal nature of the process means that we must think of a combination "thought-sound" : language takes shape "between two shapeless masses," with ideas and sounds achieving defination at the same time. To illustrate this process, Saussure imagines language as a piece of paper: thought is the front and sound is the back, one cannot cut the front without also cutting the back. Likewise, says Saussure, in language, "one can neither divide sound from thought nor thought from sound." If we were to make this division, it would be artificial, and the result would be the domain of pure psychology (ideas) or pure phonology (sounds). The domain of linguistics is precisely this area where sound and thought combine, and *"their combination produces a form, not a substance."*

The combination of thought and sound helps explain the arbitrary nature of the sign: the choice of a given piece of sound to name a 'certain ideas is, says Sassure, "completely arbitrary. Hence a linguistic system can be created only by a community since the meanings and values of words." Owe their existence solely to usage and general acceptance". What the union of thought and sounds also shows us is that one cannot start with isolated correlations of given sounds and thoughts and build up a linguistic system by adding them together. Conversely, one must begin with the entire "interdependent whole" and obtain the particular elements of the linguistic system of analysis.

Saussure makes a crucial distinction between linguistic *value* and *signification*. While he concedes that value is one elements in signification, he insists that the two terms are not identical. The value of a term in language, he states, arise from the simultaneous presence of other, dissimilar, terms that can be exchanged for it or other similar terms that can be compared with at. A word may have a certain signification or meaning but this will not be the same as its value since the latter is determined by "the concurrence of everything that exists outside it." For example, the French word *mouton* may have the same signification as the English word "sheep" but these words do not have the same value since the English language has a furthers word, "mutton," to designate a piece of meat ready to eaten, whereas the French language does not.

Summarizing, Saussure states that "in language there are only differences." He observes that "a difference generally implies positive terms between which the difference is set up; but in language there are only differences *without positive terms* ....language has neither ideas nor sounds that existed before the linguistic power." Saussure further points out that the relations and differences between linguistic terms fall into two distinct groups, corresponding to two forms of our mental activity, both "indispensable to the life of language." In discourse, the relations acquired by words are based on the linear nature of language "because they are chained together." These linear relations are "Syntagmatic." Outside of discourse, however, words can acquire many additional kinds of relationships, which are not linear: they can a be based on associations of meaning, or similarity of form (such as having the same prefix or suffix or ending). Such relations are "associative" and in these a given word is "like (the center of a constellation"; whereas a syntagm comprises a fixed order of succession and a fixed member of elements, associative relations are characterized by an indeterminate order and indefinite number.

Key notions in Structural Linguistics are the notions of paradigm, syntagm and value, though these notions were not yet fully developed in De Saussures thought. A structural paradigm is actually a class of linguistic units (lexemes, morphemes or even constructions) which are possible in a certain position in a given linguistic environment (like a given sentence), which is the syntagm. The different functional role of each of these members of the paradigm is called value (*valeur* in French).

Saussures *Course* influenced many linguists between World War I and World War II. In America, for instance, Leonard Bloomfield developed his own version of structural linguistics, as did Louis Hjelmslev in Denmark and Alf Sommerfelt in Norway. In France Antoine Millet and Emile Benveniste would continue Saussure's program. Most importantly, however, members of the Prague school of linguistics such as Roman Jakobson and Nikolai Trubetzkoy conducted research that would be greatly influential.

The clearest and most important example of Prague School structuralism lies in phonemics. Rather than simply compile a list of which sounds occur in language, the Prague School sought to examine how they were related. They determined that the inventory of sounds in a language could be analyzed in terms of a series of contrasts. Thus in English the sounds /p/ and /b/ represent distinct phonemes because there are cases (minimal pairs) where the contrast between the two is the only difference between two distinct words (e.g. 'pat' and 'bat'). Analyzing sounds in terms of contrastive features also opens up comparative scope—it makes clear, for instance, that the difficulty Japanese speakers have differentiating /r/ and /l/ in English is because these sounds are not contrastive in Japanese. While this approach is now standard in linguistics, it was revolutionary at that time, phonology would become the paradigmatic basis for structuralism in a number of different forms.

Jakobson's influence can be detected everywhere within Formalism, Czech structuralism and modern linguistics. Roman Jakobson's role in literary theory arises out of his use of two highly suggestive set of paired terms: "linguistics and poetics" and metaphor and metonymy." These terms, and the thoughts behind them, profoundly shaped the structuralist movement in anthropology, philosophy, and psychoanalysis as well as literary studies, especially in France after World War II.

As a linguist, Jakobson clarified many important concepts. Phonemes or morphemes, for example, were once thought to be the smallest units of language, but Jakobson showed them to comprise bundles of "distinctive features" that themselves were formed by binary oppositions: voiced/unvoiced, consonant/vowel, singular/plural, and so on. Furthermore, his analysis of the tendency of binary oppositions to fall into "marked/unmarked" pairs prepared the way for later ideological analyses of structures and norms-where the "unmarked" (often the male, white, Christian, heterosexual point of view) goes unexamined, functioning as the standard against which "differences" are defined.

As a reader of poetry, Jakobson pursued two kinds of analysis that are not often found together. By studying "the poetry of grammar and the grammar of poetry," he scrutinized linguistic patterns that contribute to the overall poetic effect but normally escape the notice of readers leading many critics to protest that those patterns could not have been intended by the poet. At the same time he was fascinated by the difficulty of separating a poet's life and work, not because the life explained the work but because the life was largely structured like another work. Jakobson was similar to but profoundly different from his contemporaries, the American New Critics, in several ways. Both opposed "vulgar biographism" and the "intentional fallacy", but Jakobson analyzed the myth of the poet as a function of cultural history, whereas the New Critics tuned this readings to a sense of the individual. Both Jakobson and the New Critics read texts closely, but the New Critics tended to frame interpretation within a working sense of imagination and mind, whereas Jakobson subjected the largest and the smallest patterns to linguistic and cultural analysis, without regard for individual craft. It was not that Jakobson did not believe in the unity of the human imagination, but precisely that he believed in it so much that he thought he was in no danger of departing from it. Jakobson welcomed the contributions of science to the work of literary studies while the New critics were trying to defend "humanistic" values *against* the spread of scientific "professionalism."

In his broad position paper "Linguistics and Poetics"—his concluding statement to a 1958 conference on style, published as *Style in Language* (ed. Thomas Sebcok, 1960)—Jakobson argues that what he calls the "poetic function" is at work in all verbal communication. The other five major functions of language are the *emotive* (focused on the speaker), the *conative* (focused on the addressee), the *Phatic* (focused on the channel of communication), the *metalingual* (focused on explanations of the code itself), and the *referential* (focused on the context.)

In defining the poetic function, Jakobson cites approvingly the French poet Paul Valery (1871-1945), who called poetry a "sustained hesitation between the sound and the sense." He connects verbal art to the palpability (sound, sight) of signs. The poetic function consists of making connections *within the utterance* among the properties of the words, images, and sounds in a message, using those connections ("equivalences") to generate the linguistics sequence itself. Meter, rhyme, imagery, and generic conventions are not *subsequent* to the poetic function: they *are* the poetic function. Drawing on a mathematical sense of mapping ("projecting") one function upon another, he declares that "the poetic function projects the principle of equivalence from the axis of selection into the axis of combination." What does this formula mean? While ordinary speakers select one of the terms they perceive as equivalent in order to convey a message, the poet combines what is perceived as equivalent. Poetry seeks to *maximize* redundancy; ordinary communication seeks to minimize it.

Careful to distinguish between evaluation one analytical description, Jakobson discusses the *poetic function* rather than *poetry.* He remarks about the self-reflections and sounds in the 1950s political slogan "I like like" is a classic analysis of the poetic function without claiming to be an analysis of poetry. In showing how the slogan verbally embodies "the loving subject enveloped by the beloved object," he suggests the multiple use to which the poetic function is put in everyday life, while noting that poetry employs all the "everyday" functions, too. He is more interested in how the poetic function accounts for broad linguistic behavior and effectiveness both within and outside any poetic canon. For this reason, he writes about Baudelarie, Shakespeare, Pushkin Yeats, Blake and Hopkins with the same curiosity he applies to the linguistic mechanisms of slogans, folklore, and everyday speech.

Jakobson's distinction between metaphor and metonymy in "Two Aspects of Language *and* Two Types of Aphasic Disturbances" became for hemiand many others following him—a key to language itself. Derived from the studies of aphasia (inability to speak), Jakohson detected two primordial principles of language use: similarity and contiguity (i.e. resemblance and nearness). In the vast array of normal verbal behavior, both operate at once. But in the early stages of language learning by children, in the late stages of language loss by aphasics (who can neither provide a synonym for a word or construct a sentence around it, but not both), and to some extent in literary forms like Ramanticism or realism, the outline of the two distinct principles become visible. Jakobson chooses to call these *metaphor* and *metonymy,* using the names of two rhetorical figures that had not previously been set in opposition. In metaphor, one sign is *substituted* for another because it is somehow similar to it: 'passion' becomes 'flame'. In metonymy, one sign as *associated* with another: 'wing' is associated, with air-craft' because it is part of it, 'sky' with 'aircraft' because of physical contiguity. We can make metaphors because we have a series of signs which are 'equivalent': 'passion', 'flame, 'love' and so on. When we speak or write, we select signs from a possible range of equivalences, and then combine them together to form a sentence. What happens in poetry, however, is that we pay attention to 'equivalences' in the process of *combining* words together as well as in selecting them: we string together words which are semantically or rhythmically or phonetically or in some other way equivalent. This is why Jakobson is able to say, in a famous defination, that 'the poetic function projects the principle of equivalence from the axis of selection to the axis of combination'.

The Prague school of linguistics—Jakobson, Jan Mukarovsky, Felix Vodicka and others—represent a kind of transition from Formalism to modern structuralism. They elaborated the ideas of the Formalists, but systematized them more firmly within the framework of Saussurean linguistics. Poems were to be viewed as 'functional structures', in which signifiers and signifieds are governed by a single complex set of relations. More than the Formalists, however, the Czech structuralists insisted on the structural unity of the work; its elements were to be grasped as function of a dynamic whole, with one particular level of the text (what the Prague school called the 'dominant') acting as the determining influence which 'deformed', or pulled into its own field of force, all the others. Mukarovsky distinguishes between the 'material artefact,' which is the physical book, painting or sculpture itself, and the 'asthetic object', which exists only in human interpretation of this physical fact.

With the work of the Prague school, the term 'structuralism' comes more or less to merge with the word 'semiotics'. The American founder of semiotics, the philosopher C.S. Pierce, distinguished between three basic kinds of sign. There was the 'iconic' where the sign somehow resembled what it stood for (a photograph of a person, for example); the 'indexical in which the sign is somehow associated with what it is a sing of (smoke with fire, spots with measles) and the 'symbolic' where as with Saussure the sign is only arbitrarily or conventionally linked with its referent. Semiotics takes up this and many other classifications: it distinguishes between 'denotation' (what the sign stands for) and 'connotation' (other signs associated with it): between codes (the rule-governed structures which produce meanings) and the messages transmitted by them; between the 'paradigmatic' (a whole class of signs which may stand in for one another) and the 'Syntagmatic' (where signs are coupled together with each other in a 'chain'). It speaks of 'meta languages', where one sign-system denotes another sign-system (the relation between literary criticism and literature, for instance), 'polysemic' signs which have more than one meaning, and a great many other technical concepts.

The poetic text for Lotman is a 'system of systems', a relation of relations. It is the most complex form of discourse imaginable, condensing together several systems each of which contains its own tensions, parallelism, repetitions and oppositions, and each of which is continually modifying all of the others. A poem, in fact, can only be re-read, not read, since some of its structures can only be perceived retrospectively. Poetry activities the full body of the signifier, presses the word to work to its utmost under the intense pressure of surrounding words, and so to release its richest potential.

Structuralism in Anthropology and Sociology

According to structural theory in anthropology and social anthropology, meaning is produced and reproduced within a culture through various practices, phenomena and activities which serve as systems of signification. A structuralist studies activities as diverse as food preparation and serving rituals, religious rites, games, literary and non-literary texts, and other forms of entertainment to discover the deep structures by which meaning is produced and reproduced within a culture. For example, an early and prominent practitioner of structuralism, anthropologist and ethnographer Claude Levi-Strauss in the 1950s, analyzed cultural phenomena including mythology, kinship (the Alliance theory and the incest taboo), and food preparation. In addition to these studies, he produced more linguistically focused writings where he applied Saussure's distinction between *langue* and *parole* in his search for the fundamental mental structures of the human mind, arguing that the structures that form the "deep grammar" of society originate in the mind and operate in us unconsciously. Levi-Strauss was inspired by information theory and mathematics.

Another concept was borrowed from the Prague School of linguistics, where Roman Jakobson and others analysed sounds based on the presence or absence of certain features (such as voiceless Vs. Voiced Levi-Strauss included this in his conceptualization of the universal structures of the mind, which he held to operate based on pairs of binary oppositions such as hot cold, male-female, culture-nature, cooked-raw, or marriageable vs-tabooed women. A third influence came from Marcel Mauss, who had written on gift exchange systems. Based on Mauss, for instance, Levi-Strauss argued that kinship systems are based on the exchange of women between groups (a position known as "alliances theory") as opposed to the 'descent' based theory described by Edward Evans-Pritchard and Meyer Fortes.

While replacing Marcel Mauss at his *Ecole, Pratique des Haustes Etudes* chair, Levi-Strauss writing became widely popular in the 1960s and 1970s and gave rise to the term "Structuralism" itself. In Britain authors such as Rodney Needhan and Edmund Leach were highly influenced by structuralism. Authors such as Maurice Godelier and Emmanuel Terray combined Marxism with structural anthropology in France. In the United States, authors such as Marshall Sahlins and James Boon built on structuralism to provide their own analysis of human society. Structural anthropology fell out of favour in the early 1980s for a number of reasons. D' Andrade (1995) suggests that structuralism in anthropology was eventually abandoned about the universal structures of the human mind. Authors such as Eric Wolf argued that political economy and colonialism should be more at the forefront of anthropology. More generally, criticisms of structuralism by Pierre Bourdieu led to a concern with how cultural and social structures were changed by human agency and practice a trend which Sherry Ortner has refered to as 'practice theory'.

Following Saussure, Levi-Strauss, studied hundreds of myths, breaking them into their smallest meaningful units, which he called "mythemes." Removing each from its diachronic relations with other mythemes in a single theme (such as the myth of Oedipus and his mother), he vertically aligned those mythemes that he found to be homologous (structurally correspondent). He then studied the relationships within as well as between vertically aligned columns, in an attempt to understand scientifically, through ratios and proportions, those thoughts and processes that humankind has shared, both at one particular time and across time. Whether Levi-Strauss was studying the structure of myths or the structure of villages, he looked for recurring, common elements that transcended the differences within and among cultures.

Levi-Strauss's theoretical views are set forth in *Structural Anthropology* (1958). Briefly, he considers culture a system of symbolic communication, to be investigated with methods that others have used more narrowly in the discussion of novels, political speeches, sports, and movies. For Levi-Strauss, the methods of linguistics became a model for all his earlier examination of society. His analogies are usually from phonetics (though also later from music). "A truly scientific analysis must be real, simplifying, and explanatory", he says (in *Structural Anthropology).* Phonemic analysis reveals features that are real, in the sense that users of the language can recognize and respond to them. At the same time, a phoneme is an abstraction from language—not a sound, but a category of sound defined by the way it is distinguished from other categories through rules unique to the language. The entire sound structure of a language can be generated from a relatively small number of rules.

Structuralists followed Saussure in preferring to think about the overriding *langue* or language of myth, in which each mytheme and mytheme-constituted myths fits meaningfully, rather than about isolated individual paroles, or narratives. Structuralists also followed Saussure's lead in believing that sign systems must be understood in terms of binary oppositions (a proposition later disputed by poststructuralist Jacques Derrida). In analyzing myths and text to find basic structures, structuralists found that opposite terms modulate until they are finally resolved or reconciled by some intermediary third term. Thus a structuralist reading of Milton's *Paradise Lost* (1667) might show that the war between God and the rebellious angels becomes a rift between God and sinful, fallen man, a rift that is heated by the Son of God, the mediating third term.

Some anthropological theorists, however, while finding considerable fault with Levi-Strauss' version of structrualism, did not turn away from a fundamental structural basis for human culture. The Biogenetic structuralism group for instance argued that some kind of structural foundation for culture must exist because all humans inherit the same system of brain structures. They proposed a kind of Neuroanthropology which would lay the foundations for a more complete scientific account of cultural similarity and variation by requiring an integration of cultural anthropology and neuroscience—a program also embraced by such theorists as Victor Turner.

Structuralism in Literary Theory and Literary Criticism

In literary theory, structuralism is an approach to analyzing the narrative material by examining the underlying invariant structure. For example, a literary critic applying a structuralist literary theory might say that the authors of *West Side Story* did not write anything "really" new, because their work has the same structure as Shakespeare's *Romeo and Juliet*. In both texts a girl and boy fall in love (a "formula" with a symbolic operator between them would be "Boy+Girl") despite the fact that they belong to two groups that hate each other ("Boys Groups-Girl's group" or "Opposing forces") and conflict is resolved by their death.

The versatility of structuralism is such that a literary critic could make the same claim about a story of two *friendly* families ("Boy's Family + Girl's Family) that arrange a marriage between their children despite the fact that the children hate each other ("Boy – Girl") and then the children commit suicide to escape the arranged marriage; the justification is that the second story's structure is an 'inversion' of the first story's structure: the relationship between the values of love and the two pairs of parties involved have been reversed.

Structuralist literary criticism argues that the "novelty value of a literary text" can lie only in new structure, rather than in the specifics of character development and voice in which that structure is expressed. One branch of literary structuralism, like Freudianism, Marxism, and transformational grammar, posits both a deep and a surface structure. In Freudianism and Marxism the deep structure is a story, in Freud's case the battle, ultimately, between the life and death instincts, and in Marx, the conflicts between classes that are rooted in the economic "base."

Literary structuralism often follows the lead of Vladimir Propp and Claude Levi-Strauss in seeking out basic deep elements in stories and myths, which are combined in various ways to produce the many versions of the ur-story or ur-myth. As in Freud and Marx, but in contrast to transformational grammar, these basic elements are meaning bearing.

There is considerable similarity between structural literary theory and Northrop Frye archetypal criticism, which is also indebted to the anthropological study of myths. Some critics have also tried to apply the theory to individual works, but the effort to find unique structure in individual literary works run counter to the structuralist program and has an affinity with New Criticism. The other branch of literary structuralism is semiotics, and it is based on the work of Ferdinand de Saussure.

In 1962, Roman Jakobson and Levi-Strauss published an analysis of Charles Baudelaire's poem *Les Chats* which has become something of a classic of high structuralist practice. Without toothcombing tenacity, the essay dug out a set, of equivalences and oppositions from the poems semantic, syntactic and phonological levels, equivalences and oppositions which extended right down to individual phonemes. But as Michael Riffaterre pointed out in a famous rejoinder to this critique some of the structures Jakobson and Levi-Strauss identified would simply have been imperceptible to even the most vigilant reader. Moreover, the analysis took no account of the reading *process:* it seized the text synchronically, as an object in space rather than a movement in time.

Richard Ohmann's view on literary texts, that they imitate or represent speech acts which themselves have never happened—as a way of defining 'literature' itself, though this does not in fact cover all that 'literature' is commonly taken to denote. To think of literary discourse in terms of *actual* human subjects: the real historical author, a particular historical reader and so on. Knowing about this may be important; but a literary work is not actually a 'living' dialogue or monologue. It is a piece of language which has been detached from any specific 'living' relationship and thus subject to the 'reinscriptions' and reinterpretations of many different readers. The work itself cannot 'forsee' its own future history of interpretations, cannot control and delimit these readings as we can do, or try to do, in face-to-face conversation. Its 'anonymity' is part of its very structure, not just an unfortunate accident which befalls it; and in this sense to be an 'author'—the 'origin' of ones own meanings, with 'authority' over them is a myth.

Even so, a literary work can be seen as constructing what have been called 'subject positions to understand a poem means grasping its language as being 'oriented' towards the reader from a certain range of positions : in reading, we build up a sense of what kind of effects this language is trying to achieve ('intention'), what sorts of rhetoric is considers appropriate to use, what assumptions govern the kinds of poetic tactics it employs, what attitudes towards reality these imply. None of this need to be identical with the intentions, attitudes and assumptions of the actual historical author at the time of writing, as is obvious if one tries to read William Blake's *Songs of Innocence and Experience* as the 'expression' of William Blake himself.

Literature as Julia Kristeva has argue in a manner similar to Barthe's discussion of criticism has a special relationship to semiotics both as privileged field in which to examine the semiotic functioning of meaning and as a particular "object" of semiotic study literature, she writes, "is a *particular semeotic practice* which has the advantage of making more accessible than others the problematics of the production of meaning. "In other words, the semiotic study of literature offers methods to study other cultural discursive formations – fashion, advertisements, even Disneyland. This is what de Lauretis means when she suggests that "in the last decade or so, semiotics has undergone a shift of its theoretical gears : a shift away from the classification of sign systems—their basic units, their level of structural organization—and toward the exploration of the modes of production of signs and meanings, the ways in which systems and codes are used, transformed or transgressed in social practice. While formerly the emphasis was on studying sign systems (language, literature, cinema, architecture, music, etc.) conceived of as mechanisms that generate messages, what is now being examined is the work performed through them". A good example of the "former" emphasis of semiotics (one that still has strong currency, we should add) is the systematic study of literature and "literariness" of Russian Formalism. Russian Formalism illustrates the aims and methods of structural linguistics applied to literary studies, while French structuralism offers examples of wider semiotic practices focused on literature.

The intertextual sense of the multiplicity of origins and meanings in language informs the theory of the sign set forth in Kristeva's first book *Research toward a sem-analysis,* (1969) (where sem-is from the Greek word for "sign"). This was followed by *Revolution in Poetic Language* (1974).

Kristeva finds two forces competing for expression in the language of poetry: the symbolic and the semiotic. The *symbolic* is that aspect of language that allows it to *refer.* It is systematic, prepositional, rule-bound, tied to the social order, dependent on a functional separation between the subject and the object, and capable of existing independently of its referent. The linguistics of Saussure focused on this dimension, treating language as a theoretical fiction studied in the absence of any particular speaker. The semiotic dimension of language—which cannot be known except in the moments where it breaks through the symbolic—is that aspect that bears the trace of the language user's own body and of the mother's protolinguistic presence the bobbling of the infant who tries out the vocal repertoire before he or she learns to speak, for instance, or the mother's voice prior to the baby's acquisition of language: poetic language in this sense has been called "babble, doodle, and riddle." The "Music" of poetry (and indeed prosody itself), Kristeva contends, arises out of this dimension. It is important to avoid two possible misunderstanding of Kristeva's use of these terms. Her "symbolic" is similar to Lacans, insofar as it is not symbolic of anything—not a collection of meaning—filled symbols as, say, Carl Jung, might conceive it-but is a *structure.* And the semiotic" is not the same as *semiotics,* which is the study of the functions of signs. In *Revolution in Poetic Language,* Kristeva thus maintains that all signification entails the dialectical interaction of the symbolic and the semiotic.

Ronald Barthe's theoretical development is often seen as embodying a transition from structuralist to post-structuralist perspectives, though certain of his works are characterized by a Marxian perspective. Barthes effectively extended structural analysis and semiology (the study of signs) to broad cultural phenomena, and it was he also who confronted the limits of structuralism pointing the way to freer and more relativistic assessments of texts and their role in culture. It was Barthes who made famous the notion of the "death of the author," the idea of the text as a site of free flay or pleasure, and differences such as those between "work" and "text," and "Writerly" and "readerly" works of art. As such, he anticipates many facets of post-structuralism, including certain elements of deconstruction, cultural studies, and queer studies.

Barthes' first book *Writing Degree Zero* (1953), initially published as articles in Albert Camus's journal, *Combat,* analyzes the history of literary styles in terms derived from Marx and from Sartre. In this book Barthes look at the relations between Literature with a capital *L* and the various modern forms of its demystification, from Stephen Mallorme's "vibratory near-disppearance" to Camus's "blank" style (the "zero degree" of the title). In *Writing Degree Zero,* Barthes proposes that the problem of the relationship between language and meaning is not only the main subject of modern literature, but the form of its proper engagement with history. Literature must be seen as a historical phenomenon, not transcending it to form a trans-historical institution of unshakeable human or cultural values. It is this engagement with the 'problematics of language' that allows literature to renew its purpose by challenging the limitations of inherited conventions and forms. Literary form, like language itself, is imbued with the rich and unknowable traces of all the uses to which it has already been put. It is thus always already radically historicized, grounded in the tradition of previous practices in which the writer has no choice but to work. There is thus simple free choice for writers of the mode of their creativity, nor are there any forms—like realism—which can convincingly claim to transcend linguistic conventions to produce an unadulterated engagement with the real world. Each literary form is implicated in the society which produces it, and writers inevitably exemplify social meanings outside of and beyond their won specific needs and intentions. The problematizing of language undertaken by writers from Flaubert onward insistantly reminds us that literary conventions can thus no longer be seen as pragmatic or functional options manipulated by writers seeking an outlet for their already existing ideas by way of free invention or fare choice. Writing is itself a 'compromise between freedom and remembrance,' in which the new appears only as a complication or transformation of already located conventions. In modern poetry, this disruption of the inherited takes the form of a stripping away of the normal functions of language, till words appear in their most neutal form, their degree zero. In this way 'the consumer of poetry, deprived of the guide of selective connections, encounters the word frontally, and receives it as an absolute quantity, accompanies by all its possible associations. In prose, the exemplary case is Camus' *The Outsider,* where 'the social or mythical characters of language are abolished in favour of a neutral and inert state of form', which separates the writing from the dictates of 'a History not its own'. The aim here is to create a rupture in the torture of inherited language use, which confronts the reader with both the limitations of socially situated conventions and the possibility of a language expanding beyond them. Readers or 'consumers, as Barthes sometimes call them, are thus announced as the possible site of a radical disjunction between conditioned meaning and its disruption.

A second, quite different, project Barthes undertook at the same time was an extensive study of the imagery used by the nineteenth century historians Jules Michelet. Scribbling passages on index cards, Barthes organized Michelet's "imagination" in ways that did not correspond to the explicit intentions of his writing. Like the work of the phenomenological critics Jean-Pierre Richard and Georges Poulet, Barthes's analysis was a way of structuring Michelet's writing around its unconscious "obsessions." This research was published as a book tilled *Michelet.*

Barthes' *Mythologies* (1957), is a kind of Marxian semiology of mass culture and everyday life. The object is to show how mass culture is saturated with ideological propositions ("myths") presented as if they were natural and self-evident; the result in many ways anticipates what is today called "cultural studies". Barthes combines a sharp eye for the social life of signs with a subtle critique of the naturalizations of the ethnocentric patriarchal, petit-bourgeois French worldview. Critical of the covert functions of *what-goes-without-saying,* Barthes nevertheless enjoys the exhibitions, advertisements, photographs, articles, films, wrestling matches, and commodities that provide the occasion for his little feats of writing. In the essay on soap powders, for example, he both ends up revealing that the competing products are owned by the same company and in—his descriptions of these products in terms of foam and fire, the depth of lenin and the triumph of cleanliness enjoys the process of "frothing" rhetorically himself. In fact, in a perfect illustration of how capitalism devours its critics, an executive at France's largest advertising firm found Barthe's work on advertising so compelling that he began studying with Barthes and persuaded him to work briefly as a consultant for the automaker Renault. Bathes was critical of the myth-making operation of petit-bourgeois culture, but he was also intrigued by the meaning making functions of cultural objects themselves.

Barthes' *Elements of Semiology* is in many ways a classic statement of structuralism. In the introduction to this text, Barthes states that "we are......a civilization of the written word," suggesting that there is no extensive system of signs outside of the language. He admits that objects, images and behavior could signify but only in virtue of possessing a "linguistic admixture". If such insights now seem common-place to us, that is partly because structuralism has defined the contours of much twentieth century thought. Barthes suggests that the "elements" of semiology are contained in four sets of terms: (1) language and speech; (2) signifier and signified; (3) syntagm and system; and (4) denotation and connotation.

According to the opposition between *langue* (language) and *parole* (speech out), each individual language event is allowed, even predetermined, by the existence of a 'systematized set of conventions necessary to communication', that we conventionally call a language. Because speech can only occur within the context of language, yet we only know language by way of speech, the two are in a genuinely dialectical relationship. This distinction allows the analyst to detect the general principles and possibilities are actualized. The second distinction in *Elements* is the conventional and familiar Saussurian one between the two things that constitute the sign, its material substance (signifier), and 'mental representation' or signified. Thirdly, Barthes distinguishes between system (paradigm in more conventional structuralism) and syntagm. The paradigm represents the various options that can be substituted for one another in a cultural practice, and the syntagm the logical sequence which combines them in order. Various words may substitute for one another in the same position in a sentence, and are thus in a paradigmatic relationship to one another in the same position in a sentence, and are thus in a paradigmatic relationship to one another within the same system. The order in which they appear in that sentence betrays their syntagmatic relationship. In a famous example, Barthes proposes that the menu in a restaurant replicates the same logic: the alternative dishes within a course are a system; the logical sequence in which they appear (entrees before main course, main course before dessert) is their syntagm. The final binary opposition Barthes outlines is between denotation and connotation, announcing that 'the future probably belongs to a linguistics of connotation'. This claims exhibits the contradiction at the heart of this semiotic enterprise. Connotation is seen as 'general, global and diffuse', yet Barthes calls connotation a system. This paradox foreshadows how attempts at the rigorous constitution of binary oppositions as rock-hard theoretical principles would soon come undone in Derridean deconstruction, a process of which Barthes would become perhaps one of the less philosophically rigorous but more rhetorically influential fellow-travellers. The most severe vision of Barthe's semiotic analysis appears in his treatment of the language of the fashion industry in *The Fashion System* (1967). This next work represent (especially S/Z and *Empire of Signs)* an inversion, even parody of this approach, even though the skepticism they imply towards a putatively scientific methodology always respects and relies on the semioclastic will to read across signs and texts for their unconfussed meanings. *Elements* ends with a call for a synchronic approach to language, to present not the unfolding meaning of history in process, but 'a cross-section of history'.

In his classic essay "Introduction to the *Structuralist Analysis of Narratives*" (1966), Barthes had talked of the "problem of the subject, insisting on viewing an author or persona as a grammatical rather than a psychological subject. Barthes' most well-known formulation of this probe, occurs in his essay "The Death of the Author" (1968), a phrase which has come to be associated with both Barthes and structuralism, just as the phrase "God is dead" had been attribute to Nietzsche (though in fact it had first occurred in Hegel's *Phenomenology).* Barthes begins this essay by quoting a sentence from Balzac's novella *Sarrasine:* "This was woman herself, with her sudden fears, her irrational whims, her instinctive worries." Bathes asks, who is the speaker of these words? Is it the hero of the story, or Balzac himself drawing on his experience of women? Or Balzac the author professing literary notions of feminity? Or is it universal wisdom? Barthes' answer is that we can never know, because "writing is the destruction of every voice, of every point of origin. Writing is that neutral, composite, oblique space where our subject slips away, the negative where all identity is lost, starting with the very identity of the body writing."

Barthes' argument is that as soon as narration occurs without the practical purpose of acting on reality, as soon as narrative occurs as an end in itself, "This disconnection occurs, the voice loses its origin, the author enters into his own death, writing begins". One is reminded here of Horace's statement that the voice once sent forth can never return be reclaimed by the author as his own. Barthes also points out that the idea of an individual author is a modern one: in many previous societies, the author or poet was regarded as a mediator between higher powers and humanity. Often, authorship was collective progressing through oral traditions of story telling, as was the case with the *Iliad* and the

Odyssey, conventionally attributed to Homer. The modern, individual author, says Barthes, was "a product of our society insofar as' emerging from the Middle Ages with English empiricism, French rationalism and the personal faith of the Reformation, it discovered the prestige of the individual.......It is thus logical that in literature it should be this positivism, the epitome and culmination of capitalist ideology, which has greatest importance to the 'person' of the author". Even in the present, says Barthes, our studies of literature and literary history are "tyrannically centred on the author." The newer modes of criticism (by which he presumably means phenomenological and psychoanalytical criticism), he claims, have often consolidated this obsession.

To give a text an Author is to impose a limit on that text, to furnish it with a final signified, to close the writing. This closure, in turn, collaborates with all authoritarian systems of meaning-making. A style of reading that engages with the plurality of textually as 'a multi-dimensional space in which a variety of writings, none of them original, blend and clash' challenges such authority becoming 'an anti-theological activity, an activity that is truly revolutionary since to refuse to fix meanings is, in the end, to refuse God and his hypostases—reason, science, law. Here, reading against meaning liberates us from the constraints of traditional reading institutions, the academy in particular, and allows us to animate the incommensurability, contradiction and difference implicit in textuality. Here is the most succinct version of Barthes' understanding of reading as an avant-garde activity. The later essay 'From Work to Text' (1971) develops many of these same ideas into a comparison between the traditional model of, on the one hand, the closed work located in fixed and knowable sequences of literary filiation and meaning, and the open text, on the other, which expects and inspires an active reading, 'play, activity, production, practice'. This article is largely an attempt to assimilate Julia Kristeva's idea of the 'Intertextual', that texts produce their meaning not from their own internal structures and intentions, but from their relationship with other texts. Reading is seen not as an act of consumption, but of collaboration:

Structuralism after World War II

Throughout the 1940s and 1950s, existentialism like that propounded by Jean-Paul Sartre was the dominant mood.

Structuralism surged to prominence in France after World War II and particularly in the 1960s. The initial popularity of structuralism in France led it to spread across the globe. The social sciences (in particularly sociology) were particularly influenced.

Structuralism rejected the concept of human freedom and choice and focused instead on the way that human behavior is determined by various structures. The most important initial work on this score was Claude Levi-Strauss's 1949 volume *Elementary Structure of Kinship*. Levi-Strauss had known Jakobson during their time together in New York during World War II and was influenced by both Jakobson's structuralism as well as the American anthropological tradition. In *Elementary Structure* he examined kinship systems from a structural point of view and demonstrated how apparently different social organizations were in fact different permutations of a few basic kinship structures. In the late 1950s he published *Structural Anthropology*, a collection of essays outlining his program for structuralism.

By the early 1960s structuralism as a movement was coming into its own and some believed that it offered a single unified approach to human life that would embrace all disciplines. Roland Barthes and Jacques Derrida focused on low structuralism could be applied to literature.

Blending Freud and De Saussure, the French (post) structuralist Jacques Lacan applied structuralism to psychoanalysis and, in a different way, Jean Piaget applied structuralism to the study of psychology. But Jean Piaget, who would better define himself as constructivist, considers structuralism as "a method and not a doctrine" because for him "there exists no structure without a construction, abstract or genetic".

Michel Foucault's book *The Order of Things* examined the history of science to study how structures of epistemology, or episteme, shaped the way in which people imagined knowledge and knowing (though Foucault would later explicitly deny affiliation with the structuralist movement).

In much the same way, American historian of science Thomas Kuhn addressed the structural formations of science in his seminal work *The Structure of Scientific Revolutions*—its title alone evincing a stringent structuralist approach. Though less concerned with "episteme," Kuhn nonetheless remarked at how coteries of scientists operated under and applied a standard praxis of 'normal science,' deviating from a standard 'paradigm' only in instances of irreconcilable anomalies that question a significant body of their work.

Blending Marx and structuralism another French theorist Louis Althusser introduced his own brand of structural social analysis giving rise to "structural Marxism". Other authors in France and abroad have since extended structural analysis to practically every discipline.

The definition of 'structuralism' also shifted as a result of its popularity. As its popularity as a movement waxed and waned some authors considered themselves 'structuralists' only to later eschew the label.

The term has slightly different meanings in French and English. In the US, for instance Derrida is considered the paradigm of post-structuralism while in France he is labeled as structuralist. Finally, some authors wrote in several different styles. Barthes, for instance, wrote some books which are clearly structuralist and others which clearly are not.

Reactions to Structuralism

Today structuralism is less popular than approaches such as post-structuralism and construction. There are many reasons for this. Structuralism has often been criticized for being ahistorical and for favoring deterministic structural forces over the ability of individual people to act. As the political turbulence of the 1960s and 1970s (and particularly the student uprisings of May 1968) began affecting academia, issues of power and political struggle moved to the center of peoples attention. The ethnologist Robert Jaulin defined another ethnological method which clearly pitted itself against structuralism.

In the 1980s, deconstruction and its emphasis on the fundamental ambiguity of language—rather than its crystalline logical structure—became popular. By the end of the century structuralism was seen as a historically important school of thought, but it was the movement it spawned, rather than structuralism itself, which commanded attention.

17

Deconstruction

Deconstruction is a term in contemporary philosophy, literary criticism, and the social sciences, denoting a process by which the texts and languages of Western philosophy (in particular) appear to shift and complicate in meaning when read in light of the assumptions and absences they reveal with themselves. Jacques Derrida coined the term in the 1960s, and proved more forthcoming with negative, rather than pined—for positive, analyses of the school. Like *existentialism, special, liberal, conservative,* and *postmodern,* its meaning is often so vague as to be useless.

Derrida, who is responsible for the pervasive phenomenon in modern literary and cultural theory known as "deconstruction", he himself has insisted that deconstruction is not a theory unified by any set of consistent rules or procedures, it has been variously regarded as a way of reading, a mode of writing, and, above all, a way of challenging interpretations of texts based upon conventional notions of the stability of the human self, the external world, and of language and meaning.

Husserl is one of the major influences on the development of Derrida thought and Husserl is both mentor and fail to the development of deconstruction. In Derrida's first published paper titled "'Genesis and Structure' and phenomenology" (1959) Derrida describes "two polemics which placed him [Husserl] in opposition to those philosophies of structure called *Diltheyism* and *Gestaltism*". These two polemics by Husserl and forerunners of Derrida's own destruction. Derrida notes admiringly that Husserl—

> "Ceaselessly attempts to reconcile the *structuralist* demand (which leads to the comprehensive description of a totality, of a form or a function organized according to an internal legality in which elements have meaning only in the solidarity

of their correlation or their opposition), with the *genetic* demand (that is the search for the origin and foundation of the structure)."

Derrida argues that "the objectivity of a structure is tied to the concrete genesis which must make it possible" and that "Husserl refuses, and will always refuse, to accept the intelligibility and normativity of this universal structure as Manna fallen from a "heavenly place"—or as an eternal truth created by an infinite reason". As will as demonstrating the philosophical movement of deconstruction that Derrida would make his own—Husserl is also the thinker against which Derrida publishes his first book length deconstruction in the form of *Speech and Phenomena* (1967). Derrida's "major preoccupations" in *Speech and Phenomena* are with "the impossibility of maintaining the plentitude of the present, the purity of the origin, or the self-identity of the absolute in the face of 'delay', postponement and 'originary Difference'". These early preoccupation indicate the critical engagement of deconstruction with metaphysics. For Derrida metaphysics is the appeal to originary self presence in philosophy. This appeal is typified for Derrida within Husserl's phenomenology by the alleged immediate self presence of the real in the phenomena of conscious experience.

Derrida takes the word *deconstruction* from the work of Martin Heidegger. In the summer of 1927, Martin Heidegger delivered a lecture course now published under the title, *Basic Problems* of *Phenomenology.* Given the topic of his lectures, Heidegger appropriately begins them with a discussion of the nature of philosophy and, particularly of the philosophical movement called *phenomenology.* Borrowing creatively from his teacher, Edmund Husserl, Heidegger says that phenomenology is the name for a method of doing philosophy; he says that the method includes three steps—reduction, construction, and destruction—and he explains that these three are mutually pertinent to one another. Construction necessarily involves destruction, he says, and then he identifies destruction with deconstruction *Abbau.* Heidegger explains what he means by philosophical destruction by using an ordinary German word that we can translate literally "unbuild."

The lexical and historical connection *deconstruction* to *destruction* is obvious, but Heidegger does not mean by *Abbau* quite what we mean by either *destruction* or *disassembly.* He uses *Abbau* to show that in his method the word *destruction* does not mean what we might often mean by it. He explain what he means by *Abbau*—deconstruction—to clarify further that he does not simply mean "taking things apart." As Heidegger conceived deconstruction, it was an answer to a philosophical problem: "All philosophical discussion, even the most radical attempt to begin all over again, is pervaded by traditional concepts and thus by traditional horizons and traditional angles of approach" (*Basic Problems).* Unfortunately, however, we cannot assume that these concepts, horizons, and approaches are the best ones for dealing with the things they supposedly explain. There is a world "out there." Our problem is that our only rational access to that world is linguistic, which might make us mistakenly to believe that our understanding of the world is always derivative from our language. If we add our suspicion to Heidegger's point that we have inherited our concepts and words from others who themselves had to work with inherited concepts and words and we quickly come to a question: How, then, can we think about the world productively? How can we avoid reducing understanding to something relative only to a particular language and history?

Like every other philosopher in the nineteenth and twentieth conturies, Heidegger does not believe there is an autonomous tool called reason that we use irrespective of our language, time, circumstances, or interests, to criticize ideas. Thus, since we seem unable to begin from such a rational zero point, free of any already given concepts, terms, or approaches, it appears that we are forced to repeat the past and its mistakes. If we must use concepts we've inherited from others to do philosophy (or anything else), how can we ever get to anything new? How can we get beyond whatever philosophical mistakes our intellectual forebears may have made? Aren't we condemned to historicism and cultural relativism?

Ironically, given much of the current discussion of Heidegger's work and work that derives from his, Heidegger's answer is, "No." We can use these concepts, horizons, and approaches against themselves to discover what produced them. We might, for example, think about Aristotle's discussion of form and matter, using those very terms to show their inadequacy. What, after all, is matter? Any answer I give is in terms of another form rather than in terms of matter. Questions: "What is that desk made of; what is its material?" Answer: "Wood, "But the word *wood* gives us a form, not a matter. I can ask, "What is the wood made of?" and give a reasonable answer, though one still in terms of form. As we use the terms *matter* and *form* against themselves, what starts out looking like a perfectly sensible question becomes problematic. By problematizing the distinction, we to which Aristotle was responding. Perhaps we begin to wonder—to think—in the same way that he did. If we do, perhaps we, begin to do philosophy with regards to Aristotle's questions rather than simply to repeat the scholarly exegensis of Aristotle's philosophy.

Derrida would say of this example that we can deconstruct the idea of form and matter. But what he means by *deconstruction* differs from what Heidegger means. For one thing, rather than a method or part of a method, for Derrida deconstruction is an attitude, in the root sense of that word. It is a position one has with regard to something.

Derrida's deconstruction, is different from ideological or moral criticism. Derrida does not deconstruct Heidegger's work *(Being and Time)* to show that Heidegger should have written the book better. Unlike a good book reviewer, Derrida is not repairing Heidegger's work for him, presuming that with these corrections we will have, at least in principle, a better work. Deconstructive criticism is not intended to suggest a way to make the book finally complete, but to show its *necessary* incompleteness. Deconstruction is used to show that a work does not adequately address something, not that it should have.

Deconstruction does not assume that once its work has been done everything will have been included. That would be impossible. It doesn't even assume that its work will result in the inclusion of more than was previously included; it doesn't assume that its work will make things better. That remains to be seen in each case. In sum, deconstruction doesn't assume that there is, even if only in principle, an end to the work of deconstruction. The point of deconstruction is to show where something has been omitted, not because of the blindness of the author, not because the critic is smarter or better, but because that is the way things are. These are always things I don't know, though in a very real way *that* I don't know them is part of what I know. Derrida is fascinated by this "non-knowledge" and his work circles around it.

The English word "Deconstructions" is an element in a translation series (from Husserl's *Abbau* to Heidegger's *Destruktion* to Jacques Derrida's *deconstruction)* and has been explored by Gayatri Chakravorty Spivak, Paulde Man, Jonathan Culler, Sarbara Johnson, J. Hillis Miller, Jean Francois Lyotard and Geoffrey Bennington.

These authors have resisted establishing a succinct definition of the word. When asked "What is deconstruction?" : Derrida stated, "I have no simple and formalisable response to this question. All my essays are attempts to have it out with this formidable question". There is much confusion as to what deconstruction is and determining what authority to accord to a given delimitation: a school of thought (not so in the singular), a method of reading (often so reduced by attempts at formal definition), or "textual event" (Derrida's implied characterization in the above quotation).

Most criticism of deconstruction is difficult to read and summarize. In contrast, there are many secondary texts attempting straightforward explanation of the philosophy of deconstruction, however, these works (e.g. *Deconstruction for Beginners* and *Deconstructions: A User's Guide)* have been academically criticized for being too removed from the original texts, and contradictory to the concepts of deconstruction.

A survey of deconstruction texts and secondary literature reveals a wide range of heterogeneous arguments, including claims that deconstruction can entirely sort the Western tradition, by highlighting and discrediting unjustified privileges accorded to white males and other hegemonists. On the other hand, some critics claim that deconstruction is a dangerous form of nihilism, the destruction of Western scientific and ethical values. As a rule, the political Right Wing is not sympathetic to deconstruction yet, the Left Wing's reception of deconstruction varied from hostility to co-optation:

- Many of the principal French deconstructionists have been Leftist, but Martin Heidegger place in the deconstructionist camp is complicated, as are Paul de Man's early adulthood politics. Heidegger was Rector of the University of Freiburg from 1933-34 while a Nazi Party member, de Man wrote questionably anti-Semitic articles for the right-wing newspaper *Le Soir*. (These articles were written between 1941 and 1943. This was well before de Man's critical maturity, much less his involvement with deconstructive theory; Derrida and de man met in 1966.)

- From the racial-religious perspective, deconstruction has no clear sectarian identity, e.g. Derrida's views are not sectarian. As a Jew raised in a walled Jewish community is colonial Algeria, Derrida rejected the counter-signature of anti-Semitism by Algerian Jewish institutions of the 1940s. He is atheist in terms of dogmatic theology, and has written about religion in terms precepts shared among the Abrahamic faiths. Because of the open nature of Derrida's engagement with religion, deconstruction-and-religion attraction is inter-disciplinary.
- Writers sympathetic to deconstruction tend to use idiosyncratic, imitative styles-, employing neologisms, irony, and inter-disciplinary allusions to and from the Western canon. Critics say that on deconstructing such writings they discovered it not worth the effort.

Derrida has been more forthcoming with negative than positive descriptions of deconstruction. Derrida gives these negative descriptions of deconstruction in order to explain, "what deconstruction is not, or rather *ought not to be*" and therefore to prevent misunderstandings of the term. Derrida states that deconstruction is not an analysis, a critique, or a method in the traditional sense that philosophy understands these terms. In these negative descriptions of deconstruction Derrida is seeking to "multiply the cautionary indicators and put aside all the traditional philosophical concepts." This does not mean that deconstruction has absolutely nothing in common with an analysis, a critique, or a method because while Derrida distances deconstruction from these terms, he reaffirms "the necessity of returning to them, at least under erasure." Derrida's necessity of returning to a term under erasure means that even though these terms are problematic we must use them until they can be effectively reformulated or replaced. Derrida's thought developed in relation to Hassle's and this return to something under erasure has a similarity to Husserl's phenomenological reduction or epoche. Derrida acknowledges that his preference for negative description "has been called...... a type of negative theology." The relevance, of the tradition of negative theology to Derrida's preference for negative descriptions of deconstruction is the notion that a positive description of deconstruction would over-determine the idea of deconstruction and that this would be a mistake because it would close off the openness that Derrida wishes to preserve for deconstruction. This means that if Derrida were to positively define deconstruction as, for example, a critique then this would put the concept of critique forever outside the possibility of deconstruction. Some new philosophy beyond deconstruction would then be required in order to surpass the notion of critique. By refusing to define deconstruction positively Derrida preserves the infinite possibility of deconstruction, the possibility for the deconstruction of everything.

Part of the difficulty in defining deconstruction arises from the fact that deconstruction cannot escape itself. The word is subject to the linguistic limitations and effects which it purports in its own definition. Followers of Derrida do not view deconstruction as a concept standing outside of text, which can act upon all text without itself being affected. The act of definition, in this view, is an attempt to "finish" or "complete" deconstruction, yet deconstruction is never viewed as complete, but a continuous process; 'a living philosophy' being adjusted within itself.

Nevertheless, writers have provided a number of rough definitions. One of the most popular definitions of deconstruction is by Paul de Man, who explained, "It's possible, within text, to frame a question or undo assertions made in the text, by means of elements which are in the text, which frequently would be precisely structures that play off the rhetorical against grammatical elements." Thus viewed in this way, "the term 'deconstruction' refers in the first instance to the way in which the 'accidental' features of a text can be seen as betraying, subverting, its purportedly 'essential' message". (The word *accidentally* is usually interpreted here in the sense of *incidental*).

A more whimsical definition is by John D. Caputo, who defines deconstruction thus: "Whenever deconstruction finds a nutshell—a secure axiom or a pithy maxim—the very idea is to crack it open and disturb this tranquility. Indeed, that is a good rule of thumb in deconstruction. *That* is what deconstruction is all about, its very meaning and mission, if it has any. One might even say that cracking nutshells is what deconstruction *is*. In a nutshell—Have we not run up against a paradox and an aporia [something impassable] ?—-the paralysis and impossibility of an aporia is just what impels deconstruction, what arouses it out of bed in the morning—"

Many definitions portray deconstruction as a method, project, or school of thought. For example, the philosopher David B. Allison can early translator of Derrida) stated:

> "[Deconstruction] signifies a project of critical thought whose task is to locate and 'take apart' those concepts which serve as the axioms or rules for a period of thought, those concepts which command the unfolding of an entire epoch of metaphysics. 'Deconstruction' is somewhat less negative than the Heideggerian or Nietzschean term "destruction' or 'reversal'; it suggests that certain foundational concepts of metaphysics will never be entirely eliminated—There is no simple 'overcoming' of metaphysics or the language of metaphysics."

Similarly, in the context of religious studies Paul Ricoeur (1983) defined deconstruction as a way of uncovering the questions behind the answers of a text or tradition.

Derrida states that his use of the word deconstruction first took place in a context in which "structuralism was dominant" and its use is related to this context. Derrida states that deconstruction is an "antistructuralist gesture" because "structures were to be undone, decomposed desidimented". At the same time for Derrida deconstruction involves "a certain attention to structures" and tries to "understand how an "ensemble" was constituted". As both a structuralist and an antistructuralist gesture deconstruction is tied up with what Derrida calls the "structural problematic". The structural problematic for Derrida is the tension between genesis, that which is "in the essential mode of creation or movement", and structure, "systems, or complexes, or static configurations". An example of genesis would be the sensory ideas from which knowledge is then derived in the empirical epistemology. An example of structure would be a binary opposition such as good and evil where the meaning of each element is established, at least partly, through its relationship to the other element. For Derrida, Genesis and structure are both inescapable modes of description, there are somethings that must be described in terms of structure, and others which must be described in terms of genesis," but these two modes of description are difficult to reconcile and this is the tension of the structural problematic. In Derrida's own words the structural problematic is that "beneath the serene use of these concepts [genesis and structure] is to be found a debate that—makes new reductions and explications indefinitely necessary". The structural problematic is therefore what propels philosophy and hence deconstruction forward. Another significance of the structural problematic for Derrida is that while a critique of structuralism is a recurring theme of his philosophy this does not mean that philosophy can claim to be able to discard that Derrida distances his use of the term deconstruction from post structuralism, a term that would suggest philosophy could simply go beyond structuralism. Derrida states that "the motif of deconstruction has been associated with" poststructuralism" "but that this term was" a word unknown in France until its "return" from the United States.

Deconstruction's central concern is a radical critique of the enlightenment project and of metaphysics, including in particular the founding texts by such philosophers as Plato, Rousseau, and Husserl, but also other sorts of texts, including literature. Deconstruction identifies in the Western philosophical tradition a "logocentrism" or "metaphysics of presence" (sometimes known as *phallogocentrism.)* which holds that speech-thought (the *logos)* is a privileged, ideal, one self-present entity, through which all discourse and meaning are derived. This logocentrism is the primary target of deconstruction.

One typical form of deconstructive reading is the critique of binary oppositions, or the critics of dichotomous thought. A central deconstructive argument holds that, in all the classics dualities of western thought, one term is privileged or "central" over the other. The privileged, central term is the one most associated with the phallus and the *logos.* Example include:

- speech over writing
- presence over absence
- identity over difference
- fullness over emptiness
- meaning over meaningless
- mastery over submission
- life over death

Derrida argues in *Of Grammatology* (translated by Gayatri Chakravarty Spivak and published in English in 1976) that, in each such case, the first term is classically conceived as original, authentic and superior, while the second is thought of as secondary, derivative, or even "parasitic." These binary oppositions, or "violent hierarchies", and others of their form, he argues, must be deconstructed.

This deconstruction is effected into two ways (La Double Séance). He argues that these oppositions cannot be simply transcended; given the thousands of years of philosophical history behind them, it would be disingenuous to attempt to move directly to a domain of thought beyond these distinctions. So deconstruction attempts to compensate for these historical power imbalances, undertaking the difficult project of thinking through the philosophical implications of questioning and presenting complications to show the contingency of such divisions.

The second "session" involves the emergence or eruption of a new conception. One can begin to conceive a conceptual terrain away from these oppositions: the next project of deconstruction would be to develop concepts which fall under neither one term of these oppositions nor the other. Much of the philosophical work of deconstruction has been devoted to developing such ideas and their implications, of which *difference* may be the *prototype* (as it denotes neither simple identity nor simple difference). Derrida spoke in an interview (first published in French in 1967) about such "concepts," which he called merely "marks" in order to distinguish them from proper philosophical concepts:

"—[I]t has been necessary to analyze, to set to work, *within* the text of the history of philosophy, as well as *within* the so-

> called literary text,—, certain marks, shall we say,—that *by analogy* (I underline) I have called undecidables, that is, unities of simulacrum, "false" verbal properties (nominal or semantic) that can no longer be included within philosophical (binary) opposition, resisting and disorganizing it, *without ever* constituting a third term, without ever leaving room for a solution in the form of speculative dialectics.

As can be seen in this discussion of its terms' undecidable, unresolvable complexity, deconstruction requires a high level of comfort with suspended, deferred decision; a deconstructive thinker must be willing to work with terms whose precise meaning has not been, and perhaps cannot be, established. (This is often given as a major reason for the difficult writing style of deconstructive texts). Critics of deconstruction find this unacceptable as philosophy; many feel that, by working in this manner with unspecified terms, deconstruction ignores the primary task of philosophy, which they say is the creation and elucidation of concepts. This deep criticism is a result of a fundamental difference of opinion about the nature of philosophy, and is unlikely to be resolved simply.

In literature Deconstruction has cast significant influence by denying the centrality and determinacy of meaning. As far as acknowledging textual features is concerned, deconstruction goes along with structuralism but whereas in structuralism order and meaning are affirmed, deconstruction finds shifting meanings in the text, and points out the absurdity of pinning text to one or two final interpretation, "texts are found to deconstruct themselves rather than to provide a stable identifiable meaning". The deconstructionists believe that literature is only a free play of signifiers without a centre. 'Far from presenting any meaning words carry with them a certain absence or indeterminacy of meaning' (Gayatri Chakravarty Spiuak—preface to *Of Grammatology).*

In order to understand this one must turn attention to Derrida's new concept of writing ('ecriture). According to this new concept of writing, is composed of 'difference', 'trace' and 'arche-writing'

1. Derrida uses a new word *;diffarence'* which combines 'difference' and 'deferring'. By 'differing' is meant that each sign is something that is unlike another sign and

something that is not the sign. Each sign (or word) differs from all other signs; in other words each sign is recognized by what it is not—it is something else that has to be discovered. And each sign has the capacity to postpone. No sign is perfectly adequate, it is under what Derrida calls *erasure,* a term he coins to express the inadequacy of the sign. In this manner Deconstruction rejects the Metaphysical presupposition of the presence of meaning and established the *free play of signifiers.*

2. In the opinion of the deconstructionists each sign carries the *traces* of those other signs that it is not. While accepting the basic tenets of Saussure, Derrida also reinterprets them in order to evolve his own concept of deconstruction in language. 'He agrees with Saussure's view that language is self-referential and that meaning is engendered by the difference between linguistic units. He also accepts Saussure's observation that in each sign there are traces of signs absent'.

3. This leads to his concept of 'free play of signifiers' without a centre—far from presenting any meaning words carry with them "a certain absence or indeterminacy of meaning" (Deconstruction and criticism).

Derrida believes that inspite of *difference,* the writer makes between one word and another he can never express his meaning accurately and exactly. Therefore the critic must treat words as merely traces, "He must recreate the work of art according to his own comprehension. That is why his criticism will be an endless quest and no critic can claim that he has got the true meaning of the text. Literary criticism is an endless pursuit".-When the new critics posit the presence of meaning discovered through unrevelent of symbols, images and other poetic-structural feature deconstructionists talk of 'demystification of literature which implies that literature has no mystery, no incarnation of meaning which the critics may unravel.

4. Derrida's use of the word 'ecriture' which in English would mean 'writing' has a special meaning in the deconstructionist theory. In the traditional sense written word is graphic which symbolizes the spoken word. Thus written word is the signifier of the spoken word and therefore secondary to spoken word. Derrida rejects this

> theory based on western metaphysics and which see writing as secondary. Derrida underlines the *graphocentrist* view by shifting primary stress from speech to writing. He defines writing as "inscription in general whether it is lateral or not and even of what it distributes in space is alien to the order of the voice" thus writing would include music, sculpture and cinematography. Gayatri Spivak remarks that it is "something that carries within itself the trace of a perennial alterity, the structure of the psyche, the structure of the sign. To this structure Derrida gives the name writing". "Writing then is the name of the structure always already inhabited by the trace. This is a broader concept than the empirical concept of writing, which denotes, an empirical system of notation on the material substance". Derrida calls this concept 'arche-writing' and the traditional concept *vulgar concept of writing.*

Derrida has conducted deconstructive readings of numerous major thinkers, including Plato, Rousseau, Hegel, Freud, Husserl, Levi-Strauss, and Saussure. His style and approach might be illustrated by examining two of his important essays: his seminal work, "Structure, sign, and play," Which exhibits some of the persistent concerns of deconstruction and reveals both what he owes to structuralism and his divergence from it; and "Plato's Pharmacy," which engages with issues central to the very definition of philosophy by Plato, a definition which laid the foundation of the subsequent history of philosophy.

Derrida observes that for Levi-Strauss *bricolage* is not only an intellectual activity but also *mythopoetic:* it takes myths. What does this mean? Derrida explains that Levi-Strauss's discourse on myths "reflects on itself and criticizes itself." Based on *bricolage,* it attempts to abandon" all reference to a *center,* to a *subject,* to a privileged *reference,* to an origin, or to an absolute *archia*". His discourse is decentered. It attains this status not only in virtue of employing *bricolage* but also by refusing to treat any myth as the privileged ground or source of other myths; by insisting that there is no unity or source of a myth; that such unity is merely a projection of our interpretative endeavors; that myths cannot be studied in a linear fashion according to the Cartesian principle of breaking down a problem into its component parts; in other words, by exhibiting myth to be an 'acentric structure." But in order to express this decentered notion of myth, Levi-Strauss' own discourse on myth can itself have no absolute subject or center; it must in its own strategies reflect "the form and movement of myth"; short, the discourse about myth must *itself* be a myth. Derrida quotes Levi-Strauss statement in his book *The Raw and the Cooked,* to effect that this book is itself "a kind of myth"; and this is how ethnographic *bricolage* has a mythopotie function, a function which makes the convention philosophical requirement of a center appear as mythological, as a "historical illusion".

Deconstruction is both an heir and a response to continental philosophy, but as the range of Derrida's concerns makes clear, its relevance is not confined to the philosophical discipline. Because deconstruction happens everywhere, writers interested in deconstruction pursue their interest in conversation with many other concerns, including feminism and law, as well ass literature and philosophy. Deconstruction reshapes the questions writers ask about their enterprises and challenges the boundaries assumed to divide those enterprises.

The works of Paul de Man, J. Hillis Miller, and Barbara Johnson are among many examples of deconstruction's productive engagement with literature. In *Allegories of Reading* (1979), de Man describes his approach to reading as one "in which rhetoric is a disruptive intertwining of trope and persuasion or—of cognitive and performative language. Pursuing this "disruptive intertwining" through particular attention to rhetorical figures, de Man contends that "a literary text simultaneously asserts and denies the authority of its own rhetorical mode." Miller, in *The Ethics of Reading* (1987), contends their "deconstruction is nothing more or less than good reading" and argues that "there is a necessary ethical moment in that act of reading as such." Taking authors reading their own texts as exemplary acts of reading. Miller locates ethical importance in deviation from rather than allegiance to text. Johnson, in *A World of Difference* (1987), reads literary and critical works in order to address questions such as: "What are the political consequences of the fact that language is not a transparently expressive medium?" and "How can the study of suppressed, disseminated or marginalized messages within texts equip us to intervene against oppression and injustice in the world?" Particularly concerned with issues of sexual and racial difference, Johnson shows the relevance of literary reading to such questions and also takes up questions about deconstruction's relation to feminism.

Deconstruction can be said to have had greater impact on the thinkers in cultural-philosophical areas where new tools of interpretation and perceptions have come up setting free all those that have so far remained suppressed and marginalized. Deconstruction encouraged a more liberal thinking promoting one can say various forms of feminism, multicultural studies, diasporic voices, gay and lesbian literature and post-colonial identities.

18

Reader-Response and Reception Theory

Reader-response criticism is a school of literary theory that focuses on the reader (or "audience") and his or her experience of a literary work, in contrast to other schools and theories that focus attention primarily on the author or the content and form of the work.

Reader-response criticism arose as a critical theory in response to formalist interpretations of literature. Unlike the latter, which stressed the primacy of the text and an objective interpretation of it based on established criteria, advocates of reader-response criticism focused on the importance of the reader and their individual, subjective response to the text. One of the earliest proponents of this theory was Louise Rosenblatt, who stated in her *Literature as Exploration* (1938) that "a poem is what the reader lives through under the guidance of the text and experiences as relevant to the text." The significance of Rosenblatt and other reader-response critics placed on the reader was in direct opposition to the position taken by formalist critics in the past—for them, the text was the primary focus, and its impact on the reader or the idea that the reader's response was in any way relevant in the interpretation of the work was inconceivable.

In addition to Rosenblatt, other influential reader-response critics include Stanely Fish and Wolfgang Iser, both of whom argued against regarding literary works as objects. In his essay on reader-response criticism, Steven Mailloux explains that Fish, Iser, and other reader-response critics actually had very different approaches to the critical study of literary texts. However, all of them were unanimous in their rejection of the "affective fallacy" theory proposed by William K. Wimsatt and Monroe Co Beardsley in an influential essay in 1949. In this essay, Wimsatt and Beardsley stated their misgivings about what they termed as "obstacles to objective criticism" and the dangers of "intentional fallacy" (defined as confusion between the text and its origins) and "affective fallacy" (explained as the distinction that should be made between what a text is and what it does). According to Wimsatt and Beardsey, as well as many other formalist critics, the effect of the text on the reader should be irrelevant to the study of the text because this type of approach leads to the destruction of the text as an object of "specifically critical judgment." In contrast, reader-response critics advocated the primacy of a reader's response to the text, stressing that there was no such thing as an "objectively correct interpretation," says Mailloux.

During the late 1970s and 1980s, reader-response criticism, influenced in part by trends in other disciplines, especially psychology and psychoanalytical theories, expanded to include a study of the reader as subject, a combination of various social practices, defined and positioned, socially by his or her environment. This shift from the relationship between reader and text, and their mutual impact, to a focus on self-knowledge and observation has been summarized in anthologies, including Jane Tompkin's *Reader-Response Criticism: From Formalism to Post-structuralism* (1980). Recent works by critics including David Bleich, Norman Holland, and even Stanley Fish, have also expanded the focus of reader-response theory to include the validity and significance of interpretations guided by the environments or communities inhabited by the readers. This is a departure from the earlier-held position, which emphasized the primacy of the relationship between reader and text, regardless of environment. Fish, in particular, laid out his theories regarding interpretive strategies, which, he stated, are shared by "interpretive communities" in several essays during the 1980s and later. In his study of the history of reader-response criticism, Terence R. Wright explains that while the field has expanded its boundaries to include numerous approaches, the concern reader-response critics have with the act of reading remains constant. What has changed is the awareness these theorists now have of the ways in which environment, history, politics and even sexual orientation, can affect a reader's response to a text. This expansion of criteria has led many contemporary critics to refer to this type of critical theory as reader oriented-criticism rather than reader-response criticism.

Rather than denoting a specific method or critical practice, reader-response criticism is a general term that refers to a number of different approaches of modern criticism and literary theory that focus on the responses of readers-either individual readers or readers belonging to specific categories, such as class, gender, ethnicity, etc.—to literary works, rather than on the works themselves considered as self-contained entities. It is not a single agreed theory so much as a shared concern with a set of problems involving the extent and nature of reader's contribution to the meanings of literary works, approached from various positions including those of structuralism and psychoanalysis, phenomenology, and hermeneutics. The common factor is a shift from the description of text in terms of their inherent properties to a discussion of the production of meanings within the reading process.

In this regard, one might very roughly periodize the history of modern literary theory in three stages: a preoccupation with the author (Romanticism and the nineteenth century); and conclusively concern with the text (New Criticism); and a marked shift of attention to the reader over recent years. The reader has always been the most underprivileged of this trio—strangely, since without him or her there would be no literary texts at all. Literary texts do not exist on bookshelves: they are processes of signification materialized only in the practice of reading. For literature to happen, the reader is quite as vital as the writer of the text. Where Formalism sought to sequester the text, purging all extraneous elements that might interfere with a pure perception of the words on the page, in recent decades a growing number of theoretician now assert that there is no such thing as a pure, or neutral, encounter with a text. Every work is read—or "constructed"—differently.

Reader-response criticism's emphasis on the construction of a text originates in the branch of philosophy called phenomenology. Phenomenology deals with the "understanding of how things appear." The phenomenological idea of knowledge is that reality is to be found not in the external world itself, but rather in the mental *perception* of externals. That is, all that we human beings can know—actual knowledge—is our collective and personal understanding of the world and our conclusions about it.

As a consequence of the phenomenological concept, Reader-response theory holds that the reader is a necessary third party in the author-text-reader relationship that constitutes the literary work. The work, in other words, is not fully crated until readers make a *transaction* with it by assimilating and *actualizing* it in the light of their own knowledge and experience. The representative question of the theory are these: what does this work mean to me, in my present intellectual and moral makeup? What particular aspects of my life may help me understand and appreciate the work? How can the work improve my understanding and widen my insights? How can my increasing understanding help me understand the work more deeply? To what extent does a text circumscribes or directs a particular response? Which aspects of a text may be considered inherent and objective? And which are reader-constructed and thus subjective? Also important to reader-response critics is an identification and description of the fundamental elements that inform a reader's response to a text. The theory is that the free interchange or transaction that such questions bring about leads toward interest and growth so that readers may assimilate literary works and accept them as part of their lives.

Reader-response theory recognizes the engagement of the reader within several contexts. Primarily, there is the immediate context of "concretization"—the sentence-by-sentence creation of text.

By privileging the reader and focusing on the process of reading as, at least partially, a construction of the text, Reader-response criticism has significantly contributed to discussions of issues such as the indeterminacy of meaning. Important contribution to this debate include Wolfgang Iser's *The Art of Reading* (1978), which sees readers as "actualizing" texts by filling in their "gaps" (logical and sequential holes that we must fill in) or "indeterminacies" (uncertainties) of meaning, and also Stanley Fish's *Is There a Text in this Class*? (1980), which gives the reader an even more active role as the text's true producer. All of these approaches recognize that when we read a work, especially for the first time, we do not simply move our eyes back and forth and wait for images and concepts to announce themselves. We exert great energy, making surmises, arranging details into pictures, venturing and revising predictions. We stitch the clues together, closing up "gaps" and contending with "indeterminacies". We follow the text as if it were a shooting script for a film, typing to represent the action for ourselves on our mental screens.

The larger context of Reader-Response criticism recognizes that readings of any given work are likely to differ from reader to reader, sometimes to an extraordinary extent. The reception is necessarily affected by the reader's age, gender, cultural background, personal life-experience, beliefs, and historical vantage. A high school student reading a story about adulterous passion will have one set of reactions, a middle-aged man who has divorced over accusations of infidelity will have quite another.

To see these two contexts at work, consider the opening sentences of Joyce Carol Oates's "The Lady with the Pet Dog."

> Strangers parted as if to make room for him.
>
> There he stood. He was there in the aisle, a few yards away, watching her.
>
> She leaned forward at once in her seat, her hand jerked up to her face as if to word off a blow—but then the crowd in the aisle hid him, he was gone. She pressed both hands against her cheeks. He was not there, she had imagined him.

If we have not ready the story before, then we begin in complete ignorance (though a reader who knows Anton Chekhov's story of a similar title may find certain *expectations* aroused). We must turn ourselves into detectives, readers of clues. We must simultaneously comb the sentences carefully for information and allow our imaginations free play in conjuring up possibilities. What do we learn? That there is a he and a she, that they are in a public place (a cinema, a train, at a baseball game?); that she reacts with surprise (or alarm or shock) when she catches sight of him. The suppositions we make depend in part upon logical deductions, and in part upon our own disposition as readers. One reader straightway concludes that these are old lovers; another thinks that it might be an estranged father and daughter. Most readers will probably assume that these are young or middle-aged adults, but there is no reason they could not be old people.

And on and on we go, nothing clues, making guesses, modifying the scenario. Each new sentences curtails certain possibilities, and opens others. An even more specific picture takes shape. But specificity notwithstanding, there will never be two readers who can be said to have had an identical literary experience. The human response mechanisms are too subtle and various.

The issue that arise are obvious, If readings of the same work vary according to the reader, on what grounds are interpretations to be judged? Can there be a "right" of "best" reading of the work? Or is it finally a matter of what you say versus what I say. And whom can we say is truly the "author" of the text? Indeed, since the 1960s the concept of the "death of the author" has been a popular refrain in Reader-response criticism.

Reader-response criticism, in its various forms, has gained a considerable foothold in America and European literary criticism. Nevertheless, as may be expected, the literary community is hardly unanimous on the intent, practice, and utility of the methodology. On one end of the spectrum is the position taken by E.D. Hirsch in his book *Validity in Interpretation.* Hirch affirms that while we cannot know for certain what an author intended in the creation of a work, we are nonetheless constrained by our estimate of the probable intent. In other words, the reader who would argue that *Moby-Dick* is first and foremost a work of sexual symbolism would have to contend with the legacy of evidence (assembled by critics, biographers, and historians) that suggests that Melville's motives had more to do with religious allegory and with philosophical considerations of good and evil.

Critics such as Stanely Fish, in his book *Is There a Text in This Class.* Offers the challenge of complete relativism. There is, Fish believes, no central or authorized reading of a text; there are only readings. The idea of constraining interpretation through an appeal to authorial intention is a chimera. The only way that anything approaches consensus can be reached is through the application of common "interpretive strategies," such as are likely to be found in academic communities where readers agree to certain premises.

A somewhat distinct line of Reader-response theory which emphasizes historical investigation is represented by the Reception Theory of Hans Robert Jauss.

Amy Hempel's short story "In the Cementery where Al Jolson is Buried" requires the reader to pay very close attention in order to figure put the real situation that the two friends find themselves in. The story begins on a casual, offbeat note, with one friend saying to the other, "Tell me things I won't mind forgetting—Make it useless stuff or skip it". The friend obliges with all kinds of trivia, like "no one in America owned a tape recorder before Bing Crosby did." It is not until the third paragraph that we learn that the two friends and in the intensive care unit of a hospital. As the story proceeds, section by section, we begin to piece together an understanding, one which, as will be seen, grows more complex and revealing with every new bit of information. The ultimate shock of the story is our realization that the flip comments mask a very frightening actuality: one of the friend is dying.

Much reader-response theory had its philosophical origins in the doctrine known as phenomenology, whose foundations were laid by the German philosopher Edmund Husserl. The Greek word *Phainomenon* means "appearance." Hence, as a philosophical attitude, phenomenology shifts our emphasis of study away from the "external" world of objects towards examining the ways in which these objects *appear* to the human subject, and the subjective contribution to this process of appearing. This "bracketing" of the external world is referred to by Husserl as the "phenomenological reduction," and it underlies his attempt to achieve certainty in philosophy. Husserl argues that we cannot be sure of the nature of the outside world; but we can have certainty about the nature of our own perception and about the ways in which we construct the world, the ways in which the world appears to our subjective apparatus. This emphasis on subjectivity proved to be enormously influential; it provided the foundations of the Geneva School of phenomenological criticism (including figures such as Georges Poulet and Jean Starobinski), which read literature as embodying the consciousness of its author; it exerted a considerable impact on the reception theories of Wolfgang Iser and Hans Robert Jauss; and it provided a starting point against which Martin Heidegger's thought reacted.

One can sort reader-response theorists into three groups: those who focus upon the individual reader's experience ("individualists"); those who conduct psychological experiment son a defined set of readers ("experimenters"); and those who assume a fairly uniform response by all readers ("uniformists"). One can therefore draw a distinction between reader-response theorists who see the individual reader driving the whole experience and others who think of literary experience as largely text-driven and uniform (with individual variations that can be ignored). The former theorists, who think the reader controls, derive what is common in a literary experience from shared techniques for reading and interpreting which are, however, individually applied by different readers. The latter, who put the text in control, derive commonalities of response, obviously, from the literary work itself. The most fundamental difference among reader-response critics is probably, then, between those who regard individual differences among reader's responses as important and those who try to get around them.

Individualists

David Bleich had begun in the 1960s collecting statements by influencing students of their feelings and associations. He used these to theorize about the reading process and to refocus the classroom teaching of literature. He claimed that his classes "generated" knowledge, that is, knowledge of how particular persons recreate texts. David Bleich who was associated with Holland and others in the Centre for the Psychological Study of the Arts in New York, also produced a psychological model of reader-response, but one that developed away from the ego-based theory of his colleague toward a theory of intersubjectivity based on an epistemology of the reader's initial perception and subsequent interpretation of the text. There is also a recognition of the importance of language as the articulation, both mediating and objectifying, of the self, since language ensures a distancing which enables reflection but also requires the reader as subject for its animation and in consequence cannot claim abstract objectivity. In a quasi-phenomenological spirit, Bleich claims that human attention distinguishes three kinds of entity—people, objects and symbols—and literary works fall into the third category. While the text in its mere physicality is an object, its realization as meaningful work depends on the capacity and desire for symbolization on the reader's part—that is, the reader's initial response—which is followed by a secondary symbolization, or a motivated resymbolization in which an understanding and coherent articulation of the initial response are developed as a process of interpretation. It is the reader as epistemological subject or agent who retains primacy in this process, however, which Bleich terms unapologetically 'subjective criticism' and it appears that it is the mode of attention, or response, directed by the reader at the, object which constitutes the 'perceptual symbolization' of it. This is not, however, a purely individual and arbitrary process because the decision to perceive the object as symbol—as an aesthetic object—both derives from a common immediate experience of seeing the words on the page and leads at once to a confirmation which is collective, that is the agreement of a community which determines the articulation of the resymbolization or interpretation which extends the initial reaction or perception into aesthetic understanding and enjoyment.

Bleich's idea of language as a lynchpin of objectivity, while allowing individual readers to let their imaginations wander, however subjectively, erratically, or idiosyncratically, has found favour with a new generation of reader-response critics and seems to provide a sound basis for the way that we (readers) actually read the text. As a good example of how a completely unrestrained subjectivity can actually distort the actuality of the external world, consider Vladimir Nabokov's comic novel *Pale Fire* (1962) in which the protagonist, who regards himself as the exiled king of Zembla, interprets an innocuous poem in the style of Alexander Pope by one of his colleagues at an American university as a disguised allegory of his (the ex-king's) own life. This is a delightful parody of *misreading*—the gaps between background (reality) and foregoun ("subjective misreading") are so immense that the reader can only come to the conclusion that the narrator is not only unreliable but actually mad. In this case, the reader feel a strange mixture of confusion, alienation, and yet fascination as the traditional solidarity of narrated text with implied reader in anarchically fragmented.

Michael Steig and Walter Slatoff have, like Bleich shown that student's highly personal response can provide the basis for critical analysis in the classroom. Jeffrey Berman has encouraged student responding to texts to write anonymously and share with their classmates writings in response to literary works about sensitive subjects like drugs, suicidal thoughts, death in the family, parental abuse and the like. A kind of catharses bordering on therapy results. In general, American reader-response critics have focused on individual reader's responses. American journals like *Reader Reading Research Quaterly,* and others publish articles applying reader-response theory to the teaching of literature.

In 1965, C.S. Lewis published *An Experiment in Criticism,* in which he analyzed reader's role in selecting literature. He analyzed their selections in light of their goals in reading.

In 1967, Stanely Fish published *Surprised by Sin,* the first study of a large literary work Paradise Lost) that focused on its reader's experience. In an appendix, "Literature in the Reader," Fish used "the" reader to examine responses to complex sentences sequentially, word-by-word. Since 1976, however, he has turned to real differences among real readers. He explores the reading tactics endorsed by different critical schools, by the literary professoriate, and by the legal profession, introducing the idea of "interpretive communities" that share particular modes of reading.

Fish's essay "Interpreting the Variorum" takes its title and point of departure from the then recently published "Variorum" edition (containing variant textual versions) of the poem of John Milton. Fish suggests that the controversies over meaning in Milton's sonnets are not "*meant* to be solved but to be experienced" and that "any procedure that attempts to determine which of a number of readings is correct will necessarily fail. For example, nothing that certain commentators draw opposing conclusions from exactly the same evidence, Fish warns that any analyses generated by the assumption that meaning is embedded in the text "itself" will always point in as many directions as there are interpreters." He urges that we need a "new set of questions based on new assumptions." In each of the disputes analyzed by Fish, he points out that the responsibility for judgment and interpretation is transferred from the text to its readers: the meaning of the lines at stake coincides with the experience of the readers. Meaning is not somehow contained in the text but is created within the reader's experience.

A formalist analysis, which locates meaning within the forms and verbal structure of the text itself, will ignore the reader's experience of the text, which is temporal and contains modifications and shifts of viewpoint. The central assumption of formalist analysis to which Fish stands opposite is that "there *is* a sense, that it is embedded or encoded in the text, and that it can be taken in at a single glance. "Fish calls these assumptions 'positivist, holistic, and spatial.'' The goal of such analysis is" to settle on a meaning, "to step back from the text, and then to put together or calculate'' the discrete units of significance it contains.'' Fish's objection to such an approach is that it takes the text as a self- sufficient entity and ignores or devalues the reader's activities. What we should be describing, he believes, is ''the structure of the reader's experience rather than any structure available on the page.'' The reader's activities should be ''the center of attention, where they are regarded not as leading to meaning but as *having* meaning." These activities, which include the making and revising of many kinds of decisions, are already interpretative, hence a description of them will be an interpretation. Fish points out that his approach differs from the formalist methods primarily through its emphasis on the temporal dimension of the reading process and the creation of meanings.

In his book *Is There a Text in this Class* (containing Fish's widely anthologized essay of the same title), Fish argues that what constrains interpretation is not fixed meanings in a linguistic system but the practices and assumptions of an institution. It is not the linguistic system that gives determinacy to the meaning of an utterance but rather the context of the utterance. Fish offers an anecdote about a student who asked a professor, one of his colleagues, before taking his course: "Is there a text in this class?" The professor heard this utterance in one context, assuming the question to be an inquiry about the textbook that might be required for his class. The student's question, however referred to the concept of texuality as advanced in some modern literary theory. Fish uses this example to show that his colleague having initially heard the question in one context (which includes whatever is associated with "the first day of class"), was obliged to modify this context (to embrace the concerns of modern literary theory) in order to understand the utterance. This point is that "it is impossible even to think of a sentence independently of its context," and that our making sense of an utterance and our identifying of its context occur simultaneously: we do not, as M.H. Abrams and E.D Hirsch imply, first scrutinize an utterance and then give it meaning. We hear an utterance as already embedded within, not prior to determining, a knowledge of its purposes and interests.

Fish's overall account is a sensible and balanced counter to the formalists who claim that the text is an object in its own right and that it somehow possess stable meaning independently of any reader.

In 1968, Norman Holland drew on psychoanalytic psychology in *The Dynamics of Literary Response* to model the literary work. Each reader introjects a fantasy "in" the text, then modifies it by defense mechanism into an interpretation. In 1973, however, having recorded responses from real readers, Holland found variations too great to fit this model in which responses are mostly alike but show minor individual variations.

Holland then developed a second model based on his case studies *5 Readers Reading*. An individual has (in the brain) a core identity theme (behaviors then becoming understandable as a theme and variations as in music). This core gives that individual a certain style of being—and reading. Each reader uses the physical literary work plus invariable codes (such as the shapes of letters) plus variable canons (different "interpretive communities", for example) plus an individual style of reading to build a response both like and unlike other reader's responses. Holland worked with others at the State University of New York at Buffalo, Murray Schwartz, David Willbern, and Robert Rogers to develop a particular teaching format, the "Delphi seminar," designed to get students to "know themselves."

Holland, engaged in 'constructing a post-Freudian psychoaesthetics', gives substantial and predominant force to the conscious personality and unconscious psyche of the reader in the activity of reading, employing concepts taken from American ego psychology to construct a model of the reader as enjoying the psychic pleasures and benefits of engagement with the imaginative work. His starting point is the Freudian sanctioning of artistic creativity as the therapeutic license to fantasy which, although grounded in the infantile ego and its unconscious drives, succeeds in transforming these (expressed as either desire or fear) into socially respectable and presentable imaginative forms and thereby achives an adult mediation between fantasizing ego and obdurate reality. Acknowledgement of this creatively mediating activity is developed by Holland into a theory that articulates the secondary operation implicit in it, in his view—that is, the specific mediation between reader as ego and text as object—and involves seeing the process of reading as a dynamic and mutual transaction between the text as artistic form and meaning and the reader as adaptive and defensive ego—what he terms 'the dynamics of literary response'. He claims that we as readers 'work out through the text our own characteristic patterns of desire and adaptation. We interact with the work, making it part of our own psychic economy and making ourselves part of the literary work—as we interpret it'. This approach, usually termed transactive (sometimes transactional) criticism, has the merit of recognizing that reading is itself a psychological process and that the reader—any reader—has a subjective reality, but it is perhaps simplifyingly optimistic in its conviction that the dynamics transaction with the text necessarily produces pleasure from the sublimation of traumatic unconscious processes. And although it presents the interaction of reader and text as one that is mutually transformative and explicitly rejects a dualistic Cartesian epistemology, his model retains an implicit dualism with its positing of the imaginative text on the one hand in transaction with the autonomous ego on the other.

For Holland, the literary text is the means for its reader to recreate him or herself through a unifying interpretation, a centripetal movement that brings text and self together in a movement of self-identification on the reader's part. Holland's theory has been criticized for its tendency to subordinate the text to the personality of the reader, making reading a quasi—confessional or autobiographical procedure—the reader ultimately finds only his or her own subjectivity at the core of the text. It has also, predictably, come under attack from a deconstructionist perspective which questions the unitary nature of the identity presupposed in Holland's model. Holland has sought to answer some of this criticism, and to take account of his own experimental work with readers by proposing a 'transferential' model, which moderates the emphasis on the reader as personality in favour of a stress on the activity of reading as dialectical, a negotiation between text and reader, although this returns him to the problem of dualism. But overall his theory remains strongly oriented toward a subjectivizing view of the text-reader relationship.

Experimenters

Reuven Tsur in Israel have developed in great detail models for the expressivity of poetic rhythms, of metaphor, and of word-sound in poetry (including different actors' readings of a single tune of Shakespeare). Richard Gerrig in the U.S. has experimented with the reader's state of mind during and after a literary experience. He has shown how readers put aside ordinary knowledge and values while they read, treating, for example, criminals as heroes. He has also investigated how readers accept, while reading, improbable or fantastic things (Coleridge's "willing suspension of disbelief"), but discard them after they have finished.

In Canada, David Miall, usually working with Donald Kuiken, has produced a large body of work exploring emotional or "affective" responses to literature, drawing on such concepts from ordinary criticism as "defamilarization" or "foregrounding". They have used both experiments and new developments in neuropsychology, and have developed a questionnaire for measuring different aspects of a reader's response.

There are many other experimental psychologists around the world exploring reader's responses, conducting many detailed experiments. One can research their work through their professional organizations, the International Society for the Empirical Study of Literature and Media, and International Association of Empirical Aesthetics, and through such psychological indices as PSYCINFO.

Two notable researchers are Dolf Zillmann and Peter Vorderer, both working in the field of communications and media psychology. Both have theorized and tested ideas about what produces emotions such as suspense, curiosity, surprise in readers, the necessary factors involved, and the role the reader plays. Jenefer Robinson, a researcher in emotion, has recently blended her studies on emotion with its role in literature, music, and art.

Uniformists

Wolfgan Iser exemplifies the German tendency to theorize the reader and so point a uniform response. For him, a literary work is not an object in itself but an effect to be explained. But he asserts this response is controlled by the text. For the "real" reader, he substitutes an implied reader, who is the reader a given literary work requires. Within various polarities created by the text, this "implied" reader makes expectations, meanings, and the unstated details of characters and settings through a "wandering viewpoint". In his model, the text controls. The reader's activities are confined within limits set by the literary work.

Iser's theories of reader response were initially presented in a lecture of 1970 entitled "The Affective Structure of the Text," and then in two major works, *The Implied Reader* (1972) and *The Act of Reading* (1976). After examining a number of English novels in *The Implied Reader.* Iser outlines his approach in a section of this book entitled *"The Reading Process: A Phenomenological Approach"*. Iser begins by pointing out that, in considering a literary work, one must take into account not only the actual text but also "the actions involved in responding to that text". He suggests that we might think of the literary work as having two poles: the "artistic" pole as the text created by the author, and the "aesthetic" pole refers to "realization accomplish had by the reader". We cannot identify the literary work with either the text or the realization of the text of mus lie "halfway between the two," and in fact it comes into being only through the convergence of text and reader. His point here is that reading is an active and creative process. It is reading which brings the text to life, which unfold "its inherently dynamic character". If the author were somehow to present a story completely, the reader's imagination would have nothing to do; it is because the text has unwritten implications or "gaps" that the reader can be active and creative, working things out for himself. This does not mean that *any* reading will be appropriate. The text uses various strategies and devices to limit its own unwritten implications, but the latter are nonetheless worked out by the reader's own imagination.

To explain this process, Iser draws on Roman Ingarden's concept of "intentional sentence correlatives," according to which a series of sentences in a work of literature does not refer to any objective reality outside itself. Rather, the complex of these sentences give rise to a "particular world," the world presented in the literary work. Iser's point is that the *connections* between various sentences or complexes of sentences are not established by the work itself, but are determined by the reader. A sentence in any literary work, claims Iser, characteristically "aims at something beyond what it actually says." Iser reminds us of Hueserl's observation that a group of sentences creates an expectation in the reader; but what tends to happen, says Iser, is that in truly literary works these expectations are continually modified as we go on reading; indeed, a good literary work will usually frustrate our expectations. When we read expository texts (of science or philosophy, for example), we look for our expectations to be confirmed. But we regard this confirmation in literary works as a defect, since we are likely to be bored if a text merely rehearse what we already know and if our imagination is not called upon to work. The text produced by our response when reading is called by Iser its "virtual dimension," which represents the "coming together of text and imagination."

Iser draw attention to two important features of the reading process. The first is that reading is a temporal activity, and one that is not linear. The second important feature of the reading process is that, when we are confronted with "gaps or unwritten implications or frustrated expectations in the text, we attempt to search for consistency.

According to Iser the most elements in reader-response theory is described as *actualization, realization, or concretization:* they all refer to the process whereby the signifiers of the text are brought together in the reader's mental act of cognition to create the "world" of the text. The next crucial dimension lies in the distinction between *schematized aspects* and *virtuality;* the first refers to the perception of predetermined structural patterns, elements of plot, of character or location (though, of course, the author can cheat; in Agatha Christies detective novel *The Murder of Roger Ackroyd* -1962) what should be a major foregrounded clue is quietly tucked away in a few words so that it is not until the end of the narrative that the reader realizes that the narrator of the story is himself the murderer.'

Virtuality, on the other hand, refers to the indeterminate dimension that results from the convergence of the *donnees* of the text with the individual subjectivity of the reader. Again, if the text simply says, 'The door opened suddenly and a peculiar-looking stranger went up to Tom as he sat in his insalubrious room and said, "Your time has come" we cannot deny the door, the seated Tom, or the words of the stranger; but it is entirely up to the reader to virtualize the appearance of the stranger and the degree of insalubrity of the room.

Another important German reader-response critic was Hans-Robert Jauss, who defined literature as a dialectic process of production and reception (*Rezeption*—-the term common in Germany for "response"). For Jauss, readers have a certain mental set, a "horizon" of expectations (*Erwartungshorizont)*, from which perspective each reader, at any given time in history, reads. Reader-response criticism establishes these horizons of expectation by reading literary works of the period in question.

A crucial feature of Jauss's development of reader-response theory is his emphasis upon the diachronic—the dynamics of literary history. His aim has been to elaborate a historical approach to literature which will replace the assumption of tradition (particularly a national tradition) and the canonical frame established in the nineteenth century with an interrogation of them, drawing on evidence of the historical reception of literature and, more generally, on theorizing the critical and dialectical function of reading in relating and mediating earlier and current understandings of the literary work. This project is polemically adumbrated in Jauss's celebrated essay 'Literary History as a Challenge to Literary Theory', which was his inaugural lecture at Konstanz in 1967, and formed the first chapter of his book *Toward as Aesthetic of Reception*, published in America together with his other major work in English translation, *Aesthetic Experience and Literary Hermeneutics*, both in 1982. In this essay, Jauss challenges views of literary history as given, as a canonically established body of texts, in favour of a conception of that history as dynamic, a continual process of formation, in which the ceaseless interaction between the already received and established and the new and unprecedented in literature ensures on open, ultimately indeterminable though not indefinable dynamic of change and by the same token refuses any teleological idealism. The conception can be interestingly, compared to T.S. Eliot's famous pronouncement in 'Tradition and the Individual Talent' that each 'really new' work of art alters the whole structure of the cultural tradition. While Eliot's concern is with artistic *creation,* though, Jauss is engaged in theorizing the process of artistic and cultural *reception* –the ways in which the new artwork enters the domain of the already received. As he puts it, "literature and art only obtain a history that has the character of a process when the succession of works is mediated not only through the producing subject but also through the consuming subject-through the interaction of author and public."

For Jauss, pleasure—more broadly, aesthetic pleasure experience—is important as the primary category of art and its reception, but it is no less important to consider its succession and outcome in understanding, which is where reflection, Jauss's other key term, applies. The two aspects or stages, experience and reflection, are phenomenologically distinct but yet related and both ineluctably embedded in history—here Jauss's debt to Gadamer is explicit. The hermeneutic or interpretative activity of the reader is examined not so much in general and abstract terms, in the way that aesthetic experience was analysed, as through more specific, though still family broadly conceived, instances, which occupy the later part of Jauss's study. These include identification with the hero and responses to the comic hero, as well as more closely focused discussions of French lyric, especially Baudelaire. It may be fair to say, however, that Jauss's treatment of aesthetic experience is more substantial and coherent than his discussion of hermeneutics, which tends to take on a more subsidiary and even incidental role in his theory.

Both Iser and Jauss, and the *Constance School* they exemplify, return reader-response criticism to a study of the text by defining readers in terms of the text. In the same way, Gerald Prince posits a "narratee," Michael Riffaterre posits a "superreader," and Stanely Fish an "informed reader." And many text-oriented critics simply speak of 'the "reader who typifies all readers."

Objections

Reader-response critics hold that, to understand the literary experience or the meaning of a text, one must look to the process readers use to create that meaning and experience. Traditional, text-oriented critics often think of reader-response criticism as an anarchic subjectivism, allowing readers to interpret a text any way they want. They accuse reader-response critics of saying the text doesn't exist. (Reader-response critics respond that they are only saying that to explore someone's literary experience one must ask the someone, not pore over the text.) By contrast, text-oriented critics assume that one can understand a text while remaining immune to one's own culture, status, personality, and so on, and hence "objectively."

To reader-response critics, however, reading is always both subjective and objective, and their question is not "which" but "how". Some reader-response critics (uniformists) assume a bi-active model of reading: the literary work controls part of the response and the reader controls part. Others, who see that position as internally contradictory, claim that the reader controls the whole transaction (individualists). In such a reader-active model, readers and audiences use amateur or professional procedures for reading (shared by many others) as well as their personal issues and values.

Another objection to reader-response criticism is that it fails to account for the text being able to expand the reader's understanding. While readers can and do put their own ideas and experiences into a work, they are at the same time gaining new understanding through the text. This is something that is generally overlooked in reader-response criticism.

Extensions

Reader-response criticism relates to psychology, both experimental psychology for those attempting to find principles of response, and psychoanalytic psychology for those studying individual responses. Post-behaviorist psychologists of reading and of perception support the idea that it is the reader who makes meaning. Increasingly, cognitive psychology, psycholinguistics, neuroscience, and neuropsychoanalysis have given reader-response critics powerful and detailed models for the aesthetic process.

Because it rests on psychological principles, a reader-response approach readily generalizes to other arts: cinema (David Bordwell) or visual art (E.H. Gombrich), and even to history (Hayden White). In stressing the activity of the scholar, reader-response theory justifies such upsettings of traditional interpretations as, for example, deconstruction or cultural criticism.

Since reader-response critics focus on the strategies readers are taught to use, they address the teaching of reading and literature. Also, because reader-response criticism stresses the activity of the reader, reader-response critics readily share the concerns of feminist critics and critics writing on behalf of gays, ethnic minorities, or post-colonial peoples.

19

New Historicism

New Historicism is a critical movement which flourished in the late 1970s and during the 1980s. New Historicists operate by fusing two key issues in criticism since the 1960s: the "linguistic turn" of post structuralist and deconstructive criticism, and a return to historical readings. These two impulses are aptly summarized in Louis Montrose's often repeated catchphrase: "the historicity of texts and the textualily of history." Texts, he insists (as do all New Historicist critics) are embedded in particular histories. Those histories, in turn, are embedded in language, since we only access those histories through the texts which represent them. Since all these texts use language which is seen as elusive and unfixed, "textual" history effectively calls for the kinds of close reading strategies which, as Stephen Greenbalt remarks in a recent essay, literary critics have as part of their "disciplinary tool kit." In their choice of text events to analyze, and in their manner of analyzing those events. New Historicists develop many of their ideas by fusing the ethnography of the anthropologist Cifford Geertz with the philosophic history of Michel Foucault. New Historicist essays began appearing in the late 1970s, but the ground breaking text was the 1980 publication of Stephen Greenbalt's *Renaissance Self-Fashioning: From More to Shakespeare.* This book was followed in 1983 by the founding of the journal *Representations,* initiated by Greenbalt and several of his colleagues at the University of California at Berkeley, where the journal is still published. In its volumes, and in Greenblatt's many subsequent publications, can most clearly be seen the strategies of New Historicism as well as their limitations.

Historicism began toward the end of the eighteenth century with German writers such as Herder, and continued through the nineteenth-century historians Von Ranke and Meinecke to twentieth-century thinkers such as Wilhelm Ditthey, R.G. Collingwood, Hans Georg Gadamer, Ernst Cassirer, and Karl Mannhem. Powerful historical modes of analysis were formulated by Hegel and Marx, who themselves had a profound impact on historicist thinking; and literary historians such as Sainte-Beuve and Hippolyte Taine also insisted on viewing literary texts as integrally informed by their historical milieux. Much of what passes under the rubric of the "New" Historicism is not radically new, but represents a return to certain foci of analysis as developed by previous traditions of historicism.

Historicism has been characterized by a number of concerns and features. Most fundamentally, there is an insistence that all systems of thought, all phenomena, all institutions, all works of art, and all literary text must be situated within a historical perspective. In other words, texts or phenomena cannot be somehow torn from history and analyzed in isolation, outside of the historical process. They are determined in both their form and content by their specific historical circumstances, their specific situation in time and place. Hence, we cannot bring to our analysis of Shakespeare the same assumptions and methods that we bring to Plato; the fact that they belong to different historical periods and different social, political, and economic circumstances will profoundly shape their notions of truth, of art and polity, and hence whatever meanings we might attribute to their text. In other-words, literature must be read within the broader context of its culture, in the context of other discourses ranging over politics, religion, and aesthetics, as well as its economic context.

A second feature of historicism is that the history of a given phenomenon is sometimes held to operate according to certain identifiable laws, yielding a certain predictability and explanatory power, this future is pronounced in the writings of Hegel and Marx. A third concern arises from the recognition that societies and cultures separated in time have differing values and beliefs: how can the historian "know" the past? The historian operates within the horizon of her own world view, a certain broad set of assumptions and beliefs, how can she overcome these to achieve an empathetic understanding of a distant culture? How, for example, can students fed on the epistemological fat of a New Critical diet begin to appreciate the world of the Homeric epics, the language of which we are not even sure how to pronounce, and the actions of whose characters are, by our moral standards, often bizarre? How can we avoid imposing our own cultural prejudices, not to mention on own interests and motives, on texts historically removed from us?

Thinkers such as Ditthey, Gadamer, and E.D. Hirch have offered various answers to this dilemma. Hirch's position aspires to be "objectivists," effectively denying the historical and context-bound nature of knowledge and proposing a distinction between "meaning," which embraces what the author meant or intended by his particular use of language, and "significance," which comprehends the subjective evaluation of the text according to the values and beliefs of the critic. Gadamer proposed a notion of "horizonfusion" whereby we both acknowledge that what we call the "text" is in fact a produce of a tradition of interpretation (with no "original" meaning) and that our own perspective is informed by the very past we are seeking to analyze. Recognizing both of these limitations, we can begin to effect an empathetic fusion of our own perspective is informed by the very past we are seeking to analyze. Recognizing both of these limitations, we can begin to effect an empathetic fusion of our own cultural horizon with that of the text.

Hence, the dilemma of historical interpretation can easily lead to a kind of aesthetic formalism on the one hand, which denies history any constitutive role in the formation of texts, and, on the other hand, to a historical view of texts as culturally and socially determined, a view that reduces emphasis on authorial intention and agency. The fundamental principles of historicism, then, are opposed to those of many twentieth-century movements such as Russian Formalism and New Criticism. In general, structuralism also has been a historical, focusing on synchronic analyses of language and literature. Yet structuralism differs from rigid formalism in that it does not isolate the literary text but situates it within the broader codes, sign systems, and registers of other discourses. In this sense, its endeavors are compatible with those of historicism. Also, certain adaptations of structuralism, as for example in the work of Mikhail Bakhtin, have a strongly historical dimension in which language itself is seen as an ideological phenomenon. Elements of historicism also inform hermeneutics and reader-response theory, which is obliged to take into account the different meaning that a text might have for readers of various historical periods. Indeed, the influence of Schleiermacher, usually viewed as the founder of hermeneutics, has extended not only to historists such as Ditthey and Gadamer but also to reception theorists such as Hans Robert Jauss.

The "New" Historicism which arose in the 1980s reacted against both the formalist view of the literary text as somehow autonomous and Marxist views which ultimately related texts to the economic infrastructure. It saw the literary text not as somehow unique but as a kind of discourse situated within a complex of cultural discourses—religious, political, economic, aesthetic—which both shaped it and, in their turn, were shaped by it. If there was anything new about this procedure, it was its insistence, drawn from Foucault and post structuralism, that "history" "itself is a text, an interpretation, and that there is no single history. It also rejected any notion of historical progress or teleology, and broke away from any literary historiography based on the study of genres and figures. In the same way, the "culture" in which New Historicism situated literary texts was itself regarded as a textual construct. Hence, New Historicism refused to accord any kind of unity or homogeneity to history or culture, viewing both as harboring networks of contradictory, competing, and unreconciled forces and interests.

A number of methodological features can be found to characterize 'New' Historicism-

(1) a shift from ideas to power relationships as the fundamental units for analysis and interpretation in cultural history, leading to a focus on such issues as patronage, patriarchal authority and its legitimation, the role of culture in the formation of the modern nation-state, the creation of a special role for literary production and authorship within modern culture, the delineation of separate domains of public and private space, etc.,

(2) a tendency to refuse hierarchies and dichotomies among texts of different kinds (canonical/non-canonical; high culture/mass culture; documents/fictions;

(3) the assumption that in a given historical moment, different modes of discourse (such as law, theology, moral philosophy, literature, art, architecture, cartography, chorography, choreography, costume, stage design, science of various types, etc) are rarely if ever autonomous, that by studying the permeable boundaries of the discourses constitutive of a given cultural field, the scholar can arrive at an understanding of the broader ideological codes that order all discourses in that particular culture;

(4) the symptomatic reading of this wider cultural field by means of an attention to rhetorical devices and strategies, and a consequent revival of interest in the history of rhetoric, though from a critical rather than a merely descriptive perspective;

(5) related to all above, the governing assumption that discourse and representation form consciousness rather than merely reflecting or expressing it, that culture is therefore an active force in history.

It could be argued that many of these features were already evident in the earlier *Geistesgeschichte* tradition of intellectual history (i.e. the history of ideas or of world views as expressed in such cultural institutions as religion, law, political systems, poetry, art etc.). But there is at least one major respect in which the latest type of historicism is distinguishable from the old. In most of the work identified as new historicist one senses an absence of a kind of conviction that governed earlier types of historicist criticism. In his book *Toward a New Historicism* (1972), which predated the most current use of the term, Wesley Morris identified four major types of traditional historicism:

1. the metaphysical, deriving from Hegel's transcendental philosophy, where a literary work was understood as the poetic expression of a moment in the unfolding narrative of history as the self-realization of the absolute;
2. the naturalistic or positivistic, where the literary text was treated as a medium through which a given historical epoch could be viewed by a scholar who imagined himself in the role of scientific observer;
3. the nationalistic, a relativist variant of the metaphysical, in which the literary work was viewed as expressing the native spirit of a given culture or race;

4. the aesthetic, which diverges from the other types in seeing the literary work not as the reflection or expression of an existing cultural domain but as way of *making* cultural meanings and values.

Regardless of their respective differences, all of, these types of historicism—and the version of a 'new historicism' that Morris himself sought to articulate-entailed the conviction that poetry either reflected or expressed the *human* subject, however various may have been conceptions of the nature of that subject. A poetic act was understood to express, to illustrate or to dramatize a stage in the history of consciousness or of human *paraxis,* whether of an individual or collective kind. In all its traditional forms, historicism adhered to one or another master narrative that governed the historical critic's interpretation of specific narrative or poetic acts. It is the apparent absence of such a narrative, or a certain embarrassment as its lingering presence, that characterizes much of the criticism currently, identified under the rubric 'new historicism'.

The principle that cultural practices often entail conflict and contradiction points to another factor distinguishing the current mode of historical criticism from its antecedents. Most earlier types of historicism emphasized the unifying function of culture. Even where pluratities were allowed to exist within a given cultural context, the historical critic would ultimately resolve the plural into the singular Geist of an age, a nation, a civilization or a race; or in more empirical, positivistic historical method into the more narrowly defined but still unitary political or social event, action, interest group, etc, or in the specific domain of literature, into such a notion as period-style. This tendency to contain plurality within a higher unity to reinscribe difference within the representation of the same, has been especially the case in the work of American cultural historians and is no doubt an instance of the longstanding strategy within American ideology of 'staging [pluralist] interpretation as a means of co-opting dissent'. By contrast, new historicists are often most interested in how different kinds of discourse intersect, contradict, destabilize, cancel or modify each other.

The leading proponent of "New Historicism," Stephen Greenblatt became a key figure in the shift from literary to cultural poetics and from textual to contextual interpretation in U.S. English departments in the 1980s and 1990s. Inspired by Michel

Foucault's historical investigations of medical and penal institutions and his theoretical understanding of power, the New Historicists see the literary work as a vessel tossed in a social sea of competing interests, antagonistic values, and contradictions. For Greenblatt literary works are "fields of force, places of dissusion and shifting interests, occasions for the jostling of orthodox and subversive impulses."

Greenblatt, is his introduction to The Power of Forms in the *English Renaissance* (1982) spurred the growth of the New Historicism. In this introduction, Greenblatt differentiated what he called the "New Historicism" from both the New Criticism, which views the text as a self-contained structure, and the earlier historicism which was monological and attempted to discovery a unitary political vision. Both of these earlier modes of analysis, according to Greenblatt, engaged in project of uniting disparate and contradictory elements into an organic whole, whethher in the text itself or in its historical background. The earlier historicism, moreover, viewed the resulting totality or unity as a historical fact rather than the product of interpretation or of the ideological learnings of certain groups. Such a homogenizing, procedure allows the unified vision of historical context to serve as a fixed point of reference which could form the background of literary interpretation.

Greenblatt elaborated his statements about New Historicism in a subsequent influential essay, "Towards a Poetics of Culture " (1987). He begins by noting that he will not attempt to "define" the New Historicism but rather to "situate it as a practice what distinguishes it from the positivist historical scholarship" of the early twentieth century is its openness to recent theory; Greenblatt remarks that his own critical practice has been informed by Foucault, as well as anthropological and social theory. He proposes to situate this practice in relation to Marxism, on the one hand, and post-structuralism, on the other. Citing passages from the Marxist Fredric Jameson and the poststructuralist Jean-Francous Lyotard, Greenblatt questions the generalizations made about "capitalism" in each passage. Both writers are addressing the question of the connection between art and society:

> Jameson, seeking to expose the fallaciousness of a separate artistic sphere and to celrate the materialist integration of all cliscourses, finds capitalism at the root of the false

differentiation; Lyotard, seeking to celebrate the differentiation of all discources and to expose the fallaciousness of monological unity, finds capitalism at the root of the false integration. History functions in both cases as a convenient anecdotal ornament upon a theoretical structure, and capitalism appears not as a complex social and economic development in the West but as a malign philosophical principle.

Greenblatt, further charges that both Jameson and Lyotard are trying to provide a "single, theoretically satisfactory" answer to the question of the relation between art and society. Neither of these theorists can "come to terms with the apparently contradictory historical effects of capitalism." Jameson treats capitalism as the agent of "repressive differentiation," and Lyotard treats it as the agent of "monological totalization".

In contrast to these reductive theories, Greenbalt espouses a critical practice that would recognize capitalism's production of a powerful and effective oscillation between the establishment of distinct discussive domains and collapse of those domains into one another. It is this restless oscillation... that constitutes the distinct power of capitalism", Greenblatt wishes move beyond literary criticisms familiar terminology for treating the relationship between art and society: allusion, symbolism, allegory, representation and mimesis. We need to develop, he urges looms to describe the ways in which material" is transferred from one discursive sphere to another and becomes aesthetic property," a process which is not unidirectional because the "social discourses is already charged with aesthetic energies". The New Historicism is marked by a "methodological self-consciousness," rater than the old historicist" faith in the transparency of sings and interpretative procedures." The New Historicism will view the work of art itself as "the product of a set of manipulations... the product of a negotiation between a creator or class of creators, equipped with a complex, communally shared repertoire of conventions, and the institutions and practices of society." The general movement here is away from a mimetic theory of art to an interpretative model that will "more adequately account for the unsettling circulation of materials and discourses that is ...the heart of modern aesthetic practice."

Greenblatts' works, along with that of Louis Adrain Montrose, Stephen Mullaney. Jonathan Dollimore, Catherine Belsey, and numerous other literary critics, has ensured that English Renaissance studies and New Historicism have become inextricably linked. But new historicists work has also been highly influential in studies of other historical periods, especially ninteenth-century American and British literature. Jerome McGann, for example, though not influenced so directly by Foucault as are members of the *Representations* group, has brought a New Historicist concern with social context to the criticism of British Romantic poetry. By the late 1990s literary critics seldom explicitly identified themselves as New Historicists, but the emphasis on context over text still prevailed in literary studies.

New Historists reject previous models of Elizabethan England, spurning in particular images of social wholeness and cosmic harmony. Here E.M.W. Tillyord's useful primer of Eligabethan beliefs. *The Elizabethan world Picture* (1963), became an object of derision. Tillayards decription of Renaissance beliefs in the need for harmony and order in the world were taken as an insistence that the Elizabethan world was always harmonious and cosmically ordered. For New Historicists, rather, the Renaissance was dark, fragmented, painful. It responded well to reading by anecdote because larger frameworks would not in fact make sense. England of the 1590s, then, came to seem like the first post-modern epoch in Western culture. This investment in the Renaissance was not accidental. Deconstructive and post-structuralist approaches had been successfully applied to texts from later periods, proving especially fruitful in rereading Romantic texts by William Wordsworth, P.B. Shelly and John Keats. Yet, into the 1980s, the canon of the Renaissance texts had seemed immune to new readings imprisioned in the patterns of an older historicism. Readings were historical, but they tended to absorb Renaissance ideas or events into canonical texts, and not the other way round. The canon was still sealed off, a separate, precious category, from the era which produced it. New Historists looked for a more dynamic relationship between texts and their societies. If a society could be shown to form a texts, then you could also show that texts in turn reshapped the society from which they come. For New Historicists Understood Marshall McLuhan's sound bite—the medium is the message—as a fundamental truism. If they wished to write about the forms of power, they sought also to show the power of literary forms to reshape the world. This has proved easier to assert than to prove, a beguiling possibility rather than a demonstrable fact, for lyric poems which can be shown by themselves to have changed the world turned out to be hard to find.

Michel Foucault is arguably the most influential European writer and Thinker of the recond half of the twentieth century. His unclassifiable work (is it history? philosophical? Cultural theory?) is controversial and has attracted much criticism, but the question he raised, the topics he addressed, and the positions he took have become central features of today's intellectual landscape. In literary studies, Foucault stands as a major source for post-structuralism, New Historicism, cultural studies, and queer theory, while also fueling the growing interest in literature and medicine, the examination of the institutional bases from which writers and critics operate and the interest in processess of identity formation.

Foucault begin his rather complex and sometimes paradoxical theoretical structure by redefining the concept of history. Unlike many past historians, Foucault declares that history is not linear, for it does not have a definite beginning, middle, end, nor it is necessarily teleological, purposefully going forward toward some known end. Nor can it be explained as series of causes and effects that are controlled by some mysterious destiny or all-powerful deity. For Foucault, history is a complex interrelationship of variety of discourses (the various ways—artistic, social, political and so forth—in which people think and talk about their world). How these various discourses interact in any given historical period is not random but is dependent upon a unifying principle or pattern Foucault calls the episteme: through language and thought, each period in history develops its own perceptions concerning the nature of reality (or what it defines as truth) and sets up its own standards of acceptable and unacceptable behavior, in addition to its criteria for judging what it deems good or bad, and what group of people articulate, protect, and defend the yardstick whereby all established truths, values and actions will be deemed acceptable.

To unearth the episteme of any given historical period, Foucault borrows techniques from archeology. Just as an archeologist must slowly and meticulously dig through various layers of earth to uncover the symbolic treasures of the fast, historians must expose each of the layers of discourse that come together to shape a peoples episteme. And just as an archeologist must date each finding and then piece together the artifacts that define and help explain that culture, so must the historian piece together the various discourses and their interconnections among themselves and with no discursive practices Cany cultural institution such as a form of government. For example that will assist in articulating the episteme under investigation.

Seen from this point of view history is a form of power. Since each historical era develops its own episteme, it is, in actuality, the episteme that controls how that era and its people will view reality. History, then, becomes the study and unearthing of a vast, complex web of interconnecting forces that ultimately determines what takes place in each culture or society. Why or how epistemes change from one historical period to another is basically unclear. That they change seemingly without warning is certain. Such a change accured, for example, at the beginning of the nineteenth century (the change from the Age of Reason to romanticism) and initiated a new episteme. In this new historical era variety of different relationships developed among discourse that had not evolved or did exist and were deemed unacceptable in the previous historical period. Foucault asserts that such adical and abrupt changes that cause breaks from one episteme to another are neither good nor bad, neither valid nor invalid. Like the discourses that help produce them, different epistemes exist in their own right, they are neither moral nor immoral, but amoral.

According to Foucault, historians must realize that they are influenced and prejudiced by the episteme(s) in which they live. Since their thoughts, customs habits, and other actions are colored by their own epistemes, historian, Foucault argues, must realize that they can never be totally objective about their own or any other historical period. To be a historian then, means one must be able to confront and articulate one's own set of biases before examining the various discourses (the material evidence of past events) that comprise the episteme of any given period. Such an archeological uncovering of the various discourses, Foucault believe will not unearth a monological view of an episteme that presupposes a single, overerching political vision or design, but will uncover a set of inconsistent, irregular and often contradictory discourses that will help to explain the development of that episteme, including what elements were accepted, changed, or rejected to form the "truth" and set the acceptable standards for that era.

Since New Historicists view an aesthetic works as a social production, a texts meaning resides for them in the cultural system composed of the interlocking discourses of its author, the New Historicist investigates three areas of concern:

> (1) the life of the author; (2) the social rules and dictates found within a text; and (3) the reflection of work's historical situation as evidenced in the text. Since an actual person authors a text. His, or her actions and believes reflect both individual concerns and those of the society, and are therefore essential elements of the text itself. In addition, the standards of behavior as reflected kin a society's rules of decorum must also be investigated, since these behavioral codes simultaneously helped shape and were shaped by the text. And the text must also be viewed as an artistic work that reflects upon those behavioral social codes. To begin to understand a texts significance and to realize the complex social structure of which it is part, New Historicists declare that all three areas of concern must be investigated. If one area is ignored, the risk of returning to the old historicism, with its lack of understanding concerning a text as a social production is great. And during this process of textual analysis critics must not forject to question their own assumptions and methods, for they too are products of and shaping influences upon their culture.

For the New Historicist the goal of interpretative analysis is really the formation and an understanding of a "poetics of culture" a process that sees life and its sunclry activities as being more like art than we think, more a metaphorical interpretation of reality than an analytic one. Through the practice of New Historical analysis, New Historicists believe that we will discover not only the social world of the text but also the present-day social forces working upon us as we negotiate meaning with printed material.

20

Cultural Studies

Cultural studies is an academic discipline which combines political economy, communication, sociology, social theory, literary theory, media theory, film video studies, cultural authropology, philosophy, museum studies and art history criticism to study cultural phenomena in various societies. Cultural studies researches often concentrate on how an a particular phenomenon relates to matter of ideology, nationality, ethnicity, social class, and/ or gender.

In a loosely related but separate usage, the phrase cultural studies sometimes serves as a rough synonym for area studies, as a general term referring to the academic study of particular cultures in departments and programs such as Islamic studies, Asian studies, African American studies, et al. However, strictly speaking, cultural studies programs are not concerned with specifie areas of the world so much as specific culture practices.

The term 'culture' has become virtually ubiquitous in our society. In certain circumstances and on certain occasions it still retains some of its earliest and exclusive connotations and yet we also talk frequently enough of popular culture, or black or gay cultures—even of business or management cultures - terms which might once have been considered antithetical. All such phenonena might-indeed have–come within the purview of contemporary cultural studies. Yet, in Britain, the emergence of cultural studies as a project or discipline was very much bound up with the work of figures such as Richard Hoggard and Raymond Williams, and therefore with a fairly specific history and debate which requires us to understand the significance of the term 'culture' as it circulated during the nineteenth and early twentieth centuries. Indeed, a great deal of Williams work in particular is explicitly concerned with the genealogy and connotations of the term 'culture', culminating in a particular theoretical hosition, cultural materialism which engaged out of this lengthy engagement.

The term was coined by Richard Hoggart in 1964 when he founded the Birmingham Centre for Contemporary Cultural Studies or (CCS). It has since became strongly associated with Stuart Hall, who succeeded Hoggart as Director.

From the 1970s onward, Stuart Hall's pioneering work, along with his colleagues Paul Willis, Dick Hebdige, Tony Jefferson, and Angela Mc-Robbie, created an international intellectual movement. Many cultural studies scholars employed Marxist methods of analysis, exploring the relationships between cultural forms (the superstructure) and that of the Political economy (the base). By the 1970s, however, the politically formidable British working classes were in decline. Britains manufacturing industries were fading and union rolls were shrinking. Yet, millions of working class Britons backed the rise of Margaret Thatcher. For Stuart Hall and other Marxist theorists, this shift in loyalty from the Labour Party to the Conservative Party was antithetical to the interests of the working class and had to be explained in terms of cultural politics.

At times, cultural studies' romance with agency nearly excluded the possibility of oppression, overlooks the fact that the subattern have there own politics, and romanticizes agency, overblowing its potentiality and pervasiveness. In work of this kind, popular in the 1990s, many cultural studies scholars discovered in consumers works of creatively using and subverting commodities and dominant ideologies. This orientation has come under fire for a variety of reasons.

Cultural studies concerns itself with the meaning and practices of everyday life. Cultural practices comprise the ways people do particular things (such as watching television, or eating out) in a given culture. In any given practice, people use various objects (such as iPods or handguns). Hence, this field studies the meanings and uses people attributed to various objects and practices. Recently, as capitalism has spread throughout the world (a process called globalization), cultural studies has begun to critique local and global forms of resistance to Western hegemony.

In his book *Introducing Cultural studies;* Ziauddin Sardar lists the following five main characteristics of cultural studies:

- Cultural studies aims to examine its subject matter in terms of cultural practices and their relation to power. For example, a study of a subculture (such as white working class youth in London) would consider the social practices of the youth as they relate to the dominant classes.
- It has the objective of understanding culture in all its complex forms and of analyzing the social and political context in which culture manifests itself.
- It is both the object of study and the location of political criticism and action. For example, not only would a cultural studies scholar study an object, but she/he would connect this study to a larger, progressive political project.
- It attempts to expose and reconcile the division of knowledge, to overcome the split between tacit cultural knowledge and objective (universal) forms of knowledge.
- It has commitment to an ethical evaluation of modern society and to a radical line of political action.

Since cultural studies is an interdisciplinary field, its practitioners draw a diverse array of theories and practices.

Scholars in the United Kingdom and the United States developed somewhat different version of cultural studies after the field's inception in the late 1970s. The British version of cultural studies was developed in the 1950s and 1960s mainly under the influence first of Richard Hoggart, E.P. Thompson, and Raymond Williams, and later Staurt Hall and others at the Centre for Contemporary cultural studies at the University of Birmingham. This included overtly political, left-wing views, and criticisms of popular culture as 'capitalist' mass culture; it absorbed some of the ideas of the Frankfurt School critique of the "culture industry" (*i.e.* mass culture). This emerges in the writings of early British cultural studies scholars and their influences-in the work of Raymond Williams, Stuart Hall, Paul Willis and Paul Gilroy.

Richard Hoggarts' principal contributions to the development of cultural studies are twofold: his publication of an innovative analysis of the changing patterns of working class life, *The Uses* of Literacy and his role in the development of the school for contemporary cultural studies

The significance of *The Uses of Literary* is that it was probably the first book written from a 'cultured'-in the Leavisite sense-perspective which sought to analyse in a serious way not merely the publications which were then being consumed in working-class circles, but also the ways in which these related to the dominant values of working-class life. Hoggart's intimacy with the context he describes results from his own working-class background in ceeds, though, as was the case with Raymond Williams, he was educated to the grammar school and university in ways which produced a sense of separation, even alienation, from that background. This is something which is self-consciously dealt with in the books description of the scholarship boy 'who' has left his class, at least in spirit, by being in certain ways unusual; and he is still unusual in another class, too tense and over-wound'. The consequence of this is that in his analyses Hoggart tends to combine an insider's knowingness with an outsider's judgements, and in this respect, it would be easy to accuse him of developing a merely snobbish relationship to working-class life, most notably in his disdain for the vulgarity of modern developments (notoriously, for instance, in his characterization of 'juke-box boys') who frequent milk-bars [which] indicate at once, in the nastiness of their modernistic knick-knacks, their glaring showiness, an aesthetic breakdown so complete that, in comparison with them, the layout of the living-rooms in some of the poor homes from which the costumers come seek of a tradition as balanced and civilized as an eighteenth-century town house'. However, there is a critical emphasis in his work which, though it often incorporates disdain, is arguably not redicule to this.

Leavis's attack on modernity was directed at machinery and mass standardization and focused in particular on the development of a mass media. Hoggart was influenced by Leavis's critique and is also concerned with the phenomenon and with the effects of mass consumerism in disrupting, transmuting or corrupting working-class attitudes. Invariably, change is for the worse. The 'popular publicists' he denounces disseminate an unquestioning belief in progress which is more or less synonymous with the spread of materialism (in its pejorative sense). The four general tendencies that Hoggart discerns since these are perhaps more important than any specific manifestation of them as described in the book:

1. Principles of tolerance and freedom rooted in the pragmatic working class sentiment of 'live and let live' have acquired a different inflection, enabled by-or perhaps the consequence of-the sensationalism of contemporary publications: the unwillingness to admit that freedom should have its limits. For Hoggart, 'the tolerant phrases have been joined by others in similar dress; the new depreciate the old, and together they become the ritual uniform of a shared unwillingness to admit that freedom can have its punishments. Anything goes and there is no scale.'
2. Similarly, Hoggart discerns a shift in the established principle of working-class solidarity-which enjoins suspicion of outsiders ('them and us')—since this has been debased and transformed into a form of intolerance. The popular press, in identifying themselves with, the people, promote sense that the people's ideas are not only as good as anyone else's, but are even superior because they are more representative. Hoggart illustrates this with a still recognizable pseudo democratic phenomenon: 'The popular press conduct polls on this matter and questionaries on that matter among their readers, and so elevate the counting of heads into a substitute for judgement.'
3. Materialism goes together with, and is encourages by, an unquestioning belief in progress, which is partly found up with the kudos of science. The consequence of this is a historical amnesia and glorification of youth, Hoggart's image of this process invokes explicitly Arnoldian language the wagon, loaded with its barbarians in wonderful, moves irresistibly forward: Not forward to anywhere, but simple forward for forwardness's sake'.
4. Finally, all of these processes together have produced an indifferentism (another Arnoldian term) and relativism by contributing to an endless flux of the undistinguished and the valueless to a world in which every kind of activity is finally made meaningless by being reduced to a counting of heads'. Moreover this process is paradoxically

accompanied by an abdication of responsibility and a pervasive surrendering to authority on the part of the working class.

Though Hoggarts' account of these developments involves some perspective commentary on the transformations being wrought by mass consumerism, it is manifestly the case that his work is tinged with nostalgia and conservatism. His role in the with nostalgia and conservatism. This role in the institutionalization of cultural studies, however, was of more radical and lasting significance.

Williams's relationship to the English tradition of thinking about culture is both more sustained and, ultimately, more critical than that of Hoggart. As a statement of his early position, we might consider his 1958 essay 'Culture is Ordinary'. Here he acknowledges two intellectual debts in particular, Marxism and Leavis, which perhaps inevitably produce tensions and contradictions in the essay which remain characteristic of his work up to his elaboration of cultural materialism in the 1970s. But even in this essay, we find a discernibly leftist version of the organicism which is integral to the Arnoldian ideal of a common culture, and also a recognition of the disdain which has characterized other versions of that ideal of culture. Williams, for instance, refuses simply to indulge in any blanket condemnation of modernity, citing the real improvements to working-class life which have been made by mechanization and industrialization. More to the point here, he is also contemptuous of the minoritizing, elitist view of culture, of culture as 'the outward and emphatically visible sign of special kind of people, cultivated people'. But if Williams wants to rescue culture from the minority, he also wants to defend it against those who, because of its elitist aura, would make it 'a dirty word'. Implicitly, he is referring to Marxist at this point, those who have argued that the cultural ideal was ultimately 'bourgeois'. Williams rejects this claiming not only that there is 'a distinct working class way of life which I for one value', but also that the 'arts and learning... are in a real sense a national inheritance, which is, or should be, available to everyone. In this sense, while Williams is clarity writing with the grain of postwar democratization—and indeed, much of his work in texts such as *The Long Revolution* has been directed not merely at analyzing culture, but in anguing for an expansion of democracy, even to those areas of our lives dominated by the undemocratic writ of the market—there is still an acceptance of culture's organic credentials as rooted in essentially human values. Only much later, and after a approachement with Marxist thinking, did Williams fully recongnize that culture can be marked by relations of conflict.

In the interim between the first publication of *The Long Revolution* in 1961 and that of *Marxism and Literature* in 1977, Willam's work proceeded by way of series of often radically innovative encounters with an extremely diverse set of substantive issues, ranging across the whole field of literary and cultural studies: the mass media, the novel, the drama, and the pastoral. In the work of theatre and on television a new awareness of the social conventionality of form and of the interrelationship between technology, and form is increasingly brought to bear. Willams coupling of the problem of cultural form to that of cultural technology clearly drew attention in each case to the materiality of what were in orthodoxly Marxist terms 'ideal' superstructures. This led him, in turn, to a simultaneous rejection of both technological determinism and the notion of a determined technology, and hence to a much more complex understanding of the notion of determination itself. The chronological overlap between William's work in theatre studies and that on the mass media is thus by no means merely 'coincidental'. Disparate though the work might appear, it proceeds along clearly connected lines of inquiry. And these connections are empirical and substantive as well as theoretical and methodological.

Williams was impressed both by Gramsci's work on intellectuals, which seemed to him an 'encouraging' and 'experimental' model for work in the sociology of culture, and by the wider implications of the theory of hegemony. The significance of the latter had registered initially in an essay written in 1973, entitled 'Base and superstructure in Marxist cultural Theory.' But in *Marxism and Literature* the argument is elaborated upon at much greater length. Here, as before, Williams argued against the base superstructure model for cultural analysis, on the grounds that culture is both real and material: 'From castles and palaces and churches to prisons and workhouses and schools; from weapons of war to a controlled prees... These are never superstructural activities. They are necessarily material production within which an apparently self-subsistent mode of production can alone be carried on'. Here, though, this more general materialism is decisively article lated to the theory of hegemony. The first and last chapters respectively of the book's first past are devoted to two key concepts and two keywords, deriving respectively from Leavisism and Marxism, 'culture' and 'Ideology'.

Stuart Hall is the central figure in the history and the continuing evolution of cultural studies and Marxist intellectual thought in Bristain. Hall pioneered Marxist anlyses of culture, firstly in his role as editor of the *Universities and Left Review* between 1957 and 1961, and later when he played a central role in the evolution of cultural studies. Initially, Hall's conceptions of culture owed much to the work of F. R. Leavis, even though he disagreed with leavis's politics.

In the *Universities and Left Review*, Hall promoted the study of 'lifestyles' with a view to integrating insights into culture with a broad-based socialist political analysis, and thus shared in common with the emerging generation of working-class writers an interest in the ways in which literature and politics intersected. Hall preserved with this interest when he co-authored a book with Paddy Whannel, The Popular Arts, which took as its subject the cultural politics of mass culture. The book distinguished between 'popular' and 'mass' culture in useful ways, but it also entailed a Leavisite focus on the 'quality' of popular culture. Hall and Whannel replicated the Leavisite bias Howards, 'complexity', and richness, arguing that jazz was preferable to rock 'n' roll because it was as creative as classical music. Just as film was preferable to television. The criteria by which Hall and Whannel judged popular music-such as shythmic variety, musical diversity personal expression and imagination-borrowed heavily from Leavis, and ultimately failed to analyse the possible relationships between popular culture and social struggle partly because it did not extend its analyses sufficiently far to take into account the ways in which popular music was appropriated and used by its audiences. Hall's first book-length study of popular culture thus replicated the terms of Leavisite analysis, and contained little of the political engagement which a Marxist cultural studies seemed to promise.

In contrast to United Kingdom, the American version of cultural studies initially concerned itself more with understanding the subjective and appropriate side of audience reactions to, and uses of, mass culture; American cultural-studies advocates wrote about the liberatory aspects of fandom. The distinction between American and British strands, however, has faded.

In Canada, cultural studies has sometimes focused on issues of technology and society, continuing the emphasis in the work of Marshall McLuhan and others. In Australia, there has sometimes been a special emphasis on cultural policy. In South Africa, human rights and Third World issues are among the topics treated. There were a number of exchanges between Birmingham and Italy, resulting in work on Italian leftism, and theories of postmodernism. On the other hand, there is a debate in Latin America about the relevance of cultural studies, with some researchers calling for more action oriented research. Cultural studies is relatively undeveloped in France, where there is a stronger tradition of semiotics, as in the writing of Roland Barthes. Also in Germany it is undeveloped, probably due to the continued influence of the Frankfurt school, which has developed a body of writing on such topics as mass culture, modern art and music.

Some researchers, especially in early Birtish cultural studeis, apply a Marxist model to the field. This strain of thinking has some influence from the Frankfurt school, but especially from the structuralist Marxism of Louis Atthusser and others. The main focus of an orthodox Marxist approach concentrates on the *production* of meaning. This model assumes a mass production of culture and identifies power as residing with those producing cultural artifacts. In a Marxist view, those who control the means of production (the economic base) essentially control a culture.

Other approaches to cultural studies, such as feminist cultural studies and later American developments of the field, distance themselves from the view. They criticize the Marxist assumption of a single, dominant meaning shared by all, for any cultural product. The non-Marxist approaches suggest that different ways of consuming cultural artifacts affect the meaning of the product. This view is best exemplified by the book *Doing Cultural Studies: The Case of the Sony Walkman* (by Paul du Gay et al), which seeks to challenge the notion that those who produce commodities control the meanings that people attribute to them. Feminist cultural analyst, theorist and art historian Griselda Pollock contributed to cultural studies from view-points of art history and psychanalysis. The writer Julia Kristeva and the artist Bracha L. Ettinger, are influential voices in the turn of the century, contributing to cultural studies from the field of art and psychoanalytical French feminism.

Ultimately, this perspective criticizes the traditional view assuming a passive consumer, particularly by underlining the different ways people *read*, receive and interpret cultural texts. On this view, a consumer can appropriate, actively reject, or challenge the meaning of a product. These different approaches have shifted the focus away from the *production* of items. Instead, they argue that *consumption* plays an equally important role, since the way consumers consume a product gives meaning to an item. Some closely link the act of consuming with cultural identity. Stuart Hall and Johan Fiske have become influential in these developments.

In the context of cultural studies, the idea of a text not only includes written language, but also films, photographs, fashion or hairstyles: the texts of cultural studies comprise all the meaningful artifacts of culture. Similarly, the discipline widens the concept of "culture". "Culture" for a cultural studies researcher not only includes traditional high culture (the culture of ruling social groups) and popular culture, but also everyday meanings and practices. The last two, in fact, have become the main focus of cultural studies. A further and recent approach is comparative cultural studies, based on the discipline of comparative literature and cultural studies.

Cultural studies is not a unified theory but a diverse field of study encompassing many different approaches, methods and academic perspectives, as in any academic discipline, cultural studies academics frequently debate among themselves. However, some academics from other fields have criticized the discipline as a whole. It has been popular to dismiss cultural studies as an academic fad. Yale literature professor Harold Bloom has been an outspoken critic of the cultural studies model of literary studies. Critics such as Bloom see cultural studies as it applies to literary scholarship as a vehicle of careerism by academics, instead promoting essentialist theories of culture, mobilising arguments that scholars should promote the public interest by studying what makes beautiful literary works beautiful.

Literary critic Terry Eagleton is not wholly opposed to cultural studies theory like Bloom, but has criticized certain aspects, of it highlighting what he sees as its strengthes and weakness in books such as *After Theory* (2003). For Eagleton, literary and cultural theory have the potential to say important things about the "fundamental questions" in life, but theorists have rarely realized this potential.

A more serious criticism comes from the sociology of Pierre Bourdieu, who has also written on topics such as photography, art museums, and modern literature. Bourdieu's point is that cultural studies lacks scientific method. His own work makes innovative use of statistics and in-depth interviews. Cultural studies is relatively unstructured as an academic field. It is difficult to hold researchers accountable for their claims because there is no agreement on method and validity.

Conversely, cultural studies scholars have criticized more traditional academic disciplines such as literary criticism, science, economics, sociology, anthropology, and art history.

Though a young discipline, cultural studies has established firm footing in many universities around the globe, with steadily rising enrollments, expanding numbers of departments and a robust publishing field, cultural studies steps into the 21st century as young yet successful discipline.

21

Postcolonial Criticism

Postcolonialism is a set of theories in philosophy, film, political sciences and literature that deal with the cultural legacy of colonial rule. Since the complex phenomenon of "Postcolonialism" is rooted in the history of imperialism, it is worth briefly looking at this history. The word imperialism derives from the Latin *imperium,* which has numerous meanings including *power, authority, command, dominion, realm* and *empire.* Though imperialism is usually understood as a strategy whereby a state aims to extend its control forcibly beyond its own borders over other state and peoples, it should be remembered that such control is usually not just military but economic and cultural. A ruling state will often impose not only its own terms of trade, but also its own political ideals, its own cultural values, and often its own language, upon a subject state.

The term imperialism as we know it dates back to the last half of the nineteenth century. But the concept and practice is as old as civilization itself. Both the western world and the Eastern world have seen a series of vast empires which have extended over vast territories, often in the name of bringing the blessings of their civilization to the subject peoples who were regarded as barbarians. These include the Chinese empire extending from the eleventh century B.C. to the tenth century after Christ; the Sumerian, Babylonian, Egyptian, Assyrian, and Persian empires; the empires of the Greeks, which reached a climax with the conquests of Alexander the Great; the Roman Empire, the Byzantine Empire, and the various empires of Islam which lasted until the early twentieth century.

In modern times, there have been at least three major phases of imperialism. Between 1492 and the mid-eighteenth century, Spain and Portugal, England, France, and the Netherlands established colonies and empires in the America, the East Indies, and India. Then, between the mid-nineteenth century and World War I, there was an immense scramble for imperialistic power between Britain, France, Germany, Italy, and other nations. By the end of the nineteenth century, more than one fifth of the land area of the world and a quarter of its population has been brought under the British Empire: India, Canada, Australia, New Zealand, South Africa, Burma, and the Sudan. The next largest colonial power was France, whose possessions included Algeria, French West Africa, Equatorial Africa, and Indo-china. Germany, Italy, and Japan also entered the race for colonies. In 1885 Belgium established the Belgian Congo in the heart of Africa, a colonization whose horrors were expressed in Conard *Heart of Darkness* (1899). Finally, the periods during and after World War II saw a struggle involving the countries just mentioned as well as conflict between America and the Communist Soviet Union for extended control, powers, and influence. Needless to say, these imperialistic endeavors have survived into the present day in altered forms and with new antagonists.

What concerns us is not only the history of imperialism itself but also the various narratives of imperialism. The motives behind imperialism have usually been economic. After the end of World War II in 1945 there occurred a large-scale process of decolonization of the territories subjugated by most of the imperial powers, with the significant exception of the Soviet Union and the United States, beginning with the Independence of India in 1947.

Postcolonial literature and criticism aroused both during and after the struggles of many nations in Africa, Asia, Latin America (now referred to as the "tricontinent" rather than the "third world") and elsewhere for independence from colonial rule. As a literary theory it also deals with literature written in colonial countries and by their citizens that has colonized people (s) as its subject matter. Colonized people, especially of the British Empire, attended British universities, their access to education, still unavailable in the colonies, created a new criticism-mostly literary, and especially in novels. Postcolonial theory became part of the critic's resource in the 1970; most take Edward Said's book *Orientalism* as its foundational work.

Postcolonialism deals with cultural identity in colonized societies: the dilemmas of developing a national identity after colonial rule; the ways in which writers articulate and celebrate that identity (often reclaiming it from and maintaining strong connections with the colonizer); the ways in which the knowledge of the colonized (subordinated) people has been generated and used to serve the coloniser's interests; and the ways in which the colonizer's literature has justified colonialism via images of the colonized as a perpetually inferior people, society and culture. The creation of binary opposition structures the way we view others. In the case of colonialism, the Oriental and the Westerner were distinguished as different from each other (i.e. the emotional, decadent Orient, *Vs* principled, progressive Occident). This opposition justified the "white man's burden" the colonizer's self-perceived "destiny to rule" subordinate peoples.

In *Post-colonial Drama: theory, practice, politics,* Helen Gilbert and Joanne Tompkings write: "the term postcolonialism-according to a too-rigid etymology—is frequently misunderstood as a temporal concept, meaning the time offer colonialism has ceased, or the time following the politically determined Independence Day on which a country breaks away from its governance by another state, not a naïve technological sequence which supersedes colonialism, postcolonialism is, rather, an engagement with and contestation of colonialism's discources, power structures, and social hierarchies—A theory of postcolonialism must, then, respond to more than the merely chronological construction of post-independence, and to more than just the discursive experience of imperialism.

Colonized peoples reply to the colonial legacy by *writing back to the center,* when the indigenous peoples write their own histories and legacies using the coloniser's language (e.g. English, French, Dutch) for their own purposes. "Indigenous decolonization" is the intellectual impact of postcolonialist theory upon communities of indigenous peoples, thereby, their generating postcolonial literature.

A single, definitive defination of postcolonial theory is controversial; writers have strongly criticised it as a concept embedded in identity politics. Ann Laura Stoler, in *Carnal*

Knowledge and Imperial Power, argues that the simplistic oppositional binary concept of *Coloniser and colonized* is more complicated than it seems, since these categories are fluid and shifting; postcolonial works emphasise the re-analysation of categories assumed to be natural and immutable.

Postcolonial Theory—as metaphysics, ethics, and politics—addresses matters of identity, gender, race, racism and ethnicity, with the challenges of developing a post-colonial national identity, of how a colonized people's knowledge was used against them in service of the coloniser's interests, and of how knowledge about the world is generated under specific relations between the powerful and powerless, circulated repetitively and finally legitimated in service to certain imperal interests. At the same time, postcolonial theory encourages thought about the colonised's creative resistance to the colonizer and how that resistance complicates and gives texture to European imperial colonial projects, which utilized a range of strategies, including anti-conquest narratives, to legitimize their dominance.

Postcolonial writers object to the colonised's depiction as hollow "mimics" of Europeans or as passive recipients of power. Consequent to Foucauldian argument, postcolonial scholars, i.e. the Subaltern Studies collective, argue that anti-colonial resistance accompanies every deployment of power.

Many of the debates among postcolonial scholars center on which national literatures or authors can be justifiably included in the post-colonial canon. It should be acknowledged that postcolonial theory functions as a subdivision within the even more misleading name field of "cultural studies": the whole body of generally leftist radical literary theory and criticism which included Marxist Gramscian, Foucauldian, and various feminist schools of thought among others. What all of these schools of thought have in common is a determination to analyze unjust power relationships as manifested in cultural products like literature (and film, art, etc). practitioners generally consider themselves politically engaged and committed to some variety or other of liberation process.

Postcolonial theory as already stated is applied to political science, to history and to other related fields. Taken literally, the term "postcolonial literature" would seem to label literature written by people living in countries formerly colonized by other nations-

First, literal colonization is not the exclusive object of postcolonial study. Lenin's classic analysis of imperialism led to Antonio Gramsci's concept of "hegemony" which distinguishes between literal political dominance and dominance through ideas and culture 1960s thinkers developed the concept of neo-imperialism to label relationships like that between the U.S. and many Latin American countries, which while nominally independent, had economics dominated by American business interests, often backed up by American military forces. The term "banana republic" was originally a sarcastic label for such subjugated countries, ruled more by the influence of the United Fruit Corporation than by their own indigenous government.

Second, among the works commonly studied under this label are novels like Claude Mckay's *Banjo* and Chinua Achebe's *Things Fall apart* which were written while the nations in questions (Jamaica and Nigeria) were still colonies. Some scholars attempt to solve this problem by arguing that the term should denote works written after colonization, not only those created after independence; but that would be "post-colonization" literature. Few people understand the term in this sense outside a small circle of scholars working in the field.

Third, some critics argue that the term misleadingly implies colonialism is over when in fact most of the nations involved are still culturally and economically subordinated to the such industrial states through various forms of neocolonialism even though they are technically independent.

Fourth, it can be argued that this way of defining a whole era is Eurocentric, that it singles out the colonial experience as the most important fact about the countries involved. Surely that experience has had many powerful influence; but this is not necessarily the framework within which writers from-say-India, who have a long history of precolonial literature, wish to be viewed. For instance, R.K. Narayan—one of the most popular and widely read of modern Indian writers—displays a remarkable indifference to the historical experience of colonialism, a fact which results in his being almost entirely ignored by postcolonial scholars. V.S. Niapaul is so fierce a critic of the postcolonial world despite his origins as a descendant of Indian indentured laborers in Trinidad that he is more often cited as an opponent than as an ally in the postcolonial struggle. In fact, it is not uncommon for citizens of "postcolonial" countries to accuse Americans and Europeans of practicing a form of neocolonialism themselves in viewing their history through this particular lens. Postcolonial criticism could be compared to the tendency of Hollywood films set in such countries to fous on the problems of Americans and Europeans within those societies while marginalizing the views of their native peoples.

Fifth, many "Postcolonial" authors do not share the general orientation of postcolonial scholars forward engaging in an ongoing critique of colonialism. Nigerian writers Chinua Achebe and Wole Soyinka, for instance, after writing powerful indictments of the British in their country, turned to exposing the deeds of native-born dictators and corrupt officials within their independent homeland. Although postcolonial scholars would explain this corruption as a by-product of colonialism, such authors commonly have little interest in pursuing this train of thought.

Although there has been sporadic agitation in some African quarters for reparations for the slavery era, most writers of fiction, drama, and poetry see little point in continually rehashing the past to solve today's problems. It is striking how little modern fiction from formerly colonized nations highlights the colonial past. Non-fiction writers often point out that Hindu-Muslim conflicts in South Asia are in part the heritage of attempts by the British administration in India to play the two groups of against each other; yet Indian fiction about these conflicts rarely points to such colonial causes. A good example is Kushwant Singh's *Train to Pakistan* (1956) which deals directly with the partition of India from an almost exclusively Indian perspective.

Indeed, "postcolonial" writers often move to England or North America (because they have been exiled, or because they find a more receptive audience there, or simply in search of a more comfortable mode of living) and even sometimes—like Soyinka—call upon the governments of these "neocolonialist" nations to come to the aid of freedom movements seeking to overthrow native tyrants.

Sixth, "Postcolonialism" as a term lends itself to very broad use. Australian and Canadians sometimes claim to live in postcolonial societies, but many would refuse them the label because their literature is dominated by European immigrants, and is therefore a literature of privilege rather than of protest. According to the usual postcolonial paradigm only literature written by native peoples in Canada and Australia would truly qualify.

Similarly, the label is usually denied to U.S. literature, though America's identity was formed in contradistinction to that of England, because the U.S. is usually viewed as the very epitome of a modern neo-colonial nation, imposing its values, economic pressures, and political interests on a wide range of weaker countries. The Irish are often put forward as an instance of a postcolonial European people, and indeed many African writers have been inspired by Irish ones for that reason. Yet some of the more nationalist ones (take Yeats) tended toward distressingly conservative—even reactionary—politics, and James Joyce had the utmost contempt for Irish nationalism. It is not clear how many Irish authors would have accepted the term if they had known of it.

Although postcolonial theory generally confines itself to the past half-century, it can be argued that everyone has been colonized at some time or other. Five thousand years ago Sumer started the process by uniting formerly independent city-states and Narmer similarly subjugated formerly independent Upper and Lower Egypt. Rushdie likes to point out that England itself is a postcolonial nation, having been conquered by Romans and Normans, among others.

Not only is the term "postcolonial" exceedingly fuzzy, it can also be argued that it is also often ineffective. A good deal of postcolonial debate has to do with rival claims to victimhood, with each side claiming the sympathies of right-thinking people because of their past sufferings. The conflicts between Bosnians and Serbs, Palestinians and Jews, Turks and Greeks, Hindu and Muslim Indians, and Catholic and Protestant Irish illustrate the problems with using historical suffering as justification for a political program. It is quite true that Europeans and Americans often arrogantly dismiss their own roles in creating the political messes of postcolonial nations around the world; but it is unclear how accusations against them promote the welfare of those nations. In addition, when they are made to feel guilty, countries—like individuals—are as likely to behave badly as they are to behave generously. It may make American and European scholars feel better to disassociate themselves from the crimes of their ancestors (which are admittedly, enormously bloody and oppressive, and should be acknowledged and studied), but people struggling for freedom in oppressed nations are more likely to draw inspiration from the quintessentially European Enlightenment concept of rights under natural law than they are to turn to postcolonial theory. Similarly, European capitalist market theory is far more attractive to most people struggling against poverty in these nations than are the varieties of socialism propounded by postcolonial theoreticions.

"Postcolonial" is also a troublesome term because it draws some very arbitrary lines. South African writers Athol Fugard and Nadine Gordimer are often excluded from postcolonial courses, although their works were powerful protests against apartheid and they have lived and worked for more in Africa than, say Buchi Emicheta, who emigrated to England as a very young woman and has done all of her writing there-because they are white. A host of fine Indian writers is neglected simply because they do not write in English on the sensible grounds that India has a millennia-long tradition of writing which should not be arbitrarily linked to the British imperial episode.

Of those how write in English, Anita Desai is included, though she is half German. Ngugi Wa Thiong'o is included even though he now writes primarily in Gikuyu. Bharati Mukherjee specifically rejects the label "Indian-American" though she is an immigrant from India, and Rushide prefers to be thought of as a sort of multinational hybrid (thought he has, on occasion, used the label "postcolonial" in his own writing). Hanif Kureshi is more English than Pakistani in his outlook, and many Caribbean-born writers living in England are now classed as "Black British."

Postcolonial theoretician Homi Bhabha developed the term "hybridity" to capture the sense that many writers have of belonging to *both* cultures. More and more writers, like Rushdie, reject the older paradigm of "exile" which was meaningful to earlier generations of emigrants in favour of accepting their blend of cultures as a positive synthesis. This celebration of cultural considerably, blurs the boundaries of laid down by postcolonial theory.

In practice, postcolonial literary studies are often sharply divided along linguistic lines in a way which simply reinforces Eurocentric attitudes. Latin American postcolonial studies are seldom explored by those laboring in English departments. Francophone African literature is generally neglected by Anglophone African scholars. Because of these failures to cut across linguistic boundaries, the roles of England and France are exaggerated over those of the colonized regions.

In the context of New Zealand culture, as with Australian, the issues of post-colonialism and textuatily are complicated and perhaps 'livened', by the strong oral traditions of the 'colonised', coupled with increasingly multi-cultural populations. Institutions of power are institution of inscription. Not only are there obvious language barriers between colonizer and colonized but also barriers of, the medium of expression. Aboriginal 'dreaming' and Maori oral mythology are unfortunately as traditionally inaccessible to the settler-invader as the inscripted institutions of science and law are to the colonised. Of course, colonialism and post-colonialism are directly concerned with this very process of interchange, assimilation, appropriation and re-appropriation, and the political and theoretical 'repositions' and 're-positioning' within this process. However, there is a danger of hypocrisy in post-colonial studies given that those who theorize and are involved in claiming voice for the post-colonial subject are themselves often settler subjects. As Tiffin and Lawson put it:

> The very diversity of colonial experience with its Eurocentered hierarchies has fathered a shadowy counter-hierarchy in which he or she who can most plausibly claim the kiss of the whip is accorded pre-eminent speaking position. Like the settler subject, a majority of post-colonial critics find themselves uncomfortably inside the residue of power structures they profess to oppose, and ambivalent beneficiaries

of those structures—Imperialism is a cultural effect of comprehensive power in the transmission and consumption of ideology that is not adequately registered by colours on a map.

The term 'post-colonial studies,' however, is becoming less meaningful within academic institutions in the way that commonwealth and 'new literature's of the 1970s and 1980s have already become. A Timothy Brennan has pointed out, if Britain is seen now as post-colonial too, the notions of 'Centre' and 'Periphery' on which post-colonial studies is (mistakenly) founded are now redundant. If any notions which at some point have come under the sway of British imperialism are seen as post-colonials then this term no longer does much useful distinguishing work. Such cultures are most likely to be understood in terms of a combination of both post-colonialism and post-imperialism, although what distinguishes these two terms is complex and indeterminant.

Mishra and Hodge make the basic claim for post-colonial studies that its ambiguous politics was implied in the field it brought into being: "commonwealth literature' did not include the literature of the center, which acted as the impossible absent standard by which it should be judged. The term also occluded the crucial differences between the 'old' and the 'new' Commonwealth, between White settler colonies and Blacknations that typically had a very different and more difficult route into a different kind of independence". Post-colonial studies attempted to consider and define relations between the settler or colonial-invader races and groups and the first-nation races and groups which articulated the newly emergent voice of nationhood after colonialism.

A novel which claims voice in opposition to the imperial process and which articulates a counter discursive stance to the presence of the settler invader would, on the surface, seem to offer itself to the term 'post-colonial'. An example of such writing is Ben Okris' *The Famished Road* (1991) which narrates a lyrical and local mythological response to the gradual westernization of a remote. African village, ostensibly from the position of the pre-modern colonized. However, written in the language of the imperial colonizer and by an author living in contemporary cosmopolitan London, there is an implicit collusion in the conception and writing of the novel with the culture of Imperialism. In contrast, a novel of post-imperialism may make no overt reference to the relationship between settler-invader and colonized peoples but nevertheless, read contrapuntally (with recognition to what is significantly excluded, emitted, or absent from the text), implicates the imperial culture in a relationship with complex array of international identities in the post-imperial era. One such example among contemporary novels is A.S Byatt's *Possession* (1990) a post-modern historical detective novel in which plot and characters while seminally English are nevertheless played out against a backdrop of an artistic form coterminous with Victorian imperialism (Pre-Raphaelite Poetry) and in which the narrative unfolding in the present highlights the concern for cultural identity with an American neo-imperialism. Post-colonial studies characteristically can be seen as enacting a neat reversal of colonialism, the battle for cultural dominance charqcterised by the imperial impulse continues to be played out within such discourse, albeit in changed form and in disparate ways.

From Defoe's *Robinson Crusoe* (1715) onwards the allegories of colonial expansion often brought the colonial mind up against an image only of itself. As Hugh Ridley has observed in *Images of Imperial Rule* (1983) : "Crusoe's Island, like the fictional representation of European colonies which succeeded it, is people, with figure which already lay within the traveller's mind; the journey across the world, the shipwrecks and the strange adventures lead although the protagonist by no means realizes this back to European and the European self."

Imperialism was never about the culture of the colonized and not implicitly about contact between cultures. While in economic terms imperialism was about profit, first and foremost it was about the imperialist psyche, the representation of the white European into him or herself, be this reflected in the Rousseauean idea of the 'noble savage', or in the Christian missionery project of bringing enlightenment to the 'indigenous heathen'. However, from the perspective of the colonized who may have no culturally embedded pre-existing notions of contact with others (the colonizer or imperialist) prior to colonization, it could be argued that such a process is only recently being reciprocated in literatures written from the perspective of the colonized. Again, Ben Okri's *The Famished Road* can be interpreted in this light.

As Spivak has observed, the attribution of a unified speaking voice and an authentic native 'essence' to the colonized, far from destablishing imperialistic cultural practices, actually serves to reconstitute the subject of the West. As she puts it : 'The theory of pluralized 'subject-effects' gives an illusion of undermining subjective sovereignty while providing a cover for this subject of knowledge. The much publicized critique of the sovereign subject thus actually inaugurates a subject.'

Positioning discourse from colonized peoples into discrete and knowable categories such as non-European or 'Third-World' acts so as to traduce the narratives of colonized peoples which are in turn interpolated by Western narratives of identity. Similarly, James Cifford in *The Predicament of Culture* (1988) discusses the contemporary condition of societies in which it is increasingly difficult to attach identity, meaning, or 'authenticity' to coherent culture or language or to a (presumably essentially modernist) discourse which attempts to do so.

Clifford argues that the pattern of cross-cultural influences of today no longer involves the gradual absorption of non-modern cultures to modern; rather, the non-modern has an almost equally powerful effect on the modern. Clifford does not envisage the world as populated by endangered authenticities but rather as a globalism that harbours improvisatory and combinational cultural responses in which the third world plays itself against the First, and vice versa. If, as Clifford suggests, authenticity is relational, then identities can no longer be stable, and self-other relationships are a matter of power, rhetoric, and discourse, rather than cultural 'essence'. For Clifford, 'traditional' cultures are without regret (or the nostalgia-mode of post-modernism). They are newly syncretised as part of an inevitable, ongoing process. This process is not that of modernization which is monocultural but of global interconnectedness in the legacy of imperialism. As he puts it in 'The Global Issue: A symposium': at least three processes are always going on. One is the disappearance of certain orders of difference. The second is a process of *translating orders* of difference. And the third is the creation of new orders of difference. This last, one can divide into two locally interconnected dimensions: first, imposed or neocolonial forms, stemming from an economic relationship to the state or the wider world system; and second, emergent orders which are invented out of historical debris moulded from indigenous and foreign material.

Clifford thus sees the 'new global order' a challenging tradition and traditional ways of viewing culture and subjects and mining new and often vibrant syncretized and hybrid amalgamations. As Maxwell puts it, what this means is that "the colonized have more to gain from histories that challenge the concept of identity than from histories that sustain the illusion of a unified subject." The fundamental distinction to be made throughout this debate is the understanding of post-colonialism as a means largely for the descendents of the settler groups in the colonial-imperial process to claim authenticity and autonomy and purge the guilt of empire as a process which altered pre-modern civilization. This is attempted by firstly, separating themselves from the 'original' culture; and secondly, by increasing understanding their empire as a muted and ambiguous legacy among nations, ethnic groups and selves engaged in the culture of imperialism. Given this reading post-colonial literature can be seen as a transitory phase of the wider cultural condition of the legacy of imperialism.

Aschcroft, Griffith, and Tiffin suggest that we should restrict the term post-colonial to signify *after colonialism.* "All post-colonial societies are still subject in one way or another to overt or subtle forms of neo-colonial domination, and independence has not solved the problem". After colonialism, new elites, often in the form of dictators, frequently rose and still rise to power in post-colonial countries. In Chinua Achebe's *Anthills of the Savannah,* Ikem complains about countrymen worse than thieves, "leaders who openly looted our treasury, whose effrontery soiled our national soul". Ikem refers not to the White strangers but rather to Africans who have ruled with politics similar to those of colonial oppression. With the British empire gone, African societies must look inward to find remnants of colonialism which continue to harm their nations, and perhaps, find those which are advantageous in the new world they have been thrust into. Ikem's speech directed to all Nigerians rather than to any particular class pleads, "you must develop the habit of skepticism, not swallow every piece of superstition you are told by witch doctors and professors—when you rid yourself of these things your potentiality for assisting and directing this nation will be quadrupled". Part of the danger of the term post-colonial stems from people's disregard of their responsibility for their situation. As Ikem notes in his speech, people prefer to blame other groups, perhaps even post-colonialism, for their problems and rarely comprehend that only they can help themselves. Buchi Emecheta's *The Slave Girl, Wole Soyinkas' Ake and Ken Sarowiwas A Forest of Flowers* allow us to see to what extend Aschcrofft, Griffiths and Tiffin's postcolonial theories accurately describe what African authors believe occurs in colonial and newly liberated African countries.

Frantz Fanon

A leading third world intellectual whose work helped inspire the struggle against colonialism and ground theoretically the subsequent growth of postcolonial culture, Frantz Fanon was one of the most influential thinkers of the twentieth century.

Fanon, began his writing career, publishing his first book in 1952: *Peau noire, masques blancs* (trans. 1967, *Black Skin, White Masks).* This book includes the important chapter "The Fact of Blackness, which describes Fanon's growing awareness of racism in France. The work, personal and lyrical, shows the strong influence of Fanon's psychiatric training, as he concentrates primarily on the impact of racism and colonialism on the black psyche. It also engages in a critical dialogue with French existentialism, particularly that of Jean-Paul-Sarte, and exhibits the influence of the regritude movement (which called in the 1940s and 1950s for a distinctive black cultural identity rather than complete assimilation into French culture.)

Fanon's writing based on the Algerian revolution could be seen in his essay *L' An, cinq, de la revolution Algerienne* (1959, trans, 1965, *A Dying Colonialism).* Other essays were posthumously collected and published in 1964 as *Pour la revolution Africaine* (trams. 1976, *Toward the African Revolution).* The culmination of his work, however, was the publication of *The wretched of the Earth,* just weeks before his death. This volume, which featured an impassioned introduction by Sarte, gained widespread recognition and solidified Fanon's reputation as a leading revolutionary thinker of the twentieth century.

Fanon displays a distinctive political vision, centrally informed by the European tradition of Marxist thought in a version heavily modified to reflect third world, anti-colonial perspectives. For example, in his conviction that colonialism would be ended only through violent anti-colonial struggle, Fanon was very much in accord with the Marxist view of capitalism's inevitable and. However, Fanon's reasons differed; in particular, he stressed that in the anti-colonial struggle would counteract the long-term psychological effects of the violence of colonialism itself. In addition, whereas Marx envisioned the European working class, or proletariat, as the crux of the revolution, Fanon felt that in Africa and other colonial regions, the revolution would have to be led by a coalition of peasants and social outcasts, the so-called lumpenproletariat in whom Marx saw little revolutionary potential in Europe.

Perhaps the most important aspect of Fanon's political thought was his insight into the complex interaction in colonies between class and race. Though he was intensely aware of the centrality of racism to European colonialism, Fanon as a Marxist argued that social, economic, and political oppression in the third world was ultimately more a matter of class. He makes his point most forcefully in his influential argument in *The Wretched of the Earth* that postcolonial African nations court disaster if they simply replace their white colonial bourgeois leaders with a black African postcolonial bourgeoise, while leaving the basic class structure of the societies in place.

In the important chapter "The pitfalls of National Consciousness", Fanon explores the pros and cons of nationalist attitudes in the struggle for independence from colonialism. In the chapter "On National Culture", Fanon continues his discussion of nationalism, exploring the role played by culture in the development of viable postcolonial identities for emergent African nations. Here he particularly concentrates on the importance of intellectuals in helping to develop cultural identities for emerging postcolonial nations.

During the closing decades of the twentieth century, Fanon's work was joined by that of a new wave of scholars, such as Edward Said and Hom Bhabha, who often drew on poststructuralist theorist in describing the postcolonial condition. Nevertheless, Fanon's logical but passionate arguments, rooted in a Marxist engagement with the material world, have remained a strong force in postcolonial studies.

Edward Said

Known as a literary and cultural theorist, Edward Said was born in Jerusalem, Palestine. Said's thinking has embraced three broad imperatives: firstly, to articulate the cultural position and task of the intellectual and literary critic. Said's formulations in this area, influenced by Foucault, provided a crucial impetus to the so-called New Historicism in the 1980s which was in part a reaction against the tendency of American adherents of structuralism, poststructuralism, and deconstruction either to isolate literature from its various contexts or to reduce those contexts to an indiscriminate "textuality". Said's second concern has been to examine the historical production and motivations of Western discourses about the Orient in general, and about Islam in particular-Said's own origin (or 'beginning" as he would prefer) has defined a third, more immediately political commitment: an attempt to bring to light and clarify the Palestinian struggle to regain a homeland. Some regarded him as a model of the politically engaged scholar while others viewed his enterprise as incoherent. This account of Said's work will pursue the three lines indicated above.

Beginnings (1975) was Said's first influential book. Focusing on the question "What is beginning?", Said tracs the ramifications and diverse understandings of this concept in history. Adapting insights from the Italian philosopher Giambattista Vico's *New Science* (1744), Said distinguishes between "origin," which is divine, mythical, and privileged, and "beginning," which is secular and humanly produced. In *The World, the Text, and the Critic* (1983), Said argues that critical theory has retreated into a "labyrinth of textuality" whereby it betrays its "insurrectionary" beginnings in the 1960s. Said sees even the "radical" factions of the intellectual establishment, along with the traditional humanists, as having sold out to the "principle of non-interference" and the triumph of the ethic of professionalism, a self-domestication he sees as concurrent with the rise of Reaganism. He sees contemporary criticism as an institution for publicly affirming the values of culture as understood in a Eurocentric, dominative, and elitist sense. Having thereby lost touch with the "resistance and heterogeneity of civil society," criticism has effectively presided over its own (paradoxically) cultural marginality and political irrelevance. The notion of the "text" thus dirempted from the from the "world" is what Said is at pains to combat. He effectively redefines the text as "worldly," as implication in real social and political conditions in a number of ways: the most important feature of a text is the fact of its production. The specific conditions of a text's production are constitutive of its capacity to produce meaning; they constrain their own interpretation by placing themselves, intervening in given ideological and aesthetic conjunctures. Texts are marked by an interplay between their speech and the contours of its projected reception. Moreover, as texts dislodge and displace other texts, they are essentially facts of power, not of democratic exchange. Following Foucault, Said rejects formulations of the discursive situation as one of democratic equality or political neutrality but likens it to the relation between colonizer and colonized, or oppressor and oppressed. In short, "Texts are a system of forces institutionalized by the reigning culture at some human cost to its various components."

Interestingly, Said traces the emergence of Eurocentrism itself to Renan's transference of authority from sacred, divinely authorized texts to an ethnocentric philology which diminished the status of both Semitic languages and the "Orient, a theme which is developed in *Orientalism* (1978). This is a critique of the academic field of Oriental Studies, which has been a scholarly pursuit at most of the prestigious European universities for several centuries. His focus was to show on how English, French, and American scholars have approached the Arab societies of North Africa and the Middle East. Edward Said says that the western orientalist misrepresents the Orient in these major respects:

1. West is always viewed as rational, humane, developed and superior, the Orient as under-developed and inferior.

2. Western views are based on classical texts rather than modern Oriental realities.
3. The Orient is always viewed as uniform homespun and unchanging.
4. The Orient does not have the ability to define itself, so it is the burden of the Orientalist to make an objective assessment of the East.

Orientalism by Said is a canonical text of cultural studies in which he has challenged the concept of orientalism or the difference between Fast and West, as he puts it. He says that with the start of European colonization the Europeans came in contact with the lesser developed countries of the east. They found their civilization and culture very exotic, and established the science of orientalism, which was the study orientals or the people from these *exotic* civilization.

In chapter "The Scope of Orientalism," Said explains how the science of orientalism developed and how the orientials started considering the orientals as non-human beings. The orientals divided the world into two parts by using the concept of *ours* and *theirs.* The orients were regarded as uncivilized people; and the westerns said that since they were the refined race it was their duty to civilize these people and in order to achieve their goal, they had to colonize and rule the orients. Another feature of orientalism was that the culture of the orientals was explained to the European audience by linking them to the western culture, for example, Islam was made into *Mohammadism* because Mohammad was the founder of this religion of Christ was called Christianity; thus Islam should be called *Mohammadism.* The point to be noted here is that no Muslim was aware of this terminology and this was a completely western created term, and to which the Muslims had no say at all.

Said's subsequent book *Culture and Imperialism* (1993) is effectively a continuation of the themes raised in *Orientalism* in that it examines in a more focused manner the power relations between Occident and Orient hinted at in the earlier work. Said's uniqueness as a cultural critic lay in the range of his interests, which allowed him to explore the nexus of connections between literature, politics, and religion in a global rather than national or Eurocentric context.

Gayatri Chakravorty Spivak

Born in Calcutta, India, Gayatri, Spivak was educated at both Indian and American universities, one of her teachers at Cornell was Paul de Man. She is known for her translation of, and lengthy preface to, Derrida's *Of Grammatology* and her central concern with the structures of colonialism, the postcolonial subject, and the possibility of postcolonial discourse draws on deconstructive practices, the feminist movement, Marxism, and Freud. In her influential and controversial essay "Can the Subaltern Speak?" (1983), later expanded in her book *Critique of Postcolonial Reason* (1999), she addresses precisely this issue of whether people in subordinate, colonized positions are able to achieve a voice. A "subaltern" refers to an officer in a subordinate position; the term was used by the Italian Marxist Antonio Gramsci" to refer to the working masses that needed to be organized by left-wing intellectuals into a politically self-conscious force. The term as Spivak uses it also insinuates the "Subaltern Studies Group" in India, a radical group which attempted to articulate and give voice to the struggles of the oppressed peasants of the Indian subcontinent.

The essay "Can the Subaltern Speak" perhaps her best demonstrates her concern for the processes whereby postcolonial studies ironically reinscribe, co-opt, and rehearse neo-colonial imperatives of political domination, economic exploitation, and cultural erasure. In other words, is the post-colonial critic unknowingly complicit in the task of imperialism? Is "Post-colonialism" a specifically first-world, male, privileged academic, institutionalized discourse that classifies and surveys the East in the same measure as the actual modes of colonial dominance it seeks to dismantle? According to Spivak, postcolonial studies must encourage that "postcolonial intellectuals learn that their privilege is their loss". In "Can the Subaltern speak?", Spivak encourages but also criticizes the efforts of the subaltern studies group, a project led by Ranajit Guha that has reappropriated Gramsci's term "subaltern" (the economically dispossed) in order to locate and re-establish a "voice" or collective locus of agency in post colonial

India. Although Spivak acknowledges the "epistemic violence" done upon Indian subalterns, she suggests that any attempt from the outside to ameliorate their condition by granting them collective speech invariably will encounter the following problems: (1) a logocentric assumption of cultural solidarity among a heterogeneous people, and 2) a dependence upon western intellectuals to "speak for" the subaltern condition rather than allowing them to speak for themselves. As Spivak argues, by speaking out and reclaiming a collective cultural identity, subalterns will in fact re-inscribe their subordinate position in society. The academic assumption of a subaltern collectivity becomes akin to an ethnocentric extension of Western logos—a totalizing, essentialist "mythology" as Derrida might describe it—that doesn't account for the heterogeneity of the colonized body politic.

In the third part, Spivak offers yet a further twist. She tells the story of Bhubaneswari Bhaduri's suicide not as an example of the Indian Woman's inability to speak within Western discourse but to show that Indian discourse has been so battered by the storms of (colonial) history that it, too, offers no resources for successful communication. Bhubaneshwari's suicide is misunderstood by everyone, including her own family—and no one in India seems interested in Spivak's return to and reinterpretation of the event. "Unnerved by this failure of communication," Spivak wrote her "passionate lament: the subaltern cannot speak! Fifteen years later, Spivak comments: "It was an inadvisable remark."

Further, Spivak talks usefully of a "strategic" essentialism whereby we can use essentialist language in a self-conscious way for practical, political purposes. In this essay she makes a number of suggestions that might prevent one's own position being indeterminate and merely a negative critique. She suggests that intellectuals recognize the importance of the economic sphere but without investing it with any kind of absolute or ultimate explanatory power. She adds that participation in the political process—access to citizenship, becoming a voter-will help to mobilizes the subaltern on "the long road to hegemony."

Homi K. Bhabha

Like Gayatri Spivak, Homi Bhabha extends certain tenets of poststructuralism into discourses about colonialism nationality, and culture. These tenets include a challenging of the notion of fixed identity, the undermining of binary oppositions, and on emphasis on language and discourse—together with the power of relations in which these are imbricated—as underlying our understanding of cultural phenomena. But, as in the case of Spivak, this "extension" is not a simple extrapolation of poststructuralist principles in their purity to colonial subject matter; the process of extension itself is used to display the limits of these principles and the altered nature of their applicability. Bhabha takes some of the foregoing ideas from Derrida; from Mikhail Bakhtin he draws the notion of the "dialogic" (indicating the mutuality of a relationship) in order to characterize the connection between colonizer and colonized; he draws also on Frantz Fanon's revolutionary work on colonialism, as well as on the concept of "nation" as defined in Benedict Anderson's book *Imagined Communities* (1983).

The notion of "hybridity" is central to Bhabha's work in challenging notions of identity, culture, and nation as coherent and unified entities that exhibit a linear historical development. Hybridity expresses a state of "in betweenness," as in a person who stands between two cultures. The concept is embodied in Bhabha's own life (as in the lives of many intellectuals from colonial nations who have been raised in Western institutions): born into a Pharsi community in Bombay, India, he was educated both in his native country and at Oxford University; he subsequently taught at universities on England and America, and now teaches at Harvard.

Homi Bhabha has put forward the ideas "mimicry" that denotes 'the gap between the norm of civility as presented by European Enlightenment and its distorted colonial imitation. It serves as the sly weapon of anti-colonial civility and is an ambivalent mixture of deference and disobedience. In his opinion, colonizer provides to the colonized the tools whereby the latter erodes the imperial power by building up the native resistance. This is done through 'mimicry' of the dominant power-creation of an 'in between space' and/or hybridity.,Mimicry is the outward or external imitation of the authority leading to the setting up of new structures of authority and generating new political initiatives.

Bhabha also questions the idea of the 'nation', its application to the 'heterogeneous collection of people's to bring out their 'national' character. This seems to have generated a great deal of interest in the subject, the notion of nation and nationalism coming under sharp focus. Ashish Nandy analysis of Tagore's *Gora* lays bare the subversive role of the western concept of nationalism and its effect on the growth of the protagonist's personality. Nandy says, "that nationalism colonizes his self more successfully than any imperial power could have done. This victory of nationalism Tagore implies, is ultimately a victory of the west over Indian civilization."

Bhaba's concept of 'otherness' is derived from Lacan's 'Other' and Fanon's idea of 'Other' as binary opposition between the white and the Black. In *The Location of Culture,* Bhabha cites repitition as a mode of resistance to today's neocolonialism, particularly the recolonization of migrants within the contemporary Western metropolis. For Bhabha, the human subject is not grounded in a fixed identity but rather is a discursive effect generated in the act of enunciation. When migrants, refugees, and the decolonized take up positions in Western discourse, they divide it from itself by repeating it and clear space within it for new, hybrid subjectivities. The hybrid postcolonial subject negotiates the interstices of Western discursive systems, operating in between the dichotomies of colonizer and colonized, self and other, East and West. Once a mode of Western discourse is altered through repitition moreover, it loses its "westness" and exposes itself to difference. Iteration is therefore a way of translating between cultures. It opens the possibility of an international culture of hybridity generated through discursive activity".

One interesting development is the meeting of post-colonialist triats with those of post-modernism where exploration of ancient myths and magic realism are used to understand the significance of the present, and locate one's identity. Shashi Tharoor has used myth in *The Great Indian Novel,* and Girish Karnad in *The Hayavandana and The Nag Mandala.* Influences work on a larger transnational scale where one observes African writers teaching in the Pacific islands influence Pacific island writing. The short stories of Frank Sargeson, a New Zealands, showed Australian poets ways of reproducing eommon lower and middle-class speech. Rushdie's *Midnight's Children* showed Australian, Indian and African novelists how post-modernist fabulation and self-reflexivity, could be given national political dimensions and used allegorically. The line of transmission was from Gunter Grass and Gabriel Garcia Ma'rduez through Rushdie to such commonwealth novelists as Syl Cheney-Coker, Alex Miller, and Amitav Ghosh.

Bibliography

1. Abercrombie-Principles of Literary Criticism.
2. Abrams, M.H.-A Glossary of Literary Terms.
3. Ashcroft Bill *et al.,* The Empire Writes Back: Theory and Practice in Post-colonial Literatures.
4. Bennet, Tony- Formalism and Marxism.
5. Bhabha, Homi K (ed)- Nation and Narration.
6. C.L. Wren-The English Language.
7. Connor J.D.O-Better English Pronunciation.
8. Culler, Jonathan-Literary Theory: A very short Introduction.
9. Culler, Jonathan-On Deconstruction: Theory and Criticism after Structuralism.
10. David Daiches-Critical Approaches to Literature.
11. David Lodge (ed)-Modern Criticism and Theory A Reader.
12. David Lodge (ed)-Twentieth century Literary Criticism.
13. Diamond, A.S., The History and Origin of Language.
14. Edward Said-Orientalism: Western Conceptions of the Orient.
15. Eagleton Mary (ed.)—Feminist Literary Theory A Reader.
16. Eagleton, Terry-Literary Theroy: An Introduction.
17. Frederick T. Wood-An Outline History of the English Language.
18. G.L. Brook-A History of English Language.
19. G. Yule –The Study of Language.
20. Harry Blamires-A History of Literary Criticism.
21. I.A. Richards-Practical Criticism: A Study of Literary Judgment.

22. John Algeo (ed)—The Cambridge History of English Language (Vol.VI).
23. Karl Marx-The Communist Manifesto.
24. Kenneth Burke-The Philosophy of Literary Form.
25. Muhlhauster P-Pidgin and Creole Linguistics.
26. Nowell C. Smith-Literary Criticism.
27. Patridge, E-Slang To-Day and Yesterday.
28. Peck, John and Coyle, Martin-Literary Terms and Criticism.
29. Pomorska, K-Russian Formalist Theory and its Poetic.
30. Roach, P-English Phonetics and Phonology: A Practical Course.
31. Ruthven K.K- Feminist Literary Studies.
32. Sainsbury, George- A History of English Criticism.
33. Seldon, Raman- A Reader's Guide to Contemporary Literary Theory.
34. Scott, Wilbur- Five Approaches of Literary Criticism.
35. Worsfold, Bas'l- Judgment in Literature.

Index

T

U

❑❑❑